MW00813228

Christian Humanism
in Shakespeare

Christian Humanism in Shakespeare

A Study in Religion and Literature

Lee Oser

LIBRARY OF
CONGRESS
SURPLUS
DUPLICATE

The Catholic University of America Press
Washington, D.C.

Copyright © 2022
The Catholic University of America Press
All rights reserved

The paper used in this publication meets the minimum requirements of American
National Standards for Information Science—Permanence of Paper for Printed
Library materials, ANSI Z39.48–1984.

∞

Cataloging-in-Publication data available from the Library of Congress.
ISBN: 978-0-8132-3510-3
eISBN: 978-0-8132-3511-0

I. M. Msgr. Rocco M. Piccolomini (1945–2015)

But Jesus did not commit himself unto them,
    because he knew them all,
And had no need that any should testify of man:
    for he knew what was in man.

John 2:24–25

Table of Contents

Acknowledgments

I am first and foremost grateful to my stepfather, David Kleinbard, Professor Emeritus of the CUNY Graduate Center. He and my late mother, Maureen Waters, kept a home where literature flourished. I have tried with my wife and our daughters to keep that tradition going.

I am grateful to the students in my Shakespeare classes. It has been a pleasure.

Through a generous leave policy, College of the Holy Cross gave me time to write this book.

The college's library staff has been unfailingly helpful and kind. In particular, I wish to thank Eileen Cravedi, Renee Hadad, Mark Shelton, and Slavica Zukic.

Among faculty colleagues, I wish to express my gratitude to Jeffrey Bernstein, Robert Cording, Peter Fritz, John Gavin, SJ, Richard Herrick, James M. Kee, Joseph Lawrence, Richard Matlak, Blaise Nagy, David Schaefer, Aaron Seider, Sarah Stanbury, and the late John H. Wilson, who was right about Sonnet 116.

Paul Mouton of ITS helped with technical matters.

I owe many intellectual debts, to the living and the dead. I am especially grateful to Lindsey Armstrong, John Baxter, Jeffrey Bloechl, Marie Borroff, John Briggs, Leslie Brisman, David Bromwich, Archie Burnett, James Engell, Paul Fry, John Hollander, G. K. Hunter, Robert Knapp, Benjamin Lockerd, Noah Millman, Steven Monte, James Najarian, Virgil Nemoianu, Ricardo Quinones, Christopher Ricks, William Schmitt, Matthew J. Smith, Steven Soldi, Sarah Spence, Ernest Suarez, Msgr. Thomas Sullivan, Dennis Taylor, Kevin Van Anglen, Rosanna Warren, Lauren Weiner, and Susan Zimmerman.

To a younger generation of teachers and scholars, Nicholas Bloechl, David Bonagura, Michael Casey, Matthew Clemente, Julia D'Agostino, James Fletcher, Peter Galalis, Will Hendel, Evan Hulick, Travis LaCouter, Martin Lockerd, Christopher Petter, Alex Pisano, Andrew Rhodes, Kelsey Ruescher-Enkeboll, Jake Smith, Jordan Smith, Christopher Suarez, Ryan Wilson, et al., I hope this helps.

For the distinction in my Conclusion between hypocrisy and cant, I am indebted to Theodore Dalrymple's fine essay, "The Age of Cant," which appeared in *City Journal* (August 2020).

I am grateful to my editor at CUA Press, Trevor Lipscombe, and to two anonymous readers. My errors are my own. If anyone forgives them, it will be my wife, Kate. I thank her again.

An earlier version of Chapter 2 appeared as "Bad Christians in *The Merchant of Venice*: A Rhetorical Matter," in volume 19, number 1 (March 2017) of *Literary Imagination*. An earlier version of Chapter 4 appeared as "Free Will in *Hamlet*?: Shakespeare's Struggle with the Issues of the Great Debate between Erasmus and Luther," in volume 67, number 3 (March 2018) of *Christianity and Literature*.

Brief Note on Texts, Citations, and Abbreviations

Unless stated otherwise, citations from Shakespeare are from *The Complete Works of Shakespeare*, edited by David Bevington (6th ed.); citations from Chaucer are from *The Riverside Chaucer*, edited by Larry D. Benson; biblical citations are from *The Geneva Bible: A Facsimile of the 1560 Edition* (Madison: University of Wisconsin Press, 1969). Except when quoting another's scholarship, I have modernized the Geneva Bible's spellings and occasionally clarified its punctuation, though I keep the original italics. In the case of a few classic works (e.g., Hobbes's *Elements of Law*), I have given the page number followed by a parenthesis with the traditional format for citing the work. For references to Aquinas's *Summa Theologica* and Calvin's *Institution of the Christian Religion* (1562), I use the traditional format without page numbers. Standard abbreviations apply for Early English Books Online (EEBO) and the *Oxford English Dictionary* (OED).

Abbreviations for Shakespeare's works follow C. T. Onions, *A Shakespeare Glossary*.

LC	*A Lover's Complaint*
AWW	*All's Well That Ends Well*
AYL	*As You Like It*
COR	*Coriolanus*
CYM	*Cymbeline*
HAM	*Hamlet, Prince of Denmark*
1H4	*The First Part of King Henry the Fourth*
2H4	*The Second Part of King Henry the Fourth*
H5	*The Life of King Henry the Fifth*
1H6	*The First Part of King Henry the Sixth*
2H6	*The Second Part of King Henry the Sixth*
3H6	*The Third Part of King Henry the Sixth*
JC	*Julius Caesar*
LLL	*Love's Labor's Lost*
LR	*King Lear*

Preface

Although the Elizabethans coined the term *humanist* in reference to classical scholars, the term *humanism* wasn't applied to the Elizabethans until the nineteenth century. The term *Christian humanism*, in particular, is a convenience of modern scholarship. Its usages vary considerably across religious, historical, and philological studies. Its scope resists the effort to confine it, like Ariel imprisoned in the cloven pine, inside the bounds of a single definition. Having no such definition in hand, I approach Shakespeare's plays as works of literature, created in the dialectical opening between the sacred and the secular that I have previously identified as "the radical middle." Addressing how Shakespeare fuses Christian ideas and meanings with non-Christian ideas and meanings, I present Shakespeare's Christian humanism as an effort at imaginative synthesis that varies from play to play. Its unique densities are singularly conducive to detailed literary analysis focused on the individual work. My purpose is to persuade readers that Shakespeare's Christianity is entirely relevant to his literary greatness.

Two types of argument follow. First, I observe the usual pattern of academic discourse. Over a lengthy introduction, I develop a picture of our current understanding and how we arrived there. I respond to rival critics, pointing out strengths and weaknesses. Under the banner of fair play, I lay claim to the position that Shakespeare was a Christian writer—a position that, in asserting the mutual bonds of religion and literature, challenges the field.

It is the second type of argument that holds the greatest potential for persuasion. Only after we have established our right to exist as independent critics can we argue the particulars of literary analysis. Only after we have framed our leading questions in ways that attract others can we get down to the evidence of words and meanings. At that point, as disagreements grow more interesting, a shared text becomes (among other things) a means of reviving communities of readership. In this respect, I hope *Christian Humanism in Shakespeare* will appeal to students and to general readers, as well as to my fellow teachers and colleagues who remain committed to great literature.

L. O.
December 1, 2020
Holden, Massachusetts

Introduction
Thinking of Shakespeare as a Christian

Consider it not so deeply.
(MAC 2.2.34)

The Pepper Theory

Not long ago, I submitted an essay to a literary journal at a major Catholic university. In recommending against my essay for publication, the anonymous referee stated his or her objection in an argument I shall for convenience's sake refer to as "the pepper theory":

> Shakespeare may or may not have been a Christian author. He likely was Christian, but gauging the degree of his Christian ideas is problematic, simply because a character, rather than the author directly, is always voicing them. Christian ideas and allusions do pepper his plays. But that is another matter.

The logic is impressive—because his characters stand between Shakespeare and what we can say about him, we can say little or nothing about his "Christian ideas." The author of the pepper theory is free to state that Shakespeare "likely was Christian." It hardly matters, because, as the sentence expands, the living connection between Shakespeare and Christianity is all but severed. Isn't it at least "plausible," we might ask, "that one should see signs of the maker in what he's made"?[1] In the case of Shakespeare's political views, maybe so. A presumed opening from the work to the poet's mind has given the topic abundant life. Shakespeare's sexuality is likewise deemed to be discernable through his work.[2] In the case of Shakespeare's religious views, though, this avenue of insight vanishes. All that remains of Shakespeare's "likely" Christianity is a peppering of "Christian ideas and allusions." And all that remains of Shakespeare himself is a textual entity whose personal beliefs are irrecoverable—permanently deleted from the historical record.

---

1. Tim Spiekerman, *Shakespeare's Political Realism: The English History Plays*, 14.
2. See, for example, Paul Edmondson and Stanley Wells, introduction to *All the Sonnets of Shakespeare*, ed. Paul Edmondson and Stanley Wells, 31–32.

1

In recent books and edited collections that treat Shakespeare's "Christian ideas and allusions," there is, at one and the same time, such abundance of Christian material on display, and such reticence about the author's actual beliefs, that one starts to wonder what is going on. The current consensus is to "avoid discussion of the known or conjectured religious affiliations" of Shakespeare and his fellow playwrights.[3] It is not immediately clear, we acknowledge, that one needs to identify Shakespeare as a Christian in order to discuss the biblical and religious aspects of his work. And yet, one may suspect, without resorting to conspiracy theories, that outside factors enter the picture. The widespread commitment to unbelief among American and European academics comes into play.[4]

Even so, the issue of religion shows considerable staying power in Shakespeare criticism. The best of these books and essays, which extend the most recent "turn to religion,"[5] supply a historical framework that renders any glib assumptions about Shakespeare and religion obsolete. We find ourselves in contentious territory. For that reason, an appeal to good pragmatic standards may be in order.

I would formulate this appeal as follows: if approaching Shakespeare as a Christian writer affords us a rich literary appreciation of his plays that is otherwise unavailable, if it compels our understanding through its consistency and respect for fact, then the pepper theory should be discarded. Likewise, the longstanding tendency, under various names and schools, to extricate Shakespeare from Christianity should be regarded an impediment to the growth of knowledge.

I argue in this book that Shakespeare is a Christian literary artist who criticizes and challenges Christians, but who does so on Christian grounds. He exploits artistic resources and possibilities that are specific to Christianity. I go

---

3. Brian Walsh, *Unsettled Toleration: Religious Differences on the Shakespearean Stage,* 4.

4. "The American academic world is probably as deeply invested in unbelief as its European counterpart." Charles Taylor, *A Secular Age,* 525.

5. According to John D. Cox (afterword to *Stages of Engagement,* 267, cited below), the phrase "turn to religion" (one also hears of the "religious turn") was coined by Ken Jackson and Arthur Marotti in a 2004 essay, which I cite here in its final version: introduction to *Shakespeare and Religion: Early Modern and Postmodern Perspectives,* ed. Ken Jackson and Arthur F. Marotti, 1–21. Three magisterial essays by Cox supply a helpful introduction to this "turn" and its phases: Afterword to *Stages of Engagement: Drama and Religion in Post-Reformation England,* ed. James D. Mardock and Kathryn R. McPherson, 263–75; "Was Shakespeare a Christian, and If So, What Kind of a Christian Was He?" *Christianity and Literature* 55 (September 2006): 539–66; and "Shakespeare and Religion," *Religions* 9 (November 2018): 1–11. Also helpful is Richard C. McCoy, *Faith in Shakespeare,* 7–27 (with excellent endnotes).

on to consider his relation to the Christian humanist currents of his day in Chapter 1. To begin, though, I chiefly want to present him as a Christian writer.

This modest argument puts me at loggerheads with numerous high-ranking scholars, including Stephen Greenblatt, who takes a secularizing approach to the topic of Shakespeare and religion: "His works suggest that he did have faith, of a sort, but it was not a faith securely bound either by the Catholic Church or by the Church of England. By the late 1590s, insofar as his faith could be situated in any institution at all, that institution was the theater."[6] Like the author of the pepper theory, Greenblatt advances a view of religion and literature that separates them into discrete fields of discourse, with reference, in his case, to the church and the theater. I do not deny that Greenblatt is a highly resourceful scholar of early modern religion who has elevated the topic among Shakespeareans. I am observing that his method is to toggle between religion and literature rather than to explore the depth of their coherence. This method is common. Studying the evidence, an impartial observer would tend to conclude that contemporary Shakespeare criticism does not focus on a depth of coherence that is (admittedly) unsystematic, ad hoc, differing from play to play. Rather, it runs generally along two lines: (1) it remains aloof from the quarrelsome question, or (2) more or less aggressively, it modernizes, secularizes, and in various peppery ways contains the Christian ideas and meanings in Shakespeare's plays.

A radical pepperist perusing my strongest evidence might reply by comparing Shakespeare to a versatile defense lawyer, a talented sophist who could enlist his talents to serve any rhetorical end. He had the power to fashion, as in Volumnia's admonition to her son, "words that are . . . but bastards and syllables / Of no allowance to your bosom's truth" (COR 3.2.57–59). He was like the protean (and fiendish) lover in *A Lover's Complaint*: "To make the weeper laugh, the laugher weep, / He had the dialect and different skill, / Catching all passions in his craft of will" (124–26). It is clear as a duel at dawn what my countermove must be. I must argue that Shakespeare's work reveals a personal substratum.

But to say so is not to impute to Shakespeare a modern selfhood. To approach Shakespeare as an Elizabethan person puts before us a range of issues that call into question our common assumptions about personal belief and the priority of "inwardness."[7] Instead of following those who privilege

---

6. Stephen Greenblatt, *Will in the World: How Shakespeare Became Shakespeare*, 321.

7. "Our modern notion of the self is related to, one might say constituted by, a certain sense (or perhaps a family of senses) of inwardness." Charles Taylor, *Sources of the Self: The Making of Modern Identity*, 111. For historical differentiation and clarification, see Anne Ferry, *The "Inward"*

Shakespeare's inner experience, I prefer to locate Shakespeare's Christian personhood in the religious culture that made his experience possible. Philosophically, I take my cue from Wittgenstein's axiom that "the *speaking* of language is part of an activity, or a form of life."[8] I connect Shakespeare's language-game to his "form of life." Historian Peter Marshall does so implicitly: "William Shakespeare, born in 1564, and receiving his grammar school education in Stratford in the 1570s, was very likely raised in a Catholic household, and as an adult and author he never exhibited much enthusiasm for Protestantism of the 'godly' variety. But his dramatic works are permeated with allusions to the Prayer Book and Homilies, and to the Bible, in both Bishops' and Geneva versions."[9] This strikes me as perfectly reasonable—as would a student's inferring from it that Shakespeare was not a post-Christian author. But the pepper theory allows no such inference. We cannot gauge the "degree" of Shakespeare's Christian ideas "simply because a character, rather than the author directly, is always voicing them." Shakespeare did not tell us "directly" what he was thinking when he wrote his plays. Although the density and mass of Naseeb Shaheen's *Biblical References in Shakespeare's Plays* (1999) suggest that those ideas and allusions have a collective weight, that they are not a peppery affair of the surface but possibly the core of the matter, we cannot really know. Not even if, following Shaheen, we accept that Shakespeare's biblical knowledge was individualized: "the extent of Shakespeare's allusions to parts of the Bible not read in church indicates that Shakespeare's private reading was, in fact, the main source of his comprehensive knowledge of it."[10]

We have the evidence of Sonnet 146 ("Poor soul, the center of my sinful earth"), but, as Helen Vendler points out, the "gloominess of this sonnet has little of the radiance of Christian hope."[11] George Herbert, we recall, has a small gloomy poem called "Sin's Round," which also "has little of the radiance of Christian hope." Like Sonnet 146, it exhibits "the absence of any reference to Christ, the Resurrection, or an afterlife."[12] Calvin's theology is not much cheerier than the *Rubáiyát* of Omar Khayyam. Even so, Vendler's insincere remark about "the radiance of Christian hope" holds such authority that Colin

Language: Sonnets of Wyatt, Sidney, Shakespeare, Donne, esp.1–30. For critical positions on inwardness in the Renaissance, see Katharine Eisaman Maus, *Inwardness and the Theater in the English Renaissance*, esp. 1–4.

8. Ludwig Wittgenstein, *Philosophical Investigations*, §23, his italics. I note the German: "*das Sprechen der Sprache.*"

9. Peter Marshall, *Heretics and Believers*, 543.

10. Beatrice Groves, *Texts and Traditions: Religion in Shakespeare 1592–1604*, 22.

11. Helen Vendler, *The Art of Shakespeare's Sonnets*, 614.

12. Vendler, *The Art of Shakespeare's Sonnets*, 611.

Burrow, in his Oxford edition of Shakespeare's poetry, felt obliged to memorialize it in his notes.[13] We have the evidence of Shakespeare's famous will, but its profession of Protestant faith turns out to be "entirely formulaic."[14] We have the quatrain inscribed over his grave: "Good friend for Jesus' sake forbear / To dig the dust enclosèd here! / Blessed be the man that spares these stones, / And cursèd be he that moves my bones." "Possibly," Samuel Schoenbaum commented in 1970, "Shakespeare himself composed the inscription; at any rate, the suggestion that he did would be made some seventy-five years after his death."[15] This is no longer accurate. The written record now begins with "a manuscript commonplace book of Francis Fane, compiled about 1629 ('Shakespeare Birthplace Trust MS ER.93/2')."[16] We may want to insist that any date after 1616 comes too late to relieve our aching doubts. Pointing to the gap in time between Shakespeare's death and Fane's documentation, Gary Taylor and Rory Loughnane refrain from attributing the epitaph to Shakespeare.[17] And yet, in 1629, we are well within range of living memory. Shakespeare's daughters, Susanna and Judith, were among the Stratford locals who presumably would have been able to confirm their father's authorship. Had they denied it, or identified a different author (talk about bragging rights!), the unanimous agreement between Fane's attribution and the three recorded by Schoenbaum—all appearing in the 1690s—would be entirely improbable.[18] But Shakespeare's invoking Jesus, as his protector, as he who created "the dust," as he whose forbearance should be imitated, as he who will come again in glory to judge the living and the dead, as he who will make these dead bones live, as he whose curses and blessings will never be revoked: how easily all this is lost, while we maintain a judicious silence on the question of whether or not Shakespeare wrote his own epitaph.[19] I want to underscore this point: it is hard to imagine any alleged proof of Shakespeare's Christianity that could categorically deflect our skeptical resources. In the end, we have no access to Shakespeare's consciousness. We cannot enter the inner theater of his private beliefs.[20]

13. William Shakespeare, *The Complete Sonnets and Poems*, ed. Colin Burrow, 672n.

14. David Scott Kastan, *A Will to Believe: Shakespeare and Religion*, 28.

15. S. Schoenbaum, *Shakespeare's Lives*, 3–4.

16. Gary Taylor and Rory Loughnane, "The Canon and Chronology of Shakespeare's Works," in *The New Oxford Shakespeare: Authorship Companion*, ed. Gary Taylor and Gabriel Egan, 591.

17. Taylor and Loughane, "Canon and Chronology," 417–602.

18. For these three reports, see S. Schoenbaum, *William Shakespeare: A Documentary Life*, 250.

19. See, for example, Shakespeare, *Complete Sonnets and Poems*, ed. Burrow, 728n.

20. Greenblatt traces this impasse, our having "no direct access to his thoughts," to the deadly threat of official discipline and Shakespeare's subsequent caution. Greenblatt, *Will in the World*, 173–74.

Even so, and though they are currently seen as unfashionable, pronouncements about Shakespeare's true faith have a long history. A rough sketch of the field suggests their wild abundance. In his *History of Great Britain* (1611), John Speed censured Jesuit Robert Persons for his damning portrayal of John Oldcastle. Speed included a now-famous jab at Shakespeare, on account of Falstaff's connection to Oldcastle (see Chapter 3), by referring to Persons and Shakespeare as "this Papist and his Poet."[21] Another Protestant, the Gloucestershire clergyman Richard Davies, is generally credited with conducting the earliest research on the topic. In memoranda dated 1688–1708, with a kind of minimalist flair, Davies observed of Shakespeare: "He dyed a papist."[22] Shakespeare's subsequent rise as the national poet of an imperial Protestant nation did little to attract support for Davies's curious report. In 1858, John Henry Newman advanced the Catholic position: "the most illustrious of the English writers has so little of Protestant about him that Catholics have been able, without extravagance, to claim him as their own, and that enemies to our creed have allowed that he is only not a Catholic, because, and as far as, his times forbade it."[23] A generation later, J. O. Halliwell-Phillipps suggested that Shakespeare was "an outward conformist to the Protestant faith, but secretly attached to the old religion."[24] Among Elizabethan propagandists, the derogatory term *Church Papist* was used in such cases. In 1952, H. Mutschmann and K. Wentersdorf published *Shakespeare and Catholicism*, an influential and interesting though demonstrably flawed survey of the evidence for a Catholic Shakespeare: wills; recusancy reports; genealogies; Catholics friends and associates; the sympathetic portrayal of Catholic clergy in the plays; Shakespeare's use of the Bible; his attraction to Catholic ideas.[25] Finally, the late Jesuit Peter Milward presents an example of an accomplished if uneven scholar, more pilfered than praised, who, over the course of a long career, grew sharply partisan in his assertions about Shakespeare's faith.[26]

21. E. K. Chambers, *William Shakespeare*, 2:217.

22. Chambers, *William Shakespeare*, 2:255–57.

23. John Henry Newman, *The Idea of a University*, 238.

24. J. O. Halliwell-Phillipps quoted in Kastan, *Will to Believe*, 41n6. Richard Simpson, a close contemporary of Halliwell-Phillipps, has been hailed as a pioneer in the study of Shakespeare and Catholicism. See Richard Wilson, "Introduction: A Torturing Hour—Shakespeare and the Martyrs," in *Theatre and Religion: Lancastrian Shakespeare*, ed. Richard Dutton, Alison Findlay, and Richard Wilson, 1–39.

25. H. Mutschmann and K. Wentersdorf, *Shakespeare and Catholicism*.

26. For a taste of the later Milward's partisanship, see Peter Milward, *Shakespearian Echoes: The Tragedies* and *Shakespearian Echoes: The Comedies*. I treat these in my review-essay "Shakespeare and the

On the other side of the confessional divide, Graham Holderness contends that it wasn't Catholic provocation but the force of "new scientific discoveries and theories such as evolution" that initially led scholars "to assert that Shakespeare's religious beliefs were of an orthodox Protestant complexion."[27] This would explain the silence on the topic among eighteenth-century scholars and editors, and why Coleridge did not enter upon it. In 1845 Joseph Hunter presented Shakespeare as an exemplar of the Anglican *via media*.[28] Thomas Carter published *Shakespeare, Puritan and Recusant* in 1897.[29] T. W. Baldwin, in 1943, stated that the playwright was "baptized into, trained up in, and conformed to the Church of England."[30] In the latter half of the twentieth century, historian A. L. Rowse maintained this line of thought, underscoring Shakespeare's "regular attendance at church from childhood on."[31] With a strong biblical emphasis, David Daniell in 2001 described Shakespeare as an exemplar of the "Protestant mind," the heir of Tyndale and assimilator to the stage of the Gospels in English.[32] More recently, Holderness has avouched that "Shakespeare was, both as a believing individual and as a writer, a faithful Protestant."[33] And John Cox, arguably the most important Shakespearean of his generation, leaves us with this pointed remark about Shakespeare: Christianity "defined the world he lived in, with his preference in the plays tending toward moderate Protestantism, which was the state religion of England in his day."[34]

It is easy to deprecate the excesses of those brave souls—both Catholic and Protestant—who claim to discover Shakespeare's religious meaning behind a veil of allegory. At its worst, the quest for Shakespeare's true faith can give license to a reductive impulse, the disambiguating of Shakespeare in terms of religious politics. But if generations of "Christian allegorizers" have

---

Catholic Spectrum," *Religion and the Arts* 16 (2012): 381–90. The full extent of Milward's original contributions can best be gathered from Dennis Taylor's annotated bibliography of 2006, "Peter Milward, S. J. (1925–): A Chronology and Checklist of his Works on Shakespeare, in English, Gathered in the Burns Rare Book Library, Boston College, Chestnut Hill, MA."

27. Graham Holderness, *The Faith of William Shakespeare*, 14.

28. See Schoenbaum, *Shakespeare's Lives*, 362–63.

29. Schoenbaum, *Shakespeare's Lives*, 459.

30. T. W. Baldwin, *William Shakspere's Petty School*, 221.

31. A. L. Rowse, *Shakespeare the Man*, 25.

32. David Daniell, "Shakespeare and the Protestant Mind," *Shakespeare Survey* 54 (2001): 9. And yet Daniell stops short of "making any statement about [Shakespeare's] personal beliefs" (Daniell, "Shakespeare and the Protestant Mind," 9).

33. Holderness, *Faith of William Shakespeare*, 14.

34. Cox, "Shakespeare and Religion," 1.

suffered rebuke from established critics,[35] the stinging response has on occasion smacked of an in-group closing ranks. What ought to be acknowledged is that allegory, though not a hallmark of humanism, was indispensable to the New Testament and to the entire tradition of Christian exegesis. The Hebrew prophets favored it as well—a point I will return to with respect to *King Lear* in Chapter 5. It would be odd if Shakespeare never thought in allegorical terms; obviously, he did—even while given to releasing "ironic suggestions calculated to daunt the most zealous allegorist."[36] In addressing the reach of allegory, moreover, we may bear in mind that John Foxe, making the case in *Acts and Monuments* for a Wycliffite Chaucer, described Chaucer as writing "under shadows covertly, as under a visor" so that "truth may profit the godly minded, and yet not be espied of the crafty adversary," by which he meant "the Bishops."[37] Foxe was wrong about Chaucer's being a follower of Wycliffe, but the example stands as an indicator of certain Elizabethan proclivities where literature and religion are concerned. The interest in allegory is not intrinsically misguided, but it opens a curious set of risks and rewards. Milward's later works shows an aggressive allegorizing tendency that will be most pleasing to its particular choir. But if Milward's holy grail—proof of Shakespeare's Catholic identity—has proven elusive, yet no one should be surprised that Milward's perseverance has yielded insights into the Catholic milieu of the plays. By contrast, those who insist on modernizing Shakespeare as our "secular" contemporary may find themselves writing teleological allegories that have nothing to do with Shakespeare at all.[38]

The debate over Shakespeare's churchmanship will continue. I have hardly done it justice. And who knows? Someday a scrap of parchment may emerge from some obscure attic or dusty basement, a document heartening to some, while reminding others that we are all very good at fooling ourselves.

---

35. See, for example, Kastan, *Will to Believe*, 38–40; Robert S. Miola, "Thy Canonized Bones," review of *The Quest for Shakespeare: The Bard of Avon and the Church of Rome*, by Joseph Pearce, *First Things* 185 (August/September 2008): 49–51; and Brian Vickers, *Appropriating Shakespeare: Contemporary Critical Quarrels*, 372–84.

36. René E. Fortin, "Launcelot and the Uses of Allegory in *The Merchant of Venice*," *Studies in English Literature, 1500–1900* 14 (Spring 1974): 267.

37. John Foxe, "'A Protestation to the Whole Church of England'" (1570), in *Geoffrey Chaucer*, ed. Harold Bloom, 33. I have modernized the spelling.

38. For Shakespeare's outsized role in the "ideological investment in the idea of a secular modernity," see Brian Cummings, *Mortal Thoughts: Religion, Secularity & Identity in Shakespeare and Early Modern Culture*, 4. On the Elizabethans and the "Whig view of history," see G. K. Hunter, *John Lyly*, 2–5, 350n1. See also Robert E. Stillman, *Philip Sidney and the Poetics of Renaissance Cosmopolitanism*, the comments on "presentism," 32.

But for now there is important territory to be gained by advancing the controversial proposition that Shakespeare wrote from a Christian perspective. Controversial, I say. And yet it seems perfectly fair to turn the tables on launchers of easy pronouncements: "Shakespeare's faith is not provable and a certain equivocation often lies in attempts to suggest that it is."[39] This verdict, from an excellent scholar to whom I am frequently indebted, is directed against espousers of the Catholic cause. But isn't there a "certain equiv-ocation," or at least a certain evasiveness, in the same scholar's referring to Shakespeare's "ostensibly secular drama"? *Ostensibly?* One notes the incon-gruity of Shakespeare and his "ostensibly secular drama" being "embedded" in a "religious culture" [40]—as if the crystals "embedded" in a mineral deposit might turn out (given the right diagnostic tools) to be animals or vegetables. Why not directly address why it is misleading to call Shakespeare a "secular" dramatist? In any case, to vindicate the claim that Shakespeare was a Christian author, we must rely on the massive amount of public language—outer-the-ater as opposed to inner-theater language—with which Shakespeare under-stood the Christianity of his day. Admittedly, this evidence of "deep immersion in religious questions,"[41] as Cox calls it, may be just another means of falling short. That is, it cannot furnish proof to a skeptic that Shakespeare was a Christian author. But if skepticism is inevitable, we should try to ensure that skeptical standards remain roughly equal: we should try to ensure that the skeptical reservations that arise when we consider Shakespeare's text as the work of a Christian author are not dispensed with when considering Shakespeare's text as the work of a non-Christian author, or when considering the religious dimension of other authors.

As it happens, Marlowe offers a parallel case of "an irretrievably textual being."[42] We might go further and insist that, since eleven contemporary wit-nesses[43] testified to Marlowe's "atheism" (in the murky Elizabethan sense),[44]

---

39. Groves, *Texts and Traditions*, 31.

40. Groves, *Texts and Traditions*, 188, 8–9. See *ostensible*, OED sense 2, now "the principal sense": "Declared, avowed, professed; presented (esp. untruthfully or misleadingly) as actual; stated or appearing to be genuine, but not necessarily so. Frequently implicitly or explicitly opposed to *actual* or *real*."

41. John Cox, *Seeming Knowledge: Shakespeare and Skeptical Faith*, xv.

42. David Riggs, "Marlowe's Quarrel with God," in *Marlowe, History and Sexuality*, ed. Paul Whitfield White, 19.

43. Riggs, "Marlowe's Quarrel," 19.

44. Riggs, "Marlowe's Quarrel," 20. As regards atheism in the period, Alec Ryrie's defense of French historian Lucien Febvre is enlightening. See Alec Ryrie, *Unbelievers: An Emotional History of Doubt*, 14. Those unfamiliar with Christianity may find the following reference point helpful:

we have a stronger grasp of Marlowe's inner life than we have of Shakespeare's. Then again, the witnesses may have had questionable motives, and we have no relevant testimony from Marlowe in his own hand. What we evidently are permitted to say, though, is that Marlowe's atheism was "the unintended consequence of an educational program designed to yoke literacy to belief, and eloquence to religion." Following David Riggs's essay "Marlowe's Quarrel with God," which I have just quoted, we can agree (it is a compelling thesis) that the "contradictions between self-empowerment through letters and self-abnegation before God" created a "crisis in Christian humanism." When Riggs speaks of this crisis creating "a conceptual space" to which Marlowe and others "were called,"[45] we need not assume that they discovered the reality of scientific naturalism. Their reference points were likely to have been classical. Riggs goes on to advance his thoughtful argument for Marlowe's atheism, in particular his "subordinating religion to force," by drawing evidence from *Tamburlaine the Great, Parts One and Two*.[46]

If this procedure is acceptable, though, why can't we argue that Shakespeare, while lacking the scars of a Cambridge education, discerned the Christian humanist crisis among pagan authors, biblical "inconsistencies," and "contradictory interpretations,"[47] and that he responded differently? For instance, we might pursue our point about his "frequent, deliberate, and significant" use of biblical allusions,[48] an artistic fingerprint that distinguishes him from Marlowe.[49] We might remark that the force of Shakespeare's biblical allusions is "strengthened by staging which recalls liturgy or the mystery cycles, to explore and enrich the wider concerns of his drama."[50] To maintain that such techniques were more artistic than Christian is possibly to misunderstand the relation between literature and religion. At least, we may consider the possibility that Shakespeare never saw his art as competing against religion, or as antithetical to religion, or as an alternative to religion. And yet, for some, the

---

"Unbelief, in so far as it is a sin, arises from pride, through which man is unwilling to subject his intellect to the rules of faith, and to the sound interpretation of the Fathers." Aquinas, *Summa Theologica*, II-II, q. 10, art. 1.

45. Riggs, "Marlowe's Quarrel," 20.

46. Riggs, "Marlowe's Quarrel," 28–29.

47. Riggs, "Marlowe's Quarrel," 25.

48. Hannibal Hamlin, *The Bible in Shakespeare*, 1.

49. This is not to deny Marlowe's use of the Bible. For comparison and analysis of Shakespeare and Marlowe on this point, see Roy Battenhouse, "Shakespearean Tragedy: Its Christian Premises," *Connotations: A Journal for Critical Debate* 3 (September 1993): 226–42.

50. Groves, *Texts and Traditions*, 7.

barrier to a Christian Shakespeare remains impassible by the very nature of the case: "He likely was Christian, but gauging the degree of his Christian ideas is problematic, simply because a character, rather than the author directly, is always voicing them." In the pepperist courtroom, only Shakespeare's characters can take the stand. Unlike Marlowe's characters, they cannot testify to Shakespeare's worldview (unless the case is for a post-Christian worldview). Any objection is overruled as an unwarranted raid on the inner theater of Shakespeare's religious beliefs.

Is there no getting past the obstacles to a Christian Shakespeare? Why can't the pluralistic offices of liberal modernity accommodate some version of Shakespeare as a Christian humanist? Why not a compromise solution, attributing to Shakespeare some spark of Christian purpose, yet in a way that does not endanger the non-religious reception of the work? Why not, for example, an Erasmian Shakespeare who built a theater culture based on "inclusivist . . . communitarian principles," forging a "stage-religion" in a "spirit of doctrinal minimalism," where "the player had *subsumed* the preacher's role"?[51] Though we are grateful to Jeffrey Knapp, whom I quote here, for paying mind to Erasmus (we will turn to Erasmus in Chapter 1), such a compromise pays homage to our contemporary politics more than it honors Shakespeare's historical experience.[52] Adrian Streete rightly criticizes "pluralist constructions that dominate so much of the field . . . in the service of a liberal, modern paradigm that does not pertain to the period under question."[53] Brian Walsh, analyzing the phenomenon of "religious unsettlement," likewise observes of the period: "the stakes of religious conflict became most intense, because most potentially shattering to social and political harmony, when they involved the fragmenting of a universal Christendom that might once have been taken for granted as a binding force in English society."[54] Ironically, given that Knapp presents his thesis in sharp reaction against Greenblatt's push toward secularization, there is no great gulf of feeling between Greenblatt's well-known contention that, in the first performances of *King Lear*, all Christian (Catholic and Protestant) content is "*emptied out*, even as it is loyally confirmed"[55] and Knapp's "stage-religion."

51. Jeffrey Knapp, *Shakespeare's Tribe: Church, Nation, and Theater in Renaissance England*, 28, 134, 31, 118, his italics.

52. For a lengthy and heated rebuttal of Knapp's use of the term *Erasmianism*, see Peter Lake, *How Shakespeare Put Politics on the Stage: Power and Succession in the History Plays*, 631–32n28.

53. Adrian Streete, *Protestantism and Drama in Early Modern England*, 8.

54. Walsh, *Unsettled Toleration*, 2.

55. Stephen Greenblatt, *Shakespearean Negotiations: The Circulation of Social Energy in Renaissance England*, 126. The Foucauldian key to this kind of thinking is stated earlier in the book: "the sub-

For both critics, the theater's cultural power over religion is what counts. Neither Knapp nor Greenblatt does justice to the living force of Shakespeare's theological concerns, shared by his audience, in an environment where religious language grew more troubling, not more reassuring, where it became "too dense, too marked by previous conflict, to allow easy redemption."[56] This difficult stage of theological discourse did not resolve itself into the dew of theatrical self-consciousness. It could not be neutralized by "stage-religion." If we seek to appreciate the Christian sensibility of Shakespeare's original audience, Knapp's attraction to Erasmian tolerance gets us closer than Greenblatt's acclaimed theory about the "symbolic acquisition" of religious practice as "social energy."[57] But neither gets us close enough.

The post-Christian sensibility that connects Knapp to Greenblatt is immediately evident in how both seek to contain Shakespeare's representation of evil. In this respect, Knapp's interpretation of the speech addressed by Henry V to his siblings Bedford and Gloucester at Agincourt displaces foundational Christian ethics:

> There is some soul of goodness in things evil,
> Would men observingly distill it out;
> For our bad neighbor makes us early stirrers,
> Which is both healthful and good husbandry.
> Besides, they are our outward consciences,
> And preachers to us all, admonishing
> That we should dress us fairly for our end.
> Thus may we gather honey from the weed
> And make a moral of the devil himself. (4.1.4–12)

For Knapp, this speech is evidence of the theater's church-displacing work as "an alternative site of spiritual edification," a culturally authoritative teaching moment when "the French and even the devil can be seen as 'preachers.'"[58] Though we can agree on a modest amount of "spiritual edification," the case for an "alternative site" is unconvincing. The King moralizes, delivering in the present active indicative what he discerns conditionally, "There is some soul

---

versiveness that is genuine and radical—sufficiently disturbing so that to be suspected of it could lead to imprisonment and torture—is at the same time contained by the power it would appear to threaten" (30).

56. Brian Cummings, *The Literary Culture of the Reformation: Grammar and Grace*, 417.
57. Greenblatt, *Shakespearean Negotiations*, 11.
58. Knapp, *Shakespeare's Tribe*, 130.

of goodness in things evil, / Would men observingly distil it out." The notion of "some soul of goodness in things evil" is more theologically complex, more personal and significant, than the lecture that follows. The King identifies "things evil" as "our outward consciences" and explains how this is so. Knapp is not wrong to trace a moralizing vein, but he neglects the King's concern with Judgment: it turns out that the reference to dressing "us fairly for our end" (to "dress" means to *prepare*, as at H5 4.1.185) is not entirely routine. It evokes theological questions that matter a great deal, questions that will soon erupt in Henry's colloquy with Bates, Court, and Williams. Shakespeare's airing these questions in the drama—doing so with high seriousness—doesn't in the least promote the channeling of cultural power from the church to the theater, as if the theater had the power to remake Christian reality. Like the threat of Judgment, the mystery of "some soul of goodness in things evil" has tremendous staying power. In *Henry V*, the conduct of Cambridge, Scroop, and Grey provides occasion for the King to ruminate out loud on this mystery. Scroop's betrayal, the betrayal of a beloved friend, is in Henry's view explicable by analogy: "For this revolt of thine, methinks, is like / Another fall of man" (2.2.140–41). To the Elizabethans, evil was foreseen from eternity. Evil and rebellion preceded man's creation, yet remained part of the providential plan. Scroop's inexplicable treason, "whatsoever cunning fiend it was" (2.2.110), points to one of the enduring theological puzzles. As the Church of England's "preachers" duly reminded the Queen's subjects, "Lucifer" had changed from "the brightest and most glorious angel" to "the blackest and most foulest fiend and devil."[59] The mystery and actuality of evil—Lucifer's aboriginal fall and its consequences—permeate the cosmos of Elizabeth Tudor and *Henry V*. The boys and the prisoners are about to die. We can "make a moral of the devil himself," as the King remarks, buoying his brothers' morale; and yet the vitality of evil persists.

One thinks of Iago's stubborn silence—which returns us to Greenblatt. When Iago in act five enters the stage as a prisoner, the ruined Othello comments: "I look down towards his feet; but that's a fable" (5.2.294). In Greenblatt's interpretation of this line, Othello is "holding onto a shred of the fable" that the devil has cloven heels. Given Othello's reference to the devil's disfig-

---

59. "An Homilie against Disobedience and Wylfull Rebellion," in Ronald B. Bond, ed., *Certain Sermons or Homilies (1547) AND A Homily against Disobedience and Wilful Rebellion (1570)*, 210. I have modernized the spelling. For the "Scholastic fixation on the example of Lucifer" (22–23), see Matthew J. Smith, "w/Sincerity, Part I: The Drama of the Will from Augustine to Milton," *Christianity & Literature* 67 (December 2017): 8–33; esp. 13–16.

ured body, says Greenblatt, the fact of Iago's normal human appearance undoes the "magical clarity" that the "revelation" of cloven heels would have supplied.[60] But the requirement of "magical clarity" is itself a conjuring trick. I don't see why the Elizabethan mind would have been disenchanted by Shakespeare's use of a pointed and effective contrast. The bewildered Othello is invoking popular representations of the devil—an image with no biblical warrant, by the way.[61] Stage devils had a tradition of their own. Cox supplies a valuable perspective on their appearance on the London commercial stage, during the years 1570–1642, that is, from the mid-Elizabethan period to the closing of the theaters by order of a puritanical parliament: "The ability of early audiences to tolerate inherent ambiguities in theatrical illusion is hard to overestimate. The stage devil necessarily involves an actor in a costume and thereby produces an unavoidable ambiguity at the heart of what the play presents as an instance of the uncanny."[62] This ambiguity has roots in medieval drama, and it is active in *Othello*, albeit in an important new way, that is, in Shakespeare's ability to portray "human villains as demonic."[63]

Joseph Kelly rightly observes that this dramatic innovation "did not challenge the notion of the devil, but it did raise questions about evil in human life."[64] As usual, Shakespeare was raising questions, not exploding myths. When Othello looks down, he and the audience confront the perplexing reality of evil on the ground. In terms of the playwright's artistic design, Othello grasps at the fable just as he is being stripped of the illusions that were his downfall. He has no excuse—no fable and no handkerchief. In a pathetic question addressed to Cassio, the (Christian) Moor proceeds to use the term "demi-devil" to describe his nemesis:

> Will you, I pray, demand of that demi-devil
> Why he hath thus ensnared my soul and body? (5.2. 309–310)

For Greenblatt, the modernizing revelation is, of course, that "the demi-devil is altogether human."[65] But where exactly is the dramatic force in that? Shake-

---

60. Stephen Greenblatt, *Shakespeare's Freedom*, 70–71.

61. Hence James Shapiro, in keeping with his own secularizing tendencies, misrepresents the case: "Devils should have cloven feet, but this one doesn't." James Shapiro, *The Year of Lear: Shakespeare in 1606*, 80.

62. John Cox, *The Devil and the Sacred in English Drama, 1350–1642,* 151. For the stage devil's costumes, see 5–6.

63. Joseph F. Kelly, *The Problem of Evil: From the Book of Job to Modern Genetics*, 98.

64. Kelly, *The Problem of Evil*, 98.

65. Greenblatt, *Shakespeare's Freedom*, 71.

speare's intention was to dramatize the workings of evil, on the stage and in the mind of humanity. Iago has "ensnared" Othello's "soul and body" through hellish trickery, not by debunking the devil, whom he eerily resembles.[66]

Have we put paid to the pepper theory? We found ourselves contesting the rule that the plays can reveal nothing about Shakespeare's personal religious beliefs. We suggested that our modern assumptions about the self and the meaning of inwardness are obstacles to understanding Shakespeare. We also suggested that Shakespeare's attention to the problem of evil supplies a valuable clue to the nature of his beliefs. But it may be (some will say) that Shakespeare devoted immensely detailed attention to the workings of evil without assenting to its real existence. Like Andy Warhol with his soup cans, he projected the object of his attention onto a purely aesthetic field. Confident in his isolated superiority, he was focused on the theater itself—a cultural construct in his own modernizing eyes—while making purely artistic use of the theological understanding that he deployed with consummate skill.

To tug the rope back the other way: theology, I reply, poses severe challenges to western society's recent inclination to aestheticize ethics. Theology, with its claim on reality, resists the Brechtian *Verfremdungseffekt* that Greenblatt references to illuminate his "evacuated rituals."[67] For Shakespeare's audience, theology was not easily estranged:

> Being unprepared,
> Our will became the servant to defect,
> Which else should free have wrought. (MAC 2.1.17–19)

> I have a strange infirmity, which is nothing. . . . (MAC 3.4.87)

The trained eye will read these lines quite differently from how the untrained eye will read them. To the trained eye, the density of theological language is much in evidence. To the untrained eye, "unprepared," "will," "defect," "free," and "nothing" operate within a tangential field of reference: the staggering disjunction between Macbeth's will and heaven's is all but lost. This capacity for theological resonance is a means to dramatic ironies. And our response to this type of irony, which divides the theologically savvy from the theologically naïve, raises questions about how we read Shakespeare today.

---

66. Though absolutely critical, the religious dimension of *Othello* cannot be distinctly grasped without attention to the play's historical setting. A good place to start is Emrys Jones, "*Othello, Lepanto, and the Cyprus Wars*," *Shakespeare Survey* 21 (1968): 47–52.

67. Greenblatt, *Shakespearean Negotiations*, 126, 127.

Theology held much the same fascination for Shakespeare that it held for all thinking Elizabethans. Hannibal Hamlin states an outstanding fact about the period: "Religion pervaded every aspect of life, from government to the family, the schoolroom to the public house, geography to medicine, history to husbandry."[68] Theology supplied the intellectual vocabulary for this religious culture. Likewise, Debora Shuger remarks that, during Shakespeare's lifetime, Christianity was "the cultural matrix for explorations of virtually every topic: kingship, selfhood, rationality, language, marriage, ethics, and so forth."[69] It was a time, as Brian Cummings writes, when "every Elizabethan Londoner, it seems, was a theologian."[70] For Cummings, what had changed with the Reformation was not secularization but an *intensification* of debate over matters of religion, and so we need to regain a sense for "how far a struggle over theological meaning permeated English cultural life."[71] The lines from *Macbeth* both recognize and assert the power of "theological meaning."

If knowledge of history can bring Shakespeare closer, it may also help us gain some perspective on the pepper theory. The notion of an author as a purely textual entity was unknown in Shakespeare's time. It is a more modern phenomenon, being closely connected to the emergence of the aesthetic movement. In its embryology, the basic idea can be traced back to around the mid-nineteenth century, for example, to an 1857 letter by Gustave Flaubert, on which James Joyce drew for Stephen Dedalus's description of the "mystery of the esthetic": "The artist, like the God of creation, remains within or behind or beyond or above his handiwork, invisible, refined out of existence, indifferent, paring his fingernails."[72] In 1917, T. S. Eliot, advancing his "Impersonal theory of poetry," put it this way: "the more perfect the artist, the more completely separate in him will be the man who suffers and the mind which creates."[73] The "mind which creates" is an aesthetic mind. It divides art emotions from real emotions. I do not think that Shakespeare wrote that way. In fact, I do not think that Flaubert, Joyce, or Eliot wrote that way either. Imper-

---

68. Hannibal Hamlin, "Preface," in *The Cambridge Companion to Shakespeare and Religion*, ed. Hannibal Hamlin, xii.

69. Debora K. Shuger, *Habits of Thought in the English Renaissance: Religion, Politics, and the Dominant Culture*, 6.

70. Cummings, *Literary Culture*, 286.

71. Cummings, *Literary Culture*, 281.

72. James Joyce, *Portrait of the Artist as a Young Man*, 215. For Flaubert's influence on Joyce and modernism, see Lee Oser, *The Ethics of Modernism: Moral Ideas in Yeats, Eliot, Joyce, Woolf, and Beckett*, 65–66.

73. T. S. Eliot, *The Sacred Wood*, 54.

sonality—understanding the author as a strictly textual entity—is a useful principle for isolating the more purely literary aspects of an author's labors, and for rescuing them from critics that have no real interest in literature at all. In certain conversations, its claims should be defended. At its worst, however, it dehumanizes the arts. It lends itself to a hieratic exaltation of artistic form that sacrifices the broad range of human experience to the perfected object of art—Yeats's golden bird in "Sailing to Byzantium," for example. Harold Bloom supplies an instance of this dehumanizing tendency: "We cannot know, by reading Shakespeare and seeing him played, whether he had any extrapoetic beliefs or disbeliefs."[74] This sweeping assertion—did Shakespeare *not* believe in the reality of evil?—reminds us of Eliot's remark about Henry James, "He had a mind so fine that no idea could violate it."[75] Such aestheticizing formulations, intended as bulwarks against disorder, bad taste, emotional riot, etc., impose a highly refined but narrow understanding on art and its creation.

Horace, in his *Ars Poetica*, contributed to the Renaissance movement with his lesson to would-be poets: "If you wish me to weep, you must first feel grief yourself."[76] The words of Sidney's muse, "look in thy heart and write," speak to Shakespeare as well, because what David Bevington calls "the new insistence on lifelike emotion" characterizes Shakespeare's art.[77] The Pygmalion myth, popularized by Ovid and adapted by Shakespeare in *The Winter's Tale*, directly interprets art as an expression of the artist's desire, symbolically marrying the artist to his work. Nietzsche, in *The Genealogy of Morals* (third essay, section six), seized on Pygmalion as a club to beat Kant and his bloodless heirs in aesthetic philosophy. And Ovid and Horace are not far in spirit from Mamie Dickens's record of her father's compositional practices:

> I was lying on the sofa endeavoring to keep perfectly quiet, while my father wrote busily and rapidly at his desk, when he suddenly jumped up from his chair and rushed to a mirror which hung near, and in which I could see the reflection of some extraordinary facial contortions which he was making. He returned rapidly to his desk, wrote furiously for a few moments, and then went again to the mirror. The facial pantomime was resumed, and then turning toward, but evidently not seeing, me, he began talking rapidly in a

---

74. Harold Bloom, *Shakespeare and the Invention of the Human*, 7.

75. T. S. Eliot, *The Complete Prose of T. S. Eliot: The Critical Edition: Apprentice Years, 1905–1918*, 649.

76. Horace, "Art of Poetry," in *Criticism: The Major Texts*, ed. W. J. Bate, 53.

77. David Bevington, ed., *The Complete Works of Shakespeare*, 1710 (editorial apparatus henceforth cited as Bevington); Sidney as quoted in Bevington.

low voice. Ceasing this soon, however, he returned once more to his desk, where he remained silently writing until luncheon time.[78]

From this line of physical (one might say, *Aristotelian*) testimony, it appears harder to maintain grounds for entirely separating the artist from his or her art, such as would decisively bar us from an author's emotions, intentions, and beliefs.[79] We get an idea of the author through the feelings and emotions present in the work, the sense of evil being perhaps as close as we can get to a metaphysical litmus test. We do not deny a certain proto-aesthetic flair in Touchstone's Wildean paradox, "The truest poetry is the most feigning" (AYL 3.3.17–18). Like Dickens, like other morally coherent artists, Shakespeare could distance his own moods and passions—or slip into those of others. But we are discussing the link between Shakespeare's beliefs and the *pattern* of emotions and feelings that lives on in his plays.

Shakespearean Mimesis

These emotions and feelings go the heart of the matter because they are the lifeblood of Shakespearean mimesis, that is, they tell us how Shakespeare connected his art to reality. Broaching this subject, one should acknowledge that Shakespeare gives little indication of being a purist in terms of dramatic principles. In effect, he synthesized classical and native norms. Shakespeare had looked into Aristotle and Horace. Their ideas, along with comments and commentaries of lesser known authorities, circulated through the widespread conversation about tragedy that emerged in Europe earlier in the sixteenth century, a conversation that included Erasmus, Melanchthon, Philip Sidney, Thomas Lodge, and other Christian humanists who saw tragedy in a religious light (see Chapter 5). From Shakespeare's non-iconoclastic viewpoint, it was given that Christianity lent itself to drama, because Christ imbued the cosmos with a strongly anthropocentric character.[80] The Christ who populates the mystery cycles "is the image of the invisible God" (Colossians 1:15). Likewise, the Christian personal ideal of the *imitatio Christi* "posits a relationship between the human subject and the divine object that is, at its basis, mimetic."[81]

78. Mamie Dickens, *My Father as I Recall Him*, 49–50.
79. The interested reader may wish to consult my contrast of "the Aristotelian body" and "the modernist body" (Oser, *Ethics*, 9).
80. See, for example, John 1:14 and Hebrews 1:3.
81. Streete, *Protestantism and Drama*, 2.

Shakespeare's mimetic practice is squarely at odds with Eliot's influential dictum that "the difference between art and the event is always absolute."[82] Shakespeare assumed a "fit" between his dramaturgy and the broader Christian (and more specifically Pauline) notion of human universality. By contrast, Eliot wrote out of a skeptical theory of linguistic idealism, a theory of the world as text. In fact, he changed his mind and later wrote some excellent pages on Shakespeare's relation to Aristotle and to Sidney.[83] Unlike the early Eliot, Shakespeare was a realist, though in a qualified sense. To quote A. D. Nuttall, whose theory of a "new mimesis" centers on Shakespeare: "artists always find new ways of imitating through form the indefinite richness of reality. . . . But mimesis is mimesis *of* something, or it is not mimesis."[84] Stephen Halliwell considers the same theoretical issues in his analysis of the *Poetics*: "Aristotle's terms and standards of analysis throughout the *Poetics* . . . are suspended between the dual functions of allowing the poetic structure to be treated as an artefact with properties distinctive of and intrinsic to its design within particular media, and acknowledging the kinds of reality signified and enacted by that design."[85] An English Christian, a French Marxist, a student sitting at Aristotle's feet, will have distinct ideas about "the kinds of reality signified"—a point that is crucial to the claim that Shakespeare was a Christian author.

For instance, the distinctly Christian idea of Judgment haunts *Romeo and Juliet*. Gathering from her Nurse that death has taken both Tybalt and Romeo, Juliet exclaims, "Then, dreadful trumpet, sound the general doom!" (3.2.67). Why this apocalyptic trumpet? It marks a departure from Shakespeare's source, Arthur Brooke's *Tragicall Historye of Romeus and Juliet*. How significant is it? Shakespeare intended from the start of the play for his audience to feel the eschatological pressure of predestination—to feel the plight of "star-crossed lovers" (Prol. 6) meeting their Christian doom. Brooke's poem lacks such emotional pressure because, relying heavily on the figure of Fortune, it does not tie the theme of erotic longing to the life beyond this one. Brooke's lovers are not "saints" (1.5.100). Christian eschatological references are not wholly absent from his leaden poem. They are sparse, however, and without thematic continuity. This lack is rectified in *Romeo and Juliet*. By writing a "moral prologue which outlines the whole of the play's action in advance," Shakespeare,

82. Eliot, *Sacred Wood*, 56.
83. T. S. Eliot, *The Use of Poetry and the Use of Criticism*, 32–40.
84. A. D. Nuttall, *A New Mimesis*, 181–82, his italics.
85. Stephen Halliwell, "Aristotelian Mimesis Reevaluated," *Journal of the History of Philosophy* 28 (1990): 507.

as Robert Potter points out, cues the audience's attention by reworking one of the "stock episodes of the morality play." Potter observes that, through Shakespeare's use of such Christian material, "we are invited to watch familiar moral events as interested—indeed, implicated—spectators." The reference to "the fatal loins" (Prol. 5) of Montague and Capulet conveyed the common condition known as original sin, said to be transmitted through the sexual act. The "old conventions"[86] retained their reliable grip on the Elizabethans, even as Shakespeare synthesized these Christian conventions with a classically informed image of erotic deification set up by a sexy pun on "die":

> Give me my Romeo, and when I shall die
> Take him and cut him out in little stars. (3.2.21–22)

Upon further investigation, we may remark that Juliet's "dreadful trumpet" fits into a unified design, which connects this world to the next. Catastrophe looms, and Juliet declares her "faith" is "in heaven," despite heaven's practicing "stratagems" against her (3.5.206–210). We do not find Shakespeare's design to be orthodox in any sense, but it is recognizably Christian. The dead lovers' golden statues would scandalize a Catholic or a Protestant church, but they are an apt metaphor for the play itself, a "profane" work (1.5.94), a work performed outside the *fanum*, but rich in harmonies with the church and the life of the church.

I am suggesting that Shakespearean mimesis implicates the Christian soul. And yet, for Katherine A. Rowe, former president of the Shakespeare Association of America, Shakespearean emotion has a more material basis: "Early modern drama is preoccupied by the mismatch between . . . demands for affective continuity and the essential inconstancy of humoral passions, so prone to alter with environment and occasion."[87] To advance her understanding of Shakespearean emotion, Rowe, like other scholars of the period, draws on Thomas Wright's work *The Passions of the Mind* (1600).[88] She does not mention that Wright, as befits an outspoken Roman Catholic priest and follower of Aquinas, connects his physiological analysis to "the four causes of our

---

86. Robert Potter, *The English Morality Play: Origins, History, and Influence of a Dramatic Tradition*, 123–24.

87. Katherine Rowe, "Shakespearean Tragic Emotions," in *A Companion to Shakespeare's Work: The Tragedies*, ed. Richard Dutton and Jean E. Howard, 53.

88. To the best of my knowledge, no one writing recently on Shakespeare has noted the teleological dimension of Wright's thought, with the exception of Robin Headlam Wells, *Shakespeare's Humanism*, 37.

Passions—formal, material, efficient, and final."[89] This is significant because, while Rowe addresses Shakespeare's "material phenomenology," the "material psychology of the period," and the "material soul,"[90] Wright's metaphysic entails, by contrast, a human disposition to passion that is educable and mimetic because the soul is directed toward the God of the Christians.

Let us return to *Romeo and Juliet* to test the materialist hypothesis. The Nurse gets her story straight and Juliet cries out: "Oh, God! Did Romeo's hand shed Tybalt's blood?" (3.2.71). (Brooke has Juliet apostrophizing her window: "She cryde, O cursed windowe"[91]). How powerful and resonant is this cry, this apostrophe to the God whom Aquinas called a *Deus absconditus?* Adopting the anthropological term "emotion scripts," Rowe says that these scripts "rarely come in single or unitary force."[92] We assume that, from Rowe's point of view, "affective continuity" is disrupted, a metabolic change occurring in humoral physiology, when Juliet desperately cries out to God. But, we reply, doesn't Christianity supply a "unitary force" within the Elizabethan frame of reference? Isn't it the very atmosphere within which the "inconstancy of humoral passions" occurs?[93]

I agree with Rowe that Romeo and Juliet's love affair is an experience of great passion. But I maintain that Shakespeare's understanding of passion is Christian: its tendency is to participate in Christ's Passion. When his Chorus remarks of the lovers, "passion lends them power" (2.0.13), the loan brings unforeseen consequences that reveal the dictates of providence.[94] Their "true-love passion" (2.2.104) is attested in a symbolic "orchard" (2.1.6, 2.2.63; the word does not occur in Brooke) and validated by the sanctity of marriage: "Till Holy Church incorporate two in one" (2.6.37). Their *sacrificial* deaths (5.3.304) are redemptive, uniting their families, as foretold by the Prologue, which, in a Christian spirit, requests "patient ears" (Prol. 13; cf. L. *patior, pati, passus sum*). So it is relevant, on etymological and thematic grounds, that "a term often used to describe the art of acting at the time," as Tiffany Stern informs us, "was 'passionating.'"[95] The boy actor playing Juliet needed to

89. Thomas Wright, *The Passions of the Mind in General*, ed. William Webster Newbold, 125.

90. Rowe, "Shakespearean Tragic Emotions," 54, 55, 59.

91. Geoffrey Bullough, *Narrative and Dramatic Sources in Shakespeare*, 1:314.

92. Rowe, "Shakespearean Tragic Emotions," 53.

93. An extreme test case would be Alice Arden, but a providential framework nonetheless holds.

94. See Craig Bernthal, *The Trial of Man: Christianity and Judgment in the World of Shakespeare*, 284–85n14.

95. Tiffany Stern, *Making Shakespeare: From Stage to Page*, 80.

convey her tragic suffering and her confusion, the topsy-turvy conflict in her mind between her rival loyalties, including her loyalties to this world and the next, an essential Shakespearean theme. The same goes for the actor who played Romeo—who, again with no parallel in Brooke, asks Friar Laurence: "What less than doomsday is the Prince's doom?" (3.3.9). The line highlights the moral tension of these competing loyalties, since in the Elizabethan mind the Prince's banishment of Romeo takes its lawful authority from God—a reality not lost on Romeo, who responds to Friar Laurence's bad news with pathetic vociferations about "purgatory, torture, hell itself" (18). Brooke, we note in passing, has no purgatory. A few minutes later, Romeo's "comfort is revived" (165). The relative immaturity of *Romeo and Juliet*—its moments of bathos and patches of raw writing—does not sabotage the lovers' magnificent roles, which demand actors capable of working a varied and extensive emotional register, testing and at times dissolving the borderline between comedy and tragedy. Juliet's resurrection in the tomb sails very close to comedy.[96] And this sensible intermingling is a Christian experience. Such changeable emotion is built into Christian drama, notably in the reversal pattern of *tristia* and *gaudium* that O. B. Hardison traced from the Mass through the *Quem quaeritis* trope into the earliest resurrection plays.[97] Liturgically and dramatically, Good Friday and Easter Sunday occur within sight of each other. Changeability, then, is the expression of a bedrock of belief, not a purely material index, like a thermometer, of fluctuation in environment.

In a kind of rambling foolspeak, Juliet's Nurse exhibits the dizzying Christian interplay of comedy and tragedy: the reader may consult her long and wondrous synthesis of church, sex, and apocalypse ("wormwood" twice, see Revelation 8:10), which begins, "Even or odd of all days in the year" (1.3.17).[98] Brooke's Nurse, we note, is neither liturgically minded nor weirdly eschatological.[99] Old Capulet's lament that "all things change them to the contrary" (4.5.90) would be at home in Brooke's translation, where it would die a slow death. In Shakespeare's handling, by contrast, "change . . . to the contrary"

---

96. See Groves, *Texts and Traditions*, 60–61. Groves argues that Shakespeare revised Q1 to intensify the tension between tragic and comic elements: the "ambiguous optimism of Q2 . . . sets up the audience for a greater tragic fall . . . . Shakespeare combines bawdy language and stock comic characters . . . with more fundamental comic themes, in particular the Easter resonance, to create a tragedy in which light-heartedness is integral to the tragic effect" (88).

97. O. B. Hardison, Jr., *Christian Rite and Christian Drama in the Middle Ages: Essays in the Origin and Early History of Modern Drama*, 238.

98. For background and commentary, see Groves, *Texts and Traditions*, 63–64.

99. I am indebted to Roy Battenhouse for his work on Christian eschatology in Shakespeare's tragic mimesis. See Roy W. Battenhouse, *Shakespearean Tragedy: Its Art and Its Christian Premises*, 145–49.

owes more to the rediscovery of Christian potentialities than it owes to Brooke's monotonously moralized "Fortune." Rowe's argument about alterations of "environment and occasion" fails to admit the paradox of Christian discontinuity—which lends itself to clownish humor in the Nurse's long speech, as well as when Peter demands of the musicians: "Oh, play me some merry dump to comfort me" (4.5.105–106). This restless potential for reversal ("Even or odd") is intensely Shakespearean. It serves the end of a Christian mimesis, which, resisting neo-classical pressures, is not strictly subject to the Aristotelian principle of dramatic probability.

What I take to be the most revealing Shakespearean reference to Christian mimesis is Hamlet's instructions to the players. To "hold as 'twere the mirror up to nature" (3.2.22) is to imitate "humanity" (34–35), a collective noun that, not yet atomized into billions, suits a world of Christian players with the license to universalize, that is, to imitate people of all races and all times. Hamlet in this speech makes multiple allusions to medieval cycle plays: the bad actor who would "tear a passion to tatters" (9–10) should be whipped "for o'erdoing Termagant" (13–14). The same player "out-Herods Herods" (3.2.13–14). "Pray you, avoid it," Hamlet instructs the First Player. (14). This allusive cluster does not so much suggest that Hamlet looks down his nose at the native tradition as that he is acutely aware of it.[100] Skilled players, as opposed to those made as if by "nature's journeymen" (33), speak with "th' accent of Christians" and go with "the gait" of "Christian" or "pagan" or "man." (31–2). Hamlet's Christian accent is illuminated by Cassius's remark: "How many ages hence / Shall this our lofty scene be acted over / In states unborn and accents yet unknown!" (JC 3.1.112–14). Given this overall weight of Christian reference ("pagan" is itself a Christian reference), I find it dismaying when editorial glosses on "Christians" do no better than "ordinary decent folk" or the like.[101] Nor is it self-evident, from either the play or from Hamlet's instructions, that Christians are "decent" in the least.

---

100. "The traditional actor in the role of Herod is scorned because his acting is conscious artifice." David Wiles, *Shakespeare's Clown: Actor and Text in the Elizabethan Playhouse*, ix. This is wrong in my opinion. Hamlet is not scorning the traditional actor. He is scorning the bad modern actor: "Oh, it offends me to the soul to hear a robustious periwig-pated fellow tear a passion to tatters" (3.2.8–10). Groves remarks that Hamlet's commanding the players to suit "the action to the word, the word to the action" (3.2.17–18) pleads, in effect, for the eye and for the ear. The chiasmus "harmonizes . . . the different devotional foci of Catholicism and Protestantism . . . the lingering memory of the visual stimuli of Catholicism, and the rising literary awareness inspired by Protestantism." Groves, *Texts and Traditions*, 59.

101. Bevington's note. Harold Jenkins in his Arden edition has "ordinary decent beings." William Shakespeare, *Hamlet*, ed. Harold Jenkins, 289n.

I am arguing that Hamlet's instructions exemplify Shakespeare's self-consciously Christian modernity, addressing "the purpose of playing . . . both at the first and now" (3.2.20–21). Shakespeare's dramatic "mirror" (22) is not medieval. It is humanist and Christian. It is strong enough to absorb a great deal of pressure, including witty barrages of non-mimetic punning: "By Cock, they are to blame" (4.5.62) sings the mad Ophelia, confounding Jesus Christ and the male reproductive organ. The kind of reality signified and enacted by Shakespeare's design (to echo Halliwell's terms) is, again, markedly eschatological. More obvious references, including "doomsday" (1.1.124, 2.2.239, 5.1.59), "the doom" (3.4.51), and "last trumpet" (5.1.230), combine throughout *Hamlet* with less obvious references to build apocalyptic pressure. Fainter in significance to a modern audience is the allusion to the *Dies Irae* in Horatio's lines, "And then it started like a guilty thing / Upon a fearful summons" (1.1.154–55),[102] and another to the Book of Revelation, "Wormwood, wormwood" (3.2.179). Writing about Christian souls, Shakespeare gives time and space the uncanny potential to function symbolically at any juncture, outside the bounds of natural "philosophy" (1.5.176). I will address the related topic of Hamlet's age in Chapter 4, but for now we can observe the obsessive intrusion of Christian eternity into the play's unfolding *now*. It starts with the Ghost's shuttling in and out of time. It affects our sense of place. The Ghost is "here," and then "here" (1.1.146–47), and then, haunting the realm beneath the stage, *"hic et ubique"* (1.5.165).[103] Space is tensed and tinctured by the reality of Judgment. Old Hamlet is murdered in an archetypal "orchard" (1.5.60). The Prince expatiates on Denmark's being "a prison" (2.2.244, 52): "I could be bounded in a nutshell and count myself a king of infinite space, were it not that I have bad dreams" (2.2.255–57). Soon we hear of "what dreams may come" (3.1.67). Gertrude's "closet" serves, we suggest, as her "private chapel" (*closet*, OED 2), where in penitence she confesses her sins. From an Augustinian and therefore traditional Christian viewpoint, what compels Shakespeare and his *Hamlet* into new territory is not so much his great reasoning powers in a mimetic context where reason speaks for the human soul as the image of God in man. It is, rather, his alertness to the soul's distance from God, that is, to the soul's

---

102. *Ingemisco tamquam reus*. The line is from the famous *Dies Irae*, by Thomas of Celano (13th c.). See *The Hymns of the Breviary and Missal*, ed. Matthew Britt, OSB, 204.

103. Greenblatt links this Latin phrase to traditional "Catholic practice in England . . . specifically connected to a belief in Purgatory." Stephen Greenblatt, *Hamlet in Purgatory*, 234–35.

unlikeness to God.[104] Horatio's testimony to Hamlet about the ghost's identity, "A figure *like* your father" (1.2.200, my emphasis), wavers between likeness and unlikeness. Given stress by poetic consonance, the ambiguous resemblance of "figure" and "father" puzzles our hold on truth. A "figure" might be anything—a human figure, a rhetorical figure, a figure in typology. Laertes receives Hamlet's "offered love *like* love" (5.2.249, my emphasis).

To be sure, the play-world of Christian mimesis was not bound by tragedy. Shakespeare's alertness to man's incorrigible fallenness was often quickened by his comic instinct, as in the case of Nell Quickly:

> "How now, Sir John?" quoth I. "What, man? Be of good cheer." So 'a cried out, "God, God, God!" three or four times. Now I, to comfort him, bid him 'a should not think of God; I hoped there was no need to trouble himself with any such thoughts yet. (H5 2.3.17–21)

It strains credulity to think that such instinctive wit was the profit-driven work of instrumental reason, a clever bit of Shakespearean invention intended to amuse the house with low and sentimental comedy. It is necessarily subjective to say so, but the comic irony doesn't feel like a shtick. It is too terribly serious. It doesn't enforce the audience's class prejudices: it negates them. It completes the theme of Falstaffian repentance with a power that reaches beyond words to everyone's deepest terrors and desires, to the fear of Judgment and the hope of salvation.

Athens and Jerusalem

Commenting on "the uneasy and unstable alliance of classical and Christian elements" that characterized the Renaissance, Paul Cantor calls into question the notion of a "grand and successful synthesis . . . under the label 'Christian humanism.'" He writes: "Any investigation of the phenomenon ought to begin with a frank admission of how deeply problematic the concept is, of how many tensions and contradictions lie concealed beneath what appears to be a simple label." Cantor is absolutely correct. "One can see how difficult it is to fuse Christianity and classicism," he observes. "The Achilles

---

104. "A human being is a major kind of thing, being made 'in the image and likeness of God' [Genesis 1:26–27] not by virtue of having a mortal body but by virtue of having a rational soul and thus a higher status than animals." Augustine, *On Christian Teaching* (*De Doctrina Christiana*), trans. R. P. H. Green, 16 (I.xxii). "*[I]nveni longe me esse a te in regione dissimilitudinis.*" Augustine, *Confessions: Books 1–8*, ed. and trans. Carolyn J.-B. Hammond, 328 (7.10).

of Homer's *Iliad* is the classical hero *par excellence*, and it would be hard to imagine a less Christian figure."[105] This comment overlooks the Book of Revelation, where Christ himself wields a "sharp sword" (19:15), but the point is well taken. For Cantor, "attempts at arriving at a higher synthesis of antithetical values can end up highlighting the conflicts between them."[106] No doubt this is true. Where my emphasis differs from Cantor's is in my concern for Shakespeare's attention to the conflict, preeminent in *Hamlet*, between antithetical values. To the extent that Hamlet's psyche is never fully integrated, to the extent that it suffers imbalances and disorders, it reflects the disintegration of Christendom. Likewise, Shakespeare's protracted deliberations on Caesar, like the topical resonances of his classical plays, suggest that he identified and exploited conflicts of feeling between the classical and the Christian worldview as well. He was not Aquinas. He did not attempt a synthesis of all knowledge: his effort at synthesis varied from play to play. A history of antitheses—classical versus Christian, Catholic versus Protestant—had chemically altered the materials that he had to work with.

The question to pursue, in light of Cantor's criticism, is how well did Christian *truth* survive this history of ruptures and upheavals? Its role as Augustine understood it suffered. Its abstract power as "that through which" dialectic is true declined.[107] Geoffrey Shepherd's insight into the humanist agenda is apt: humanists "believed that truth, by virtue of its nature, requires exemplification and finds its confirmation only in the complexity of existence."[108] Shakespeare is complex in this truth-seeking sense, which engages the central tensions and contradictions of Elizabethan civilization. In Shakespeare's Christian humanism, the "higher synthesis" of Hellenism and Hebraism, of Athens and Jerusalem, is not systematic, but nonetheless it engages truth.[109] It becomes a means of assimilating and addressing the great issues of a changing world, from theology to the arts, from history to law, from the economies of market towns to the challenges of international trade, from the teachings of Aristotle to the incursions of natural philosophy, from the power of the Virgin Queen to the role of women in society. In the adaptability of its construction materials, this working synthesis served as a bridge to the past, including folkways it altered

---

105. Paul Cantor, *Shakespeare: Hamlet*, 2, 3, 3.

106. Cantor, *Shakespeare: Hamlet*, 12.

107. Augustine, *Soliloquies: Augustine's Inner Dialogue*, trans. Kim Paffenroth, 78.

108. Geoffrey Shepherd, introduction to *An Apology for Poetry*, by Sir Philip Sidney, ed. Geoffrey Shepherd, 20.

109. For "Athens and Jerusalem" in European culture, see Rémi Brague, *Eccentric Culture: A Theory of Western Civilization*, trans. Samuel Lester, 24–26.

at a touch. It joined past and present, the sacred and the secular. It was never more exacting for his audience than when Shakespeare connected the Delphic imperative "Know thyself," a humanist commonplace,[110] to the pressing cause for interest in such knowledge, namely, the imminent reality of Judgment. Shakespeare's assimilation of salvation history and classical learning to the realities of contemporary life must have amounted, for Elizabethan theatergoers, to an intensely entertaining pedagogical and moral experience, which, I suggest, is practically the whole point of Shakespeare's art.

"Literature" and Christian Writing

Unlike later writers and critics, Shakespeare does not distinguish literature from Christian writing. Elsewhere, I have argued that Shakespeare, like Sidney, "is best understood as negotiating a serious place for literature and drama in a deeply religious culture."[111] This position, which I maintain, is challenged and complicated, not contradicted, by Cummings's daunting observation, "'Literature' in its modern sense . . . is not a useful term in the Elizabethan and Jacobean period."[112] Before giving unqualified assent to this remark, we would need to inquire into what exactly we mean by "'literature' in its modern sense." Cummings cites Sidney's *Apology* in support of his position. It is certainly a text where literary and theological concerns converge. *Christian humanism* as a generic label evokes Sidney's *Apology*, as it does epics by Spenser and Milton. But while these works, if we take them seriously, force us to contemplate the relation between literature and theology, we are not bound to assume that "'literature' in the modern sense" is *atheological*. We may prefer the term *paratheological*, that is, *closely related to theology*.[113] The problem we face is that many contemporary critics of Shakespeare are natural-born pepper theorists, uninterested in the profound theological dimension of literature. For scholars of Spenser and Milton, of Donne and Herbert, this is not necessarily the case. But the stakes are higher where Shakespeare is concerned.

---

110. For Platonic, Stoic, and Ciceronian uses of the "Delphic maxim," see Rhodri Lewis, *Hamlet and the Vision of Darkness*, 20–21. For its Christian humanist assimilation by Erasmus and Thomas More, see Wells, *Shakespeare's Humanism*, 11. For Calvin's version, see John Calvin, *The Institution of the Christian Religion*, 1.1.1. For general background and its bearing on Shakespeare's Christian humanism, see Rolf Soellner, *Shakespeare's Patterns of Self-Knowledge*. Soellner's approach (and greater emphasis on Montaigne) complements my own.

111. Lee Oser, "Imagination, Judgment, and Belief in *A Midsummer Night's Dream*," 49.

112. Cummings, *Literary Culture*, 286.

113. See Lee Oser, *The Return of Christian Humanism: Chesterton, Eliot, Tolkien and the Romance of History*, 3.

Unless we acknowledge how permeable the membrane was between literature and theology in Shakespeare's time, we must expect an artificial barrier to divide them. The barrier is common, though its outlines may differ from critic to critic. Alison Shell, an authority on Catholicism and literature during Shakespeare's period, supplies a sophisticated version. She describes Shakespeare as "someone constantly ready to appropriate religious matter wherever it enhances artistic vision, but who invariably subordinates it to the requirements of the individual artefact." Shell argues by way of A. W. Schlegel's distinction between organic and mechanical form: "Because the truth-claims insisted upon by Christianity . . . have an intrinsically overriding quality, they can be seen as imparters of mechanical form—and hence artistically inferior."[114] Schlegel was a critic of depth and insight, but he was galvanized by the romantic drive for originality. "The whole of Shakespeare's productions bear [sic] the certain stamp of his original genius," he tells us.[115] It follows that, for Shell, Shakespeare is an organic writer, not subject to dogmatic truth-claims, which, being unoriginal, must invariably weaken the literature they inhabit. One can agree that the Bible offered Shakespeare a storehouse of first-rate material: in this regard, Shakespeare "exploited religious allusion." One can admire, in Shell's discussion of *King Lear*, her remarks on Cordelia's spiritual condition: Cordelia is a pagan who deserves to be saved, and so the playwright, for purposes of dramatic interest, is "setting up the question of whether this is going to happen." But the matter is trickier than it seems. Where, exactly, do we draw the line when it comes to dogmatic truth-claims? Is the existence of evil a dogmatic truth-claim that Shakespeare wasn't subject to? What of moral agency? Or Judgment?

Shell sets up too strong an opposition between Christianity and Shakespeare, limiting Christian literature to the more devotional end of the spectrum. In her reading of *Measure for Measure*, for example, she twice characterizes the original audience's participation as "voyeuristic," an exotic word of late origin that serves her notion of Shakespeare's saying "more about human weakness inside the play than outside."[116] In other words, for Shell, Shakespeare gets the spectators focusing on fictional characters, while offering them a vacation from the reality of sin as it applies to everyone in the theater. Granted, we may say that *Measure for Measure* has a voyeuristic dimension,

114. Alison Shell, *Shakespeare and Religion*, 231.
115. A. W. Schlegel, "Shakespeare," in *Criticism: The Major Texts*, ed. W. J. Bate, 423.
116. Shell, *Shakespeare and Religion*, 46, 194, 170, 174 ("invitation to voyeurism"), 171.

particularly in Angelo's attempted seduction of Isabella. Shell shows a refreshing sensitivity to the play as entertainment. My pushback, so to speak, is that the Elizabethans expected and enjoyed a greater quotient of morality in their entertainment than we do. Accordingly, for Shakespeare and his audience the theatrical conditions that invited Christian voyeurism were, in the popular biblical sense, a "snare" (e.g., 2 Timothy 2:26). My purpose here is not to invoke the anti-theatrical tradition in all its severity. Rather, I want to suggest that Shakespeare liked snares: he liked to set moral traps for his audience, and they enjoyed the game and its rules. In this respect, Shakespeare could rely on the eschatological pressure that impels a Christian man or woman to be constantly on the lookout for the end: "Keep awake therefore, for you know neither the day nor the hour" (Matthew 25:13). "Take heed: watch & pray: for you know not when the time is" (Mark 13:33). "You also must be ready, for the Son of Man is coming at an unexpected hour" (Luke 12:40). "Be alert at all times" (Luke 21:36).[117] The irony of the beam and the mote (Matthew 7:3–5) would also have applied.

Angelo and Isabella trade insights into human psychology—our capacities for mercy and justice, our uses and abuses of power, our troublesome sexuality—that "tent" us "to the quick" (HAM 2.2.598), beyond the breezy pleasures of moral or sexual tourism. No voyeuristic impulse could short-circuit the Christian humanist cue that Shakespeare supplies through Escalus's thematic *know thyself* speech:

> Let but your Honor know,
> Whom I believe to be most strait in virtue,
> That, in the working of your own affections,
> Had time cohered with place, or place with wishing,
> Or that the resolute acting of your blood
> Could have attained th' effect of your own purpose,
> Whether you had not sometime in your life
> Erred in this point which now you censure him,
> And pulled the law upon you. (MM 2.1.8–16)

"Let but your Honor know" is a resonant phrase, couched in a disconcerting pause, an effect of the line's brevity. It registers an appeal to a humanistic *topos* of high seriousness. In Escalus's delivery of this speech to Angelo, especially in the references to "you" and to "him," that is, respectively, to Angelo and

---

117. See also, for instance, Matthew 24:42.

Claudio (but not just to Angelo and Claudio), one can readily imagine the actor cocking his eye at individual playgoers—touching them with the sharp imperative of self-scrutiny.

Inherent in the audience's form of life, the capacity of Christians to connect with Christ at any moment shouldn't be overlooked: it is a powerful legacy of the mystery plays that Shakespeare makes his own. Lucio's devilish habit of forcing himself on the Christlike Duke is a prime example. To follow Groves: "The York cycle shares this sense of the devil being someone Christ has difficulty shaking off, and stresses the awkward, intrusive intimacy of the situation."[118] The intimate way in which the audience experienced the Jesus-Lucifer agon reinforces our sense that Schlegel's taxonomy of organic and mechanical form is inadequate: given Shakespeare's keen awareness of his Christian audience's imaginative capacities, it becomes difficult to say what is mechanical and what is organic. The Bible and sacred history are vivified through the power of audience participation. It is no small consideration that the medieval English theater survived well into Shakespeare's lifetime—and that its remnants and memories outlived its performance.[119] Shakespeare's stage was a "free open platform," as G. R. Kernodle observed, but its physical "background" was "a complex symbol, combined out of several age-old medieval symbols."[120] These included, above and below the stage respectively, "the heavens" and "hell."[121] Shakespearean drama was rooted in the past and yet imaginatively fluid within its traditional boundaries. Religious signifiers resounded with new suggestiveness across this post-medieval stage. Duke Vincentio's likeness to Christ could readily suggest Duke Vincentio's unlikeness to Christ. Isabella's resemblance to Mary played out against Catholic and Protestant ideas of her—and of what it meant to be an Elizabethan woman.

If the current tendency is to modernize, to secularize, to contain the religious and theological meanings of Shakespeare, a strong exception arises with respect to the Eucharistic controversy. Anthony Dawson, for example, locates his work in a critical conversation about the shift from a late medieval "incarnational aesthetic" to a Protestant "distrust of externals and a corresponding

---

118. Groves, *Texts and Traditions*, 177. For more on the mystery plays and *Measure for Measure*, see 162–66.

119. See Kurt A. Schreyer, *Shakespeare's Medieval Craft: Remnants of the Mysteries on the London Stage*, esp. 1–11; and Groves, *Texts and Traditions*, 33–39.

120. G. R. Kernodle, "The Open Stage: Elizabethan or Existentialist?" *Shakespeare Survey* 12 (1959): 3, 2.

121. See Stern, *Making Shakespeare*, 24–25.

turn away from physical signs toward inner conviction."[122] Dawson, in discussing the controversy, enlists the theology of Richard Hooker in order "to suggest that in Shakespearean theater analogous habits of thought are in play." Hooker, as Dawson explains, maintained that the reality of God's presence depended on the spirit with which the communicant received the sacrament: with his receptionist theology, Hooker advanced a *via media*, navigating a path between God's purely symbolic representation at the Lord's Supper and God's real presence in the Eucharist, known to Catholics as "the Blessed Sacrament." This *via media* serves Dawson in turn to advance his analogy, to argue that "theatrical representation was understood and deployed in terms that derive from the Eucharistic controversy." Two more points stand out in Dawson's comparison of Eucharistic theology and Shakespearean drama: (1) theatrical representation so conceived is marked heavily by "meta-theatrical mediation," regarding which Dawson turns to more modern writers, Diderot and William Archer, for clarification; and (2) "relations between theology and theater" exist "without hollowing out the religious field."[123] Though I am skeptical of the heavy work that Diderot, in particular, does in this argument, I recognize, of course, that "metatheatrical reflections upon the shortcomings of dramatic fiction and metadramatic pleas for audience response and imaginative participation" were a "marked feature" of the Elizabethan theater.[124] I appreciate Dawson's unwillingness to hollow out the religious field. The weakness of Dawson's argument lies in his premise, unsupported by contemporary testimony, that Elizabethan audiences brought Hooker's receptionism with them into the playhouse, parsing for their pleasure all the mediations of absence and presence that metadramatic analysis can contrive, while, at the same time, vacationing from the intrusive reality of Judgment—of which Shakespeare's writing unsparingly reminds them. I suspect that many in Shakespeare's audience knew about Hooker's Eucharistic theology. So far so good. I would add, in support of Dawson's position, that Shakespeare's allusions to the Eucharistic controversy must have registered immediately: in *Hamlet*, for instance, we note Ophelia's "baker's daughter" and "God be at your table" (4.5.43–44), as well as Hamlet's obsession with the physical transformation

122. Anthony B. Dawson and Paul Yachnin, *The Culture of Playgoing in Shakespeare's England: A Collaborative Debate*, 21. I note that this fashionable notion of an "incarnational aesthetic" imports a conceptual category, the "aesthetic," into a worldview that does not recognize the "aesthetic."

123. Dawson and Yachnin, *The Culture of Playgoing*, 26, 28, 29.

124. Susannah Brietz Monta, "'It is requir'd you do awake your faith': Belief in Shakespeare's Theater," in *Religion and Drama in Early Modern England: The Performance of Religion on the Renaissance Stage*, ed. Jane Hwang Degenhardt and Elizabeth Williamson, 115.

of corpses.[125] What I reject is Dawson's making this theology the basis of a sweeping theory of audience psychology. Dawson wants to have it both ways. He does not want to deny the power of contemporary religion, yet he wants to import that power into the theater in order to aestheticize it, sacrificing its greatest claims on the audience in order to do so.

Theological Sensitivity

I would urge the importance of what Cummings calls Shakespeare's "theological sensitivity."[126] A reciprocal sensitivity among Shakespeare scholars would be welcome. The once-vigorous rapport between theology and literature has faded: we are well past the modernist period, when such giants as Franz Rosenzweig, Karl Barth, Jacques Maritain, and Reinhold Niebuhr commanded the attention of poets and fiction writers.[127] Roy Battenhouse, who was alert to these matters, blamed the Hegelianism popular among Christian theologians for the predominance of what he described as A. C. Bradley's "crypto-theologizing": "a theologizing of a gentlemanly but insinuating kind . . . masked . . . behind a fashionable reserve."[128] Battenhouse traced an intellectually progressive line of thought from Bradley's *Shakespearean Tragedy* (1904) to Roland Frye's *Shakespeare and Christian Doctrine* (1963), where Frye concluded that "Shakespeare's works 'make no encompassing appeal to theological categories.'"[129] We can insist on a reductive approach to theology, so that it works like a radio either blasting or silent. But such an approach does not require theological sensitivity. The difference between "theological categories" and theology resembles the difference between "religious matter" (Shell's phrase) and religion. In each case, the former term affects the direction of the discussion by deciding the nature of the topic. Greenblatt has in effect circled back to Frye's position: "Shakespeare was not a theologian, and his work does not meddle in doctrinal claims."[130] We notice the slippage from "theologian" to "doctrinal claims." Bloom likewise says that Shakespeare has "no theology."[131] If we take Greenblatt and Bloom to mean that Shakespeare has no theological idols and defers to no systematic approach, I can readily

125. I am indebted to Margreta De Grazia, "Soliloquies and Wages in the Age of Emergent Consciousness," *Textual Practice* 9 (1995): 67–92.

126. Cummings, *Mortal Thoughts*, 235.

127. See, for example, Anthony Domestico, *Poetry and Theology in the Modernist Period*.

128. Roy Battenhouse, *Shakespearean Tragedy: Its Art and Its Christian Premises*, 69.

129. Frye, quoted in Battenhouse, *Shakespearean Tragedy*, 69.

130. Greenblatt, *Shakespeare's Freedom*, 3.

131. Harold Bloom, *The Western Canon: The Books and Schools of the Ages*, 56.

agree with them. Shakespeare's theological language is eclectic and coheres only within the unities of particular works of art. Shakespeare is an artist, not a theologian. But I think in fact that, as regards Shakespeare and theology, Greenblatt and Bloom simply insist on what they want to be true.

Given the strong historical ties between Christianity and literature,[132] the recent impulse to set them apart may amount to a long walk off a short pier. One recalls John Henry Newman's remark that theology is "the secret assumption, too axiomatic to be distinctly professed, of all our writers."[133] This comment is consistent with Shuger's provocative observation that "materialisms remain illicitly dualist."[134] I am suggesting, then, that a heightened sensitivity on our own part to the history of Christianity and literature leads to a heightened sensitivity to Shakespeare's place in that history and to how he engages theological language and controversy. Critics who erect a barrier between Shakespeare and Christianity, at least to the extent that they do so, and despite whatever else is gained, are de-theologizing and modernizing their subject matter. For the next several pages, then, dislodging this barrier is the purpose of pressing the case against leading critical tendencies.

Pressing the Case

For Richard McCoy, in his highly readable *Faith in Shakespeare*, Shakespeare's theological interests turn out to be, upon lengthy and disinterested examination, wholly beside the point. McCoy adduces as a normative principle for Shakespeare criticism Samuel Taylor Coleridge's celebrated notion of "the willing suspension of disbelief for the moment, which constitutes poetic faith."[135] For McCoy, the credibility of Shakespeare's "characters and stories derives from no higher power than literature."[136] McCoy thus puts his weight behind the

132. For Christianity's part in preserving classical literature, see Ernst Robert Curtius, *European Literature and the Latin Middle Ages*, trans. Willard R. Trask; see also Brague, *Eccentric Culture*, 152–78. For a rival view, see E. K. Chambers, *The Medieval Stage*, esp. 1:1–22 and 2:2–3. For Christianity and the sources of medieval drama, see Hardison, *Christian Rite*, which is critical of Chambers. For how monastic discipline prepared the grounds for numerous renaissances great and small, see Christopher Dawson, *The Making of Europe*, 15–22. For Christianity and western literature more broadly, see Erich Auerbach, *Mimesis: The Representation of Reality in Western Literature*, trans. Willard R. Trask. For theology's creative links to western literature, see Oser, *Return of Christian Humanism*, esp. 21–35, which culls key passages from G. K. Chesterton.

133. Newman, *Idea of a University*, 51.

134. Debora K. Shuger, "Subversive Fathers and Suffering Subjects," in *Religion, Literature, and Politics in Post-Reformation England, 1540–1688*, ed. Donna B. Hamilton and Richard Strier, 61.

135. Samuel Taylor Coleridge, quoted in McCoy, *Faith in Shakespeare*, 4.

136. McCoy, *Faith in Shakespeare*, ix.

artificial barrier that separates literature from theology where Shakespeare is concerned. Cox's critique of McCoy is exactly right: "A theory of faith in dramatic illusion must be pertinent to [the medieval cycle plays] as to Shakespeare's putatively nonreligious drama."[137] McCoy fails to show how his theory could survive this test. I would take Cox to have settled the matter, but David Kastan, citing McCoy, likewise regards Coleridgean disbelief as a foundation for contemporary Shakespeare criticism: "What is demanded from us is neither belief in God nor trust in His word, but only 'that willing suspension of disbelief' in the fictions that Shakespeare has created."[138] I want to acknowledge that Kastan, one of the eminent literary scholars of our time, does not write in the backwash of a naive secularism. He is both acute in observing that "'secular' has become itself . . . a contested notion,"[139] and judicious in citing Charles Taylor's authoritative account of religion's demotion to being "one option among others," hence not antithetical to secularity.[140] Even so, he is less pluralistic than he might be. His statement appears to reject the counterdemand for "belief in God" and "trust in His word" as requirements for understanding Shakespeare, but it is hard to imagine what rising critical school prompted this bold rejection of Christian hermeneutics. One might imagine, to the contrary, that someone's "belief in God" might occasionally yield a vein of insight into an author as profoundly connected to Christianity as Shakespeare was. Kastan does not deny this. He eschews smugness and cheap shots. But with the suggestion of facing resistance, he liberates us from a Christian sensibility that is marginal at best and endorses a post-Christian sensibility that, as Eliot said in a different context, owns all the best advertising space.

In their return to Coleridge, Kastan and McCoy perceive that personal belief invariably enters literary study, even if it does so in terms of disbelief. Since Eliot addressed this matter with admirable clarity, we may refer to him once again: "If you deny the theory that full poetic appreciation is possible without belief in what the poet believed, you deny the existence of 'poetry' and 'criticism'; and if you push this denial to its conclusion, you will be forced to admit that there is very little poetry that you can appreciate, and that your appreciation of it will be a function of your philosophy or theology or something else."[141] To limit a work's potential readership to those who share its

---

137. Cox, "Afterword," 273–74.
138. Kastan, *Will to Believe*, 11, and, for Kastan's acknowledgement of McCoy, 14n30.
139. Kastan, *Will to Believe*, 5.
140. Taylor, *A Secular Age*, 3; quoted in Kastan, *Will to Believe*, 13n14.
141. T. S. Eliot, *Selected Essays*, 230.

author's beliefs would, in the mature Eliot's view, hurt the cause of literature. The open-minded depth of response to the art of writing that Eliot calls "full poetic appreciation" is itself the fruit of education and culture. It is rooted in traditional practices[142] that the unprecedented rise of anti-humanism—one thinks of Greenblatt as Foucault's American disciple—has withered. In this professional context, what McCoy and Kastan propose is the maintenance of fairly conservative norms—hence the appeal to Coleridge. At the same time, McCoy and Kastan are reticent to defend the philosophical or theological assumptions behind these norms. Such reticence, I suggest, is no longer a luxury we can afford if we want a real Shakespeare, by which I mean a Shakespeare who is more than hermeneutic fodder in a materialist archive. As we shall see in analysis of individual plays, the real Shakespeare understood his philosophical and theological assumptions very well, because he wrestled with them in his writing.

An irony in the recent Coleridge-izing of Shakespeare bears commenting on as a symptom of scholarly reaction against Christianity. Study of the *Biographia Literaria* reveals that "the willing suspension of disbelief for the moment, which constitutes poetic faith"[143] was never intended by Coleridge to address the issues of personal belief that engage McCoy, Kastan, and Eliot. We find that the phrase "poetic faith," to which McCoy gives such weight, was intentionally and deeply connected through Coleridge's metaphysics to Christian morality.[144] If we consider the case closely, McCoy is found to rely not so much on Coleridge, as on an aestheticizing interpretation of Coleridge. The actual, historical Coleridge would have rejected McCoy's position in favor of Cox's: "In most of Shakespeare's plays, moral recognition is inseparable from faith, so ethical questions are addressed by addressing religious ones."[145] When McCoy remarks on the "basis for an enduring faith in Shakespeare that is good enough for me," he echoes not Coleridge but

---

142. A "practice depends on a mode of understanding it which has been transmitted often through many generations." Alasdair MacIntyre, *After Virtue*, 221.

143. Samuel Taylor Coleridge, *Collected Works*, 7.II: 6–7 (*Biographia Literaria*, ch. 14), ed. James Engell and W. Jackson Bate; quoted in McCoy, *Faith in Shakespeare*, 4.

144. Though it makes no apparent impact on his argument, McCoy in an endnote quotes the distinguished Coleridgean James Engell: "the essential motives for Coleridge's philosophical inquiries—motives that remain even when he deals with the imagination—are moral and strongly connected with the Christian religion." James Engell, *The Creative Imagination*, 332, quoted in McCoy, *Faith in Shakespeare*, 161n78. With respect to poetic faith, Coleridge's synonymous concept of "negative faith" (see McCoy, *Faith in Shakespeare*, 5, 17) is developed along specifically moral lines in the *Biographia Literaria* (Coleridge, *Collected Works*, 7B: 216–18).

145. Cox, *Seeming Knowledge*, xiv.

Walter Pater, who famously wrote: "What is this song or picture, this engaging personality presented in life or in book to *me*?"[146] To paraphrase Don
Corleone: it was Pater all along. Kastan's position is much the same, a magisterial aestheticism of the first-person plural: "What is demanded from us."
What is demanded of us, in the case of well-written books addressing Shakespeare and religion by McCoy and Kastan, is a latter-day Epicureanism, which
distinguishes the learned and the tasteful from the barbarous and the ideologically crude.

If the representatives of this fine Epicurean hermeneutic were more
interested in theology; if they gave more weight to the historically fertile relations between Christianity and literature; if they were less disposed to classify
under one and the same sociological rubric what Anthony Julius calls "confessional communities";[147] if they were occasionally suspicious of their own
enlightened prejudices, they might not have expended such labor in reshaping
the study of Shakespeare and religion into yet another (and another) occasion
for modernizing Shakespeare. Consider, for instance, Kastan's push toward a
less Christian *Hamlet*, which evidences the allegedly naturalistic force of the
"mind's eye": "'The mind's eye' sounds familiar, a timeworn cliché, but it was
new . . . . [The] phrase provides an explanation for the spectral appearance,
deflecting the unnerving thought that it is some real, protoplasmic entity
apprehensible by sense." And again: "Always for Hamlet there is a slight gap
between . . . what is seen only in the 'mind's eye' and what can actually be
seen."[148] It is true that the phrase was relatively new *in English*. But if we suspect that Shakespeare read Augustine in Latin, we head off in the very opposite of Kastan's direction. To quote G. R. Evans in her work *Augustine on Evil*,
there are those who see demons: "The effect of the demons is not to change
the substance of things but to work upon the *oculus mentis*, the eye of the
mind." And there are "those who have understanding, for they 'see' with the
oculus mentis."[149] The Latin phrase is found not only in the writings of Augustine but in the Latin texts of other theologians as well.

When framing the celebrated controversy surrounding John Shakespeare's
"Spiritual Testament," Kastan writes as a pyrrhonist, one who is persuaded

---

146. Walter Pater, *Works*, 1:viii, his italics. For commentary on Pater's continuing significance,
see Oser, *Return of Christian Humanism*, 95.
147. Anthony Julius, "The Fantasy of Free Speech," *Times Literary Supplement* 6043 (January
25, 2019): 14.
148. Kastan, *Will to Believe*, 123, 140.
149. G. R. Evans, *Augustine on Evil*, 108, 158.

by the impossibility of judging a question on one side or the other. At stake in the matter is the Shakespeare family's relation to Roman Catholicism, a topic where prejudice—whether Catholic or anti-Catholic—can be difficult to overcome.

The famous document, discovered in 1757 and now lost, was a handwritten copy of a formulary written during plague-time by Cardinal Charles Borromeo, Archbishop of Milan. Possibly it arrived in England through the hands of Jesuit missionaries attempting to succor Catholics who, like Old Hamlet, could not receive the sacrament of extreme unction. (We note that John Shakespeare, whether unaneled or not, died in September, 1601—within the pale of *Hamlet's* dates of composition.) Kastan observes that in 1923 Herbert Thurston, SJ, discovered the original document's long-lost template in the printing presses of the Counter-Reformation. This finding would eliminate the possibility that the Spiritual Testament was an eighteenth-century forgery, unless a forger had near-miraculous access to the formulary, as well as a co-conspirator in the man who discovered the document. In a generous note to the author, Kastan put the case this way, citing the influential work of historian Robert Bearman: "Is it more probable that an amateur Stratford antiquarian (who . . . was not a Catholic) found an English translation of the Borromeo testament, of which no other English version was known until 1966, and that he decided to forge evidence of John Shakespeare's enduring Catholicism? Or that a manuscript version of the Borromeo testament, also of which no other example is known, reached John Shakespeare [as Bearman says the father of the most famous of all Englishmen] and that he, or someone acting for him filled in the blanks of the formulary. . . . Each seems to me almost equally improbable, and yet one of them has to be true."[150] The "amateur Stratford antiquarian" would be a man of dubious character named John Jordan. On the subject of Jordan's tangled web, Schoenbaum has this to say: "The discrepancies in Jordan's testimony are hardly reassuring (he *was* a rogue), but they do not prove the testament a fraud."[151] Moreover, Schoenbaum supplies an important fact in the case: despite Jordan's maintaining that the man who found the document had not shown it to the owner of the house, Thomas Hart, the fact is that Hart "informed [Edmond] Malone that he remembered the discovery of the document."[152]

---

150. David Kastan, email to author, February 12, 2019. I appreciate that these words, from a formidable, exacting, and generous scholar, are entirely fair-minded.

151. Schoenbaum, *Shakespeare's Lives*, 124.

152. Schoenbaum, *Shakespeare's Lives*, 124.

So it is notable that, in the face of longstanding testimony, Kastan should impugn the witness of Joseph Moseley, the master bricklayer who "[a]llegedly" discovered the document on April 27, 1757.[153] The suspicious adverb is Kastan's addition to his sources. And since Kastan devotes pages to neutralizing the Spiritual Testament, we might point out that the document was discovered "between the rafters and the tiling of the western Shakespeare house on Henley Street,"[154] not so oddly, as Kastan has it, in the roof: "one might reasonably wonder why it was in the roof."[155] No, one might not reasonably wonder why it was found in the roof. Moseley was tiling the roof and found the document, as Stanley Wells is right to say, "in the rafters."[156] Nor does Kastan address the contested phraseology of the Spiritual Testament, an aspect of the case where Bearman, in an essay that was quickly received as authoritative, was simply wrong, as Dennis Taylor observes, to build a case for forgery.[157] At the highest level of academic authority, the upshot of Kastan's work conspires, like circumstances beyond our control, with more assertive readings. In his *Dictionary of National Biography* entry on Shakespeare, Peter Holland has this to say about the document: "Transcribed by the great Shakespeare scholar Edmond Malone, who later came to doubt its authenticity, it is now lost and its link to John Jordan, a Stratford man well known for inventing materials to satisfy the increasing thirst for Shakespeariana, puts it under suspicion. In the unlikely event that it was genuine it would suggest that John Shakespeare was a Catholic."[158] And yet, we say, great scholars make mistakes; Malone did not foresee the 1923 and 1966 findings; Jordan's involvement is neither surprising nor fatal to the case; Hart remembered the document's discovery; Old Hamlet and John Shakespeare (whose grandson was named Hamnet/Hamlet) appear to have some things in common. And while Holland includes Bearman among his sources, he too seems never to have heard of Dennis Taylor. Groves is another who defers to Bearman, but she and her readers are well served by a fair-minded note, "recusancy often ran in

153. Kastan, *Will to Believe*, 22. I am indebted here to Dennis Taylor, cited below.
154. Schoenbaum, *Shakespeare's Lives*, 123.
155. Kastan, *Will to Believe*, 24.
156. Stanley Wells, *Shakespeare: For All Time*, 24.
157. Dennis Taylor, "Bearish on the Will: John Shakespeare in the Rafters," *Shakespeare Newsletter* 54 (Spring 2004): 11,16, 24, 28. Taylor's article is a response to Robert Bearman's "John Shakespeare's 'Spiritual Testament': A Reappraisal," *Shakespeare Survey* 56 (2003):184–202. For the argument about the will's phraseology, see Taylor, 16, 24.
158. Peter Holland, "William Shakespeare," *Oxford Dictionary of National Biography*, accessed online June 20, 2019.

families and the appearance of John Shakespeare's granddaughter, Susanna, on a recusancy list (6 May 1606) makes the case for recusancy in Shakespeare's family highly plausible."[159]

But to return to Kastan's argument: the skeptical qualifications pile up to justify his pyrrhonist conclusion: "There is no way to establish if the Spiritual Testament is authentic and, even if we could, there is no way to determine what the document represented for John Shakespeare."[160] I take this to mean that we could not logically infer John Shakespeare's allegiance to Roman Catholicism even if we agreed on the will's authenticity, as those who have studied Taylor's painstaking rebuttal of Bearman have grounds to do. "But even if we could be certain," we are told, "that the Spiritual Testament established that John Shakespeare lived and died a Catholic, it would still tell us nothing about *William* Shakespeare's faith."[161] *Nothing* is a strong word. One needn't assume that the poet William Shakespeare was a Catholic in order to be able to appreciate his religious background. I am not promoting a Catholic Shakespeare. But with such crushing evidentiary standards, we must yield the authority of the humanities to the sciences, where numbers supply the vacancy of literature, and where human intuition does not trespass on the field of knowledge.

McCoy presides over the epistemological territory that we encountered earlier with the problem of "gauging the degree" of Shakespeare's "Christian ideas." In the following statement, he walls off literature from religion by asserting that religious conviction is impervious to doubt:

> As the philosopher of religion, Anthony Kenny, explains, "The common characteristic of faith in almost all religious traditions is its irrevocability. A faith that is held tentatively is no true faith. It must be held with the same degree of certainty as knowledge," and, Kenny adds, "In some traditions the irrevocability of faith is reinforced by the imposition of the death pen-

159. Groves, *Texts and Traditions*, 28n6. Lois Potter, suggesting that John Shakespeare's allegiance to Rome might have "changed with times" after Queen Mary's death, detects no connection between father and granddaughter in terms of religion. The incriminating document in the rafters was, one must assume, forgotten and left to rot. Potter proposes numerous non-Catholic reasons why Susanna did not take communion on Easter Day, 1606, and why she subsequently failed to appear at court to account for her actions. See Lois Potter, *The Life of William Shakespeare: A Critical Biography*, 44 and 351–52. By contrast, Catholic apologist Joseph Pearce, who is, incidentally, a font of good English prose, places Susanna's recusancy in the Warwickshire context of the Gunpowder Plot and its aftermath. See Joseph Pearce, *The Quest for Shakespeare: The Bard of Avon and the Church of Rome*, 151–53.

160. Kastan, *Will to Believe*, 25.

161. Kastan, *Will to Believe*, 26, his italics.

alty for apostasy, which is the abandonment of faith." Religious conviction was supposed to be even more absolute in Shakespeare's time.[162]

For several reasons, I find this approach flawed. First, in fixing on a "common characteristic of faith," McCoy discounts the consequential differences between "religious traditions." Second, he discounts how history shapes and informs religious experience. To take a prominent example, French theologian Sebastian Castellio, condemning Calvin's imposition of the death penalty against Protestant heretic Michael Servetus, developed "a form of rational mysticism that required doubt as a condition of trust."[163] He rejected "Calvin's account of faith as knowledge."[164] Third, McCoy disregards how, in Susannah Monta's words, "pastoral theology often consoles spiritually uneasy readers by acknowledging that in this world faith is always mixed with doubt."[165] From pastoral theology it is a short step to the texture of personal experience. In England, Ben Jonson and John Donne were far from alone in suffering self-division over their religious loyalties. The doubts occasioned by such personal crises may not have descended to Marlovian depths, but the clash of theological possibilities was vertiginous. Did one have doubts about purgatory? Free will? The number and efficacy of sacraments? McCoy supplies a supporting quotation from Hooker: "If the things which we believe be considered in themselves, it may truly be said that faith is more certain than any Science."[166] And if we go back to the eminent authority cited by McCoy, we find that Kenny's quotations from Aquinas and Newman support McCoy's position.[167] But here is a different kind of language-game: "As you can see, God so orders this corporeal world in its external affairs that if you respect and follow the judgment of human reason, you are bound to say either that there is no God or that God is unjust."[168] That is Martin Luther addressing Erasmus. Cummings remarks: "Luther's scandalous flirtation with atheism is the more shocking because it comes from the century's most radical fideist."[169]

---

162. McCoy, *Faith in Shakespeare,* 4, quoting Anthony Kenny, "Knowledge, Belief, and Faith," *Philosophy* 82 (July 2007): 394.

163. Dominic Erdozain, *The Soul of Doubt: The Religious Roots of Unbelief from Luther to Marx,* 63.

164. Erdozain, *The Soul of Doubt,* 64.

165. Monta, "'It is requir'd,'" 116. Monta supplies a wide range of examples.

166. McCoy, *Faith in Shakespeare,* 4.

167. Kenny, "Knowledge, Belief, and Faith," 394–395.

168. Luther, quoted in Cummings, *Literary Culture,* 404. The passage can be found in Martin Luther, *On the Bondage of the Will,* in *Luther and Erasmus: Free Will and Salvation,* ed. E. Gordon Rupp and Philip S. Watson, 330.

169. Cummings, *Literary Culture,* 405.

McCoy and Kenny overlook what may strike us as a paradox, that the Christian world can spark intenser doubts than the post-Christian world does. Scientific naturalism eliminates hell and all that; agnosticism lives more or less equably with doubt; but the threat of Judgment gives an equally sharp edge to what we know and what we don't.[170]

Religious doubt is an important feature of the Shakespearean stage. The suicidal despair that Edgar recognizes in his father, the blinded Gloucester, is a type of religious doubt expressed in a pagan setting with overt reference to Christianity. Henry V doubts his Christian legitimacy, Hamlet his God-given senses. Macbeth doubts "th'equivocation of the fiend / That lies like truth" (5.5.43–44). Sonnet 146, as we have seen, "has little of the radiance of Christian hope." It follows that McCoy might have exercised more care before pronouncing on the epistemology of doubt in Shakespeare's writing. He might have considered its relation to Calvin's "arrogant verities,"[171] or to Luther's radical fideism, or to what Cox identifies as "the history of religious skepticism in the sixteenth century."[172] This history is beyond complex. It encompasses not just the skepticism of Erasmus and More, or the Christian pyrrhonism of Montaigne, or the intellectual currency of Lucian and of Sextus Empiricus. It is really a matter of the epistemological ground shifting under England and Europe. All this affected Shakespeare, for whom skepticism and Christianity may have been strange bedfellows, but they were bedfellows nonetheless. Further, and of no less importance: an Elizabethan audience knew intimately well that Jesus had asked, "when the Son of man cometh, shall he find faith on earth?" (Luke 18:8). That he cried on the cross, "My God, my God, why hast thou forsaken me?" (Matthew 27:46, see also Mark 15:34). A Christian could despair, lack signs of assurance, feel desolate and forsaken. The argument from doubt cannot serve the case for a post-Christian Shakespeare unless it gives attention to qualia that in this case do not concern the post-Christian critic.

---

170. It is symptomatic of our current muddle, where Christian culture is concerned, that a major Chaucer scholar observes of the *Canterbury Tales*: "Cut off from a sure sense of relation to the divine, or of their place in a traditional hierarchy, the pilgrims question their own status." Winthrop Wetherbee, *Chaucer: The Canterbury Tales*, 9. On this reading, radical doubt antedates Shakespeare's period by two centuries.

171. Erdozain, *Soul of Doubt*, 62.

172. Cox, *Seeming Knowledge*, 4; on Christian skepticism and Shakespeare, see xii, 1–14, and 228–38. See also Soellner, *Shakespeare's Patterns*, esp. 131–49. For Shakespeare in relation to Montaigne and Sextus Empiricus, see Ronald Knowles, "*Hamlet* and Counter-Humanism," *Renaissance Quarterly* 52 (Winter 1999): 1052–57. For Erasmian skepticism, see Erika Rummel, "Desiderius Erasmus" (under the heading "Methodology"), *Stanford Encyclopedia of Philosophy*, https://plato.stanford.edu/entries/erasmus/, accessed January 15, 2020.

A Paradigm Shift

To gain additional perspective on the modernizing of Shakespeare, we can go back in time to the dawn of modern science. The relevant phenomenon is that, as the new light emerges over the horizon, Shakespeare's "rhetorical universe" is setting in the west. I refer by this phrase to Shakespeare's deep grounding in rhetoric, a paramount literary concern throughout the present study. The playwright was born in 1564, the same year as Galileo, the year of Michelangelo's death. He died in 1616, the year the world also lost Cervantes, while Galileo lived on until 1642, the year the theaters closed in England. Thomas Hobbes was born in 1588 and died in 1679. Aubrey in his *Brief Lives* says that Hobbes met Galileo in the 1630s, though the meeting is not well documented. Descartes and Hobbes met in 1648. What matters to us is that Hobbes's defense of the new science inaugurates a mechanistic worldview. The shift is most evident in the emergence of mathematical ideas foreign to Shakespeare, in "innovations rooted in precise mathematical formulation of lawful relationships between basic physical properties."[173] Galileo was arguably truer to this approach than Hobbes was, but it is Hobbes's attack on rhetoric's authority that illuminates the retrograde position of Shakespeare.

In *The Elements of Law* (1638), Hobbes contrasts the humble *mathematici*, who employ "evident demonstration," against the quarrelsome *dogmatici*, who argue rhetorically. The former, says Hobbes, are known for "teaching," the latter for "persuading." The *dogmatici* "take up maxims from their education, and from the authority of men, or from custom."[174] To speak as Kastan does of the "fictions" that Shakespeare created would not, from a Hobbesian point of view, be to appreciate their literary character, but to recognize their dubious rhetorical pedigree. For Shakespeare, imagination was an indispensable aid to rhetorical invention. It was one of the "inward wits," a psychological faculty "occupying the area between the body and the soul."[175] For Hobbes, by contrast, "imagination" was "conception remaining, and by little and little decaying from and after the act of sense." Hobbes continues: "From the same cause . . . there appear unto us castles in the air, chimeras, and other monsters which are not in *rerum natura* . . . . And this composition is that which we commonly

173. James Davidson Hunter and Paul Nedelisky, *Science and the Good: The Tragic Quest for the Foundations of Morality*, 34.

174. Thomas Hobbes, *The Elements of Law: Natural & Politic*, 66–67 (1.13). I am indebted to Quentin Skinner's discussion in *Forensic Shakespeare*, 311–14.

175. E. Ruth Harvey, *The Inward Wits: Psychological Theory in the Middle Ages and the Renaissance*, 2.

call FICTION of the mind."[176] Hobbes wrote these words in direct rebuttal to the long dead Sidney, who had granted poetry "another nature" that felicitously included the making of "Chimeras," even as he (Sidney) rejected the belittling of poetry as "wholly imaginative" and building "castles in the air."[177] Hobbes's attack, moreover, took in not only the fables and allegories, the dreams and miraculous wonders of imaginative poetry, but the adages and proverbs of the classical rhetorical tradition, the common currency of Shakespeare's education as a writer. Erasmus's instruction book for rhetorical and oratorical training, *De Copia*, a mainstay of Shakespeare's humanistic education,[178] represents the kind of older learning that Hobbes condemned. One infers that, for Hobbes, its influential lessons were so much mental clutter. Hobbes's one-sided polemics got the job done. Later in the seventeenth century, the long quarrel between the Ancients and the Moderns drew to a close.[179] The power of the poetic imagination languished until the era of Burke and Wordsworth.

We confront the reality of a paradigm shift. Under the impetus of scientific discovery Hobbes attacked the authority of Shakespeare's rhetorical universe. He could see that the Elizabethan language-game was over. Superbly various and coherent in its day—perfect enough for writers to achieve a "unity of effect of purpose and effect at every level, from their overall plan to the smallest details of language"[180]—it was too wedded to an outdated form of life to survive. Shakespeare and his form of life had slipped into the past. To quote a famous passage from Wittgenstein: "new language-games, as we may say, come into existence, and others become obsolete and get forgotten. (We can get a *rough picture* of this from the changes in mathematics.)"[181] We cannot reduce Shakespearean wisdom to Hobbesian pragmatism: "The end of knowledge is power . . . and the scope of all speculation is the performance of some action or thing to be done."[182] Shakespeare is related to Hobbes as Judgment is to "power." For Shakespeare, "the scope of all speculation" leads not to "the performance of some action" for practical gain or utility, but to the performance of some action in the face of divine scrutiny. The Elizabethans are

---

176. Hobbes, *Elements of Law*, 8, 10 (1.3).
177. Sir Philip Sidney, *An Apology for Poetry*, ed. Geoffrey Shepherd, 100–101.
178. T. W. Baldwin, *William Shakspere's Small Latine & Lesse Greeke*, 2:176–96.
179. See Margreta de Grazia, "Revolution in Shake-speares Sonnets," in *A Companion to Shakespeare's Sonnets*, ed. Michael Schoenfeldt, 63.
180. Brian Vickers, introduction to *English Renaissance Literary Criticism*, ed. Brian Vickers, 14.
181. Wittgenstein, *Philosophical Investigations*, §23, his italics.
182. Hobbes, quoted in Frederick Copleston, SJ, *A History of Philosophy*, 5:3.

not "early modern" in the same sense that Hobbes is "early modern." They were not born skeptics.[183] The subject-object dualism characteristic of scientific thought was foreign to their self-understanding. Fact and value had not yet uncoupled.

Shakespeare's Christian Rhetoric

The study of rhetoric dominated Shakespeare's education. His thought is dyed in it. Though I will be analyzing Shakespearean rhetoric in detail in several chapters, it merits an initial comment in this Introduction, since it is a clear and indispensable marker of Shakespeare's historical reality as a Christian writer.

His teachers taught the young Shakespeare to divide speech or oratory into three basic types. Although the lesson went back to Aristotle,[184] Elizabethan schoolmasters usually took Cicero as their model, or the pseudo-Ciceronian *Rhetorica ad Herennium*. For our purposes, it will be helpful to turn to the vernacular rhetorician Thomas Wilson, author of *The Arte of Rhetorique*, an inexpensive handbook that Shakespeare quoted and may have owned.[185] Classifying the three basic types of speech as "causes," Wilson underscores their importance: "Nothing can be handled by this art but the same is contained within one of these three causes. Either the matter consisteth in praise or dispraise of a thing; or else in consulting whether the cause be profitable or unprofitable; or lastly whether the matter be right or wrong."[186] Wilson refers to the first cause as "demonstrative," the second as "deliberative," and the third as "judicial." He explicates all three causes in terms of rhetorical place-topics (or topics of invention), the traditional means for stocking speeches and expressing and amplifying the matter at hand. He also supplies lengthy examples for imitation. One of his examples of deliberative oratory is "An Epistle to Persuade a Young Gentleman to Marriage, Devised by Erasmus, in the Behalf of His Friend," a well-attested source for Shakespeare's Sonnets 1–17. It is important to note that the three causes or basic types of speech frequently go by other names, respectively to Wilson, the epideictic, the political, and the forensic or legal. They are everywhere in Shakespeare

---

183. I am following Wittgenstein: "why should the language game rest on some kind of knowledge?" Ludwig Wittgenstein, *On Certainty*, §477.

184. Aristotle, *Rhetoric*, in *The Basic Works of Aristotle*, ed. Richard McKeon, 1358a36–1359a5.

185. Skinner, *Forensic Shakespeare*, 3, 46–47.

186. Thomas Wilson, *Wilson's Arte of Rhetorique, 1560*, ed. G. H. Mair, 11. I have modernized the spelling.

and "may," as Wilson instructively remarks, "every of them be contained in any one of them."[187]

As regards what I have called Shakespeare's rhetorical universe, the crucial paradox—I cannot stress this point enough—is Christianity's power to undo the classical scheme. Unlike Wilson, Shakespeare is constantly aware of this paradox, which asserts that a human judge, whether a character or a member of the audience, may see things quite counter to how the divine Judge sees them. In this respect, Christ in the Beatitudes teaches the universal need for surrendering worldly mores in order to achieve unworldly, spiritual ones. It is a lesson in turning the world upside down. Saint Paul codifies this message in deceptively simple terms: "We *are* fools for Christ's sake" (1 Corinthians 4:10, italics in original). Paul is most himself when urging that worldly wisdom can alienate us from God. Like some other thinkers of a high order, including Luther, he has an anti-intellectual streak: "God has chosen the foolish things of the world to confound the wise" (1 Corinthians 1:27). If we assume the hidden reality of God's plan for salvation and redemption in Christ, then the deliberations of the state become inherently suspect: "And we speak wisdom among them that are perfect: not the wisdom of this world, neither of the princes of this world, which come to nought. But we speak the wisdom of God in a mystery, *even* the hid *wisdom*, which God had determined before the world, unto our glory. Which none of the princes of this world have known: for had they known it, they would not have crucified the Lord of glory" (1 Corinthians 2:6–9). In Chapter 1, I will examine the paradox of Christian folly, including its rhetorical effects and mystical potential, with emphasis on the impact of Erasmus. For now, I would like to bring this lengthy Introduction to a close with some remarks on the Stratford-upon-Avon of Shakespeare's birth. These concern the playwright's father, the status of whose Spiritual Testament we looked at earlier. Here I want to consider Shakespeare's local formation as an author. This formation, at the intersection of two worlds, Catholic and Protestant, can still be glimpsed by the ordinary tourist.

Stratford-upon-Avon

Schoenbaum's *William Shakespeare: A Documentary Life* gathers what we know about John Shakespeare's tenure as chamberlain and acting chamberlain, in the Stratford of the early to mid-1560s. Tasked with administrating "borough property and revenues," the older Shakespeare was one of the "cus-

187. Wilson, *Wilson's Arte of Rhetorique*, 11.

todians of Stratford's purse-strings." It was a busy and stressful time in his life. The Guild Chapel was

> being Protestantized—workmen whitewashed the frescoes and took down the rood-loft; they installed seats for the priest and his clerk, and perhaps a communion board where formerly the altar stood. Vicar Bretchgirdle's house in Church Street underwent needed repair. A new classroom in the upper story of the Guild Hall replaced the old schoolhouse in the quad. Meanwhile the pestilence came and spent itself. Through it all the acting chamberlain kept the books, although he was slightly tardy in presenting his account for the plague year.[188]

Our chief concerns are how all this upheaval was remembered by those who lived through it, and whether William Shakespeare had any personal memory of these events. The raw facts give us something to go on. The plague struck in the summer of 1564, barely months after the poet's birth. According to Malone, it carried off "more than two hundred souls—from one-sixth to one-seventh of the entire population."[189] Vicar John Bretchgirdle died of it in 1565, having baptized baby William the previous year. The "needed repair" of Bretchgirdle's house went forward in 1563,[190] not long before it was boarded up.[191] John Shakespeare's "tardy" report for 1564, dated 21 March, 1565, includes the receipt for removing the symbolic rood-loft.[192] Given the "significant presence of both Catholics and Protestants" in Stratford,[193] I suspect that, to the Catholics and to those whose sympathies for the old faith were not dead and cold, the coincidence of a plague's breaking out, and carrying off the vicar, while the town was engaged in eliminating the traces of the old faith under his leadership, was not a little striking.[194] Presumably there were Protestants in Stratford who associated the Catholic faction with the devil and his works. With laborers suddenly in shorter supply, with a classroom being built "in the upper story of the Guild Hall," as well as, next door in the

---

188. Schoenbaum, *William Shakespeare*, 30–31.

189. Schoenbaum, *William Shakespeare*, 24. Schoenbaum's paraphrase.

190. B. Rowland Lewis, *The Shakespeare Documents: Facsimiles, Transliterations, Translations and Commentary*, 1:57.

191. For the standard "plague-orders" of the Elizabethan authorities, see A. L. Rowse, *The Elizabethan Renaissance: The Cultural Achievement*, 282–83. See also ROM 5.2.9–11.

192. Richard Savage and Edgar I. Fripp, eds., *Minutes and Accounts of the Corporation of Stratford-upon-Avon*, 1:138.

193. Andrew Hadfield, "Shakespeare: Biography and Belief," in *The Cambridge Companion to Shakespeare and Religion*, ed. Hannibal Hamlin, 21.

194. For the "importance of residual Catholicism," see Groves, *Texts and Traditions*, 27.

adjacent chapel, the demands for carpentry work, dismantling of the rood-loft, and limewashing of the Doom painting, it is likely that the improvements proceeded on an irregular schedule.

The illustrated booklet that is available for five pounds at the Guild Chapel, across the street from the Shakespeare homesite of New Place, includes an impressive re-creation of the great Doom painting, which was repeatedly covered after the Reformation. It still stands above the chancel arch, but in its current state of preservation it is faded and partially obstructed by a ceiling. Commissioned by Hugh Clopton early in the sixteenth century, the original work featured simple drawing, a palette of primary colors, and a symmetrical use of space. A haloed Christ sits in Judgment, while the Virgin Mary and John the Baptist, both haloed, kneel to his lower right and left, respectively. Further to her right a pair of tiara'd popes stand in the company of those meeting Saint Peter, while, to the left of Saint John, grotesque devils chain and torment the damned. As in the paintings of Hieronymus Bosch, Judgment is individualized. The booklet's anonymous author dangles an intriguing morsel concerning the poet's father:

> Surviving council records show that in 1563 John Shakespeare authorized payment of 2s for "defasyng ymages in ye chappell." Whether they were all covered at that time or at a later date is unknown. William Shakespeare was born in 1564 and it is quite possible the paintings, or some of them, were still visible during his lifetime. Speculation also surrounds John Shakespeare's willingness to follow the orders he was given. . . . What we do know is that rather than the paintings being defaced, they were largely limewashed over instead (only the face of the Archangel Michael in the Allegory of Death painting can be seen to have been clearly 'defaced'—literally scratched-away). This limewashing actually served to protect the paintings.[195]

The report of two shillings paid in 1563 for the defacing of images is confirmed by John Shakespeare's report as chamberlain dated 10 January, 1564.[196] The choice to limewash the paintings and not to deface them is interesting. The technique's general "reversability" became an established fact.[197] Granted that significantly more defacing occurred than the visitor's booklet suggests,[198]

---

195. Anon., *The Edge of Doom: The History and Hidden Wall Paintings of the Guild Chapel*, 6.
196. Lewis, *Shakespeare Documents*, 1:57.
197. Eamon Duffy, *The Stripping of the Altars: Traditional Religion in England c.1400–c.1580*, 583.
198. See Edgar I. Fripp, *Shakespeare: Man and Artist*, 1:134; and, more recently, Kate Giles and Jonathan Clark, "The Archaeology of the Guild Buildings of Shakespeare's Stratford-upon-Avon,"

the limewashing may not have been done out of purely artistic concerns. It may represent a compromise in terms of accommodating the Elizabethan state, or, more personally, a compromise between John and his wife, Mary, who came from "an old Catholic family" and may have influenced the date of William's baptism in order to avoid an infelicitous holy day.[199] As suggested above, it may have been incomplete.[200] And the fact that John Shakespeare supervised the work is at least potentially consistent with the case for his recusancy. So was, it may be, his inability to read. Those pictures may have represented his preferred approach to salvation history.

Let's skip ahead a few years. William Shakespeare was five when the Northern Rebellion broke out in November, 1569. Its short-lived attempt to replace Queen Elizabeth with a Catholic, Mary, Queen of Scots, led to a number of anti-Catholic measures affecting the town. William Butcher, a Catholic sympathizer[201] and third in succession from the late Bretchgirdle, "was deprived of his vicarage at the moment of the outbreak." In the fall of 1571, John Shakespeare's first act as Chief Alderman under bailiff Adrian Quyney was "to get rid of the Romanist vestments remaining at the Gild [sic] chapel."[202] It is curious that these vestments lingered so long.[203] Here is another interesting survival within the future playwright's own range of experience: the Guild Hall (or Guildhall) retains "remnants of mural painting and artscribbling in evidence in Shakespeare's day."[204] These wall paintings "are religious, the remnants of a reredos in the priests' private chapel in the Guildhall. The paintings show(ed) the Holy Trinity with the Virgin Mary to one side and John the Evangelist to the other. He was originally thought to be John the Baptist but . . . in March 2016 a new figure—definitely John the Baptist—was uncovered on one of the beams."[205] Though we have no particular storyline

in *The Guild and Guild Buildings of Shakespeare's Stratford: Society, Religion, School and Stage*, ed. J. R. Mulryne, 165–66.

    199. Fripp, *Shakespeare: Man and Artist*, 1:38. For a more recent account of Mary Shakespeare and her background, see Hadfield, "Shakespeare," 22.

    200. Giles and Clark, "The Archaeology of the Guild Buildings," 166.

    201. Peter Milward, *Shakespeare's Religious Background*, 17.

    202. Fripp, *Shakespeare: Man and Artist*, 1:48 (*sic*).

    203. Groves remarks on "the widespread refusal to destroy vestments, mass books, and chalices" during the Reformation. Groves, *Texts and Traditions*, 39.

    204. Fripp, *Shakespeare: Man and Artist*, 1:135n3.

    205. Lindsey Armstrong, email to author, March 26, 2020. I am deeply grateful to Dr. Armstrong, who is General Manager of Shakespeare's Schoolroom and Guildhall. See also Kate Giles, "Digital Creativity and the Wall Paintings of 'Shakespeare's Guildhall,' Stratford-upon-Avon," *Internet Archaeology* 44 (2017): https://intarch.ac.uk/journal/issue44/6/toc.html.

in which to place these facts, they document the Reformation's impact on John Shakespeare's Stratford. They commemorate an intense time that doubtless became part of the local lore, to be remembered and discussed by the townsfolk for decades. We can infer that a fly on the Guild Chapel wall would have heard some interesting things. In the words of that remarkable man, Edgar Fripp: "When John Shakespeare laid down his office as deputy bailiff on 4 October 1572, his mind, unless we have strangely misunderstood him, was agitated by these matters of Church and State, and his eldest son, in his ninth year, heard not a little about them."[206] A peculiar trace of the playwright's memory of his father's 1564 report—that is, his memory of the talk it occasioned—may persist in King Edward's lamentation: "But when your carters or your waiting vassals / Have done a drunken slaughter and *defaced* / The precious *image* of our dear Redeemer" (R3 2.1.122–24, my emphasis).[207]

The Guild Chapel is not the only local building that invites scrutiny. Milward states it was under Bretchgirdle's "supervision that [Holy Trinity Church] was brought into conformity with new regulations."[208] If we could present evidence of the Protestantizing work at the Holy Trinity Church being interrupted, we might link it to Catholic countercurrents in John Shakespeare's Stratford. Moreover, the idea that the new regulations injured old loyalties fits with what Shakespeare tells us about his countrymen. One thinks of "the people" remaining loyal to Rosalind and her father, banished to the Forest of Arden, which bears the maiden name of Shakespeare's mother, Mary Arden (AYL 1.2.271–72).[209] One thinks also of Gloucester's loyalty to the old king, his older son's godfather. Such potentially Catholic vestiges are consistent with our main suggestion here, which is not that Shakespeare was (or was not) a crypto-Catholic, but that this period of religious change in Stratford bequeathed to the future playwright a powerful Catholic/Protestant binary, a series of impressions more black-and-white than gray, in need of resolution and yet resistant to it. We must consider not only his father's direct involvement in events, but his own inhabiting their intimate consequences, including the new schoolroom in the Guild Hall (just beyond the Guild Chapel on his

---

206. Fripp, *Shakespeare: Man and Artist*, 1:52. More recently, see Sylvia Gill, "Reformation: Priests and People," in *The Guild and Guild Buildings of Shakespeare's Stratford: Society, Religion, School and Stage*, ed. J. R. Mulryne, 51.

207. Fripp, *Shakespeare: Man and Artist*, 1:37n1.

208. Milward, *Shakespeare's Religious Background*, 17.

209. For a "significant parallel between the tragic situation of the English Ardens and that of the exiled Duke Senior in *As You Like It*" (117), see Peter Milward, "Religion in Arden," *Shakespeare Survey* 54 (2001): 115–21.

walk to school), the nearby Holy Trinity Church, and New Place, a childhood landmark directly across the street from the chapel and a symbol, when Shakespeare purchased it in 1597 for sixty pounds, of the living past.

Do we have evidence that may point to the Protestantizing work at the Holy Trinity Church being interrupted? Naturally it is hard to say. English-heritage writer Val Horsler observes a "remarkable pre-Reformation survival" in "the *mensa*, or stone altar table, which . . . originally graced the chapel of St. Thomas of Canterbury in the south aisle." According to Horsler, "It was rediscovered beneath the floor there when the organ was moved at the end of the nineteenth century; three of its original five incised crosses, representing the wounds of Christ, can still be seen." But there is something more: "Another survival is in one of the three sedilia, the original medieval seats for the priests, on the south wall of the sanctuary. The two nearest the altar have carved Tudor roses under their canopies; but the third retains the face of Christ—unexpected in a church where all the other faces of Christ have been systematically chiseled away. It may be a vernicle—a representation of Christ's face as it was miraculously transposed upon the cloth with which St. Veronica (hence its name) wiped his face as he carried his cross towards Calvary."[210] In my first visit to Stratford, in 2011, one had little way of knowing about this strange survival. Normally, the stone canopy above the priest's stone seat can be seen by no one but the seat's occupant. It is otherwise entirely hidden from view. But in 2019, at the time of my most recent visit, the stewards of the church had placed a mirror on the sanctuary floor before the third sedilia, mere feet from Shakespeare's epitaph, angling it so that guests could see the image of Christ's bearded face under the canopy above the seat. Assuming that this remarkable survival was not an accident of budgetary circumstances, forgetfulness, or blind fate, one wonders, did the Shakespeares know? Did Vicar Bretchgirdle fall ill before the work of defacement could be completed? Did the image's survival mark an act of recusancy, nostalgia, or respect for one's ancestors? Did it represent a tacit or explicit compromise? Whatever the answers to these questions, the startling juxtaposition of carved Tudor roses against a pre-Reformation image of Christ supplies as concise an introduction to Shakespeare's mind as one could ask for.

---

210. Val Horsler, *Holy Trinity Church Stratford-upon-Avon: A Visitor's Guide to Shakespeare's Church*, 17.

CHAPTER 1

Theological Comedy in
A Midsummer Night's Dream

To dramatize for his audience their own conflict between worldly and spiritual priorities, the fierce paradox that is built into their faith, Shakespeare plays a game of wisdom and folly. His primary instruments for this Christian reversal of perspective are his fools and clowns, who have a topsy-turvy knack for unsettling what Geoffrey Hill calls "the world's routine of power."[1] Moreover, as Robert Bell observes: "The importance of Shakespeare's fools and scourges of folly is underscored by the fact that such characters rarely exist in Shakespeare's source materials."[2] Of course, Shakespeare's practice of moral disorientation makes no sense at all unless we understand his audience. Craig Bernthal reminds us of their religious frame of mind: "The drama of choosing between heaven and hell displays a mindset that in sixteenth- and seventeenth century England was virtually inescapable. Spiritually, people confronted judgment every day of their lives."[3]

To fathom Shakespeare's rhetorical game of wisdom and folly, we can turn to the sad state of Helena in Act 3 of *A Midsummer Night's Dream*. Helena uses demonstrative rhetoric in dispraise of herself, and she does so to great effect. By wisely seeing herself as the fool that she is, she implicitly invites others to participate in an act of self-discovery. She comes to play the part of a fool, and to confirm the truth in Puck's resonant couplet, spoken earlier in the scene to Oberon: "Shall we their fond pageant see? / Lord, what fools these mortals be!" (3.2.114–15). Puck's judgment hovers over the following exchange, elevating Helena's insights and imbuing them with a touch of judicial rhetoric, a hint of judgment and eschatology, that is, as Thomas Wilson might say, "contained in" her demonstrative rhetoric:

---

1. Geoffrey Hill, *Collected Critical Writings*, 80.
2. Robert H. Bell, *Shakespeare's Great Stage of Fools*, 80.
3. Craig Bernthal, *The Trial of Man: Christianity and Judgment in the World of Shakespeare*, xxx.

HELENA

    To Athens will I bear my folly back

    And follow you no further. Let me go.

    You see how simple and how fond I am.

HERMIA

    Why, get you gone. Who is't that hinders you?

HELENA

    A foolish heart, that I leave here behind.

HERMIA

    What, with Lysander?

HELENA

    With Demetrius.

(3.2.315–320)

Just past the textual halfway point of *A Midsummer Night's Dream*, Helena is ready to call it quits. Her close friends appear to be mocking her. As her frustration mounts, she experiences a change from ignorance to knowledge, akin to what Aristotle called *anagnorisis*, meaning recognition or discovery, which is most effective when it happens between persons and alters their feelings toward one another. To be accurate, Helena from the start is sensitive to love's folly and its effects, comparing herself to Demetrius: "as he errs, doting on Hermia's eyes, / So I, admiring of his qualities" (1.1. 230–31). But she must descend further in folly in order to experience the reversal, or *peripeteia*, that accompanies, in a quasi-Aristotelian manner, her recognition scene. It is the Christian invertibility of folly and wisdom that structures this change. Responding to Helena's self-criticism, Hermia follows her initial command, "get you gone," with a sharp question introduced by an interrogative pronoun: "Who is't that hinders you?" Interestingly, Helena's reply, "A foolish heart," does not directly answer Hermia's question. Helena does not come out and say, "My foolish heart." Why not? To quote Neil Rhodes on Elizabethan rhetorical practices: "The object of *ex*pression was to create an *im*pression, out there, on somebody else, and for the expression to make an impression the speaker must express something felt within as an emotional truth."[4] Dramatically, Helena needs to create a strong impression, since, among the mad lovers in this scene, one person's "emotional truth" might seem to be transitory and vaporous. She produces a unifying signifier and holds it up for inspection: "A foolish heart," that's *who*. Can anyone sympathize with a "foolish heart"? Any

---

4. Neil Rhodes, *Shakespeare and the Origins of English*, 15, his italics.

takers? Hermia misses the point. She proceeds to her next question, "With Lysander?" and Helena confesses, "With Demetrius," in a beautiful stepped line that strengthens the suggestion of substitution within a given pattern. At first blush, Hermia's question ("With Lysander?") strips Helena of her riddle. To be sure, Hermia is in no mood for riddles, and in no mood for doing right by Helena. But if we can gain a broader perspective on our desires, as Helena appears to do, we see that, for Shakespeare, Helena's purpose goes beyond answering Hermia's question and satisfying Hermia's curiosity: Helena's appeal to the bonding of hearts lays the groundwork for a shared recognition of common folly.

In her pathetic confession to Hermia, Helena speaks as a spectator of her own life's drama, while directing her words at an audience (Hermia) who does not as yet recognize what is at stake for herself. And yet, as Helena admits defeat and resolves to withdraw from the society of her friends, her confession to Hermia anticipates her return to their company: spectators and fools, all. It is a moment of thematic climax that Shakespeare has carefully prepared, as when Lysander pleads with Hermia: "I mean that my heart unto yours is knit, / So that but one heart we can make of it" (2.2.53–54); or when Demetrius explains why Hermia no longer excites him: "My heart to her but as guest-wise sojourned, / And now to Helen is it home returned" (3.2.171); or when Helena chides Hermia for forgetting their "ancient love," when they "grew together . . . two seeming bodies but one heart" (3.2. 208–215). "A foolish heart" unites them, though, for now, Helena alone appears to recognize it in herself. For now, she remains isolated. The reversal of fortune doesn't happen with the prescribed Aristotelian swiftness.

Before it can happen, the mutual recognition of folly must take place. When Helena argues with Demetrius, pursuing him outside the city, Shakespeare is again laying the groundwork for the broadening of sympathies through the coming of self-knowledge:

> Nor doth this wood lack worlds of company,
> For you, in my respect, are all the world.
> Then how can it be said I am alone
> When all the world is here to look on me? (2.1.223–26).

The word *company* links Helena's isolation here to her last words in Act 3, Scene 2, an invocation of sleep: "Steal me awhile from mine own company!" (436). Her "company," in the latter instance, is not only herself, but, as she ingenuously suggests in her meekness and her folly, Demetrius, Lysander, and Hermia, all of whom collapse nearby. Bottom and Titania are only a little further off, and waiting in the wings are all the "company" of actors (1.2.1).

And the audience? Helena, we notice, has already invited "the world" to "look on": "Nor doth this wood lack worlds of company . . . When all the world is here to look on me." In effect, Shakespeare connects the theatrical nature of civilized experience, as exhibited in Helena's acceptance of the role she has played, to the Christian paradox that folly can be a form of wisdom. In dispraising herself, Helena states that she is a fool, and, by a gradual process of implication, reveals who the others are. And because it is humble, true, and mortifying to human pride, her confession of foolishness pulls her larger audience into the ever-expanding "company" of folly: as Peter Quince suggests, "for if we meet in the city, we shall be dogged with company, and our devices known" (1.2.94–95). "Company" here signifies everyday Athenians, who are much like the mixed crowd of Londoners watching the play. As a fool who knows she's a fool, Helena summons the audience to an implicit confession, a rite of dispraise: *mea culpa, mea maxima culpa*. The underlying strong force of this social alchemy is a sense of self that is pre-Cartesian in its play of mind, and pre-Hobbesian in its anthropology. To be clear: *A Midsummer Night's Dream* is not overtly religious like *Everyman* or *The Second Shepherds' Play*. But I dissent from the verdict that it "is not a 'Christian play' in any meaningful sense."[5] Only on a superficial level can the meaning be prescinded from the paradoxical Christian rhetoric that makes the meaning possible. Is there a comedy among the Greek and Roman classics, or in all of world literature, that invites us to sympathize with folly, to see ourselves universally as "fools," and thus to humble ourselves collectively and wisely for our own common good? The Romans had their witty parasites, and powerful fools have populated the world's stages from India to China and beyond, but not with this liturgical quality of universal affect, emanating from a young woman, no less.

The Christian paradox that folly can be a form of wisdom found major literary expression earlier in the sixteenth century. It appeared in a work of high originality and great renown, Erasmus's *Praise of Folly* (1511, rev. 1514). The character of Folly (*Stultitia*) is a kind of court or university lecturer (the setting is indistinct), who delivers a mock encomium spoken in praise of herself, her followers, and her vast worldly influence. The satire is aimed not at

---

5. Hannibal Hamlin, *The Bible in Shakespeare*, 111.

institutions, but at the mediocrities who unfortunately represent them. Five centuries ago, the book charmed readers throughout Europe, and it infuriated many theologians.[6] Thomas Chaloner Englished it for the Elizabethans,[7] but I suspect that Shakespeare knew the *Stultitiae Laus* or *Moriae Encomium*—the alternate title features a Greek pun honoring Thomas More—in its choice original Latin.

In her classic work *The Fool: His Social and Literary History*, Enid Welsford makes two points that may serve to introduce the topic of Erasmus's lessons for Shakespeare. First, Erasmus seized on a tension in the Renaissance idea of fooling, between "the fool as a worthless character that lurked beneath the veneer of wealth, learning, and respectability" and the wise fool as a "truth-teller whose real insight was thinly disguised as a form of insanity": with this tension he created a springboard for "variations of meaning," "ambiguities of definition," and "reversal and counter-reversal of accepted judgments."[8] Walter Kaiser offers a complementary take on the subject: "The outlandish costume of motley assigned to the medieval fool distinguished him sharply from other human beings; but the contribution of the Renaissance to this figure was precisely that of making him just like everyone else."[9] In Shakespeare's handling, this expansion of the field included not only the fool Polonius, but the well-dressed gentlefolk in the best seats. William Empson classified the "Shakespearean use of *fool*" as "a rather generalized memory of the Erasmus doctrine,"[10] but we may suggest that the "memory" was sharper than that.[11] In recent years, Rhodes has made the large but justifiable claim for "the dramatic development" by Shakespeare "of opposing concepts of salutary folly and deluded wisdom from *The Praise of Folly*."[12] Rhodes helps us to think of Erasmus as opening a new path in European literature and Shakespeare's developing its possibilities. To support this suggestion, we can

---

6. See, for example, Erasmus's well-known 1515 letter to Martin Dorp, in Erasmus, *The Praise of Folly and Other Writings*, ed. and trans. Robert M. Adams, 228–51.

7. Erasmus, *The Praise of Folie*, 1549, 1560 (?), and 1577, ed. Clarence H. Miller.

8. Enid Welsford, *The Fool: His Social and Literary History*, 239.

9. Walter Kaiser, *Praisers of Folly: Erasmus, Rabelais, Shakespeare*, 14.

10. William Empson, *The Structure of Complex Words*, 124, his italics.

11. For an overview of book inventories and statistical analysis documenting Erasmus's "continued popularity and cultural importance" (65) into Shakespeare's period, including the *Stultitiae Laus*, see Gregory D. Dodds, *Exploiting Erasmus: The Erasmian Legacy and Religious Change in Early Modern England*, 64–66, 291n21. For further background on Shakespeare and Erasmus, see Stuart Gillespie, *Shakespeare's Books: A Dictionary of Shakespeare's Sources*, 152–60. I wish to express my general debt to Gillespie.

12. Rhodes, *Shakespeare and the Origins*, 56–57.

cite Robert Weimann and Douglas Bruster: "Erasmus must have appealed especially to all those intent on unfixing those static abstractions in the late moral and interlude plays, with their allegorical versions of disorder, sin, and vice."[13] After Erasmus, virtue and vice could change from being static abstractions to ambiguous elements in complex and fluid scenarios. Likewise, Bell comments on Folly's "unstable ironies": "The strange affinity between advocate and adversary of folly must have intrigued Shakespeare, whose stage of fools dramatizes similarly incongruous connections."[14] We have grounds, then, for considering *The Praise of Folly* a breakthrough book for Shakespeare, suggesting complicated ways to think about folly and wisdom.

I turn now to Welford's second point: "half-seriously, half-mockingly, Erasmus defends the creative vital instincts of humanity against the encroachment of . . . analytic reason."[15] Erasmus and other humanists characteristically championed rhetoric against the dialectal "intricacies of the Realists, Nominalists, Thomists, Albertists, Scotists," etc.[16] In her cracked theological enthusiasm, Folly humorously exaggerates the more absurd questions that attracted scholastic interest: "Whether there is more than one filial relationship in Christ? Whether the following proposition is possible: God the Father hates the Son. Whether God could have taken on the nature of a woman, of the devil, of an ass, of a cucumber, of a piece of flint? And then how the cucumber would have preached, performed miracles, and been nailed to the cross?"[17] For the learned doctors, as J. V. Cunningham observes, reason "is the principle of distinction and its method is division." Shakespeare, when he desired it, as in *The Phoenix and the Turtle*, could excel at scholastic reasoning.[18] He could ape and mangle it as well. Bottom prefers wordplay to logic when he tells us, "I will get Peter Quince to write a ballad of this dream. It shall be called 'Bottom's Dream,' because it hath no bottom" (4.1.212–14). It was enough to drive a dialectician mad. Erasmus had punned on his friend Thomas More's name with the title *Moriae Encomium*. Shakespeare's "Flute, the bellows mender" puns on

13. Robert Weimann and Douglas Bruster, *Shakespeare and the Power of Performance: Stage and Page in the Elizabethan Theatre*, 90.

14. Bell, *Shakespeare's Great Stage*, 79.

15. Welsford, *The Fool*, 240.

16. Erasmus, *The Praise of Folly*, ed. and trans. Clarence H. Miller, 90. For the ancient distinction between rhetoric and dialectic, see Miriam Joseph, CSC, *Shakespeare's Use of the Arts of Language*, 18–19.

17. Erasmus, *Praise of Folly*, ed. Miller, 88–89. See Miller's excellent notes.

18. See J. V. Cunningham, "'Essence' and the *Phoenix and Turtle*," *English Literary History* 19 (December 1952): 275.

the Latin *follis*, which means not "folly" but "bellows." The poet knew that "from the Latin word for bellows the name *fool* or *fou* was coined."[19] His love of wordplay—the source of Bottom's fibbing "Phibbus" (1.2.30)—and his refusal to subordinate experience to logic are Erasmian and humanistic qualities, which challenge scholastic assumptions.

This relative independence from the logicians is one aspect of what John Cox calls Shakespeare's "skeptical faith." As Cox explains, Shakespeare is "closely akin" to Erasmus because "he is more doubtful about those who know than he is about what they know."[20] Put another way, both Erasmus and Shakespeare direct scrutiny against pretentions to knowledge, not against core Christian truth. Both respond to new realities in the age of humanism, and both respond to the age-old ubiquity of pride and self-love. Both writers marshal the spirit of play to attack the pose of logical certitude, questioning its terms, premises, and conclusions, impugning the motives of its fleshy practitioners, mocking its excesses. For both, fools and folly invite us to be skeptical about unexamined claims to knowledge and authority.

The Erasmian art of challenging the reader had impressed Sidney and Spenser before Shakespeare's mind absorbed it entirely. This art of teasing, testing, and prodding the reader into a state of heightened moral perception gathers up a rich skein of influences—a tradition of moral complexity indispensable to understanding Shakespeare's art. Plutarch, in his famous essay from the *Moralia*, "How the Young Man Should Study Poetry," had argued on the basis of "plausibility": "imitation that does not show an utter disregard of the truth brings out, along with the actions, indications of both vice and virtue commingled; as is the case with that of Homer, which emphatically says good-bye to the Stoics, who will have it that nothing base can attach to virtue, and nothing good to vice, but that the ignorant-man is quite wrong in all things, while, on the other hand, the man of culture is right in everything." Plutarch found support in Euripides: "The good and bad cannot be kept apart / But there is some commingling."[21] Sidney took the same lesson from Ovid's *Ars Amatoria*, and connected it directly to *The Praise of Folly*.[22] Shakespeare's Friar Laurence comments: "Virtue itself turns vice, being misapplied / And vice sometime by action

---

19. Kaiser, *Praisers of Folly*, 5.

20. John Cox, *Seeming Knowledge: Shakespeare and Skeptical Faith*, xii. Cox also draws attention to the relevance of More. In my view, More's ordeals of conscience plumb epistemological depths that anticipate Newman's *Grammar of Assent*.

21. Plutarch, *Moralia*, trans. Frank Cole Babbitt, 1:133 (25 C–D).

22. Sir Philip Sidney, *An Apology for Poetry*, ed. Geoffrey Shepherd, 121.

dignified" (ROM 2.3.21–22). Bacon in *The Advancement of Learning* (1605) would observe: "For it is not possible to join the wisdom of the serpent with the innocence of the dove, except men be perfectly acquainted with the nature of evil itself . . . so as, except they plainly perceive that you know as much of their corrupt opinions and depraved principles as they do themselves, they despise all honesty of manners and counsel."[23] Milton, who fully digested *The Praise of Folly* and praised its author,[24] likewise seized on a scriptural warrant for recognizing moral complexity. In his *Areopagitica* (1644) he states: "Good and evil we know in the field of this world grow up together almost inseparably. . . . It was from out the rind of one apple tasted, that the knowledge of good and evil, as two twins cleaving together, leaped forth into the world. And perhaps this is that doom which Adam fell into of knowing good and evil, that is to say, of knowing good by evil." Milton goes on to make a point that memorably overstates the humanist break from scholastic ethics: "That virtue therefore which is but a youngling in the contemplation of evil, and knows not the utmost that vice promises to her followers, and rejects it, is but a blank virtue, not a pure; her whiteness is but an excremental whiteness; which was the reason why our sage and serious poet Spenser, whom I dare be known to think a better teacher than Scotus or Aquinas, describing true temperance under the person of Guyon, brings him in with his palmer through the cave of Mammon and the bower of earthly bliss, that he might see and know, and yet abstain."[25]

In *The Praise of Folly*, Erasmus addresses society as a satirist, without resort to overt moralizing. This way of thinking was congenial to Shakespeare's art, which, on the moral level, is not didactic but interrogatory. In *The Praise of Folly*, the frame or standard of the satire occasionally pokes through the carnivalesque atmosphere, but Folly, like Saint Paul, is wary of praising human wisdom. Erasmus does not so much discard as hold in reserve the inwardly demanding morality of the *Enchiridion Militis Christiani*, that is, *The Handbook of the Militant Christian* (1503), in which the Pauline doctrine of Christian foolishness is earnestly laid out.[26] Instead, he is facetious in the Renaissance sense of the word—nimbly ironical. He had caught the tone of Lucian: gabby and irreverent, skeptical and droll.

---

23. Francis Bacon, quoted in the editorial notes to Sir Philip Sidney, *The Defense of Poesy Otherwise Known as An Apology for Poetry*, ed. Albert S. Cook, 95.

24. John Milton, *Complete Poems and Major Prose*, ed. Merritt Y. Hughes, 728.

25. Milton, *Complete Poems and Major Prose*, 728–29.

26. Erasmus, *The Handbook of the Militant Christian*, in *The Essential Erasmus*, ed. and trans. John P. Dolan, 40. William Tyndale translated the work in 1533 as *The Manual of the Christian Knight*.

Like the Shakespeare of *A Midsummer Night's Dream*, the Erasmus of *The Praise of Folly* brings Athens and Jerusalem into witty and provocative conjunction. As Barbara Swain observed decades ago, Erasmus's "sermon on wisdom— or folly—beckons with one hand to Solomon and Ecclesiastes, as all meditations on wisdom or folly must, but stretches out the other to the whole 'rout of poeticall gods.'"[27] Folly pays her respects to Venus and Diana, to Apollo and Vulcan, to Pan and Priapus, to almighty Jupiter, while building toward a rhapsodic encounter with Saint Paul. In her peroration, she quotes the passage from First Corinthians that the Athenian Bottom garbles as he wakes from his enchanted slumber, and she finds the heart of her paradox in the fool's experience of wisdom. She also locates this paradox, earlier in her lecture, in a figure deeply associated with Theseus's city. Erasmus was a lover of Socrates, whom Folly praises for much the same reason as the god at Delphi praised him. The oracle declared that no one was wiser because, unlike all the other Athenians, he "declined the epithet of 'wise.'"[28] Socrates, through his intellectual humility, comes to exemplify the interplay of wisdom and folly. He is, as Erasmus writes with no great irony in his *Colloquies*, "Saint Socrates."[29] In defending *The Praise of Folly* in a highly publicized letter to a young theologian, Martin Dorp, Erasmus elaborates: "I find it enough to have learned the saying of Socrates, that I know nothing at all, and to devote my energies to helping other people with their studies."[30] It was Socrates's serene exposure of the ignorance or folly of his fellow citizens that provoked his execution; we are reminded that blasphemy in Erasmus's Europe could result in an auto-da-fé. Like Shakespeare, Erasmus took real risks. Having infuriated the monks and theologians who felt themselves abused by Folly's praise, and having shown an all but Lutheran zeal for reform, he eventually "appeared on many lists of forbidden books, and the first Roman Index of Forbidden Books (1559) listed him among authors whose books were prohibited without exception."[31]

We must be careful not to advance the case for Erasmus's influence on, as it were, all fronts. Shakespeare must have reflected on Erasmus's failures, his decline into ineffectiveness, his lost dream of "intellectual and cultural

---

27. Barbara Swain, *Fools and Folly during the Middle Ages and the Renaissance*, 139.

28. Erasmus, *Praise of Folly and Other Writings*, ed. Adams, 24.

29. More accurately, it is the character Nephelius who says, "Pray for us, Saint Socrates!" Erasmus, "The Religious Feast," in *Praise of Folly and Other Writings*, ed. Adams, 201.

30. Erasmus, Letter to Martin Dorp, in *Praise of Folly and Other Writings*, ed. Adams, 237.

31. See Charles G. Nauert, *Humanism and the Culture of Renaissance Europe*, 172–73. The quotation is from page 173.

synthesis."[32] Though conscious of Erasmus's "philosophy of Christ,"[33] Shakespeare didn't champion it. The famous phrase evokes Erasmus's more pious ambitions, the side of his educational program that, according to G. K. Hunter, blunted the progress of the humanist movement in England in the later sixteenth century. Hunter writes: "for Erasmus, the end of education is *sapiens et eloquens pietas*, active Christian virtue rendered effective in the service of the community by the power to write and speak."[34] I note that, while Hunter does not employ the term *Christian humanism*, he warns against applying the term *anti-religious* to the English humanist movement: "It sought to turn religious ideals and energies towards the amelioration of life in this world and to achieve an order in this life corresponding to the religious vision of man's worth."[35] Historian Charles Nauert traces a kind of "'apostolic succession' from Erasmus's English friends through all the religious changes under Henry, Edward, and Mary, down to the men who carried through the Elizabethan settlement in 1558–59."[36] Inevitably, this Christian idealism met its match in the political animal. I note that Gregory Dodds connects the failure of Erasmus's legacy after 1580 to the rival soteriology of English Calvinism.[37] According to Hunter, though, the humanist situation suffered from an unbridgeable gap between the ideal and the real. Charting the careers of the humanist successors of the three major founders, Erasmus, More and Colet, Hunter observes a decline in influence and identifies its cause: "The Humanist assumption that learning could teach a man to live piously in the world of politics could not bring with it the creation of a learned Civil Service."[38]

The current of Christian humanism that runs directly from Erasmus to Shakespeare will elude us if we identify it too strictly with the idealism—a lofty blend of piety and pedantry—behind the original impetus. This is what happens in C. S. Lewis's critique of English humanism in the sixteenth century, in which Lewis rarely passes up an opportunity to give the humanists a good kick in the shins. Lewis's opposition here is one of those ironical turns

---

32. Louis Bouyer, *Erasmus and His Times*, 218.

33. "Erasmus used the expressions 'philosophy of Christ,' 'Christian philosophy,' 'heavenly philosophy,' and 'philosophy of the Gospel' interchangeably." Léon-E. Halkin, *Erasmus: A Critical Biography*, 284.

34. G. K. Hunter, *John Lyly*, 24, 29.

35. Hunter, *John Lyly*, 13.

36. Nauert, *Humanism*, 196.

37. Dodds, *Exploiting Erasmus*, 64–65.

38. Hunter, *John Lyly*, 24, 29. In *2 Henry the VI* (4.7), Lord Saye's noble but ineffectual defense of his judicial record is, as Bernthal observes, an epitome of Christian humanist sentiment. See Bernthal, *Trial of Man*, 42–43.

that face the literary historian as times and circumstances change. One could argue (it is a complicated case) that Lewis was a Christian humanist in the tradition of Chesterton and Tolkien. But the present topic puts our focus on the Elizabethans. For Lewis, "the facts seem consistent with the view that the great literature of the fifteen-eighties and nineties was something which humanism, with its unities and *Gorboducs* and English hexameters, would have prevented if it could, but failed to prevent because the high tide of native talent was then too strong for it."[39] In what sense, we wonder, can dismissing humanism as a neoclassical dead-end do justice to *The Praise of Folly*? Expanding our view, we may recognize the benefits of Shakespeare's grammar school education: "Without humanism . . . there could have been no Elizabethan literature: without Erasmus, no Shakespeare."[40] Hunter takes Lewis's mixed reception of humanism as a comment, not so much on humanistic practice, as on humanistic theory. He observes Lewis's capacity for dwelling "unfairly"[41] on the pietistic elements in humanistic education. In *The Tudor Play of Mind*, an important book that contributed to the wide-reaching resurgence of rhetorical studies at the University of California at Berkeley in the 1970s and 80s, Joel Altman upholds Hunter's account while noticing artistic continuities in English humanism.[42] Altman, like T. W. Baldwin before him, is rightly attentive to Erasmus's influence on the English grammar school curriculum. Undoubtedly, Erasmus's commitment to teaching Christian boys to argue *in utramque partem*,[43] the art of formal controversy and articulating two sides of a question, made a great and fertile impression on Shakespeare's young mind. In this respect, Altman's view coheres with my own, the difference being my concern for Erasmus and Shakespeare as Christian humanists.

Shakespeare was well educated by Elizabethan grammar school standards, which were, as Baldwin has documented for all time, Erasmian in the extreme.[44] Because he was a popular entertainer, not a university man with vain hopes of becoming a courtier or ambassador, Shakespeare never knew

39. C. S. Lewis, *English Literature in the Sixteenth Century Excluding Drama*, 19.

40. Emrys Jones, quoted in Rhodes, *Shakespeare and the Origins*, 59.

41. Hunter, *John Lyly*, 21.

42. Joel B. Altman, *The Tudor Play of Mind: Rhetorical Inquiry and the Development of Elizabethan Drama*, 196–97.

43. Altman, *Tudor Play of Mind*, 43–44.

44. T. W. Baldwin, *William Shakspere's Small Latine and Lesse Greek*. Baldwin's magnum opus was published in two volumes in 1944. C. S. Lewis published *English Literature in the Sixteenth Century Excluding Drama* the same year. He published his brilliant but Erasmus-neglecting essay "Variation in Shakespeare and Others" in *Rehabilitations and Other Essays* five years earlier, in 1939. It appears that Lewis's sense of Erasmus was not informed by Baldwin's monumental research. A pity.

the frustrations of a Gabriel Harvey. He never subscribed to the humanist program for achieving political influence (Hunter's "learned Civil Service"). Despite Jeffrey Knapp's claim to the contrary,[45] whatever sympathy Shakespeare felt for Erasmus's *Complaint of Peace* was always tinged by competing realities—it was never an ideological foundation. The *argumentum in utramque partem* prevailed. Had his political instincts been deflected by Erasmian idealism, it is doubtful Shakespeare would have survived artistically. Shakespeare's Christian humanism, which was inseparable from his consciousness of history, comprehended the clash between Erasmian idealism and political reality.

I find, then, that Shakespeare's Erasmus is a Christian satirist, skeptical and urbane, spectacularly erudite, the master rhetorician whom Wilson cited in his *Arte of Rhetorique*. Erasmus's grueling debate with Luther also left its mark, as did Erasmus's enlightened respect for women. For Shakespeare and his tribe, Erasmus became a representative figure of the history of the Reformation—a sympathetic character in Anthony Munday's *Sir Thomas More*, revised by Henry Chettle, Thomas Dekker, Thomas Heywood, and none other than Shakespeare himself.[46] But the author of *A Midsummer Night's Dream* was not attracted to Erasmus because of his pious educational program or his lost dream of a renewed and united Europe, neither of which had much bearing on life in post-Reformation England.

Of all Erasmus's writings, it is *The Praise of Folly* that most adopts a proto-Shakespearean perspective. Provocative rather than prescriptive, it lectures no princes about the necessity of virtuous conduct and peace. Folly naturally claims to be responsible for war, and she briefly slips out of character with a few sage remarks, such as, "War is such a monstrous pursuit that it's proper only for beasts, not men."[47] Her perspective on European civilization anticipates—more acutely than the broad concept of the *theatrum mundi*—Shakespeare's premise of life as a play: "Each plays his assigned part till the stage manager comes forth and takes them off stage. Indeed, he often assigns

---

45. Jeffrey Knapp, *Shakespeare's Tribe: Church, Nation, and Theater in Renaissance England*, 56.

46. *Sir Thomas More* is a discarded play in which, it is widely accepted, Shakespeare had a hand—Hand D, to be precise. The play was evidently composed in the early 1590s. Whoever sponsored it saw sufficient potential in Anthony Munday's plot, and sufficient interest in More and his celebrated friend, to justify financing an extensive revision for the stage. After this major investment of time and work, the Master of Revels quashed the project, anxious over its political resonances. See Vittorio Gabrieli and Giorgio Melchiori, introduction to *Sir Thomas More*, by Anthony Munday, 23, 27.

47. Erasmus, *Praise of Folly and Other Writings*, ed. Adams, 72. By contrast, *The Education of a Christian Prince* condemns the folly of war at length. See Erasmus, *The Education of a Christian Prince*, ed. Lisa Jardine, trans. Neil M. Cheshire and Michael J. Heath, 102–110.

one actor several roles, so the performer who just now acted a king in purple majesty presently comes back a humble servant in rags. They are all but shadows of real persons, yet there's no other way to put on the show."[48] This idea of society as a theater of "shadows" (*adumbrata*)[49] coheres with Puck's "If we shadows have offended" (5.1.418): at first "we shadows" signifies the fairies, but then it includes all the characters, as Puck goes on to ask for general applause, speaking for the entire company by maintaining the first-person plural, "we will mend. . . . If we have unearnèd luck . . . We will make amends ere long" (425, 427, 429). Peter Quince as stage manager and the doubling of parts also come to mind.[50] As the zenith of Erasmian wit, *The Praise of Folly* lent an attractive luster to the Erasmian rhetorical legacy as a whole, highlighting its playfulness, its interest as a game.

It was the Elizabethans' lively investment in the question of salvation that made the game worth playing. The 1590s was a time of simmering tension between strict adherents to Calvin's views on assurance, that is, those who preached the comforting doctrine of certainty of election (or, less comfortingly, certainty of damnation), and those scholars and ecclesiastics, including Peter Baro and Lancelot Andrewes, who saw spiritual benefits in not knowing whether they were saved.[51] The crisis—for that is what it was—came to a head with the drawing up of the Lambeth Articles in 1595. In essence, the Lambeth articles maintained "that God from all eternity had predestined by an unchangeable decree a definite number of persons to salvation, and that the elect were saved not because God had foreseen their merits but through His good pleasure alone."[52] Had they been formally approved by the government, the Lambeth Articles would have increased the power and authority of the stricter breed of learned Calvinists, armed as they were with Ramist logic, explanatory diagrams, and hatred of Catholic theology. Baro, having inflamed the hardliners against him, lost his Divinity Chair at Cambridge, from which he fled in 1596, dying penniless in London a few years later. His disciple

---

48. Erasmus, *Praise of Folly and Other Writings*, ed. Adams, 28. For the history of "the play metaphor," see Anne Righter, *Shakespeare and the Idea of a Play*, 59–62.

49. Erasmus, *Stultitiae Laus*, §29.

50. For Brett Gamboa, the "casting patterns" of a *Midsummer Night's Dream* and *Romeo and Juliet* suggest "that—quite early in his career—doubling was a central part of Shakespeare's theatrical vision and a superior means to deepen audience engagement." Brett Gamboa, *Shakespeare's Double Plays*, 136.

51. See Brian Cummings, *The Literary Culture of the Reformation: Grammar and Grace*, 287–96, and Dodds, *Exploiting Erasmus*, 112–15.

52. *The Oxford Dictionary of the Christian Church*, ed. F. L. Cross and E. A. Livingstone, 945.

William Barrett converted to Rome. Andrewes, on the other hand, stayed in the Church of England. We may recognize that passages in Richard Hooker's *Of the Laws of Ecclesiastical Polity*, the first four books of which were published in 1593, suggest a margin for human agency within broadly Calvinist parameters; but, during his lifetime, Hooker's impact on this theological war zone was close to nil.[53] In the immediate aftermath of the crisis, the Queen banned further disputation.[54] Even so, the next decade witnessed the rise of English Arminianism, indicating that official suppression had neither muzzled the controversy nor curtailed its broader theological and political significance.

The English were, in fact, debating the very grounds of the Reformation. The positions of Baro and Andrewes stand, as Brian Cummings writes, in "contradiction to Calvin. They endorse a view of the co-operation of the will that is Calvin's first principle to deny."[55] Earlier in the century, Erasmus and Luther had staked out the Catholic and Protestant positions in a war of books that electrified Europe, and that I believe held much significance for Shakespeare's development as a playwright. Subsequent to the Erasmus-Luther debate, Calvin took considerable pains to illuminate and to justify "how God worketh in the hearts of men."[56] Marlowe's *Doctor Faustus*, which first appeared around 1590, dramatized this operation with disturbing energy, inspiring an extensive debate over "the freedom of Faustus's will vis-à-vis salvation."[57] In 1547, the Council of Trent, despite intramural sparring between Augustinians and Thomists, had defended its traditional authority on these matters. During Elizabeth's reign, mainstream Puritans who inclined toward even the slightest concession to free will could be accused of harboring Catholic sympathies. Record exists of the anti-Calvinist position at Oxford in the 1580s,[58] and it must have taken root at Cambridge before the crisis erupted. The Family of Love, a half-forgotten sect that was influential during Elizabeth's reign, also believed in free will.[59] *Church Papists*, a term dating from around 1580,

53. Cummings, *Literary Culture*, 314–16. See Richard Hooker, *Of the Laws of Ecclesiastical Polity: Preface, Book I, Book VIII*, 58 (1.3.1) and 73 (1.7.6–1.7.7).

54. Peter Lake, *Moderate Puritans and the Elizabethan Church*, 228.

55. Cummings, *Literary Culture*, 295.

56. John Calvin, *The Institution of the Christian Religion* (chapter heading to 2.4). I have modernized the spelling.

57. Paul R. Sellin, "The Hidden God," in *The Darker Vision of the Renaissance: Beyond the Fields of Reason*, ed. Robert S. Kinsman, 178.

58. In the career of Anthony Corro. See Nicholas Tyacke, *Anti-Calvinists: The Rise of English Arminianism c. 1590–1640*, 58–60.

59. See Peter Lake, "Religious Identities in Shakespeare's England," in *A Companion to Shakespeare*, ed. David Scott Kastan, 60.

expressed the frustration if not contempt of rival groups of Catholics and Puritans toward those who regularly attended Church of England services, yet (from the hot Puritan point of view) "had not fully repudiated the Pelagian, merit-mongering and idolatrous mental habits and assumptions that characterized the religion of real Papists."[60] Throughout Shakespeare's lifetime, the Catholic elements in the debate had proven uncannily perdurable. The English church, like the English nation, like Christendom itself, remained torn on this crucial question.

The 1595 crisis flared up close to the date when *A Midsummer Night's Dream* first appeared on the London stage. Topicality being essential, it isn't surprising that Shakespeare imported the crisis into Fairyland. We learn that "Judith Phillips, a London cunning woman, was whipped through the City in 1595 after being convicted for extracting large sums of money from gullible clients prepared to pay for the privilege of meeting the Queen of the Fairies."[61] I want to suggest that Shakespeare found means to respond to the "Protestant myth that fairy-beliefs were an invention of the Catholic Middle Ages."[62] His creative breakthrough was to translate the conceptual link between fairy lore and Catholicism, scorned by Protestant Reginald Scot in his *Discovery of Witchcraft* (1584),[63] into the jostling registers of the predestination controversy. To admit this view, we must as always take account of Shakespeare's audience and the theological temper of the time. One reason theology mattered to Shakespeare was because it mattered to his audience.

It is the predominance of theology in Elizabethan culture that leads me to pause our Erasmian trajectory in order to establish the crucial relevance of a well-known Chaucerian subtext. Scholars long have recognized that *The Knight's Tale* influenced *A Midsummer Night's Dream*. In her 1978 book, *Shakespeare's Chaucer*, Ann Thompson pieces together the scholarly background, including "the framing action of the wedding of Theseus and Hippolyta, the setting in Athens nearby the woods (in which two rivals intend to fight over a girl), the hunting scenes, and the final wedding celebrations." Thompson

---

60. Lake, "Religious Identities," 66.

61. Keith Thomas, *Religion and the Decline of Magic*, 613. Phillips's "clients" remind one of Dapper's gullibility in Jonson's *Alchemist*.

62. Thomas, *Religion and the Decline of Magic*, 610. Thomas concedes that this "myth . . . may well have had some effect."

63. See Geoffrey Bullough, *Narrative and Dramatic Sources in Shakespeare*, 1:395–97. Bullough notes Scot's "tone of stern protestant reproof for the popish beliefs of Bodin and other writers" (371). For more on Scot and fairy lore, see Jesse M. Lander, "*A Midsummer Night's Dream* and the Problem of Belief," *Shakespeare Survey* 65 (2012): 42–57.

gathers a string of telltale verbal parallels, provoking one of her shrewdest observations: "Shakespeare refers to May rather more than we might otherwise expect in a play ostensibly set on a midsummer night." Further, she draws our attention to an important 1945 essay by Dorothy Bethurum, in order to make a suggestion that we can tuck away in the back of our minds for now, namely, "that the fairies in the play might be a lighter version of the supernatural influences in the poem."[64] In *The Swan at the Well*, published in 1985, E. Talbot Donaldson notes other suggestive verbal parallels but offers his most original contribution in comparing Chaucerian self-parody in *The Tale of Sir Thopas* to Shakespearean self-parody in "The most lamentable comedy and most cruel death of Pyramus and Thisbe" (1.2.11–12).[65] More recently still, Harold Bloom takes a strong position that I suspect is basically right (though Erasmus is missing in action): "Shakespeare actually owed more to Chaucer than to any other precursor, including Ovid, Christopher Marlowe, and William Tyndale."[66] My aim here, in considering this scholarly tradition, is to understand Shakespeare's encounter with the Elizabethan Chaucer, a figure who, unsurprisingly, was drawn into the vortex of religious controversy.

For the inescapable John Foxe, Chaucer was a Wycliffite. In his second edition of the *Acts and Monuments of These Latter and Perilous Times* (1570), popularly known as the *Book of Martyrs*, Foxe represented Chaucer as a critic of Romish religion and "the Morning Star of the Reformation." He placed Chaucer's name on an honor roll of early "faithful witnesses" of the true church. Seizing on Chaucer's supposedly Wycliffite attitudes toward the "superstitious sects of Friars," Foxe praised Chaucer as one who "(no doubt) saw in Religion as much almost, as even we do now, and uttereth in his works no less, and seemeth to be a right Wycliffian."[67] Foxe was wrong about Chaucer's being a Wycliffite—a point we touched on in the Introduction. He was relying on texts that are no longer admitted to the Chaucerian canon. Even so, his instincts in the matter have proven sufficiently intriguing to later scholars to command a certain respect. Elizabethans persuaded by Foxe's take on Chaucer were not necessarily ideological dupes. John Wycliffe was Chaucer's close contemporary. Both moved in the circle of John of Gaunt, both targeted clerical luxury, both scorned pious fraud and godless superstition. Leaving

---

64. Ann Thompson, *Shakespeare's Chaucer: A Study in Literary Origins*, 88, 89, 90.
65. E. Talbot Donaldson, *The Swan at the Well: Shakespeare Reading Chaucer*, 7–29.
66. Harold Bloom, introduction to *Geoffrey Chaucer*, ed. Harold Bloom, xi.
67. John Foxe, "'A Protestation to the Whole Church of England'" (1570), in *Geoffrey Chaucer*, Bloom's Classic Critical Views, ed. Harold Bloom, 32, 33. I have modernized the spelling.

aside other points of comparison,[68] I want to underscore, in the words of Erasmus, Wycliffe's popular association with the doctrine of predestination, "the doctrine which Wyclif taught and Luther asserted, that whatever is done by us is done not by free choice but by sheer necessity."[69]

This is relevant to us because Chaucer is at his most elaborately fateful in *The Knight's Tale*.[70] The poem is not exactly a romance in the traditional, medieval sense. It is a hybrid, a philosophical romance featuring a heavy dose of philosophical consolation deriving largely from Boethius. Its philosophical climax is Theseus's First Mover speech, which addresses God's foreknowledge and intention: "Wel wiste he why, and what thereof he mente" (2990). With the curious exception of suicide, the main characters have no choice but to give in to what the gods—along with certain rigid social codes—have predetermined. As the riddle of fate unfolds and we learn the destinies of Palamon, Arcite, and their beloved Emily, human freedom proves to be an illusory effect of not knowing the future. It is active only in contemplation of the "faire cheyne of love" (2988). We learn to see the wisdom of Theseus's advice, "To maken vertu of necessitee" (3042) in the "foule prisoun of this lyf" (3061). To quote the Knight-narrator, "Be it of werre, or pees, or hate, or love, / Al is this reuled by the sighte above" (1671–72). So it strikes us that Foxe's appropriation of Chaucer seizes on elements that are, with respect to *The Knight's Tale*, impressively coherent.[71] To a sophisticated reader, Chaucer's philosophical romance is as much a comment on the nature of romance as it is on the workings of the cosmos. One could say the same thing about *A Midsummer Night's Dream*. In any case, I am suggesting, especially given Foxe's Wycliffite Chaucer, that the profound impact of *The Knight's Tale* on *A Midsummer Night's*

68. For example, see the nineteenth-century German scholar Hugo Simon, whose work is excerpted in Bloom, *Geoffrey Chaucer*, 345–58.

69. Erasmus, *On the Freedom of the Will*, in *Luther and Erasmus: Free Will and Salvation*, ed. E. Gordon Rupp and Philip S. Watson, 41. Erasmus was not entirely correct on this point. The historical Wycliffe, though a predestinarian, followed the orthodox belief in free will. He was "not a strict determinist." Geoffrey Shepherd, "Religion and Philosophy in Chaucer," in *Writers and Their Background: Geoffrey Chaucer*, ed. Derek Brewer, 283.

70. The words *fortune* and *destinee* supply the concept of fate in *The Knight's Tale*, appearing ten and five times, respectively. The English word *fate*, offspring of the Latin *fatum*, is first attested in Chaucer's *Troilus and Criseyde*, where it occurs three times, its only instances in all of Chaucer's works. In the OED, there is a lengthy silence between Chaucer's and Shakespeare's uses of the noun. Bottom and Flute (Chaucer also supplies the first attestation of *flute*) use the word *Fates* three times between them, in reference to the classical goddesses. Puck gets the sole non-mythological usage: "Then fate o'errules, that, one man holding troth, / A million fail, confounding oath on oath" (3.2.92–93).

71. An impediment to a Wycliffite reading of *The Knight's Tale* is Arcite's funeral. For committed Lollards, funeral rites were *verboten*.

Dream may be approached through the theme of predestination—which, conversely, is the theme of free will.

In his portrayal of Theseus, Shakespeare breaks from the mold of Chaucer's stern lawgiver when the duke abruptly rules against Egeus's paternal claim on Hermia. The action is calculated to surprise, since Theseus is overruling "the law of Athens . . . Which by no means we may extenuate" (1.1.119–20). It is an act that looks very much like a free choice, as Theseus's unexpected decision takes precedence over Egeus's "will," which is a funny way of talking about the Athenian law: "Egeus, I will overbear your will" (4.1.178). Insofar as it has the power to unify the realms of political and spiritual authority, Theseus's decision cooperates with Oberon's ability to set Fairyland to rights. It is a kind of cosmic action, which will be ratified in the "temple" (4.1.1.179). But it flouts the legal situation of the opening scene. The play to a large extent hinges on a moment when it is morally at odds with itself.

In terms of free will and its theological significance, we can read Theseus as representing, in his syncretistic world, the Pauline concept of Christ's releasing humanity from bondage to "our law" (1.1.44). Egeus's demand for his daughter's "obedience" (37) is likewise suggestive of the Ten Commandments. Theseus's expression "die the death" (65) is definitively rooted in the Old Testament.[72] Given this context, his sudden reversal redounds with a grace suggestive of his will's freedom from bondage. To be sure, a grace that supersedes what was assumed to be the unmerciful example of the Old Testament is, from our standpoint, a problematic grace, but here it is:

> Egeus, I will overbear your will;
> For in the temple, by and by, with us
> These couples shall eternally be knit. (4.1. 178–80)

This display of spontaneous freedom serves almost invisibly to fulfill what might be called Oberon's prophecy, an unusual octet rhyme spoken to Titania the previous night. Theseus's freedom to overrule the Athenian law is undetermined (that is, it appears to be caused solely by his own agency) in the natural world, in the world the Athenians can see, but it is determined from the perspective of the supernatural world. Oberon has already foreseen what will happen to the couples, and the felicity of their fall depends on Theseus's changing his mind.

---

72. Naseeb Shaheen, *Biblical References in Shakespeare's Plays*, 145.

Edmond Malone pointed out over two centuries ago that Oberon and Titania, upon their reconciliation, "can now fulfil the purpose which brought him to Athens: to endow Theseus and Hippolyta's marriage with joy and prosperity."[73] We hesitate at the word *now*. Oberon and Titania cannot fulfill their original purpose until one remaining impediment is removed. The unhappiness of the four noble youths would have tarnished the wedding festivities of Theseus and Hippolyta. Hence the need for Theseus to "overbear" Egeus's "will." But even if the great scholar missed a small detail, we cannot tax Oberon with such mortal shortcomings. As he dances with Titania near or around the sleeping lovers, his intense rhyming creates the impression of a powerful will at work:

> Now thou and I are new in amity,
> And will tomorrow midnight solemnly
> Dance in Duke Theseus' house triumphantly,
> And bless it to all fair prosperity.
> There shall the pairs of faithful lovers be
> Wedded, with Theseus, all in jollity. (4.1.86–91)

By juxtaposing supernatural and natural circumstances, and then uniting them in the cosmic symbolism of music and the dance, Shakespeare entertains the paradox of God's foreknowledge coexisting with human freedom and human potential. This perspectival opening develops as Oberon links the cosmic occasion of present dancing to future dancing and blessings to be bestowed on Theseus's "house" and the "faithful" newlyweds. In effect, Shakespeare distinguishes the action of grace in the supernatural and natural realms, and encourages his audience to work through the problem of seeing "these things with parted eye, / When everything seems double" (4.1.188–89).

Before further considering how the predestination crisis impacted Shakespeare's play, we have some more catching up to do with Chaucer. The philosophical question at the heart of *The Knight's Tale* is, how do two nearly identical beings achieve their individual destinies? After Duke Theseus has conquered their city, Palamon and Arcite are discovered badly wounded in the rubble of Thebes, "Two yonge knyghtes liggynge by and by, / Bothe in oon armes . . . and of sustren two y-born" (1011–1012, 1019). The cousins are imprisoned together and fall in love with the same girl. Emily's limits as a

---

73. Edmond Malone, paraphrased by editor Harold F. Brooks in William Shakespeare, *A Midsummer Night's Dream*, ed. Harold F. Brooks, 91n.

character-type ensure that her personal response cannot tilt the scales one way or the other. The whole poem is a controlled experiment in the quirks of fate. Individuation is the work not of man but of his destiny.

In *The Knight's Tale*, Theseus experiences a change of heart in part two, where the marvelous coincidences typical of medieval romance assert their sway. Arcite, pining after Emily, has disguised himself in order to return to Theseus's city. Palamon, having escaped his Athenian prison-tower, conceals himself in the woods. One fine morning, Arcite leaves Athens "to doon his observaunce to May" (1500). The sworn rivals meet by chance when Palamon, hiding "in a bussh" (1517), overhears Arcite's love-complaint. Honoring their chivalric code, they agree to fight it out in full armor the next day. And that is naturally when Theseus, out on a hunting expedition with his household in tow, happens upon them battling in the woods like wild boars. By his own law, Theseus is bound to put the men to death. When Palamon points out that both he and his cousin have transgressed, the duke readily assents to their joint execution. But at that moment Hippolyta, the unsuspecting Emily, and the other women present fall "on hir bare knees adoun" (1758) to beg for mercy on the cousins' behalf. Chaucer slips in his favorite line: "For pitee renneth soone in gentil herte" (1761). And Theseus, reflecting on his own past experience as "a servant" of love (1814), cools down. His decision to build an amphitheater in the grove where the men were fighting, and to arrange a tournament there so that they can pursue their rivalry in high chivalric style before the world, is widely approved. He leavens the law with pity and mercy, validating the poem's Christian dimension.

When Chaucer's Theseus relents, he embarks on an oration that speaks not only to Palamon and Arcite, but (we might say) to Lysander and Demetrius as well: "Who may been a fool but if he love? . . . And yet they wenen for to been ful wyse / That serven love, for aught that may bifalle" (1799, 1804–1805). The confusion of folly and wisdom that characterizes the typical lover is a cause for pity, as it is in Shakespeare's play. Chaucer, developing his strong thematic interest in pity and mercy, goes so far as to have Theseus allude to the Lord's Prayer: "I yow foryeve this trespas every deel" (1825). But human folly lacks the connection to spiritual insight that characterizes Erasmus and Shakespeare. In *The Knight's Tale*, the god of love shoots his unshunnable arrows, and Theseus remains what the Knight-narrator calls him, "lord and governour" (861). He heeds the dictates of destiny and philosophizes to justify them. But he does not have his counterpart's capacity for swift and stunning reversal. His lack of freedom marks a limitation not only in his range of experience, but in human potential as well.

Shakespeare revisits Chaucer's problem of individuation by means of what R. Chris Hassell, Jr., calls the four lovers' "pasteboard qualities."[74] It can be hard, especially for newcomers, to remember which young lover is which. Theseus in the opening scene confronts Hermia with choices that would seem to be defining: "either prepare to die . . . Or else to wed . . . Or on Diana's altar to protest / For aye austerity and single life" (1.1.86–90). The presence of "Diana's altar" connects Hermia to Chaucer's Emily. But while Hermia is clearly more willful than fair Emily, does she accomplish more? Is she actually freer than Helena, who complains to Demetrius, "You draw me, you hardhearted adamant!" (2.1.195). Other than running off with Lysander and rejecting his polite advances, Hermia acts in ignorance and fails to realize her own destiny. And yet Shakespeare begins the play by dramatizing the reality of momentous choices, a plot-driver that is heightened by Hermia's defiance, "My soul consents not" (1.1.82). Will a higher power intervene? Will Hermia cooperate with that power, or will she defy it? Or be a puppet in any case? To the shorter Hermia's great indignation, Helena in fact calls her a "puppet" (3.3.288), and Hermia immediately echoes back the term. To be an echo is to be another's double (as the rhetorical term *anadiplosis* would suggest). Hermia and Helena are so interchangeable that at one point Shakespeare simply rhymes their names (3.2.155–56).

Shakespeare may be said to elaborate on a Chaucerian state of affairs where individuation is not primarily the work of the individual, and self-fashioning is not much in evidence.[75] Both in the larger play, and in the play within the play that shows the playwright flexing his metadramatic muscles, the mechanicals perform their allotted parts, acting "man by man, according to the scrip" (1.2.2–3) and "everyone according to his cue" (2.2.71). "You shall see," Pyramus sagely informs Theseus, "it will fall pat as I told you" (5.1.185–86). Likewise, the youthful lovers, whose passions and conflicts are parodied in "The most lamentable comedy and most cruel death of Pyramus and Thisbe," are servants of their destinies, and it is Helena's personal achievement to recognize their position. As in Chaucer, willful characters adapt to what reality offers them. But in Shakespeare, the experiential gap between will and reality widens tellingly.

Lysander and Demetrius are willful beings, alike in their willfulness, alike in conforming to type. Fortunately for them, they are in a comedy. At the

---

74. R. Chris Hassell, Jr., *Faith and Folly in Shakespeare's Romantic Comedies*, 63.

75. The word *fashion* "does not occur at all in Chaucer's poetry." Stephen Greenblatt, *Renaissance Self-Fashioning: From More to Shakespeare*, 2.

height of his folly, Lysander justifies his headlong attraction to Helena in a speech that recalls Folly's madcap enthusiasm for "dialectical precision":[76]

> The will of man is by his reason swayed
> And reason says you are the worthier maid.
> Things growing are not ripe until their season;
> So I, being young, till now ripe not to reason.
> And, touching now the point of human skill,
> Reason becomes the marshal of my will
> And leads me to your eyes . . . . (2.2.121–27)

For Aquinas and his scholastic heirs, "reason" illuminated the choices facing the "will of man." The reasoning soul worked with the willful body in apprehending and acting on choices. Form and matter cooperated according to their hierarchical relationship. Lysander's speech resembles a passage from the *Summa Theologica*: "that act whereby the will tends to something proposed to it as being good, through being ordained to the end by reason, is materially an act of the will, but formally an act of the reason."[77] The whole system of definitions, distinctions, and divisions is a permanent testament to reason's capabilities. And yet we are likely to find Lysander's speech, as a species of logical discourse and deliberative oratory (delivered rather perversely in heroic couplets), to be anything but rational. Of course, it is the love-juice talking.

Or is it the Reformation talking? I want to suggest that the Elizabethan audience appreciated the theological humor. They got the joke, which is not only on theology, but on humanity as well. They could see Lysander's effort at dialectical argument for the farce that it is, though he doesn't see it that way, nor does Helena. As Lysander repeats the words *will* and *reason* again and again, their hierarchical relationship is humorously undone and reversed. Will takes the upper hand, while falsely declaring that it remains subordinate to reason. To adduce that high theological authority, the learned Puck, the situation is preposterous: "And those things do best please me / That befall preposterously" (3.2.120–21). The word *preposterous* evidently entered the English language through a 1533 translation of Erasmus's *Enchiridion* (OED 1a and 2). The preposterous result in this case is an Erasmian lesson in preposterous wisdom (*praepostera sapientia*).[78] Our logical terminology (and our logical self-

---

76. Erasmus, *Praise of Folly*, ed. Miller, 90.
77. Aquinas, *Summa Theologica*, I–II, q. 13, art. 1.
78. Erasmus, *Stultitiae Laus*, §29.

understanding) can withstand the pressures of experience about as well as Pala-mon and Arcite can honor their obligations to Theseus. Were this a tragedy, we might be in the bedroom scene of *Hamlet*. Lysander's false premise, "The will of man is by his reason swayed," is the comical cousin to "reason panders will" (HAM 3.4.89), with its Lutheran indictment of humanity. The author of *A Midsummer Night's Dream* keeps these darker potentialities firmly in check.

Shakespeare develops his theological slapstick by means of one of his char-acteristic devices, the dishonoring of oaths. In the following passage, Lysander's abrupt rejection of Hermia resounds well beyond the lovers' concerns:

> The heresies that men do leave
> Are hated most of those they did deceive,
> So thou, my surfeit and my heresy,
> Of all be hated, but the most by me! (2.2.145–48)

In a nation known for "confounding," as Puck says, "oath on oath" (3.2.93), everyone was a potential heretic with a price to pay. Cummings supplies the relevant context: the 1534 Act of Succession, "enforced by an oath of alle-giance" (famously refused by Thomas More), "was only the beginning of a rash of public swearing enforced by government. . . . Almost every revolution of religion and politics . . . was accompanied by a new oath of allegiance to it." [79] Given the ruptures of English history in the sixteenth century, the satir-ical thrust of these lines must have been keen. In particular, the relation of free will and heresy was a hot topic that could get you in hot water. The hard laughter, painful in one way, was healthy in another—a form of comic cathar-sis. [80] I will return to this matter of Shakespeare's investment in comical release.

The curious fact that Lysander and Demetrius both apparently lose their free will through the intervention of the love-juice, while Lysander alone is restored to his condition at the start of the play, throws the problem of free will into high relief. We may protest that Demetrius is a puppet who has no choice, given Oberon's determination to bind him to Helena. Or we may sug-gest that this particular question was theologically compelling to Shakespeare's

---

79. Brian Cummings, *Mortal Thoughts: Religion, Secularity & Identity in Shakespeare and Early Modern England*, 145 and 148.

80. John Briggs's analysis of the tragic effects of *The Spanish Tragedy* and *Hamlet* illuminates my analogous claim for *A Midsummer Night's Dream*: "Their plots displace yet somehow re-enact [personal and political/philosophical] conflicts for cathartic ends, each complicating and redirecting the protagonist's (and by analogy the audience's) desire . . . in ordeals of wonder and woe that induce reflection." John Channing Briggs, "Happiness, Catharsis, and Literary Cure," in *The Eudaimonic Turn: Well-Being in Literary Studies*, ed. James O. Pawelski and D. J. Moores, 125.

original audience. As an instrument of Oberon's power, which is as close as we get to the will of God in this play, Puck comments aloud while wrapping up the business in the woods:

> Jack shall have Jill;
> Naught shall go ill;
> The man shall have his mare again, and all shall be well. (3.2.461–63)

Like the Jacks, the Jills have two natures, beastly and celestial, appetitive and rational.[81] If the "man shall have his mare again," it is because "man" symbolically wears an ass head. He is a "Jack" ass. It will be a marriage of true minds.[82] Oberon's application of the love-juice to Demetrius's eyelids—"Sink in apple of his eye" (3.2.104)—restores what the young man comes to think of as his "natural taste" (4.1.173) for Helena.[83] We are led to ask whether Demetrius has been restored to his place in the cosmic order by a grace he never understands. This is basically the Erasmian lesson that Hassel gleans from the play as a whole: the lovers' experience "(like that of the audience) is a carefully developed liberation from their conceptions that love (or transcendental knowledge) has secure rational and sensual foundations, or that it can somehow be earned or deserved."[84] Then again, if "merit" counts (Theseus drops the m-bomb at 5.1.92),[85] Demetrius's resisting the temptation to rape Helena in the second act (2.1.214–19; see TMP 4.1.14–19) may be considered meritorious enough to ring Reformist alarm bells. If Demetrius, by treating Helena justly, has earned merit in the eyes of God, the salvific effect of his just act could be his soul's release, through the angelic offices of Oberon, from idolatrous bondage to Hermia. On the other hand, if we accept Demetrius's apparent merit as merely the predetermined function of divine grace, those Reformist alarm bells cease.[86]

---

81. "Man is made of two natures, one corporeal and terrestrial, the other divine and celestial; in the one he resembles beasts, in the other those immaterial substances which turn the heavens." Sixteenth-century humanist G.-B. Gelli, quoted in Theodore Spenser, *Shakespeare and the Nature of Man*, 11–12.

82. One may suggest that the current interest in bestiality with respect to Bottom and Titania risks losing the metaphysical thread. See, for example, Hugh Bonneville, *Shakespeare Uncovered.*

83. Peter Holland, introduction to *A Midsummer Night's Dream*, by William Shakespeare, ed. Peter Holland, 68.

84. Hassel, *Faith and Folly,* 63.

85. Compare "See, see, my beauty will be saved by merit! / Oh, heresy in fair, fit for these days!" (LLL 4.1.21–22). Hassel refers to Theseus's use of *merit* as a "pun." See R. Chris Hassel, Jr., *Shakespeare's Religious Language: A Dictionary*, 213.

86. See Calvin, *Institution*, 2.5.2.

Theological possibilities abound. Although the *apple of one's eye* appears to have become "a common expression"[87] by Shakespeare's day, we might remember its biblical links to God's protection, as in Psalms 17:8. Or we might think of "Eve's apple" (SON 93.13) as metonymic for the Fall. Demetrius's pleasure in his "natural taste" does not wholly foreclose the possibility of his relapsing into madness.[88] Or, more happily, does the apple of Demetrius's eye, like the apples in Juliet's orchard, retain some trace of Eden before the Fall? Along similar lines, does Oberon's herbal "liquor" whose "virtuous property" is to remove "all error" (3.2.367–68) savor of baptismal waters?

It may be helpful to pull back a little, to remember that Shakespeare wrote plays, not theological tracts. A wild night in the woods doesn't mean the death of reason. Shakespeare, in subjecting reason to folly, was not militating against Thomism, on the one hand, or against Calvinist logic, on the other. A master of wit, he was playing with theological language, including the language of controversy: "And this same progeny of evils comes / From our debate, from our dissension / We are their parents and original" (2.1.115–17). If "debate" and "dissension" lead unhappily to "evils," Titania's reference to her and Oberon's being "their parents and original" points to Adam, Eve, and original sin. Evil is prior to experience, part of the landscape, and not a social problem to be engineered out of existence by the power of art.

While Erasmus afforded Shakespeare a satirical perspective on theological controversy, I am not connecting the play to Erasmian folly in such terms as *doctrinal minimalism* or *charitable forbearance*[89]: its laughter is too hard, the questions too charged, the confessional divisions too real, and, historically, we are too late in the game. As I suggested earlier, if Erasmus's "philosophy of Christ" impressed Shakespeare, it was partly due to its conspicuous lack of success. And yet Erasmus was in no sense a parochial thinker. He was a great Catholic reformer who wrote with full Pauline consciousness: "no devout man ought to approve of revolution."[90] His idealistic effort at non-revolutionary transformation informs one of the most important of his adages, "The Sileni of Alcibiades," an essay that highlights Socrates's Silenic appearance: "with his peasant face, glaring like a bull . . . he might have been taken for some blockheaded

---

87. Shaheen, *Biblical References*, 150.

88. Shakespeare uses "natural" adjectivally in *Twelfth Night* to mean "half-witted." C. T. Onions, *A Shakespeare Glossary: Enlarged and Revised throughout by Robert D. Eagleson*, 178.

89. Knapp, *Shakespeare's Tribe*, 31, 33.

90. Erasmus, *The Adages of Erasmus*, ed. William Barker, 264 (see also Romans 13:1–7).

country bumpkin."[91] Coincidentally, Will Kemp, the great comic actor who played the role, was famous for his clownish appearance and "ill face."[92] Erasmus extends his Silenic conceit, from seeing beyond appearances to reality, to seeing beyond the surface of the letter to its spiritual truth—a cultivating of insight that can be disseminated among the "Christian people who are the Church."[93] To be sure, "bully Bottom" (3.1.7, 4.2.19) the weaver is no Saint Socrates, but he shows an interesting penchant for Socratic and Pauline knowledge. His clowning has its depths. It catches something of the Reformation's commitment to the spiritual potential of the common worker.

In his *Paraclesis* (Gk. "summons" or "exhortation"), originally published in 1516 as a foreword to his Latin translation of the New Testament, and first Englished in 1534, Erasmus says of ordinary laymen and laywomen who live and preach "the spirit of Christ": "he is truly a theologian, whether he is a ditch-digger or a weaver."[94] This essential text of western history, though not a call to revolution, is an epochal statement on behalf of the powerless, a vigorous affirmation of the spiritual dignity and intellectual capacity of women, a pushback against clerical exclusivism, a proverbial trumpet-blast heralding a Christian renewal on jarringly Christian terms. A brief, pithy, and dangerous little tract, the *Paraclesis* enjoyed tremendous popularity. It might aptly be called the founding document of the Reformation. It is true that the association of weavers and Christians goes back as far as the jeering, second-century Greek philosopher Celsus. It is also true that Erasmus decided to revise the *Paraclesis*, reevaluating but not abandoning his hopes for "the motley crowd."[95] I do not suggest that Shakespeare wrote the role of Bottom chiefly as a spiritual statement on behalf of working people. The moral simplicity of the mechanicals is appealing, but "Kemp the jig-maker"[96] was too clownish for Bottom to exemplify the Christian weaver in a pure sense. Because Shakespeare knew what Erasmus could not have known, his sense of history was less hopeful than Erasmus's, his knowledge of original sin more disturbing.[97] Consequently, he modified the early object of Erasmus's veneration (the idealized weaver)

---

91. Erasmus, *Adages*, 243.

92. David Wiles, *Shakespeare's Clown: Actor and Text in the Elizabethan Playhouse*, 24.

93. Erasmus, *Adages*, 253.

94. Erasmus, *Praise of Folly and Other Writings*, ed. Adams, 122.

95. Erasmus, *Praise of Folly and Other Writings*, ed. Adams, 131.

96. Wiles, *Shakespeare's Clown*, 55.

97. "Some one [*sic*] said: 'The dead authors are remote from us because we *know* so much more than they did.' Precisely, and they are that which we know." T. S. Eliot, *The Sacred Wood*, 52, his italics.

with delectable touches of vanity, molded him to comedy, and infused him with the mystical wisdom of Folly.[98]

In 1968, scholar Thelma N. Greenfield first proposed a connection between Erasmus and Bottom.[99] As Greenfield observes, Folly quotes Paul's First Letter to the Corinthians (1 Corinthians 2:9) in her climactic spiritual ascent, where she claims as her own the happiness of lovers and the beatific vision of Christians. I note a parallel between Folly's reference to a mystical and dreamlike state of indeterminacy "whether waking or sleeping" (*uigilantes an dormientes*[100]) and Demetrius's language after the lovers have awoken: "Are you sure / That we are awake? It seems to me / That yet we sleep, we dream" (4.1.191–93). It will be helpful to compare Folly's reference to Corinthians with Bottom's waking speech. Folly first:

> Nevertheless it happens that, because the life of the pious is nothing but a meditation and a certain shadow (as it were) of that other life, they some-times experience a certain flavor or odor of that reward. And this, even though it is like the tiniest droplet by comparison with that fountain of eter-nal happiness, nevertheless far surpasses all pleasures of the body, even if all the delights of all mortals were gathered into one. So much beyond the body are the things of the spirit; things unseen, beyond what can be seen. This, indeed, is what the prophet promises: "Eye hath not seen, nor ear heard, nor has the heart of man conceived what things God has prepared for those who love him." And this is Folly's part, which shall not be taken from her by the transformation of life, but shall be perfected. Those who have the privilege of experiencing this (and it happens to very few) undergo something very like madness: they talk incoherently, not in a human fashion, making sounds without sense . . . . [In] short, they are completely beside themselves. Soon after, when they come to themselves, they say they do not know where they have been, whether in body or out of it, whether waking or sleeping. They do not remember what they heard or saw or said or did except in a cloudy way, as if it were a dream.[101]

And now Bottom's version:

98. Falstaff also catches this comical falling off: "I would I were a weaver; I could sing psalms or anything" (1H4 2.4.130–31).

99. Thelma N. Greenfield, "*A Midsummer Night's Dream* and *The Praise of Folly*," *Comparative Literature* 20 (1968): 236–44. For extensive treatment of the Pauline subtext, see Hassel, *Faith and Folly*, 52–76; for related materials, see Weimann and Bruster, *Shakespeare and the Power of Performance*, 91–92, 240n55.

100. Erasmus, *Stultitiae Laus*, §67.

101. Erasmus, *Praise of Folly*, ed. Miller, 137–38.

I have had a most rare vision. I have had a dream, past the wit of man to say what dream it was. Man is but an ass if he go about to expound this dream. Methought I was—there is no man can tell what. Methought I was—and methought I had—but man is but a patched fool if he will offer to say what methought I had. The eye of man hath not heard, the ear of man hath not seen, man's hand is not able to taste, his tongue to conceive, nor his heart to report, what my dream was. I will get Peter Quince to write a ballad of this dream. It shall be called "Bottom's Dream," because it hath no bottom. (4.1.203–214)

Though Bottom's "rare vision" may smack of the flesh, it is more than a profane bungling of a major Christian text. It unfolds before us as a kaleidoscopic commentary on election, salvation, the Bible, the limits of our knowledge, the good of *eros*, and the spirit's home in God. It captures the fool's unaccountable capacity to stand for wisdom. And while Shakespeare's audience would have been prepared to discuss the verse, "We are fools for Christ's sake" (1 Corinthians 4:10), they would have assented to Bottom's metamorphosis for one very good reason: the image of a man with an ass head[102] was symbolically credible. It is relevant here that the word *man*, which Bottom keeps repeating, has thematic currency in the play, especially among the mechanicals when we first meet them in Act 1, Scene 2. And as Bottom informs us elsewhere, "I am a man as other men are" (3.1.41). What, then, was "man"? As we have seen with our Jacks and Jills, man was a celestial jackass. It is a good strong joke that makes us laugh at ourselves. "What do you see?" Bottom asks. "You see an ass head of your own, do you?" (3.1.111–12).

But if folly rules in the Athenian woods, the point is not to explode theology as so much intellectual nonsense (as if Shakespeare were channeling the spirit of H. G. Wells's *Outline of History*); rather, in its cathartic power, Shakespeare's fantastical synthesis releases its audience from the morbid "fear" (3.1.12, 20, 26, 39) instilled by a dangerous theological situation. The threat of imminent death worries Quince and company: "That would hang us, every

102. Weimann and Bruster comment on Folly's Pauline text and Bottom's garbling of it: "Erasmus had to defend himself from such staggering audacity. Yet Shakespeare's treatment adds a further piece of contrariety by confounding, at least by implication, the supreme spiritual taste of blessedness with the bottomless bliss of sensual rapture. All this is experienced under the pre-Christian mask of the ass's head" (*Shakespeare and the Power*, 91). If Weimann and Bruster think that Shakespeare was intent on shoving a gobbet of raw paganism down the Elizabethan gullet, then they have in a sense gone heresy hunting: they are pulling in the same direction as anti-theatricalist Stephen Gosson (see Bullough, *Narrative and Dramatic Sources*, 1:v).

mother's son" (1.2.71). Robert Southwell, SJ, arguably a poetic influence on the play and possibly Shakespeare's distant relation, was hanged at Tyburn in February, 1595.[103] Behind the mechanicals' ludicrous fears about frightening the ladies, one senses that other, graver threats have been comically sublimated. A cast of fools, trapped in the labyrinth of theology, has made a miraculous escape.

To complete this chapter's engagement with predestination and free will, I want to pursue the suggestion, made many years ago by Dorothy Bethurum, that, in Thompson's words, "the fairies in the play might be a lighter version of the supernatural influences in the poem."[104] How, then, do we judge the parallel between the planetary gods who arbitrate the destiny of Chaucer's lovers, and the fairies who intervene in the affairs of Shakespeare's Athenians? The similarity is not just that pagan machinery resolves the plot both in *The Knight's Tale* and in *A Midsummer Night's Dream*. It is relevant that what occurs within the natural range of perception—Bottom being the exception to the rule—is juxtaposed against what occurs within the supernatural range of perception. Through its blend of pathos and folly, *A Midsummer Night's Dream* achieves considerable intimacy with its audience. Unlike *The Knight's Tale*, it sympathetically reaches across class boundaries. But it works a similar magic by making us privy to the supernatural world over which the characters have no control, but which has control over them.

In Chaucer, the Knight-narrator engages us with an ascending hierarchy of knowledge, from the limited range of human knowledge to the higher mysteries of divine foreknowledge. On the mortal level, each member of the Arcite-Palamon-Emily love triangle is partly informed about the future by his or her tutelary god. On the next level, Venus and Mars expect satisfaction, having respectively promised Palamon and Arcite their hearts' desire. But how can both Venus and Mars be satisfied when they are at odds? At this level, Jupiter turns his plot-dilemma over to Saturnus, who somehow must satisfy everyone. At the highest level of foreknowledge, Saturnus keeps his answer to the riddle of fate to himself. We don't learn how he plans to accommodate

---

103. See Lee Oser, "Imagination, Judgment, and Belief," *Literary Imagination* 16.1 (2014): 46–47.

104. To be precise, Bethurum does not speak of the fairies being a "lighter version." She says, "In both stories . . . the resolution is brought about by supernatural aid, by planetary intervention in *The Knight's Tale* and by Puck and Oberon in *A Midsummer Night's Dream*." Dorothy Bethurum, "Shakespeare's Comment on Medieval Romance in *A Midsummer Night's Dream*," *Modern Language Notes* 60 (1945): 89.

Venus and Mars's contradictory demands until his backchannel connection to Pluto is revealed on the day of the great tournament.

The gloomy power of Saturnus in *The Knight's Tale* is replaced by the airy power of Oberon in *A Midsummer Night's Dream*. I do not see this exchange as marking a growth in human freedom per se, but as expressing Shakespeare's idea of human freedom within religious limits, where the power of fate is more humanized: I see it as a playful expression of the poet's urbane Christian skepticism.

Like Saturnus, Oberon will come to foresee the action and to set it in motion. In the first half of the play, though, Titania not only thwarts Oberon's will, but the plot runs away from the "king of shadows" (3.2.347) when Puck misapplies the love-juice to Lysander. In the second half, Oberon's increasingly hands-on resolution of the plot reflects his full recovery as an arbiter of fate and ambassador of God's will.

This angelic role is almost baroque in its elaboration. A profuse verbal sign of Oberon's complicated activity is the repetition of the modal auxiliary *shall*. In Oberon's frequent usage, *shall* joins a sense of foreknowledge with a sense of predestination. We note that the underlying ambiguity of *shall*, between knowledge or belief, on the one hand, and the seemingly predestined activity of moral agents, on the other, is inherent to the English language and has significant theological ramifications.[105] When Bottom says, "It shall be called 'Bottom's Dream,' because it hath no bottom," he knows or believes what is going to happen, and he is implying that Peter Quince is predestined to write and to title the ballad accordingly. The same form (*shall*) is "used for expressing the speaker's degree of commitment to truth and for getting other people to do things."[106] Another example: we understand the law "Thou shalt not bow down to them," that is, to any "similitude" or "graven image" (Exodus 20:4–5), as a divine and therefore an omniscient imperative with a binding claim upon us. And yet we also know that one may possibly fail to fulfill the law, or, some would say, necessarily fail to do so. Oberon's power grows the more absolute as he fuses the epistemic and deontic aspects of *shall*,[107] that is, its two senses of (a) foreknowledge (or belief) and (b) predestination for moral agents. Spoken at his master's behest, Puck's folkloric ditty ("Jack shall have Jill; / Naught shall go ill; / The man shall have his mare

---

105. See Cummings, *Literary Culture*, 215–17.
106. F. R. Palmer, quoted in Cummings, *Literary Culture*, 216.
107. See Cummings, *Literary Culture*, 215

again, and all shall be well") does this kind of work. Its compelling use of *shall* combines knowledge of the future with a sense of moral necessity, evoking but not invoking the highest level of divine authority. By the end of the play, Oberon has ascended very high indeed up the great chain of being:[108]

> Now, until the break of day,
> Through this house each fairy stray.
> To the best bride-bed will we,
> Which by us shall blessèd be;
> And the issue there create
> Ever shall be fortunate.
> So shall all the couples three
> Ever true in loving be;
> And the blots of Nature's hand
> Shall not in their issue stand;
> Never mole, harelip, nor scar,
> Nor mark prodigious, such as are
> Despisèd in nativity,
> Shall upon their children be.
> With this field dew consecrate,
> Every fairy take his gait,
> And each several chamber bless,
> Through this palace, with sweet peace;
> And the owner of it blest
> Ever shall in safety rest.
> Trip away; make no stay;
> Meet me all by break of day. (5.1.396–417)

The word *shall* occurs six times in this valedictory passage. Only in the first instance does Oberon address the matter of agency ("To the best bride-bed

---

108. By way of Cardinal Robert Bellarmine's *De Ascensione Mentis in Deum per Scalas Creaturarum* (*The Mind's Ascent toward God by means of the Ladder of Creatures*, 1614), Arthur O. Lovejoy discusses the intrinsic tension in Christianity between the scholastic belief in the real cosmic plenitude of the great chain of being and the opposing tendency to deny "that the manifold of finite things has any existence" (92). This dialectical instability affords grounds for Puck's describing the fairies as "shadows" (5.1.418) and helps clarify the great chain of being's cosmic significance in the play. See the classic work of intellectual history, Arthur O. Lovejoy's *Great Chain of Being: A Study of the History of an Idea*, 67–98, esp. 90–93. On the other hand, C. S. Lewis is undoubtedly correct about the "profound disharmony of atmospheres" in what he calls "the Medieval Model": this disharmony, between sublunary and translunary experience, explains "why all this cosmology plays so small a part in the spiritual writers, and is not fused with high religious ardor in any writer . . . except Dante." C. S. Lewis, *The Discarded Image: An Introduction to Medieval and Renaissance Literature*, 120.

will we, / Which by us shall blessèd be"), but this statement of his and Titania's role imbues the speech as a whole with a sense of cosmic duty being fulfilled by moral agents. The speech closes powerfully with three consecutive
commands. It is of theological interest that Oberon is telling the fairies what
to do, that he foresees what they will do, and that he describes what must necessarily happen to fairies and mortals both. On the mortal level of knowledge
and action, by contrast, we overhear a divine promise about "the couples
three" being "true in loving" and blessed in their "issue," in a future dependent
in either Protestant or Catholic terms on God's grace, as suggested here by
apotropaic incantation. Oberon activates the Catholic possibility of free will
within the traditional framework of divine foreknowledge by adding the Catholic holy-water touch of "field dew consecrate,"[109] while mixing in signs of
Calvinist assurance. The convoluted pattern of fate, which joins the mortal
and immortal worlds, appears in the seeming contradiction of straying to obey
Oberon's commands: "each fairy stray." For this to make sense to us, we must
see and hear "double," a doubleness expressed in rhyming couplets that com-
press the play's most salient formal feature, that is, its Chaucerian use of heroic
couplets. Puck's final entrance with his mood-altering "If we shadows have
offended" (5.1.418) deflates the angelic rhapsody and deflects the anti-theatrical charge against Shakespeare and his audience of doting on idols.

The difference between Chaucer and Shakespeare reflects a change from
literalness to metaphoricity. In this respect, we may recall Erasmus's summons
to see beyond the surface of the letter to its spiritual truth. No doubt the
further we travel from literalness, the more we invite hermetic symbolism.[110]
A Midsummer Night's Dream does not preclude such divagations, and the author
may dabble in them here and there, but his theological topicality and engagement with Chaucer tend to limit their scope. *The Knight's Tale*, despite a few
satirical and humorous flourishes, possesses a heavy earnestness deriving from
its philosophical investments. Chaucer's Theseus explains cause and effect as

109. Working through Keith Thomas's position that the line of argument descending from
Scot is "grossly unfair" (see Thomas, *Religion and the Decline*, 610) because English belief in fairies
preceded Roman Catholicism, and because the medieval church was anti-fairy, Phebe Jensen concludes: "instead of denying the connection between Catholicism and fairies, Shakespeare embraces
it when he gives Oberon, Titania, and their crew a positive sacramental role." Phebe Jensen, *Religion
and Revelry in Shakespeare's Festive World*, 109. For the Sarum Missal and the "blessing of the bridal
bed," see David N. Beauregard, *Catholic Theology in Shakespeare's Plays*, 82–83.

110. For the combined influence, alongside Saint Paul and Apuleius, of Pico, Cornelius
Agrippa, and Bruno, see Frank Kermode, "The Mature Comedies," in *Early Shakespeare*, ed. John
Russell Brown and Bernard Harris, 211–27.

if in a metaphysical fable. The Knight-narrator demonstrates no awareness that his eavesdropping on the gods and his attention to planetary influences merely push the chain of causality back one step, beyond mortal sight, but no closer to explaining the ultimate riddle. For this reason, one might say that the lovers' saga in *The Knight's Tale* is a kind of unwitting play within a play. Emily and her two knights are puppet-mortals directed by puppet-gods. Shakespeare's play, climaxing in the essential foolery of its play within the play, examines the riddle of fate through the playwright's historically self-conscious artistry, prophylactically allusive and elusive, informed not only by Chaucer and Chaucer's Elizabethan reception, but by religious polemic. By the time Shakespeare was thirty, two of his most important contemporaries, Kyd and Marlowe, were dead, charges of "atheistical and heretical opinions"[111] ringing in the London air. The sleeping dogs slept lightly, and one never knew from what corner they might spring. William Cecil, Lord Burghley was "used to playing both sides"[112] of the dangerous controversy over predestination. Shakespeare had every reason to avoid literal explanation: "If we shadows have offended." What does Puck literally stand for? Or Titania? Just how divine is Oberon, and what exactly is his relation to angels and to nuns? It is folly to ask. We are wiser to make comparisons: to negotiate likeness and unlikeness. Where the Knight's philosophical romance offers answers— answers that immediately get their comeuppance at the hands of the unruly Miller—*A Midsummer Night's Dream* poses highly topical questions. Shake-speare's method is not to tell his audience what to think about free will and predestination. The play's theological power serves his Christian humanist purpose, which is healing laughter at human folly, as the great tangle of human ignorance, Christian truth, and religious debate comes under comical consideration. One is reminded of Thomas More's "fantastic trilingual pun," where the name Raphael Hythloday translates into English from Hebrew, Greek, and Latin to mean "God heals . . . through the nonsense . . . of God."[113] But of course that is a very strange thought.

In its eclectic take on the predestination crisis, Shakespeare's Christian humanism is *paratheological* and not *atheological*. It is theology's fraternal twin, similar at the molecular level, but with its own aims. As a work of literature, *A Midsummer Night's Dream* encourages a modicum of tolerance in theological

111. Stanley Wells, *Shakespeare & Co.*, 97.
112. Cummings, *Literary Culture*, 298.
113. Thomas More, *Utopia*, ed. and trans. Robert M. Adams, 6n9.

matters. As a social lubricant that people were willing to pay for, it should not be construed as being indifferent to religious tensions that troubled virtually every thinking Elizabethan. I agree with the verdict that Shakespeare disliked radical Puritanism, and certainly he defied Jesuit opinion regarding love poetry. (Erotic devil that he is, Puck comes down on the sacred side of things.) But where great religious traditions are concerned, a genuine tolerance does not result from abandoning one's convictions. It results from exposure to other intelligent points of view. Its civilizing effect is grounded on a mature willingness to recognize one's own ignorance, to recognize, as well, that the tension between wisdom and folly is maddening, humbling, and inescapable for us all. This kind of work occurs primarily in the cultural sphere, in the dialectical opening between the sacred and the secular that I have called "the radical middle."[114] Such work is by its nature always vulnerable to discipline and punishment, from pedants, priests, and politicians, from all agents and managers of grievance.

The Merchant of Venice, the subject of the next chapter, is an especially controversial product of the radical middle. It is a deeply challenging play that recent history has made painful. It has driven many conscientious critics to lay literature aside in an effort to set things to rights; and yet we will find that the root of the problem goes back to Shakespeare's theological and biblical humanism. What many have found unconscionable stems from potentialities that were native to his paratheological medium, as the folly that saves the Athenian lovers becomes, among the worldly Venetians, more sinful in its effects. My response, in keeping with the larger aims of the present book, will be to recover Shakespeare's Christian intention. As we shall see, the playwright did not lose sight of the predestination crisis in the works that followed *A Midsummer Night's Dream*. Its dramatic import would occupy his mind for years.

---

114. Lee Oser, *The Return of Christian Humanism: Chesterton, Eliot, Tolkien and the Romance of History*, 5. See also Jens Zimmermann, introduction to *Re-envisioning Christian Humanism: Education and the Restoration of Humanity*, ed. Jens Zimmermann, 1–15.

CHAPTER 2

Moral Figures in
The Merchant of Venice

Though justice be thy plea, consider this,
That in the course of justice none of us
Should see salvation.

(MV 4.1.196–98)

The learned band of scholars attuned to Shakespeare's rhetoric—Baldwin, Joseph, Rhodes, Skinner, Sloane, Trousdale, Vickers, and others cited in these pages—affords a means to consider Shakespeare's moral intention, a means unavailable to critics not so attuned.[1] I have my disagreements with Brian Vickers, but the student of Renaissance literature will be hard pressed to find a more important lesson than the following: "Where we expect literary criticism to constitute a *poetics*, a reasoned account of how a work of literature exists as an autonomous artefact, independent of its effect on readers, the Renaissance understood literature as being essentially a form of *rhetoric*, with an explicit or implicit design on its readers, intended to arouse their feelings and direct them to some moral end."[2] If Elizabethan literature is moral by design, one would assume that Shakespeare's rhetoric expresses his moral intention. I have stated my methodology: I argue for locating Shakespeare's beliefs in the worldview embedded in his works. In this respect, Shakespeare's moral intention—deducible from the pattern of his rhetoric—is heavily marked by Christianity's power to undo judgment in the classical sense. It follows that Shakespearean rhetoric in its moral design is less a means of persuasion than a Christian game of moral interrogation. It may encourage us to applaud a speech; on a more unified level, though, it invites us to scrutinize that speech. It does not encourage us to affirm what is without parallel in our

---

1. For a valuable defense of literary intentionality, see Christopher Ricks's side of a fine discussion, Quentin Skinner and Christopher Ricks, "Up for Interpretation *or* What Is This Thing that Hearsay Is Not?" *Literary Imagination* 14 (2012): 125–42.

2. Brian Vickers, introduction to *English Renaissance Literary Criticism*, ed. Brian Vickers, 1, his italics.

own private experience; rather, through its moral questioning, it spurs a Christian audience toward greater self-knowledge. To say this is not to deny the reality of private experience, but only to recognize—in the sense of Wittgenstein—its expressive limits.

With this rhetorical form of authorial intention in mind, I turn to *The Merchant of Venice* and to the landmark scholarship of Barbara Lewalski. In her 1962 essay "Biblical Allusion and Allegory in *The Merchant of Venice*," Lewalski tempers her allegorical reading of the play by recognizing moral subtleties in the clash of Jew and Christian. She finds "a thematic counterpoint to the opposition of Old Law and New, suggesting the disposition of Christians themselves to live rather according to the Old Law than the New." The "play does not," she thoughtfully observes, "present arbitrary, black-and-white estimates of human groups, but takes into account the shadings and complexities of the real world."[3] And yet, despite her erudition, despite her sensitivity to "shadings and complexities," and despite "Biblical Allusion and Allegory in *The Merchant of Venice*" ranking among the most cited essays devoted exclusively to the play,[4] few scholars today would endorse Lewalski's allegorical approach.

Nonetheless, if there is currently little appetite for Christian allegories of Shakespeare, John Cox's work affords means for at least appreciating Lewalski's understanding of the play. The key lies in Cox's exposition of Shakespeare's Christian skepticism, whereby Shakespeare's "continuing reflection on the narrative of salvation history . . . is rendered *allusively*, not *allegorically*, and . . . does not fully reveal meaning in either comedy or tragedy, because the plays consistently imagine human beings in the fallen world, well short of apocalypse . . . and therefore encumbered by imperfection, both in themselves and in what they know."[5] This is excellent criticism. But Cox's distinction between allusion and allegory, important as it is, creates a difficulty. The difficulty lies in gauging the degree to which salvation history is activated by a particular allusion, be it biblical or theological, literary or dramatic—as in the haunting of the Shakespearean stage by the mysteries and moralities. Cox uses the phrase "does not fully reveal meaning" to indicate the limited scope of allusion. Right as he is, we must at the same time remain aware that the audience's response is critical in drawing the line between allusion and allegory.

---

3. Barbara K. Lewalski, "Biblical Allusion and Allegory in *The Merchant of Venice*," *Shakespeare Quarterly* 13 (1962): 334.

4. My source is Google Scholar. Accessed April 10, 2020.

5. John Cox, *Seeming Knowledge: Shakespeare and Skeptical Faith*, xii–xiii, my emphasis.

If salvation history is real to you, then allusions will awake sympathetic vibrations, evoking a fuller register of meanings. In this respect among others, the Elizabethans were different from us.

Cox describes imperfect characters burdened with a flawed grasp of reality. Shakespeare has a way of drawing us, as it were, into their imperfect circle. In the previous chapter, we followed Cox in remarking that Shakespeare's Christian skepticism is "closely akin"[6] to that of Erasmus. Both writers remain skeptical of human motives and the human capacity for self-knowledge, though neither calls into question the core teachings of Christianity. Here we may consider how rhetoric in *The Merchant of Venice* serves Shakespeare's Christian skepticism by probing the common depths of ignorance where moral judgment is concerned: the gaps in what the characters know, in what we know about them, and, finally, in what we know about ourselves. Shakespeare, I suggest, complicates this problem of moral knowledge by adapting Erasmus's Pauline conceit in *The Praise of Folly*, "it seems to me that the Christian religion taken all together has a certain affinity with some sort of folly and has little or nothing to do with wisdom."[7] Being a form of debate, the contest between worldly wisdom and Christian folly encourages close rhetorical analysis. So it is fitting to approach *The Merchant of Venice* both through analysis of rhetorical figure, as well as through analysis of forensic oratory or what Thomas Wilson, in his *Arte of Rhetorique,* referred to as "judicial" rhetoric.[8] On both levels, figural and judicial, the debate between wisdom and folly provokes our judgment—and our lapses of judgment.

When are we wise and when are we foolish? How can we judge? Thomas Sloane locates Erasmian humanism in a rhetorical tradition, going back to Cicero's *De Oratore*, that shuns the more Platonic insistence on "definition and division" in favor of a practice of "pro-con reasoning."[9] To quote Sloane: "A lesson I find deep in the core of Erasmian humanism is the *via diversa*, the doctrine that . . . truth is so complex—and maybe in its variety so ungraspable— that one has to approach it through different, untried, even multiple avenues."[10] One thinks inevitably of the blinded Gloucester: "And that's true too" (LR 5.2.11). The rhetorical term *elenchus* (Gk. "cross-examining; testing; argument of refutation") also comes to mind, that is, the pursuit of "argument

---

6. Cox, *Seeming Knowledge*, xii.
7. Erasmus, *The Praise of Folly*, ed. and trans. Clarence H. Miller, 132.
8. See Introduction.
9. Thomas O. Sloane, *On the Contrary: The Protocol of Traditional Rhetoric*, 26, 31, 33.
10. Sloane, *On the Contrary*, 8.

for the sake of argument" tending toward "'a state of *Aporia*.'"[11] Because Shakespeare's skepticism is not anti-foundational, *The Merchant of Venice* is not a debunking of Christian moral truth, per se, but an insistence upon its humbling complexity. The emphasis falls on the pursuit of truth through "multiple avenues." As I have suggested, wisdom and folly supply the main terms of Shakespeare's game of pro and con: they and their cognates weave in and out of *The Merchant of Venice*, inviting our acquiescence, our disagreement, our judgment. Gratiano's speech to Antonio, beginning "Let me play the fool" (1.1.79–104), first awakens our ears to the debate of wisdom and folly; Shylock's warning to his daughter about gazing "on Christian fools with varnished faces" (2.5.34) sticks in our minds; the epithet "wise" serves to praise Jessica lavishly: "She is wise . . . wise, fair, and true" (2.6.54, 57); Portia derides "these deliberate fools" who "have the wisdom by their wit to lose" (2.9.80–81); Shylock enthuses, "O wise young judge, how I do honor thee!" (4.1.222); Bassanio and Antonio are acquitted by the "wisdom" of Balthasar (4.1.408). As in *A Midsummer Night's Dream*, though with increasing eschatological pressure, Shakespeare wants us to think these terms through and to decide for ourselves where and when folly is "salutary" and wisdom "deluded."[12]

By way of John Russell Brown's Arden edition of *The Merchant of Venice*, Lewalski focuses on the "'Moral' appended to the casket story in the medieval *Gesta Romanorum* that is almost certainly Shakespeare's source for this incident."[13] Lewalski refers to "History 32" of the *Gesta Romanarum*, translated and "Now Newly Perused and Corrected by R. Robinson" (1595).[14] Its Moral explicates the allegorical adventures of the geste's heroine, including her final test by an emperor, who "sheweth this Mayden three vessells, that is to say, God putteth before man life & death, good & evill, & which of these he chooseth he shall obtaine."[15] As one can see, the effect of the original Moral is to deliver wisdom with the force of revelation: the reader is handed the truth, not lured into its pursuit. What I want to take from Lewalski, by way of Cox, is that Shakespeare connects Portia's father's will "allusively" to the presence and will of God, which are never "fully" revealed to us, at least not to the degree that they are revealed to us in the allegorical Moral. At the same

---

11. Richard A. Lanham, *A Handlist of Rhetorical Terms*, 62. Lanham quotes G. B. Kerferd, *The Sophistic Movement* (1981).

12. Neil Rhodes, *Shakespeare and the Origins of English*, 56–57 (cited in Chapter 1).

13. Lewalski, "Biblical Allusion," 336.

14. William Shakespeare, *The Merchant of Venice*, ed. John Russell Brown, 172.

15. Quoted in Lewalski, "Biblical Allusion," 336.

time, the effect of the allusion is complicated, as we have suggested, by the audience's knowledge of the literary source, the transparently allegorical geste. The *Gesta Romanarum* was popular among the Elizabethans, who enjoyed its piety and may have found it a consoling reminder of simpler times. Our relative ignorance of this medieval favorite, by contrast, weakens not only Shakespeare's allusion to it but the entire effect. Insofar as the allegory lived in the Elizabethan mind, it could be recalled by Shakespeare's allusion, which would then have suggested that Portia was acting under God's providence, that she was (on an eschatological level) facing absolute scrutiny as regards her filial obedience, even though the state of her soul was not transparent to the audience, as the heroine's soul was for readers of the pious, medieval geste.

Writing for the popular stage, with a Christian audience in mind, Shakespeare found it dramatically valuable that intelligence is not a moral virtue. Intelligence is not the same as wisdom. Theologically, it is a dangerous endowment. Portia's wit is established at once, when she remarks to Nerissa: "It is a good divine that follows his own instructions. I can easier teach twenty what were good to be done than to be one of the twenty to follow my own teaching" (1.2.14–17). A dilemma (Gk. "double proposition") emerges, since to know the law means to know our fallen condition, which means to recognize our sinfulness, which, as the Reformers argued, the law cannot ameliorate. This theological dilemma, with its biblical roots in Romans 3:20, speaks to what Luther called "the bondage of the will." For Luther, "the words of the law are spoken, not that they might assert the power of the will, but that they might illuminate the blindness of reason. . . . The whole nature and design of the law is to give knowledge, and that of nothing else save of sin, and not to discover or communicate any power whatever."[16] Chapter 4's discussion of *Hamlet* will focus on Erasmus and Luther's debate over free will, the great theological crux of the Reformation. At present, a close concern will inform our analysis of *The Merchant of Venice*, namely, the immeasurable distance between God and fallen humanity out of which Luther's theology erupts. Lewalski is surely right to notice that when Shylock claims "the Law," he becomes "subject to what Paul terms the 'curse' of the Law, since he is unable to fulfill its conditions." She cites Galatians 3:10: "For as many as are of works of the Lawe, are under the curse: for it is written, Cursed is every man that

---

16. Martin Luther, *The Bondage of the Will*, in *Erasmus & Luther: Discourse on Free Will*, ed. and trans. Ernst F. Winter, 108.

continueth not in all things, which are written in the booke of the Lawe, to do them."[17] She acknowledges, as I have noted, the general problem of Christian fallibility in "the disposition of Christians themselves to live rather according to the Old Law than the New." But Lewalski does not pursue how the Pauline "curse" might also apply to the play's Christians. She does not examine the reality of Christian fallenness in terms of individual psychology or its theological ramifications. In Act 1, Scene 2, for example, Portia's dilemma implies her own need, despite her intellect, for the extralegal spiritual aid that Christians call grace.

As certain ominous rumblings may already have suggested, in an analysis of this kind, a host of rhetorical figures must sooner or later come trooping in, kitted out with their Greek and Latin names, all about as cheery as row seven of the periodic table. Let us precede their triumphal march with Erasmus's droll warning, "Every definition is a misfortune."[18] That being said, I would observe that Portia expresses her theological dilemma about the law through the figure *inter se pugnantia*, which "points out discrepancy between theory and practice."[19] Miriam Joseph, in her valuable study *Shakespeare's Use of the Arts of Language*, cites Portia and then turns to Henry Peacham's *Garden of Eloquence* (1577, rev. 1593) for corroboration: "Inter se pugnantia, is a form of speech by which the orator reproveth his adversary, or some other person of manifest inconstancy, open hypocrisy, or insolent arrogance. . . . Thou therefore which teachest another, teachest not thy self; thou that preaches a man should not steal, yet thou stealest [Rom. 2]."[20] Peacham refers us to the second chapter of Romans, where Paul distinguishes between Gentile and Jew in order to take hypocrites to task, presenting salvation as a spiritual dispensation that moves inwardly, in defiance of legalistic and ceremonial displays. Portia's use of inter se pugnantia differs from Peacham's model insofar as Portia plays both parts: "orator" and "adversary." Her handling of the figure is the more complex, eliciting multiple points of view: it invites us to distinguish between Portia's theoretical wisdom and her practical folly, to appreciate her wisdom in reproving her folly, to share her respect for moral principle, and to wonder how deep that respect goes.

---

17. Lewalski, "Biblical Allusion," 340.

18. Erasmus, quoted in Lanham, *Handlist*, 78.

19. Miriam Joseph, CSC, *Shakespeare's Use of the Arts of Language*, 138.

20. Henry Peacham, quoted in Joseph, *Shakespeare's Use*, 324–25. I have modernized the spelling.

It may strike us that inter se pugnantia is suited not only to Christians reproving Christian hypocrisy,[21] but also to supplying the kind of irony that, in *The Merchant of Venice*, has served the interpretive purposes of hostile critics, particularly in the years since the Holocaust. In his well-known monograph, *The Harmonies of the Merchant of Venice*, Lawrence Danson rightly stands his ground against those whose ironical readings emphasize Christian hypocrisy in the play to the extent that its Christianity (including the Christianity of Portia) is dismantled and disgraced.[22] Unlike Danson, though, I place Shakespeare's rhetorical ironies at the heart of his writing. I argue that they serve the playwright's moral purpose, inviting us to judge the characters and ourselves in the dual light of their self-knowledge and our own.

On the surface of things, Portia conducts herself reasonably well. She might strike a naïve admirer, or even a G. K. Chesterton, as an embodiment of virtue.[23] But by the highest Christian standards, or in light of the severe Augustinian scrutiny of the Reformers, she betrays failings that, when we start to notice them, give an uncanny depth to her character. To take a key instance: compared to those bad guessers, Morocco and Aragon, Portia tends to comes off well. They serve as her comic foils, unless, that is, one prefers charges of racism against her on account of her ungenerous response to Morocco, in particular. Such charges would not be groundless. But they will distract us from Shakespeare's intention unless we enter into his worldview. To appreciate the debate of wisdom and folly, to appreciate the ground rules of the game that Shakespeare and his audience are playing, it will be helpful to place Portia's "*ex post facto* racism" in an Elizabethan perspective.[24]

Shakespeare has little to offer in terms of modern racial ideology.[25] He is not averse to caricature, but his understanding resists the dehumanizing

---

21. Shakespeare's use of inter se pugnantia may comment on the Protestant-Catholic conflict that Nicole Coonradt detects in the play. Coonradt asks a compelling question: "Could Shakespeare have had in mind the conversion not of Jews, but those within Christianity? After all, forced Christian conversions from Catholicism and Protestantism had been anything but rare and were the agonizing reality for most Elizabethans." Nicole M. Coonradt, "Shakespeare's Grand Deception: *The Merchant of Venice*—Anti-Semitism as 'Uncanny Causality' and the Catholic-Protestant Problem," *Religion and the Arts* 11 (2007): 92.

22. Lawrence Danson, *The Harmonies of the Merchant of Venice*, 1–18.

23. Chesterton calls Portia "the most splendid and magnanimous woman in literature." G. K. Chesterton, "The Heroines of Shakespeare," quoted in John Gross, *Shylock: A Legend and Its Legacy*, 270.

24. On Portia's "*ex post facto* racism," see Gorman Beauchamp, "Shylock's Conversion," *Humanitas* 24 (2011): 78–79.

25. For a good introduction to contemporary attitudes about race, see William Harrison, *The Description of England: The Classic Contemporary Account of Tudor Social Life*, 444–50.

project of ideological racism. Why? Because, rhetorically, he always assumes
the human species definition, "Man is a rational animal." This assumption is
woven into the fabric of his work. Basic to communication and congenial to
wit, it commands the audience's assent.[26] The standard definition of man as
a rational animal informs, for instance, the terms with which Portia mocks
another one of her suitors, the bibulous German, "When he is best he is a
little worse than a man, and when he is worst he is little better than a beast"
(1.2.86–87). One's race did not alter the definition of man. Morocco says to
Portia, "Mislike me not for my complexion, / The shadowed livery of the
burnished sun" (2.1.1–2). His "complexion" is a "livery." To judge from the
stage directions, *a tawny Moor all in white* (2.1.s.d.), the actor may have worn a
lighter face-paint than the actor who played Aaron the Moor, "blacked up in
some form of body make-up, his head possibly covered with a tight-curled
black wig."[27] In both cases, the non-essential nature of race found its elaborate theatrical expression. Its exoticism, artistic resonance, and other associations, positive and negative, were consequential matters, but they did not
disrupt the unity of humankind. Therefore, to return to the pivotal matter
of discerning wisdom and folly, the implication follows that, when Portia is
first informed by a servant that Morocco is coming, she should know better
than to judge him by appearances. That is, she ought to pay attention to what
her "*holy*" and "*ever virtuous*" (1.2.27) father intends (I underscore the adjec-
tives to catch the allusive and/or allegorical suggestion), and take her father's
"meaning" (1.2.30) to heart. Yet she fails to do so when she replies, "If he
have the condition of a saint and the complexion of a devil, I had rather he
should shrive me than wive me" (1.2.127–29). The antithesis "condition of
a saint / complexion of a devil" makes it clear that skin color is the issue
here: a black man could certainly be "a saint."[28] So while Portia acknowledges
that "complexion" is no impediment to holiness, yet she wants to marry a
man whose appearance pleases her in a distinctly worldly sense. Then again
(let us play pro and con), if we are persuaded that Portia is no saint,[29] we
may want to be wary of leaping to the opposite extreme of judgment. It is

26. Compare Gadshill the thief: "*homo* is a common name to all men" (1H4 2.1.96). Bevington's
gloss is helpful: "the Latin name for man applies to all types."

27. Ian Wilson, *Shakespeare: The Evidence: Unlocking the Mysteries of the Man and His Work*, 88.

28. See also Revelation 7:9, as well as popular medieval and Renaissance artwork of the Ado-
ration of the Magi, the "three wise men" visiting the infant Jesus (Matthew 2:1–12).

29. Hugh Short reviews the anti-Portia literature in his impressively recalcitrant "Shylock Is
Content: A Study in Salvation," in *Shakespeare Criticism: Merchant of Venice: New Critical Essays*, ed.
John W. Mahon and Ellen Macleod Mahon, 199–212.

mere groundless cynicism to hold that she cheats to get her way when Bassanio arrives in Belmont, destined by the logic of romance to choose the right casket. Most importantly, the fact that the state of her soul can never be revealed to us in this life is a moral and not a neutral fact: we are not the final Judge.

As if to oppose our authority on moral matters, a powerful character takes the stage to deliver the multifaceted lesson that our judgment is skewed. It is Shylock, of course, who most powerfully challenges our perception of wisdom and folly. His effect on the Elizabethans was cruder than ours in some respects and subtler in others: cruder as comedy, but subtler in its moral insinuations. His initial dialogue, with Bassanio, is marked by echoing and repetition, which intensify into oppositions that test our moral response. Rhetorically, Shakespeare creates ironic dissonance through a battalion of figures, including the fallacy of the false assumption, or *secundum quid*, which, as Joseph explains, "assumes that what is true in some respect is true absolutely, or contrariwise."[30] When Shylock comments, "Antonio is a good man," and Bassanio replies, "Have you heard any imposition to the contrary?" (1.3.12–14), Shylock explains that he means "good" in a qualified sense (i.e., financially solvent) that does not extend to Bassanio's absolute sense of the term. When Shylock tosses back "assured" at 1.3.28, Shakespeare's ironic wit is similarly in force: Bassanio has just used the word to mean that "Shylock may trust Antonio, whereas Shylock means that he will obtain legal assurances."[31]

I want to distinguish at this point an Erasmus-inflected approach to the play where self-knowledge of "the enemy within" is the grounds of forgiveness,[32] from an ahistorical approach, whereby Shylock is morally separable from the Christians, in effect relieving Shakespeare of his sense of Christian hypocrisy, and silencing his Christian ethics. Given the common currency of ironical tropes like secundum quid, and especially their role in Act 1, Scene 3 in implicating Christians in sinful behavior, I am led to question John Drakakis's understanding of the Jew as devilish antagonist: "The unfixing of meaning evident in this initial exchange is consistent with Antonio's own claim, later in the scene, that the Jew is a 'devil' who challenges the very probity and

---

30. Joseph, *Shakespeare's Use*, 195.

31. Bevington's note.

32. "If you wish to be forgiven, you, who have loved what you should have hated and who have hated what you should have loved, must attack the enemy within." Erasmus, *The Essential Erasmus*, ed. and trans. John P. Dolan, 70. The passage is from the *Enchiridion Militis Christiani* (*The Handbook of the Militant Christian*) (1503). In the same work, Erasmus writes: "The crown of . . . God-given wisdom is to know yourself" (42).

stability of language itself [i.e., "The devil can cite Scripture for his purpose" (1.3.96)]. The Jew's verbal repetitions . . . and his telling gloss on the adjective 'good' . . . require to be read symptomatically as evidence of the propensity to a devilish duplicity that owes its scriptural origin to St Matthew's gospel."[33] While Drakakis is perceptive in noting Shylock's verbal repetitions, he overrules Shakespeare's moral intention when he interprets Shylock's language as posing an exceptional threat (the "unfixing of meaning") to the rhetorical action. Nothing could be further from the truth. Rhetorically and theologically, no one escapes. There was nowhere to escape to. The Venetians are playing the same language-game as Shylock. They and he are both duplicitous.

When Antonio enters the scene at 1.3.37, the repetition of "kindness" drives the rhetorical action:

> SHYLOCK   This is *kind* I offer.
> BASSANIO   This were *kindness*.
> SHYLOCK   This *kindness* I will show.
>   Go with me to a notary, seal me there
>   Your single bond; and, in a merry sport,
>   If you repay me not on such a day,
>   In such a place, such sum or sums as are
>   Expressed in the condition, let the forfeit
>   Be nominated for an equal pound
>   Of your fair flesh, to be cut off and taken
>   In what part of your body pleaseth me.
> ANTONIO   Content, in faith. I'll seal to such a bond
>   And say there is much *kindness* in the Jew.
>   (1.3.140–52, my emphasis)

Bevington helpfully glosses "kind" as "kindly," but, rhetorically speaking, this is just the kindly fin of the shark. Shylock's awkward use of "kind" (in place of "kindly"), while a grammatical solecism and an example of *anthimeria*, "the substitution of one part of speech for another,"[34] allows Shakespeare to hammer into his dialogue an argument from conjugates ("kind," "kindness"), a rhetorical move by which the author insinuates his doubts about human kindness.[35] As Jay Halio observes, the "kindness" that Shylock "will show"

---

33. John Drakakis, introduction to *The Merchant of Venice*, by William Shakespeare, ed. John Drakakis, 45.

34. Joseph, *Shakespeare's Use*, 62.

35. While I agree with Bevington's gloss on "were" (141) as "would be, if seriously offered," I think Bassanio's meaning is connected to his effort to clarify Shylock's solecism.

signifies the ways of human*kind*, in particular, still following Halio, "the nature of revenge."[36] Through the punning figure *antanaclasis*, which "in repeating a word shifts from one of its meanings to another,"[37] Shylock inverts the normal meaning of "kindness." When Shylock is done proposing his "merry sport," Antonio returns the volley: "there is much kindness in the Jew." Further, when Shylock goes on to explain, referring to Antonio, "To buy his favor I *extend* this friendship" (1.3.167, my emphasis), Shakespeare evokes the *extension* and *intention* of terms. Since Antonio has already referred to "friendship" and "friend" in denouncing Shylock for usury (1.3.131–32), Shylock's subsequent appeal to friendship enforces the logic of contraries. The rhetorical extension of "friendship" is "the set of people" actually in a state of friendship with Shylock. The Christians of Venice may exhibit various shades of humor, courtesy, and etiquette toward him, but Shylock has only enemies among them. The rhetorical intention of "friendship" is definitional: it is "the sum of qualities which make" for friendship, such as "loyalty, congeniality, mutual affection, unselfish devotedness, trustworthiness, fidelity."[38] Because these qualities are void, the only possible "bond" between Shylock and the Christians must be contractual, legal, financial: Shylock offers to "buy" Antonio's "favor." Shylock's barbed extension of "friendship" implicates Antonio and Bassanio in the general negation of virtue, a sting that lingers despite Antonio's effort to shake it off by saying, for Bassanio's benefit, just as Shylock exits: "Hie thee, gentle Jew. / The Hebrew will turn Christian; he grows kind" (1.3.176–77). This last instance of punning on "kind" has a nervous feel because it sustains the negative, ironic mood, where extension and intension of terms (much like the opening of the caskets) reveal their contraries. The pun "gentle"/"Gentile" is likewise morally double-edged: they may hardly realize it, but the Christians have not been kind; the Gentiles have not been gentle. The critical point is not that we should exonerate Shakespeare of the charge of Christian anti-Semitism, an offense that history must judge. The point is that Antonio and Bassanio share responsibility with Shylock for the rhetorical game they have been playing: they could not have played it so well without him.

Curiously, though, we don't yet know where the game is headed. Antonio's upcoming run of bad luck is highly improbable, and Jessica has not yet eloped, altering the bond's significance from a self-caricaturing jest to a blood debt.

---

36. Jay Halio, introduction to *The Merchant of Venice*, by William Shakespeare, ed. Jay Halio, 46.
37. Joseph, *Shakespeare's Use*, 165.
38. Miriam Joseph, CSC, *The Trivium: The Liberal Arts of Logic, Grammar, and Rhetoric*, 77–78.

For the moment, "the bond as text . . . floats free."[39] Even so, for the morally alert in Shakespeare's original audience, their identification with the Gentiles heralds doubts and scruples about Christian behavior.

Venice's lowest common denominator is Lancelot the clown, most likely played by the great and conspicuous Will Kemp. His part is significant—*dense* in the sense of *Dichtung*—but too limited to achieve the depths of Bottom or Falstaff. He is integral to my argument because, through the rhetoric of his foolspeak, he draws our attention to the gap between Christian theory and Christian practice, between ideals and reality. His dilemma of choosing between "the fiend" and his "conscience" is at once a cruder, more sophisticated, and funnier version of Portia's dilemma (which it serves to comment on) of knowing the law only in order to break it: "in my conscience, my conscience is but a kind of hard conscience to offer to counsel me to stay with the Jew. The fiend gives more friendly counsel" (2.2.25–28). Portia does not speak of her conscience. No one does but the clown, and he obsesses over it. In his word-juggling, Lancelot implies a distinction between "the faculty" and "the content" of conscience, that is, between conscience and what he calls "counsel," between conscience as "lawgiver" and conscience as "the law he gives."[40] We get the sense that Lancelot is rebelling against his "inner nagger."[41] If we like, we can excuse his disloyalty to his master because his master is a bad man: "Certainly the Jew is the very devil incarnation" (24–25). But it is not clear that the conscience-defying clown is justified in the eyes of heaven.

Lancelot, it should be acknowledged, has something of the trickster and moral Vice about him.[42] His prankish reunion with his father, Old Gobbo, plays mischievously on Isaac's blessing of the trickster, Jacob, in Genesis 27.[43] His warning to Jessica, "the sins of the father are to be laid upon the children" (3.5.1–2, see Exodus 20:5), and his logical deduction, "for truly I think you are damned" (3.5.5), satirize, to follow Steven Marx, "the Calvinist theology of predestination."[44] In this latter instance, we might say that Shakespeare,

39. Craig Bernthal, *The Trial of Man: Christianity and Judgment in the World of Shakespeare*, 112. Bernthal makes a related point: "The bond is proposed as a jest by Shylock, burlesquing Christian folklore that would have Jews, in an unholy inversion of the Eucharist, eating Christian flesh and drinking Christian blood" (98).

40. C. S. Lewis, *Studies in Words*, 209.

41. Lewis, *Studies*, 195.

42. I am indebted to David Wiles but disagree with his categorically identifying Lancelot as a "moral Vice." David Wiles, *Shakespeare's Clown: Actor and Text in the Elizabethan Playhouse*, 8.

43. See René E. Fortin, "Launcelot and the Uses of Allegory in *The Merchant of Venice*," *Studies in English Literature, 1500–1900* 14 (Spring 1974): 266–68.

44. Steven Marx, *Shakespeare and the Bible*, 115.

through his fool's license, seizes on the element of jurisdictional overreach in the Calvinist attachment to logic, which "dictated that it is a necessary truth about a person that either he is saved *or he* is condemned."[45] Summing up Jessica's chances of salvation, Lancelot poses yet another dilemma, "I fear you are damned both by father and mother. Thus when I shun Scylla, your father, I fall into Charybdis, your mother" (3.5.13–15). Jessica seizes the dilemma by the horns, "I shall be saved by my husband. He hath made me a Christian" (3.5.17–18). But Lancelot, not to be outdone, responds with the figure *metalepsis*, dubbed by Puttenham the "*far-fet*" or far-fetcher:[46] "Truly, the more blame he! . . . This making of Christians will raise the price of hogs. If we all grow to be pork eaters, we shall not shortly have a rasher on the coals for money" (3.5.19–24). Lancelot's "we" is more comical than vicious, more salubrious than wicked: it serves to reveal all human beings as mundanely self-interested, regardless of creed, and prepared now and in the future to subordinate otherworldly to worldly concerns. Through metalepsis, Lancelot demonstrates something less than the power of prophecy but something nonetheless prophetic—a practical gift for seeing human reality as in itself it really is.[47] By word and deed, he suggests it's not easy in this fallen world to be converted at heart: the pun-heavy point about Lancelot's impregnating a "Moor" (3.5.37) speaks volumes.

In his last extended turn (his dialogue in Belmont is brief, though it is significant that he gets there), not only does Lancelot speak his mind about the way Christians actually behave, but his wordplay cues Lorenzo's exemplary recognition of a moral power lurking behind the clownish humor. At first, Lorenzo responds to Lancelot's gratuitous punning, "How every *fool* can play upon the word!" (3.5.41, my emphasis). But Lancelot stays on the attack. His verbal fencing serves his crafty purpose of avoiding work, but when at last he acquiesces and does his job, he inspires a moral reflection from Lorenzo, which—a detail to be returned to—foreshadows Portia's strategy in the next scene: "and I do know / A many *fools*, that stand in better place, / Garnished like him, that for a tricksy word / Defy the matter" (3.5.64–67, my emphasis). It would be wrong, then, to interpret Lancelot's role as purely subversive. A descendent of the old Adam with a touch of Plautus's "cunning servant," he

45. Brian Cummings, *The Literary Culture of the Reformation: Grammar and Grace*, 257, his italics.

46. George Puttenham, *The Arte of English Poesie* (1589), 193, his italics. Students enjoy the following example: if you are walking through a city park and a shady-looking fellow asks you if you want to buy a "plane ticket," that is an example of *metalepsis*.

47. With a salute to Matthew Arnold.

is a morally ambiguous figure who plays his part in nudging the audience along the *via diversa* of truth.

It is a pity that we have no drawing or description of Shylock on the Elizabethan stage. My guess is that it is was competition with the deceased Marlowe, a need to get past Marlowe's insane, two-dimensional, but mesmerizing Barabas, that provoked the unexpected depths of character in a comic villain whose assumedly "red beard and wig and bottle nose" were the readily identifiable stage properties of his type.[48] Shylock in his agony delivers more than a satirical attack on Christian hypocrisy: his intelligence rebuffs the stock responses befitting a stock figure. As I have suggested, Shakespeare aimed to throw the moral burden of self-knowledge back at his audience, who were as prone to non-Christian behavior as the Venetians on the stage. The Lopez affair notwithstanding,[49] David Kastan is right about the historical circumstances:

> There were no real Jews, or at least very few real Jews, and that small number was practicing in secret. Jewishness, therefore, can be no more than a metaphor in the play, a condensation of a set of contrasts with Christian norms: the old law versus the new; the letter versus the spirit; justice versus mercy; getting versus giving—and if these are, as they are, implicitly negative contrasts, they nonetheless function within a purely symbolic economy rather than a social one, and demand to be understood as such.[50]

By the 1590s, this "purely symbolic economy" had already done considerable satirical service, as when Erasmus's Folly, commenting on the lack of charity among monks, has Christ return to wonder, "*Whence cometh . . . this new race of Iewes?*"[51] More's *Utopia* plies a similar vein.[52] Satirical Protestants compared Catholics to Jews on account of their stubborn devotion to the old faith.[53] Background material in sources and analogues for the play reveals much the same thing. In the *Gesta Romanorum*,[54] in Anthony Munday's novel *Zelauto* (1580), in Robert Wilson's morality play *The Three Ladies of London* (1584,

48. Halio, introduction, 10.

49. "The most notorious case of Jewish criminality in Elizabethan England is of course that of doctor Roderigo Lopez . . . who was tried and executed in 1594 for an alleged plot to poison Queen Elizabeth." James Shapiro, *Shakespeare and the Jews*, 73.

50. David Kastan, *A Will to Believe: Shakespeare and Religion*, 89–90. For an opposing view, see Shapiro, *Shakespeare and the Jews*. For Shylock and the anti-Semites, see Gross, *Shylock*, esp. 312–323.

51. Erasmus, *The Praise of Folie*, ed. Clarence H. Miller, trans. Thomas Chaloner, 87, italics in original. "'Vnde nam hoc,' inquiet, 'nouum Iudaeorum genus?'" Erasmus, *Stultitiae Laus*, §54.

52. Thomas More, *Utopia*, ed. and trans. Robert M. Adams, 17.

53. Beatrice Groves, *Texts and Traditions: Religion in Shakespeare 1592–1604*, 26.

54. Geoffrey Bullough, *Narrative and Dramatic Sources in Shakespeare*, 1:447–48.

repr. 1592), and, as Drakakis notes, in so-called "usury tracts," Elizabethans learned that "Jews could imitate Christians in the same way that Christians could imitate Jews."[55] Marlowe's "bottlcd-nosed knave" riveted the moral lesson to farcical satire: "for this example I'll remain a Jew."[56] And Shylock's bold answer to Portia, "My deeds upon my head!" (4.1.204), commonly recognized as an allusion to Matthew 27:25, casts a revealing light on Northumberland's response to Richard II, "My guilt be on my head" (R2 5.1.69), as well as on Canterbury's response to King Henry V, "The sin upon my head, dread sovereign" (H5 1.2.98). This mass of background material does not reflect Saint Paul's construction of a debate "between Christian and Jew . . . as a will contest between heirs."[57] That is, it does not share Paul's historical concern with Christians and Jews as rival heirs to God's promise. To the Elizabethan mind, that question had been settled long ago. Rather it supports Shakespeare's intention to lure us—in our complacency, in our need for a cheap laugh at another's expense, in our self-righteousness, in our lack of charity and mercy—into the purely symbolic role of the Jew. Whether a person realizes that he or she has taken the bait is not for Shakespeare to say, exactly, but the pressing reality of Judgment and the ever-present framework of salvation history (however allusive, however allegorical) make that realization count.

As we have seen, Portia, Lancelot, and Jessica experience dilemmas. With Jessica's elopement, Shylock experiences a dilemma of his own that confirms his fall into evil while humanizing his anguish and complicating our response to him. We first learn of Shylock's dilemma through Solanio's report: "I never heard a passion so confused, / So strange, outrageous, and so variable" (2.8.12–13). What we hear second-hand is the stammering of a man in a world of pain: "My daughter! Oh, my ducats! Oh, my daughter! / Justice! The law! My ducats, and my daughter!" (2.8.15–16). Since we do not actually see Shylock saying these things, the actor playing Solanio would be our interpretive guide to Shylock's state of distraction. The unsympathetic Solanio describes a man who experiences "a passion" that is foreign and bizarre. Shakespeare wrenches the Christian keyword "passion" into an unexpected context, evoking Christ's Passion and, despite a strong element of caricature, exhibiting the moneylender's powerful capacity for suffering, as Shylock looks distractedly

55. Drakakis, introduction, 33.
56. Christopher Marlowe, *The Jew of Malta* (3.3.9–10 and 4.1.194), ed. James R. Siemon.
57. Marx, *Shakespeare and the Bible*, 120.

from loss to loss, not knowing which loss is worse. We may follow Lewalski: Shylock's choice reveals, "not his lack of love for his daughter, but his pitiable inability to determine what he loves most."[58] Resolving his dilemma at fury's height, Shylock later exclaims to Tubal, "I would my daughter were dead at my foot, and the jewels in her ear! Would she were hearsed at my foot, and the ducats in her coffin!" (3.1.83–85). But this horrific burst of feeling (an instance of the figure *ara*, or cursing) is emotionally counterpointed by Shylock's poignant reference to his dead wife. His brief remembrance of the nobly named "Leah" (3.1.114), namesake of the wife of Jacob and daughter of Laban, touches both Shylock's deeper interest in the story he tells Antonio and Bassanio about Jacob and Laban (1.3.75–86), and his grief for the woman he has lost. In a play where rings matter a great deal, we cannot dismiss the pathos of Shylock's response when he hears from Tubal of Jessica's trading his ring for a monkey: "It was my turquoise; I had it of Leah when I was a bachelor. I would not have given it for a wilderness of monkeys" (3.1.114–16).[59] Possibly, "my turquoise" indicates superficiality and greed, but "wilderness" is a powerful word in Jewish sacred history, resounding, in the Geneva Bible, of the Israelites' journeys in the wilderness (Exodus 13, etc.). Coming from Shylock, it suggests the diminishment of a larger awareness.

If Shylock accrues sympathy points in Act 3, Scene 1, he nonetheless shows himself to be highly rebarbative. The rhetorical action that flows from his encounter with Salerio and Solanio in this scene, and that climaxes in his "I am a Jew" speech (succeeded almost immediately by the entrance of Tubal with news of Jessica), begins where we left off in Act 1, Scene 3, with the figures secundum quid (false assumption) and antanaclasis (a type of punning); but now the language on both sides bristles with open hostility. Even so, Shylock and his enemies play by the same rules. The use of puns to twist and reverse meaning, to deploy the fallen tropes of a fallen species, is characteristic of both sides—as when Gratiano in the fourth act cries at Shylock whetting his knife: "Not on thy sole, but on thy soul, harsh Jew, / Thou mak'st thy knife keen" (4.1.123–24). The author's commitment to this punning action is

58. Lewalski, "Biblical Allusion," 330.

59. "That Shylock is greedy and malicious in no way destroys the pathos of his anguish over the loss of Leah's ring." Camille Slights, "In Defense of Jessica: The Runaway Daughter in *The Merchant of Venice*," *Shakespeare Quarterly* 31 (Autumn 1980): 360. Director Robin Russin would agree: "Beyond Jessica's elopement and theft of Shylock's treasure, what constitutes the moment of greatest pathos in the play is Tubal's revelation that she traded away an item of little financial worth to her father, but of enormous emotional importance." Robin Russin, "The Triumph of the Golden Fleece: Women, Money, Religion, and Power in Shakespeare's *The Merchant of Venice*," *Shofar* 31 (2013): 117.

obvious, since he was willing to pay a steep price for it, laboring hard in the following passage to catch his first pun:

SOLANIO   And Shylock for his own part knew the bird was fledge, and
           then it is the complexion of them all to leave the dam.
SHYLOCK   She is damned for it.
SALERIO   That's certain, if the devil may be her judge.
SHYLOCK   My own flesh and blood to rebel!
SOLANIO   Out upon it, old carrion! Rebels it at these years?

                                                              (3.1.27–34)

Salerio calls Shylock "the devil," much as Solanio had done a moment earlier: "here he comes in the likeness of a Jew" (3.1.19–20). The punch line (Shylock as Jew, devil, and judge) must have been infernally funny to the Elizabethans. But in terms of the playwright's fitting his parts together into a whole play, it was the theme of Judgment that commanded his attention: "dam / damned" was worth the extra scribbling for the way it evokes original sin and eschatological concerns that implicate everyone in the playhouse. Shylock's reference to "flesh and blood," like Salonio's farcically false assumption ("old carrion!"), relays the message that the flesh is incorrigibly fallen. Similarly, Gobbo's "flesh and blood" (2.2.88) alludes by *metonymy* (effect for cause) to what Shylock calls "the work of generation" (1.3.80), the producer of more beastly flesh and blood. A little later in Act 3, Scene 1, Salerio, still conversing with Shylock, asks about Antonio's "flesh": "What's that good for?" (3.1.49). Shylock replies: "To bait fish withal. If it will feed nothing else, it will feed my revenge" (3.1.50–51).[60] The punning figure antanaclasis, which suits the play's duplicity, occurs as "feed" shifts in meaning from the concrete to the abstract. Revenge is on Shylock's mind, but it is also on the playwright's, with a more apocalyptic understanding of its significance, an understanding that reaches to the judgment seat of Christ.

That Shylock's "I am a Jew" speech shares many characteristics with forensic oratory has the effect of positioning the audience as a jury. It is Shylock's last attempt at anything like persuasion—as Quentin Skinner remarks, he makes no such attempt in the courtroom.[61] And though the setting on the street is informal, Shylock clearly speaks as a plaintiff, pleading his case in

---

60. Note also "to feed upon / The prodigal Christian" (2.5.15), Shylock's comment on Bassanio's dinner invitation.

61. Quentin Skinner, *Forensic Shakespeare*, 146–47.

impressive prose, stirring memories of classical oratory in the minds of the educated. We can identify three of the six parts of a formal oration as defined in the *Rhetorica ad Herennium*. Shylock begins with his *narratio,* his narration of the facts of the case. He proceeds to his *confutatio,* refuting Antonio's argument or "reason." And he concludes, it must be said, rather artfully (*conclusio est artificiosus orationis terminus*).[62] He omits the other three parts, the *exordium, divisio,* and *confirmatio:*

> [Antonio] hath disgraced me, and hindered me half a million, laughed at my losses, mocked my gains, scorned my nation, thwarted my bargains, cooled my friends, heated my enemies; and what's his reason? I am a Jew. Hath not a Jew eyes? Hath not a Jew hands, organs, dimension, senses, affections, passions? Fed with the same food, hurt with the same weapons, subject to the same diseases, healed by the same means, warmed and cooled by the same winter and summer, as a Christian is? If you prick us, do we not bleed? If you tickle us, do we not laugh? If you poison us, do we not die? And if you wrong us, shall we not revenge? If we are like you in the rest, we will resemble you in that. If a Jew wrong a Christian, what is his humility? Revenge. If a Christian wrong a Jew, what should his sufferance be by Christian example? Why, revenge. The villainy you teach me I will execute, and it shall go hard but I will better the instruction. (3.1.51–69)

Given C. L. Barber's remark, "Shylock thinks to claim only a part of humanness, the lower part, physical and passional,"[63] one infers that Shylock has in mind the same human flesh he would "bait fish withal" (3.1.50). Martin Yaffe's Shylock is not "self-pitying," as Barber's is, but forced into his role: "Reacting in kind . . . to Antonio's treatment of him . . . Shylock is led to understand both himself and others around him in terms of their common animal characteristics."[64] But whether Shylock is self-pitying, or a victim, or both, I think the key effect for the audience is his suddenly wielding the art of rhetoric like a master. In a short space of time, he goes from being mocked by Salerio and Solanio to dominating the stage, rising eloquently in his own defense, and shattering the silence surrounding Christian duplicity: "If a Jew wrong a Christian, what is his humility? Revenge." He argues copiously from example, as if he had absorbed Wilson's *Arte of Rhetorique,* and given it a sharp twist:

62. Anon., *Rhetorica ad Herennium,* trans. Harry Caplan, 8–12 (I.iii.4).

63. C. L. Barber, *Shakespeare's Festive Comedy: A Study of Dramatic Form and Its Relation to Social Custom,* 182.

64. Martin D. Yaffe, *Shylock and the Jewish Question,* 64.

The *Ethnic* Authors stir the hearers, being well applied to the purpose.
For when it shall be reported that they which had no knowledge of God,
lived in brotherly love . . . the Christians must needs be ashamed of their
evil behavior, and study much to pass those which are in calling much
under them, and not suffer that the ignorant and Pagans' life, shall coun-
tervail the taught children of God. . . . If an unlearned man will do no
wrong, a learned man and a Preacher, must much more be upright and
live without blame.[65]

The twist is that Shylock does not stir his hearers with examples that contrast
"ethnic" virtue and Christian vice: instead, he has Christian vice exampling
ethnic vice—talk about "multiple avenues" of truth. Shylock's cynical reference to "Christian example" reprises, moreover, the "discrepancy between
theory and practice" that Portia had introduced through the figure *inter se
pugnantia*, and that Lancelot had dramatized in turn.

We cannot shake off a disturbing sense that Shylock's perverse eloquence
sets the rhetorical tradition at odds with itself. One thinks of that noble orator
Hamlet concluding his encomium for "man," "And yet, to me, what is this
quintessence of dust?" (2.2.309). Behind Shylock's deliberations on human
"kindness," one senses the ripening of Shakespeare's tragic disposition, his
looming preoccupation with our species's depravity. Logically, "Jew" is Shylock's minor term, "man" his implicit major, and his middle term comprises
numerous adjuncts and characteristics, including "eyes, hands, organs, dimen-
sions, senses, affections, passions," use of "weapons," capacity to be "healed"
by skilled "means" or to "die" by "poison," a sense of right and "wrong," etc.
The implicit conclusion is *a Jew is a man*. The syllogism can be fleshed out as,
"All Jews have eyes, hands, weapons, etc.; all things with eyes, hands, weapons,
etc. are men; so all Jews are men." The species definition of man is ironically,
pointedly, at work. Were Antonio the speaker, his argument or "reason" would
have been, "*You* are a Jew." But the language-game is always duplicitous, erect-
ing and dismantling barriers. Shylock is quite capable of saying with contempt,
"*You* are a Christian." Going on the rhetorical attack, he assumes, falsely, that
his knowledge of the case is sufficient. In his mind, to be plaintiff and to be
judge are not, as Portia would say, "distinct offices" (2.9.61). The nine questions
that follow (beginning "Hath not a Jew eyes?") animate the figure *epiplexis* (Gr.
"rebuke") or *percontatio* (L. "thorough investigation"), where "one asks questions,

---

65. Thomas Wilson, *Wilson's Arte of Rhetorique, 1560*, ed. G. H. Mair, 190–91 (I have modernized the spelling). The scriptural basis is Hebrews 10:28–29.

not in order to know, but to chide or reprehend."[66] Cicero is the all-time master of this figure, a hallmark of his celebrated prosecutions of the monsters Verres and Catiline. Not only are we hearing a massive rebuke, then, but its distinguished prose has a recognizably classical and Ciceronian aura. The irony is deeply layered and yet available both to Reformist and to Catholic sensibilities. Shylock's speech combines great rhetorical art and logic in order to deprecate the rational animal that employs them. Reason, as Luther argued, was not a very nice lady. Luther comes to mind as well for his classical learning and enormous psychological penetration, all of which he directed against Erasmian humanism. Shylock seizes command of the stage, wielding a dignified and quasi-Ciceronian cadence in a powerful oration, to deliver an indictment against *all* his hearers: he makes a case very like the Reformers', that *man* remains at root a fallen being, prone to irrational, beastly behavior, more educable in "revenge" and "villainy" than in mercy, forgiveness, and virtue.

There is one element of the plot that seems to like to trick me. More than once I have tripped over the fact that Shakespeare places the scene of Shylock's "I am a Jew" speech right before the long scene in Belmont (3.2), where Bassanio chooses the correct casket, leading to the betrothals of the two couples (the second being Nerissa and Gratiano), followed by the arrival of romantic couple number three, Jessica and Lorenzo, accompanied by Salerio, who carries a letter from Antonio bearing news of financial disaster. The effect of this arrangement of materials (which may explain my confusion) is to separate a pivotal speech of a distinctly judicial character, that is, Shylock's scathing indictment of Antonio, from the courtroom scene itself, in which Portia, disguised as Balthasar, "a young doctor of Rome" (4.1.153–54), conspiring with Nerissa disguised as a clerk, descends on Venice in order to defend Antonio from Shylock's deadly rage. It seems to me now that the courtroom scene, through its very prominence, can distract us from the unity and the scope of Shakespeare's larger design, in which relevant testimony occurs throughout the work. The play never ceases to entertain the question (in Thomas Wilson's words) of "whether the matter be right or wrong." Pretty much everyone is on trial—including the audience.

Earlier I suggested that Lorenzo's reflection on Lancelot's fooling, "and I do know / A many fools, that stand in better place, / Garnished like him, that for a tricksy word / Defy the matter" (3.5.64–67), ironically anticipates Portia's triumph as Balthasar. It is a curious and elaborate triumph. After

---

66. Joseph, *Shakespeare's Use*, 256.

pleading with Shylock to "be merciful" (4.1.180), after eloquently instructing him in the "quality of mercy" (4.1.182), after conceding the strength of his repeated demands for "the law," and after deciding in Shylock's favor, Portia abruptly turns the tables: "This bond doth give thee here no jot of blood; / The words expressly are 'a pound of flesh'" (4.1.304–305). As Skinner has remarked, the "sudden reversal happens because Portia is able to show that the legal issue around which the trial resolves is not *iuridicalis* but *legalis*."[67] In other words, it is not a case for determining whether something was done injuriously (*iure an iniuria factum sit*),[68] but a case where controversy arises in the letter or interpretation of the letter (*in scripto aut e scripto aliquid controversiae nascitur*).[69] Lorenzo's comment about a "tricksy word" defying "the matter" bears directly on Portia's actions because, to lift a point from Skinner, the "term *res* was . . . usually applied to describe the 'matter' (as the vernacular rhetoricians liked to say) that was taken to stand in need of investigation in a judicial case."[70] Portia as Balthasar manages to "defy the matter" by cleverly sidestepping the juridical issue and seizing—Shylock-like—on the letter of the law. Her maneuver, while its primary sources lie elsewhere (scholars point to Ser Giovanni Fiorentino's *Il Pecorone* as the likely source), recalls what Cicero in *De Officiis* calls "chicanery and an excessively clever but malicious interpretation of the law,"[71] regarding which he recounts the famous story of the Roman Quintus Fabius Labeo, who cheated the Neopolitans and the Nolans out of land by following the letter of a treaty that he himself had brokered. Of special interest in this section of *De Officiis* is how Cicero amusingly berates the Romans for failing to live up to Roman standards. In this way he sets an important precedent for Erasmian humanism, which attacks Christian follies, and for Shakespeare's assimilation of such moral ideas and satirical techniques.

Skinner, in observing that the notion of equity is strikingly absent from the courtroom scene, duly notes that it "is true that the exercise of mercy is held to be a consequence of successfully appealing to the ideal of equity as opposed to the letter of the law."[72] Portia pleads eloquently for mercy, but she does not first appeal to Shylock's or to anyone else's notions of equity. And why not? Because to do so would mean to invite a *narratio* on both sides.

67. Skinner, *Forensic Shakespeare*, 225.

68. Anon., *Rhetorica ad Herennium*, 42 (I.xiv.24).

69. Anon., *Rhetorica ad Herennium*, 34 (I.xi.18).

70. Skinner, *Forensic Shakespeare*, 21.

71. *Existunt etiam saepe iniuriae calumnia quadam et nimis callida, sed malitiosa iuris interpetatione.* Marcus Tullius Cicero, *On Duties* [*De Officiis*], trans. Walter Miller, 34 (I. x. 33).

72. Skinner, *Forensic Shakespeare*, 215.

It would mean considering both Antonio's and Shylock's intentions in light of each man's character and experience, thus possibly eliciting sympathy for "the Jew." Shylock's obvious villainy serves an important comic purpose, because it shields his enemies from moral scrutiny that the comedy could not endure. In this respect, Portia's repeated use of the metonymically reductive term *Jew* conveniently reduces Shylock to a stock type, recalling Marlowe's *Jew of Malta*.[73] But her Shylock is not the sum and total of Shakespeare's Shylock. The playwright does, in fact, give us a *narratio* that humanizes the Jew and inspires degrees of pity for him. As we have seen, Shylock gets his own *narratio* at the beginning of the "I am a Jew" speech. Moreover, we can understand Tubal's report (in the same scene, 3.1) of Jessica's selling Leah's ring as the testimony of a witness in the case.

Shakespeare was well aware of the ancient concept of equity.[74] The demands of equity test our judgment where the letter of the law cannot accomplish the work of justice, due to mitigating or complicating circumstances in the individual case. Let us bear in mind, moreover, that each true Christian "is judged by his own intentions. And it is through his own intentions, according to Augustine, that man reforms the divine image within himself."[75] Equity would inspire mercy both by honoring the need for individualized justice and by attuning the courtroom and the audience to their uncharitable intentions and hence to their own inadequacy as judges (see Portia's lines at 4.1.196–98, this chapter's epigraph). From Shakespeare's viewpoint, the demands of equity had a contemporary aspect as well, being "at some variance with the scholastic tradition in theology which reserves to conscience a priori powers of discrimination between truth and falsehood." Conscience in a legal sense had become "a term of adjustment, of flexibility in relation to the individual case." In fact, the "legal concept of 'conscience,'" brought to our attention by Lancelot the clown, was "the guiding light" in the English court of Chancery, the "law court charged with reflecting the interests of justice or equity against the strict letter of the law."[76] The problem

---

73. "For *metonymy* we could substitute *reduction*." Kenneth Burke, *A Grammar of Motives*, 503, his italics.

74. Skinner, *Forensic Shakespeare*, 214. For sixteenth-century background, see Brian Cummings, *Mortal Thoughts: Religion, Secularity & Identity in Shakespeare and Early Modern England*, 77–79. For equity in the court of Chancery under Queen Elizabeth, with reference to *The Merchant of Venice*, see George W. Keeton, *Shakespeare's Legal and Political Background*, 132–50, esp. 137.

75. Kathy Eden, *Poetic and Legal Fiction in the Aristotelian Tradition*, 131. I am indebted to Eden throughout this paragraph.

76. Cummings, *Mortal Thoughts*, 79, 77.

touches the career of no Englishman more memorably than that of Thomas More.

Antonio, who introduces the problem of self-knowledge at the very start of the play—"I have much ado to know myself" (1.1.7)—is particularly difficult to judge by his intentions. In light of Shylock's star testimony against Antonio in Act 3, Scene 1, we may take the merchant's cruelty toward Shylock to be an expression of zealotry, monomaniacal in its obsession with usury, a flawed imitation of Christ. Our perception of his behavior toward Shylock is complicated by the fact that the bearbaiting Elizabethans looked on cruelty differently from how we do, seizing with gusto on its grotesquely comic elements. For instance, in the Towneley cycles, which were performed until 1576, the torturers of Christ "turn their actions into jests."[77] The passionate Shylock is, to some extent, both devilish and provocatively Christlike in his role as comic butt. After all, Christ did not go around spitting at people (1.3.110, 115). He was the one spat upon (Matt. 26:67 and 27:30). Whatever we make of all this, there remains a serious argument for Antonio's redeeming himself in the courtroom scene. For Lewalski, the Antonio of Act 4 "becomes . . . a perfect embodiment of Christian love."[78] Certainly, if we understand Antonio's demand of Shylock that he "presently become a Christian" (4.1.385) as playing on the trope of Christian money-lenders imitating Jews (the symbolic Jew), then Antonio's powerplay looks much less sinister—the demand takes on a comical aspect. Gorman Beauchamp and Hugh Short have recently defended the absolute goodness of Antonio's charity and Shylock's conversion, and have done so intelligently.[79] Antonio, no less than Bassanio, was willing to "'give and hazard all he hath'" (2.7.16). But still, I would contend that Antonio's role in the forced conversion of Shylock can be justified only by the charity of Antonio's intentions (I do not refer to Antonio's *beliefs*: Antonio's beliefs are clear enough). And these remain opaque on our side of the veil. Shylock's sudden illness, after saying, "I am content" (4.1.391), concludes his defeat in the bruising contest between Jew and Christian, in which Antonio finally and decisively crushes his antagonist. Shylock's great mockery of Bassanio, "What, wouldst thou have a serpent sting you twice?" (4.1.69), had

---

77. V. A. Kolve, *The Play Called Corpus Christi*, 191.

78. Lewalski, "Biblical Allusion," 331.

79. See Gorman Beauchamp, "Shylock's Conversion," *Humanitas* 24 (2011): 55–92, and Short, "Shylock Is Content." Todd Pettigrew's argument that "Shylock's agreement does not constitute a genuine religious conversion" merits consideration as pushback against such readings. See Todd H. J. Pettigrew, "The Christening of Shylock," *Literary Imagination* 21 (November 2019): 274.

briefly demonized the Christians—a "fleering frumpe" if there ever was one.[80] A tremendous clash of wills has excited but not settled our judgment of the principals. Antonio, in my reading, may indeed try to imitate Christ, but I would argue that the play is too skeptical about human nature to relieve our doubts about his success. We remain, after all, "in a fallen world . . . well short of apocalypse . . . encumbered by imperfection."

So we are shaken by a curious crack in the hall of earthly justice. The "traditional allegory of the Parliament of Heaven"[81] still applies to Portia, Shylock, and Antonio, insofar as this tradition hovers ironically (more dissonantly than Lewalski would allow) over the judicial proceedings in Venice: Portia, Shylock, and Antonio are both like and unlike the traditional figures of Mercy, Justice, and Christ, respectively. To be clear, the truth of salvation history is not subjected to irony. It is our moral blindness, the human claim to know the immediate relevance of salvation history, that is so subjected. Shylock's manic drive for revenge tumbles him into the devil's camp, but Portia's curious indifference to equity suggests that she is giving a kind of highly eloquent biblical lip-service to mercy, though we cannot fully sift her motives or her conscience. And Antonio, from start to finish, is a blend of virtue, anger, and melancholy—hardly an ideal subject for allegorical identification.

If we notice the disorienting gap between earthly justice and Judgment, we will also notice the ironies latent in Shylock's merciless exclamation, which is gleefully echoed by a vengeful Gratiano, "A Daniel come to judgment!" (4.1.221, 331, 338). Shakespeare knows that he has lured everyone in the theater into playing the role of judge. We are all would-be Daniels "come to judgment." Given this shared situation, and given the premium that Portia places on Christian mercy, it is interesting that Daniel himself, in the Apocryphal book that Shylock has in mind, doesn't show the least interest in it. He traps the lustful elders by interrogating them separately about Susanna's alleged adultery; when their stories conflict, they are summarily executed "according to the law of Moses" (Susanna: 62). Mercy is off the table. Overlooking this inconsistency, Lewalski wields the biblical background to support her allegorical reading: "the name Daniel, which means in Hebrew, 'The Judge of the Lord,' was glossed in the Elizabethan Bibles as 'The Judgment of God.'" Moreover, "Portia has assumed the name 'Balthasar' for the purposes of her disguise, and the name

---

80. Puttenham, *Arte of English Poesie*, 201.

81. Lewalski, "Biblical Allusion," 339. For Lewalski, Shylock's role as the Devil is "superadded" to his role as Justice.

given to the prophet Daniel in the Book of Daniel is Baltassar—a similarity hardly accidental." Lewalski scores her main point along Christian exegetical lines: "Daniel in this book [the Book of Daniel] foreshadows the Christian tradition by his explicit denial of any claim upon God by righteousness, and his humble appeal for mercy."[82] For Lewalski, as we shall see, Gratiano's mocking echo of Shylock isn't vengeful: it is entirely appropriate. James Shapiro unearths yet more of the Elizabethan context: "It is worth considering what else the invocation of Daniel might have meant to Shakespeare's audiences, for even if the reference might have recalled the story of Susanna, Elizabethans did not consider this narrative as separate from the rest of Daniel: as the Geneva Bible notes, it was often joined 'to the end of Daniel' to 'make it the thirteenth chapter.' In scores of sermons and tracts produced in the late sixteenth century, Daniel called to mind first and foremost the Jewish prophet who foresaw the final judgment, an event precipitated by the conversion of the Jews."[83]

Acknowledging this densely layered source material, I want to suggest that Shakespeare, in writing his play, was sensitive to Daniel's ruthlessness against the elders—a very different Daniel from the prophet who prays for forgiveness by denying "any claim upon God by righteousness." Shakespeare's biblical sensitivity has the effect of setting up the Elizabethan audience to fail, to fall into laughter, to respond nervously and superficially to Gratiano's cheerleading in the court scene and its obfuscation of exhausting ambiguities and moral nuances—Gratiano, who at least had the wisdom to say, "Let me play the fool" (1.1.93, 79). The playwright, I am arguing, was alert to *contraria*, to discord and contrariety within the Bible, despite its infallible authority.[84] The same phenomenon is referred to by the "exegetical trope" *contradictio*.[85] *Contraria*, the broader term, belonged among the rhetorical topics of invention that Shakespeare studied as a schoolboy.[86] Erasmus, unlike Luther, Calvin, or

---

82. Lewalski, "Biblical Allusion," 340. Lewalski cites Daniel 9:18. See also Halio's note at 4.1.220 in William Shakespeare, *The Merchant of Venice*, ed. Jay Halio, 199.

83. Shapiro, *Shakespeare and the Jews*, 133.

84. In a Reformist spirit, Thomas Wilson insisted on the Bible's infallible authority: "The history of God's book to the Christian is infallible, and therefore the rehearsal of such good things as are therein contained, move the faithful to all upright doing, and amendment of their life" (190; I have modernized the spelling). By contrast, Christopher Marlowe, according to Richard Baines's famous letter, bragged about quoting "a number of Contrarieties oute of the Scripture." Baines, quoted in Christopher Marlow, *Doctor Faustus*, 128–29, ed. David Scott Kastan. This charge would have evoked the closet atheism of Marlowe's Cambridge education. See David Riggs, "Marlowe's Quarrel with God," in *Marlowe, History and Sexuality*, ed. Paul Whitfield White, 15–37, esp. 25–26.

85. See Cummings, *Mortal Thoughts*, 190.

86. See T. W. Baldwin, *William Shakspere's Small Latine and Lesse Greek*, 2:115.

Thomas Wilson, was "vexed by conflicting interpretations to which scripture is subject. The mere existence of controversy over some issues . . . leads him to conclude that scripture leaves these matters finally obscure. The problems of interpretation thus define for him the limits of what is sayable about any doctrine." [87] Such problems obstructed the Bible's authority. Not only could the devil quote Scripture, but Scripture itself could exhibit, if not a "devilish duplicity," then enough inconsistency to puzzle and dismay those longing for solid answers—as when Richard II sets "the word itself / Against the word" (R2 5.5.13–14) in his cell at Pomfret Castle. [88]

In my skeptical Christian reading of *The Merchant of Venice*, Portia as Daniel may well allude to the Judgment of God, but she surely does not stand for it—unless we are foolish enough to believe that she does. The allegorical framework in the background is activated to deny her an easy place in the allegory. And as the storm of criticism surrounding her would suggest, she is more than a little ambiguous in nature. As a romance heroine she can seem at times both a character and a metatheatrical crux flaunting improbability: her dressing up as Balthasar while somehow intuiting that the Duke would send for her cousin Bellario; her hilarious "Your wife would give you little thanks for that" (4.1.286), breaking the tension of the legal proceedings with Nerissa and Shylock joining in—almost a Mel Brooks schtick; her restitution of Antonio's ships; these and other instances lead one to conclude that for Shakespeare neither the plot nor the pleasure of metadrama is the soul of the play. These have their place, but the soul of it lies in the questions of conscience put to a Christian audience. Given the tendency to aestheticize Shakespeare through metadramatic analysis, it is worth underscoring that, as an agent of Shakespeare's theatrical self-consciousness, Portia does not alienate us from the action of the play; rather, she serves Shakespeare's moral intention. Portia in her turn as judge is designed to provoke our judgment of her character. She is not as enthusiastically vindictive as Gratiano is, but Lewalski's argument that the allusions to Daniel "greatly enrich the irony when Gratiano flings the title [of Daniel] back in Shylock's face"[89] holds true under two conditions that do not necessarily obtain: first, if the impurity of Christian motives escapes our notice; and, second, if the imperfection of Christian interpretation never concerns us. In the first respect, let us add to what we

87. Cummings, *Literary Culture*, 172.

88. See excellent readings of this passage by Alison Shell, *Shakespeare and Religion*, 133, and by Cummings, *Mortal Thoughts*, 189–91.

89. Lewalski, "Biblical Allusion," 341.

have observed so far, that Gratiano and his friends share a striking tendency "to confuse the religious ideal of contempt for this world with the aristocratic affectation of contempt for money."[90] In the second respect, Christian interpretation is complicated not only by biblical *contraria,* but by the audience's lively moral investment, which must inevitably produce rival interpretations and rival emphases—Shakespeare's comical appropriation of the conflict that Erasmus, in debating the limits of biblical exegesis, had shunned in his famous retreat from "assertions."[91]

Mindful of warring judgments, let us recall the words of the "schedule" (2.9.55) that Portia's father had deposited in the silver casket: "The fire seven times tried this; / Seven times tried that judgment is / That did never choose amiss" (2.9.63–65). As Richmond Noble noted years ago, these words refer to the twelfth Psalm, which Lewalski quotes from the "Psalter for the *Book of Common Prayer,* in the *Bishops Bible* [*sic*], 1584, verses 3, 7: 'The Lorde shal roote out al deceptful lippes: and the tongue that speaketh proude things . . . The woordes of the Lorde are pure woordes: even as the silver whiche from the earth is tryed, and purified seven times in the fyre.'"[92] To a Catholic, this passage carries purgatorial overtones; to Protestant and Catholic alike, it indicates the severe distance between pride and purity. We may say respectfully that, after all these decades of response to her pioneering and indispensable work, Lewalski's "judgment" has been "tried." But Shakespeare's play demands that its readers and critics, like its characters, be tried as judges again and again. Portia and her friends exhibit many virtues. Like most of us, they are commendable in their own eyes, by their own customs and usages. But their pursuit of justice is flawed by the highest Christian standards—which ironically survive in the accusations of a superior mob of post-Christian Balthasars.

The Merchant of Venice is a fallen comedy that weighs our fallen flesh from start to finish. The curious metaphysics of "a pound of flesh" is essential to Shakespeare's wit. So too is our own built-in fallibility in trying to gauge the fallenness of others. The flesh of Shylock's imagination haunts even Belmont in Lorenzo's reference to "this muddy vesture of decay" (5.1.64).[93] Likewise, the Jew's indignation and his version of events trouble our consciences long

---

90. Marx, *Shakespeare and the Bible,* 105.

91. Erasmus, *On the Freedom of the Will,* in *Luther and Erasmus: Free Will and Salvation,* ed. E. Gordon Rupp and Philip S. Watson, 37.

92. Lewalski, "Biblical Allusion," 337n26. See also Richmond Noble, *Shakespeare's Biblical Language,* 78 and 165.

93. Akin to the shift of perspective from Belmont to "the floor of heaven" (5.1.58) is the shift of perspective from Cleopolis to the New Jerusalem in *The Faerie Queene* (1.x.58).

after the too-happy ending. Honorable within honorable limits, Portia's forensic brinksmanship is, from an ulterior perspective, a bravura display of rhetorical control, where persuasion and judgment bear the grave weight of human imperfection. Her plea for mercy is powerful and moving, but her excellent performance and triumphant use of a "tricksy word" operate on a worldly plane. Shakespeare, like his audience, believed in a Judgment with "no trifling strife about words,"[94] and he wrote with it in mind.

As Shylock's most unforgettable speech would indicate, the playwright had moved beyond his rhetorical training to see rhetoric not so much in the light of reason, as in the glare of will and appetite. Collating the sources of his second tetralogy, which now looms before us, he registered the clash of perspectives between writers: the rivalries and hatreds, the uses of crass and subtle propaganda, the frequently impossible claims to knowledge. His unsparing intelligence continued to penetrate and explore a world of religious and rhetorical *contraria*, the world that Erasmus tried to heal through skepticism and charity—the legacy of Christian humanism in crisis. Shakespeare's response to this crisis was, as I have suggested, quite different from Marlowe's. Unlike the Marlowe of *Tamburlaine* and *The Jew of Malta*, Shakespeare carefully maintained the ulterior perspective of sacred history and Judgment. Nonetheless, Shakespeare's response to the tensions within Christian humanism was similar to Marlowe's in one respect: it compelled him to break new ground. For Shakespeare, this meant reexamining Christian England from top to bottom, and doing so with a more mature skepticism than he had exercised in the first tetralogy. The intellectualism of systematic theology, the clarity of Lutheran exegesis, Calvin's representation of faith as knowledge, the glittering myth of the Tudor regime: none of them matched truth to experience in the way their more zealous adherents claimed. The question was how to judge history, how to get the truth of history onto the stage, without offense to one's conscience, and with only the tainted art of rhetoric with which to avoid error.

---

94. John Calvin, *The Institution of the Christian Religion*, 3.12.1. I have modernized the spelling.

CHAPTER 3

The *Henriad*

A Skeptical Christian Writes History

God pardon all oaths that are broke to me!
God keep all vows unbroke are made to thee!

(R2 4.1.215–16)

Predestined or not, we now make our way to the four major history plays—*Richard II*, *1 Henry IV*, *2 Henry IV*, and *Henry V*—that Alvin Kernan memorably called the *Henriad*. Kernan explains: "these four plays are not an epic in the usual sense—there is no evidence that Shakespeare planned them as a unit[1]—but they do have remarkable coherence, and they possess that quality which in our time we take to be the chief characteristic of epic: a large-scale, heroic action, involving many men and many activities, tracing the movement of a nation or people through violent change from one condition to another."[2] Kernan's judgment about the plays' "remarkable coherence" is not in doubt. For our purposes, though, it is not "heroic action" but "a large-scale" sequence of oaths that strengthens the links between the four plays. This structural interest leads us first to the Christianity of the Gospels.

Oaths and Sermons

To read the Sermon on the Mount (Matthew 5–7) is to encounter Christianity at its least political. For a Marxist, it must be acknowledged, there is no such thing as an *apolitical* anything. But with respect to Christ's message, the word should not be cancelled. No stranger to Marxism, W. H. Auden implied as much in his commentary on Jesus: "He decisively rejected the political solution. The whole of His direct teaching is concerned with the relation of the

---

1. As early as 1944, Tillyard had argued that "Shakespeare conceived his second tetralogy as one great unit." E. M. W. Tillyard, *Shakespeare's History Plays*, 267. Norman Rabkin subsequently submitted further evidence of a unified design: "already in *Richard II* Hotspur—a character completely unnecessary to the play—has been made practically a generation younger than his model." Norman Rabkin, *Shakespeare and the Problem of Meaning*, 36.

2. Alvin Kernan, "*The Henriad*: Shakespeare's Major History Plays," in *Modern Shakespearean Criticism: Essays on Style, Dramaturgy, and the Major Plays*, ed. Alvin B. Kernan, 245. I do not suggest that the term originated with Kernan; its origin is obscure.

individual to God and to his neighbor, irrespective of the political system under which he may happen to live."[3] Put another way: the Sermon on the Mount constitutes Jesus' foremost "message of the inbreaking of God's kingdom."[4] It certainly does not teach prudence (*phronesis*) in the Aristotelian sense. To an Aristotelian, to any practical person, it seems designed to turn the world upside down. Its unsettling effect is not relieved by the fact of its author's crucifixion. In the words of biblical scholar Rudolf Schnackenburg, it "remains a storm center for all Christians."[5] We cannot fathom Christianity or Christian humanism without engaging the Sermon on the Mount.

Seated on a mountain, attended by disciples, Jesus starts to preach. First come the Beatitudes, "Blessed *are.* . . ." Then comes the litany of "extreme demands,"[6] including one that especially concerns us:

> You have heard that it was said to them of old time, "Thou shalt not forswear thyself, but shalt perform thine oaths to the Lord." But I say unto you, Swear not at all, neither by heaven, for it is the throne of God: Nor yet by the earth: for it is his footstool: neither by Jerusalem: for it is the city of the great King. Neither shalt thou swear by thine head, because thou canst not make one hair white or black. But let your communication be, Yea, Yea: Nay, nay. For whatsoever is more than these, cometh of evil. (Matthew 5:33–37)

This is a text to which Shakespeare returned many times.[7] Its effect was to drive a wedge between Christ and Caesar, for the simple reason that Caesar's empire—from Rome to Jerusalem—was built on oaths. The physical metaphor of a wedge may fail to capture the inner force of the action, its exacting claim on the conscience. It is this inner force that boggles the practical mind, so that Jesus must, in his disturbing fashion, repeat himself. Later in the Gospel of Matthew, the Pharisees present him with a coin, a denarius, featuring, it would appear, an image of the Roman Emperor Tiberius, whose divine title was inscribed along the curving edge. (The denarius is represented by the abbreviation "*d.*" in the tavern reckoning that Peto fetches from Falstaff's pocket in *1 Henry IV*.) The Pharisees want to know if it is right to pay taxes. Christ replies, "Render therefore unto Caesar the things which are Caesar's;

---

3. W. H. Auden, *The English Auden: Poems, Essays and Dramatic Writings 1927–1939*, 343.
4. Rudolf Schnackenburg, *All Things are Possible to Believers: Reflections on the Lord's Prayer and the Sermon on the Mount*, vii.
5. Schnackenburg, *All Things*, vii.
6. Schnackenburg, *All Things*, vii.
7. Twelve times, according to Naseeb Shaheen, *Biblical References in Shakespeare's Plays*, 801–802. In addition, it is alluded to in a dialogue between Cassius and Brutus (JC 2.1.113–40).

and unto God the things that are God's" (Matthew 22:21).[8] This seemingly simple reply—it is actually a command—stirs up doubts about questions that are not so easy to answer. What exactly is owed to Caesar? What exactly is owed to God? What is the relationship between earth and heaven?

Coins, which proliferate throughout the *Henriad*, are oaths made of metal.[9] The King's "word," as Richard II observes during his abdication, is "sterling" (4.1.265). To cite one of Falstaff's quips, one needed the "blood royal" (2H4 1.2.128) to coin a royal—worth ten shillings. To cite another, the Prince "will not stick to say his face is a face royal" (2H4 1.2.22–23). The English monarchy could not have survived without the exclusive royal prerogative for minting coins. During the reigns of Richard II, Henry IV, and Henry V, the two sides of a gold noble displayed, respectively, the sovereign's image and an ornate cross. A number of Elizabethan coins featured the Queen's profile on the obverse side and a biblical inscription in Latin on the reverse. Quantities of these were minted at the Tower of London, "Julius Caesar's ill-erected tower," as Richard's unhappy Queen remarks (R2 5.1.2). If English coins served to bolster the social order with an ideal image of church and state, nonetheless they could not distract the alert Christian conscience from the violence that underlay that social order. This extraordinary mayhem was not easy to legitimize.

To say the least, the Elizabethan state endured an uneasy relation with the Gospels. Both the homily "Against Swearying and Perjurie" and Article 39 of the Church of England show it laboring to preserve its Caesarian due against the primitivist rigor of Anabaptists and nonconforming Puritans. "Against Swearying and Perjurie" belongs to the first Book of Homilies (1547), which Queen Elizabeth made the backbone of her effort to secure religious unity and conformity. Though the book is largely the fruit—authorially and editorially—of Cranmer's genius, the young Queen reissued it in 1559, and forcefully imposed it on the English pulpit.[10] Scholarship has struggled to recover the feeling on the Elizabethan street with respect to this homily and other, similar expressions of the Queen's policy. If the man on the street happens to be Shakespeare, the feeling has proven to be particularly elusive.

---

8. Here I anachronistically quote the King James Version (1611) simply because it is more resonant.

9. For numismatic and economic references in *1 Henry IV*, including how coinage "specifically focuses attention upon the relation of value and political authority," see David Scott Kastan, introduction to *King Henry IV Part 1*, by William Shakespeare, ed. David Scott Kastan, 62–69.

10. See Ronald Bond, introduction to *Certain Sermons or Homilies (1547) and A Homily against Disobedience and Wilful Rebellion (1570)*, ed. Ronald Bond, 8–11.

Since the landmark work of E. M. W. Tillyard, *Shakespeare's History Plays* (1944), analysis of Shakespeare's politics has focused on the issues that Tillyard raised. His "orthodox" position has been galvanized into a kind of poststructuralist life-in-death by New Historicists, for whom "all literary productions serve the interests of the *dominant* ideology," while dissents from Tillyard include, to give a few examples, Shakespeare as democrat, as republican, as Essex man, and as Catholic recusant.[11]

A key passage in "Against Swearying and Perjurie" occurs when the homilist tries, in his discussion of oaths, to wriggle free from the grip of Matthew 5:33–37:

> Lawful swearing cannot be evil which bringeth unto us so many godly, good and necessary commodities. Wherefore, when Christ so earnestly forbad swearing, it may not so be understood as though he did forbid all manner of oaths, but he forbiddeth all vain swearing and forswearing, both by God and by his creatures, as the common use of swearing in buying, selling and in our daily communication, to the intent every Christian man's word should be as well regarded in such matters, as if he should confirm his communication with an oath.[12]

From the zealous angle of nonconforming Puritanism, it was impossible to overlook such unwarranted accommodation of the state's interest. From that angle, Christ could not have approved the authorities' investment in the countless oaths that knit together the fabric of the commonwealth: from the monarch's coronation oath to subjects' oaths of allegiance, from the oaths of magistrates and juries to apprentices' oaths to their masters, from schoolmasters' oaths and soldiers' oaths to church oaths and baptismal vows.[13] The author of Article 39 upholds the same reasonable principles: "As we confess

---

11. On *Richard II* and "the deposition of the rightful king," Tillyard writes: "In doctrine, the play is entirely orthodox." Tillyard, *Shakespeare's History Plays*, 297. For Tillyard on the "Tudor Myth," see 39–42. For the New Historicist recasting of Tillyard's "orthodox" Shakespeare, see Tim Spiekerman, *Shakespeare's Political Realism: The English History Plays*, 11 (quoted above, his italics) and 24. For Shakespeare as democrat, see Annabel Patterson, *Shakespeare and the Popular Voice*. For Shakespeare's republican milieu, see Andrew Hadfield, *Shakespeare and Republicanism*. For Shakespeare as an Essex man, see Peter Lake, *How Shakespeare Put Politics on the Stage* (discussed below). For Shakespeare as Catholic recusant, see Joseph Pearce, *The Quest for Shakespeare: The Bard of Avon and the Church of Rome*.

12. Bond, *Certain Sermons*, 130. I have modernized the spelling throughout.

13. For oaths as "essential to the implantation of the Reformation," see Jonathan Michael Gray, *Oaths and the English Reformation*, 8; for oaths as a means of resistance to Elizabethan authority, see 210–212.

that vain and rash swearing is forbidden Christian men by Our Lord Jesus Christ, and James his apostle [see James 5:12], so we judge, that Christian religion doth not prohibit, but that a man may swear when the magistrate requireth, in a cause of faith and charity, so it be done . . . in justice, judgment, and truth."[14] To the Reformed mainstream, Puritan and Conformist alike,[15] this represented a respectable compromise with the Sermon on the Mount. It fulfilled the sense of "dual loyalty" that "the Christian, from the very beginning, has owed to God and Caesar, or, in political terms, to Church and State."[16] Actually, that is Bertrand Russell's characterization of the typical medieval outlook, which Luther and Calvin revised. In their terms, we should speak not of a dual loyalty to church and state, but of negotiating the two kingdoms of earth and heaven. None found it easy to do. Some found it well-nigh impossible. To quote Luther: "Whoso then can judge rightly between the law and the Gospel, let him thank God, and know that he is a right divine."[17]

The anxiety created by Matthew 5:33–37 spurred defensive measures by the state and satirical measures by the defenders of their own sanity. One can detect this line of satire, for example, when Hotspur teases his wife, Lady Percy:

> HOTSPUR   Come, Kate, I'll have your song too.
> LADY PERCY   Not mine, in good sooth.
> HOTSPUR   Not yours, in good sooth! Heart, you swear
>   like a comfit maker's wife. "Not you, in good sooth,"
>   and "as true as I live," and "as God shall mend me,"
>   and "as sure as day,"
> And givest such sarcanet surety for thy oaths
> As if thou never walk'st further than Finsbury.
> Swear me, Kate, like a lady as thou art,
> A good mouth-filling oath, and leave "in sooth,"
> And such protest of pepper-gingerbread,
> To velvet-guards and Sunday citizens.
>   (1H4 3.1.243–254)

14. From "The Thirty-Nine Articles," in Christopher Marlowe, *Doctor Faustus*, ed. David Scott Kastan, 250.

15. I deploy the terms "Reformed mainstream," "Conformist," and "Puritan" in accordance with the usages and explanations of Peter Lake, "Religious Identities in Shakespeare's England," in *A Companion to Shakespeare*, ed. David Scott Kastan, 57–84.

16. Bertrand Russell, *A History of Western Philosophy*, 306.

17. Martin Luther, *Commentary on Galatians*, quoted in Duncan B. Forrester, "Martin Luther and John Calvin," in *History of Political Philosophy*, ed. Leo Strauss and Joseph Cropsey, 324–25. I am indebted to Forrester's essay.

A champion of honor who betrays his oath of fealty to Henry IV, Hotspur commands a greater field than Finsbury, where, during Elizabeth's reign, the London citizenry liked to promenade on summer Sundays. In his words to his wife, "Swear me, Kate, like a lady as thou art, / A good mouth-filling oath," young Percy aims a jibe at those who lack his capacity for battle and other excitements of the blood. In his aristocratic eyes, the good citizens are true to type, but not much else. The sarcanet of the metaphor "sarcanet surety" is a fine soft silk but "flimsy."[18] The passage is a catalogue of not very "godly . . . commodities" (to quote the homily), from the "comfit maker's" sweetmeats to "pepper-gingerbread," "velvet" (the proud fashion of well-to-do wives), and the aforementioned "sarcanet." Hotspur thinks that London's mercantile Puritans employ their chaste oaths out of mere propriety. He is not persuaded by their religious appearances. Likewise alert to hypocrisy, Falstaff refers to one "Master Dommelton" (2H4 1.2.29), a thriving Puritan merchant and purveyor of satin—just the type of person that Hotspur had satirized. Hearing that Dommelton has refused his worthless "bond," Falstaff lampoons the "rascally yea-forsooth knave" (2H4 1.2.32 and 35–36). We may feel the force of Matthew 5:33–37 in the citizens' oath "yea-forsooth," though some editors hear little more than Dommelton's obsequious manner. The Puritan topicality is evident in Falstaff's wordplay on *security* (37, 41, 42). Indignant because Dommelton has insisted on a "guarantee of payment,"[19] Falstaff hints theologically at Dommelton's unwarranted *securitas* in his own election.[20]

Because they condemned the regimen of oaths, hated the theater, despised the required homilies or set sermons, rejected the bishops, satirized the establishment, were godlier and potentially more hypocritical than others, and so on, the active, zealous Protestants who dissented from the Elizabethan Settlement did their part to encourage a vein of anti-Puritanism in Shakespeare. Scholars have long recognized that Shakespeare's original idea was to portray the proto-Puritan Lollard martyr Sir John Oldcastle, Lord Cobham, as a latter-day Vice and Lord of Misrule. Simply from the Epilogue to *2 Henry IV* we know that Shakespeare was compelled to change Oldcastle's name to Falstaff. Studying this background, Kristen Poole has argued that Falstaff "catalyzed

---

18. Bevington's note.

19. Bevington's note on "bond."

20. For the theology of *securitas* in the 1590s, see Brian Cummings, *The Literary Culture of the Reformation: Grammar and Grace*, 295. Also, James C. Bulman cites a sermon by Archbishop Edwin Sandys warning against "security" as a form of spiritual sloth. See William Shakespeare, *King Henry IV, Part 2*, ed. James C. Bulman, 188n.

and epitomized the early modern representation of the stage Puritan"[21] by following a pattern established by the grotesquely comical Martin Marprelate tracts (1588–89). Their anonymous author(s) had set out in seven tracts to "mar prelates," that is, to render ridiculous the English bishops. These nonconformist pamphlets delivered the satirical goods, inspiring their conservative targets to return the favor in the form of "anti-Martinist" writings. A number of scholars have followed Poole in documenting similar aspects of the Falstaffian background. We note that when he signs his letter to Hal, "Thine, by yea and no" (2H4 2.2.124), Falstaff adopts the common Puritan idiom of Matthew 5:33–37, repeated later in the play by Justice Swallow (3.2.9). Hannibal Hamlin observes that references "to yea and nay were common among Puritan writers," citing as examples William Perkins's famous *Golden Chaine* and cartographer John Norden's *Progresse of Pietie*. Hamlin evidences the power of this "catch-phrase" by quoting its pointed uses in the writings of anti-Puritan writers, including the champion of episcopacy and future archbishop Richard Bancroft and the author of an anonymous play printed in 1595, *A Knack to Know a Knave*.[22] Like Poole and Hamlin, Peter Lake and Beatrice Groves are oriented toward Falstaff's mimicry of pseudo-godliness among the godly.[23]

I want to resist this narrowing of Falstaff in order to pursue his *literary* significance within the religious culture that Shakespeare inhabited. To start, I want to ask whether his prevailing mood is one of comedy or satire. To the extent that we read *1 Henry IV* as leaning toward comedy, one may recall C. L. Barber defending his position against L. C. Knights. Such differences are important from a literary standpoint because the recent emphasis on anti-Puritan satire, with its acute historical sensitivities, tends to neglect the broader comedic effects of Falstaff's saturnalian comedy. For Barber, whose contribution to the field may reasonably be called permanent, "the dynamic relation of comedy and serious action is saturnalian rather than satiric."[24] For Knights, on the other hand, the key is satire: "Once the play is read as a whole the satire on war and policy is apparent."[25] I suggest that we make sense of this critical

21. Kristen Poole, *Radical Religion from Shakespeare to Milton: Figures of Nonconformity in Early Modern England*, 21.

22. Hannibal Hamlin, *The Bible in Shakespeare*, 258.

23. Hamlin, *The Bible in Shakespeare*, 259–62; Lake, *How Shakespeare Put Politics*, 335–40; Beatrice Groves, *Texts and Traditions: Religion in Shakespeare 1592–1604*, 131.

24. C. L. Barber, *Shakespeare's Festive Comedy: A Study of Dramatic Form and Its Relation to Social Custom*, 205.

25. L. C. Knights, "Notes on Comedy," in *Determinations: Critical Essays*, ed. F. R. Leavis, 128. Knights's position goes back at least as far as Hermann Ulrici (1806–84). See Tom McAlindon, *Shakespeare's Tudor History: A Study of Henry IV Parts 1 and 2*, 4.

impasse, of the apparent tension between satirical rowdiness and saturnalian release, by recognizing not only the grotesque, comical power of the stage Puritan, but also the influence on Shakespeare of bawdy, exuberantly comical, and intelligent satire outside the Marprelate controversy: one thinks especially of Chaucer, but also of Rabelais.[26] My gist, in any case, is that Falstaff exceeds the topical satire of the stage Puritan, without negating it, by realizing something more universal, namely, the comical possibilities inherent in the daily clash between Christian theory and Christian practice.

To pursue this line of argument about Falstaff's comical capacities, I need to return to the origin and effects of Matthew 5:33–37. As stated in the Introduction, one of my general purposes is to challenge the tendency to deploy terms such as "confessional communities" in ways that manage to obscure the essential connection between Shakespeare and Christianity. With respect to Matthew 5:33–37, scholar John Kerrigan may be said to represent this tendency.

In his massively researched *Shakespeare's Binding Language*, John Kerrigan refers frequently to the prohibition of oaths in the Sermon on the Mount. His initial citation of the text is characteristic of his approach: "For now, it is enough to notice that it [Matthew 5:33–37] marks a break in Judaeo-Christian tradition that could not be entirely resolved by such texts as 'Against Swearying and Periury.'"[27] It should be noted that Kerrigan is a formidable and tough-minded critic who does not hesitate to expose the deficiencies of the scholars who precede him. And while it would be captious to impugn his knowledge of Christianity on such slender grounds as his attributing the Epistle to the Hebrews to Saint Paul,[28] his intellectual milieu is nonetheless one where the many readers credited in his preface did not spot an error that would strike a Christian scholar immediately. My main concern is that, for Shakespeare, it was fundamentally impossible for "such texts as 'Against Swearying and Peri-ury'" ever to resolve what Kerrigan refers to as "a break in Judaeo-Christian

26. For the Wife of Bath and Falstaff, see, for example, Harold Bloom, *The Western Canon: The Books and Schools of the Ages*, 118–19, and E. Talbot Donaldson, *The Swan at the Well: Shakespeare Reading Chaucer*, 129–39. Poole documents Rabelais's influence on the anti-Martinist Thomas Nashe (Poole, *Radical Religion*, 26). For more on Rabelais, see Anne Lake Prescott, who suggests Rabelais's direct influence on the Shakespeare of *King Lear*, but who argues more generally for Rabelais as a cultural force: "Spenser and his imitators were less likely to mention Rabelais than were Ben Jonson and his tribe . . . [Rabelais] was more likely to find explicit notice among the swaggering young, the self-consciously masculine, the cosmopolitan elite, and people with a touch of what was to be called a 'libertin' mentality." Anne Lake Prescott, *Imagining Rabelais in Renaissance England*, 136–38, x.

27. John Kerrigan, *Shakespeare's Binding Language*, 12.

28. Kerrigan, *Shakespeare's Binding Language*. The error is not uncommon. See Marjorie Garber, *Shakespeare After All*, 174.

tradition." It was characteristic of Shakespeare to be extremely sensitive to Christian hypocrisy in "such texts." Kerrigan, by contrast, presents as a fairly minor consideration what was actually a defining turn. He is insensitive to the fact that Christ's command is *sui generis*. It stands apart not only from the norms of Judaism, but from those of Islam, Hinduism, and Buddhism as well. It is not at home in any political dispensation. It signifies not so much "a break" from Judaism as a radical departure, something hard and uncompromising: "For whatsoever is more than these, cometh of evil." Cummings's reminder that, in 1583, "Archbishop Whitgift revived the practice of *ex officio* swearing in order to inveigle Presbyterian sectaries into giving themselves away"[29] underscores the reality that those dissenting sectaries were honoring a distinctly Christian imperative.

For the Shakespeare of the *Henriad*, it was everyman's Christian destiny to fail to align the kingdom of God and the kingdom of England—as a Christian Caesar, King Henry V would be the fleeting exception. For the Elizabethans, more generally, this spiritual dilemma meant either dying a martyr's death (an unpopular option), or, more commonly, experiencing qualms of conscience in the face of official pressures. Matthew 5:33–37 retained its power to disturb regardless of where one fell on the religious spectrum. For this reason, I hesitate to identify Falstaff too narrowly as a vehicle of Shakespeare's "rabid anti-puritanism."[30] Whitgift's cynical maneuvering suggests how the state could "corrupt a saint" (1H4 1.2.90), but we should bear in mind that difficult compromises were everywhere. They were the order of the day, a fact of life for the Elizabethan compromise and its Elizabethan compromisers. When Falstaff called it a "bad world" (2.4.130), he was addressing its universal badness. The particular joke might have been on the godly, but the universal joke resonated with all the Lord's hypocrites.[31]

Before examining the rash of false oaths that characterizes *Richard II*, I want to go a little further on the subject of historical Christianity and its challenges to Shakespeare criticism. In this spectacular drama written entirely in verse, Shakespeare's exposure of oath-breaking, of the raw violence of Richard's overthrow, of the brutal deposition and assassination of a duly

---

29. Brian Cummings, *Mortal Thoughts: Religion, Secularity & Identity in Shakespeare and Early Modern England*, 153.

30. Lake, *How Shakespeare Put Politics*, 587.

31. "Aristotle himself . . . says that Poetry is *philosphoteron* and *spoudaioteron*, that is to say, it is more philosophical and more studiously serious than history. His reason is, because poesy dealeth with *katholou*, that is to say, with the universal consideration, and the history with *kathekaston*, the particular." Sir Philip Sidney, *An Apology for Poetry*, ed. Geoffrey Shepherd, 109.

"anointed" king, might be read as a bleak and unsparing satire on the divinity of Christian kingship, centering on the triumph of Bolingbroke—whether understood as a schemer or an opportunist—and extending to the mundane changeableness, self-justification, and toadying of lesser men. In a sense, the play's form, its symmetrical arrangement, ritualistic patterns, and lapidarian prosody, provides a glittering foil to its dark content. Study of *Richard II* may lead us to conclude that more affinity exists between Shakespeare and Nietzsche than between Shakespeare and Paul or Luther. Even if we grant the historical interest of Paul's command against rebellion (a comment on Matthew 22:21, i.e., Caesar's coin), "Let every soul be subject unto the higher powers: for there is no power but of God: & the powers that be, are ordained of God" (Romans 13:1); even if we grant that the play invites historical questions about passive obedience and the divine right of kings, yet we may remain indifferent to the Christian nature of the work as a whole. From our perspective, Shakespeare could have raided the Bible purely for "aesthetic" purposes, while the doctrine of divine right, and Richard II's absurd belief in it, may seem no more than the excrescences of a dead religion.[32] The more we are committed to a post-Christian version of Shakespeare, the likelier we are to catch hints of modern nihilism in the brutal tale of Richard's fall.

And yet, though such hints may seem discernable, they occur only if we amputate Shakespeare's biblical worldview. To Shakespeare's Bible-reading contemporaries, Paul's command against rebellion gathered up a great knot of textual connections.[33] The Geneva Bible with its running cross-references is itself a kind of sacred hypertext, which, to risk understating the case, strongly attracted the most intensely biblical of the major Elizabethan playwrights. The Christian meekness enjoined by Paul in Romans 13:1 extends the spirit of the Beatitudes (Matthew 5:3–12). It is grounded in Jewish teaching (Wisdom: 6:1–3) and sustained by the First Letter of Peter (2:13–17 and 3:13). As the Tudor homilies make clear, Paul's injunction can be connected to David's refusal to take the life of Saul (see below). At the same time, Romans 13:1 meshes with any number of other statements by Paul, including

---

32. For the doctrine's major characteristics, see John Neville Figgis, *The Divine Right of Kings*, 5–6. I am indebted in this sentence to Figgis's exceptionally brilliant opening pages.

33. Figgis lists the following related texts: 1 Sam. 7:10–18; Prov. 8:15; Dan. 4; Luke 20:25; John 19:11; 1 Pet. 2:13–17; and Ps. 51:4, the last being a "favorite argument to prove that kings are accountable to God alone." *The Divine Right of Kings*, 7–8. For the Elizabethans' variegated reception of Romans 13:1–7, see Thomas Fulton, "Political Theology from the Pulpit and the Stage: *Sir Thomas More*, *Richard II*, and *Henry V*," in *The Bible on the Shakespearean Stage: Cultures of Interpretation in Reformation England*, ed. Thomas Fulton and Kristen Poole.

two key instances. First, though less obviously, there are the remarks (frequently cited in this book) from his writings to the church at Corinth, regarding the subversion of worldly wisdom by Christian folly. Second, there are his providence-oriented remarks to the Athenians on the fate of nations (Acts 17:26–27).

Providence and Politics

Shakespeare's biblical grasp of providence holds throughout the *Henriad*, being essential to its grand design. If we are Elizabethans, we always know that, behind the spectacular action, providence is going about its business. Being unable to grasp how or why it is doing so, observing the apparent godlessness on display before us, we encounter the precariousness of our knowledge. But this abiding condition of ignorance is (as I have argued) unrelated to modern nihilism. Quite the opposite is true. The providential aspect of Romans 13:1 subjects English history to Shakespeare's riddles of inversion, forcing his audience to interrogate their apparent knowledge and their apparent good.

Shakespeare's scrupulous handling of providence is characteristic of his skeptical mind; his resistance to propaganda is characteristic of his respect for truth. The study of providence required a capacity for skepticism, not about God's having a plan, but about our ability to know it. Providence was shamelessly politicized during the Tudor period. In Thomas More's *History of King Richard III,* a work at once Christian and skeptical, and a known influence on Shakespeare, the author puts an appeal to "God's special providence" into Richard's lying mouth.[34] A related issue was the status of miracles, a sub-branch of providence that remained tensely unresolved in the sixteenth century. A certain skepticism toward miracles, though often taken as a touchstone of Shakespeare's post-Christian sensibility,[35] was nothing new. More, whose Utopians "venerate miracles,"[36] had great success mocking the future Richard III's attempt to stage a miracle at Paul's Cross.[37] The Reformation's general decree against miracles, despite its efficiencies in winnowing Roman Catholics from Protestants, never gained absolute sway over Protestant clergymen.[38] Protestant zealots, in par-

34. Thomas More, *History of King Richard III,* in *Richard III: The Great Debate: Sir Thomas More's History of King Richard III [and] Horace Walpole's Historic Doubts on the Life and Reign of King Richard III,* ed. Paul Murray Kendall, 99.

35. See, for example, Richard C. McCoy, *Faith in Shakespeare,* 46, 141–43.

36. Thomas More, *Utopia,* ed. and trans. Robert M. Adams, 82.

37. More, *History of Richard III,* 87–88.

38. See Alexandra Walsham, *Providence in Early Modern England,* 226–32.

ticular, had "natural recourse to notions of providence and of direct intervention in the human world described under that rubric."[39] In general, one could
still swear by a miracle, *if it were true*.[40] Hence the problem of "seeming knowledge" (AWW 2.3.4–5). Shakespeare comments ambiguously on the Reformation
by putting the official Protestant line on miracles into the mouth of a Catholic
Archbishop of Canterbury: "miracles are ceased" (H5 1.1.68). The simplest
explanation for such a move is that Shakespeare was anticipating Henry V's
miraculous victory over the French, and using it to expose a faithless and schem-
ing prelate, in this case a Catholic. I think this is right but would further suggest,
given the deliberate anachronism, that the more general problem of authoritative
pronouncements about providence, rather than specific Catholic or Protestant
instances, also comes under scrutiny.

I sense that, by now, my prioritizing of religion over politics in the *Henriad*
will have raised a few hackles. Two noted political thinkers, Allan Bloom and
Harry Jaffa, saw the history plays very differently, reading them in a neo-Aris-
totelian light. They saw Shakespeare as constructing a world of "political
heroes": "the dramatist who wishes to represent man most perfectly will
usually choose political heroes. Because of his artistic freedom, he can paint
his figures more characteristically, less encumbered by fortuitous traits, than
can a historian."[41] Tim Spiekerman in *Shakespeare's Political Realism* has
advanced Bloom's position in a reading of the *Henriad* that, privileging Shakespeare's presumed insights into the political reality behind religion, rides
roughshod over Shakespeare's skeptical technique.[42] A major force in Spiekerman's book is Machiavelli, whose contempt for conscience, which "is not
directly treated in classical philosophy,"[43] betrays a classical bias that distorts
Shakespeare's ideas and meanings. More recently, James Knowles has high-
lighted the Elizabethan reception of Lucan, Tacitus, and Machiavelli, in order
to present *1 Henry IV* as essentially a political commentary, devoid of religious
content. For Knowles, the "play articulates a bleak critique of aristocratic culture and the possibilities of political action where militarism and terror out-
strip debate and law."[44] This vein of interpretation is too thin, I say, because

39. Lake, "Religious Identities," 79.
40. See the fascinating though slightly outdated essay by Robert Weston Babcock, "Saints'
Oaths in Shakespeare's Plays," *The Shakespeare Association Bulletin* 6 (July 1931): 86–100.
41. Allan Bloom with Harry V. Jaffa, *Shakespeare's Politics*, 9.
42. Spiekerman, *Shakespeare's Political Realism*, 59–152.
43. Timothy Potts, *Conscience in Medieval Philosophy*, 1.
44. James Knowles, "*1 Henry IV*," in *A Companion to Shakespeare's Works: The Histories*, ed. Richard Dutton and Jean E. Howard, 416.

Knowles promotes a "rational attitude"[45] that Shakespeare discredits. I will return to this point of controversy, which concerns both Shakespeare's approach to providential action and his Christian skepticism about instrumental thinking.

The distinguished historian Peter Lake has pronounced upon "the gulf separating 'politics' from 'religion'" in the two tetralogies.[46] The thematic use of oaths in the *Henriad* flies in the face of this bold assertion. So, too, does Jean-Christophe Mayer's observation that the "plays containing the most allusions to religion in the whole of the Shakespearean corpus are the dramatist's English history plays."[47] What I especially maintain, however, is that Shakespeare's universalism owes more to Christianity's inherent suspicion of politics, and to its explicit call for radical self-criticism, than it owes to political philosophy or to partisanship. We cannot verify whether or not Queen Elizabeth said, "know you not I am Richard II"—her alleged response to the staging of a play performed by Shakespeare's company, the Lord Chamberlain's Men, on the eve of the Essex rebellion in February, 1601.[48] We cannot even verify that the play in question was Shakespeare's. Granted, it is a politically impressive fact that the deposition scene was omitted from the three quartos of *Richard II* published in Elizabeth's lifetime. No doubt it resonated. I am not for a moment denying Shakespeare's great interest in the political situation around him. Unlike the New Historicists, I think that "Shakespeare is an author from whom we can learn something significant about politics."[49] But I deny that "the struggle for political power is the central concern" of the English history plays.[50] That it is an indispensable concern, I do not doubt. It is an impressive surface. But "central" is more than a little wrong: it is entirely misleading.

To follow Lake, we may ask, did politics in the 1590s eclipse the abiding religious concerns of the theater-going public? How deeply was Shakespeare impacted by the political crisis that attended the heirless Queen's final decade? By speculating on Shakespeare's ties to Robert Devereux, Second Earl of Essex, Lake connects the playwright to a cross-denominational milieu in which "the important thing was not so much men's religious beliefs but their political

45. Knowles, "*I Henry IV*," 429.

46. Lake, *How Shakespeare Put Politics*, 600.

47. Jean-Christophe Mayer, "Providence and Divine Right," in *The Cambridge Companion to Shakespeare and Religion*, ed. Hannibal Hamlin, 151.

48. See Lake, *How Shakespeare Put Politics*, 266–67, and Mayer, "Providence and Divine Right," 163.

49. Spiekerman, *Shakespeare's Political Realism*, 4.

50. Spiekerman, *Shakespeare's Political Realism*, 9.

loyalties."[51] From one point of view among others, this may be true. But Lake's analysis, for all his superb erudition, betrays an impulse to reduce Shakespeare's writings to a story in which Essex's career predominates. Lake searches the plays for "contemporary resonances," which is to say, for circumstantial evidence to support his case. No doubt he supports it. But Shakespeare presents a wealth of circumstantial evidence for anybody capable of picking out a rabbit or a duck. And, in the end, any critic whose approach boils down to the decoding of particulars will lack the means of identifying Shakespeare's universal appeal.

Consider Shakespeare's famous description of Henry V comparing him as a "conquering Caesar" to "the General of our gracious Empress" (H5 5.0.28 and 30). This compliment to Essex is both serious and superficial. It is serious because it is patriotic. Shakespeare and his company are wishing Essex success in the Irish wars and honoring the Queen. It is superficial because it is patriotic. The glory of the world takes a palpable hit when Christianity asserts its moral authority: "Render unto Caesar. . . ." As a "lower" type of Caesar (H5 5.0.29), the figure of Essex in *Henry V* is not impervious to the profound Christian ambivalence toward Caesar. What we experience is a layered form of perception that goes deeper even than the massive fissures occasioned by the Reformation. Expressive of historical continuity, not historical rupture, the figure of Essex, like the *Henriad* itself, is Shakespeare's means of considering and managing new experience, of reappraising the world in serious, Christian terms. The reader misunderstands me who infers that Shakespeare was writing to defend either Roman Catholic or Protestant orthodoxy. He was not. As he writes in Sonnet 110 ("Alas, 'tis true, I have gone here and there"), he was prone to looking "on truth / Askance and strangely" (5–6). Confessing pride and error, the poet swears "by all above" (6) that, even as his "blenches" (7; i.e., his times of straying) kept him young, experience taught him to see his "best of love" (8) in right relation to his personal salvation ("my heaven," 13). If we read the figure of Essex as one of the poet's "worse essays" (8), or simply as one of his "essays," such writing takes its place in a work of Christian mimesis. In other words, it idolizes neither politics nor the self and its desires, but defers like Sonnet 110 to an ultimate jurisdiction.

As we saw with Hotspur's amusement at middle-class manners, the *Henriad* blends historical and contemporary references. I agree with Mayer's remark that Shakespeare's drama "seeks to establish a dialogue between an

---

51. Lake, *How Shakespeare Put Politics*, 586.

ideologically conflicted past and a religiously and politically troubled present."[52] A case in point is Richard's faith in the divine right of kings, which touches pre-Reformation debates between king and parliament, as well as Reformation debates between king and pope.[53] We are met with more than a light smattering of historical interconnections. But what was the purpose of the "dialogue" that Mayer observes? The political purposes that it had, I suggest, were secondary to, and shaped by, the Christian humanist means by which Shakespeare inquired into the battle for secular power. Shakespeare's goading his audience to recognize the limits of their historical and spiritual knowledge correlates to his biblical grasp of providence. His lesson for them emerges through his epistemological technique, which is to maintain a skeptical distance from major inferences of cause and effect. These rhetorical topics of invention might serve a historian's purposes or a lawyer's, but they cannot produce an account of human motives, or of events themselves, remotely equivalent to God's. This skepticism combines with Christian theology and historical parallelism to structure the playwright's crisscrossing between times. It is Shakespeare's Christian skepticism, in particular, that shapes his historical consciousness of, and his ambivalence toward, the Reformation, its causes and effects, its antecedents and consequences.

Richard II

Two characters appear on stage. One of them, King Richard, opens the play by addressing the other, who is his uncle and his liegeman: "Old John of Gaunt, time-honored Lancaster, / Hast thou according to thy oath and bond / Brought hither Henry Hereford, thy bold son. . . ?" (R2 1.1.1–3). Richard's sonorous appeal to his kinsman's "oath and bond" launches a theme that will carry us into all four plays of the *Henriad*. This is not the ideal realm of Erasmus's *Education of a Christian Prince*, where the prince honors his baptismal vows to renounce Satan and all his works, and where the people, swearing their allegiance to a benevolent and rightful prince, distrust "actors in a drama who come on the stage decked with all the pomp of state."[54] Thomas More had likewise advanced the unflattering metaphor of state and stage.[55] In fact, we are close to the world that Shakespeare absorbed from More's *History of King*

---

52. Mayer, "Providence and Divine Right," 165.

53. See Groves, *Texts and Traditions*, 93.

54. Erasmus, *The Education of a Christian Prince*, ed. Lisa Jardine, trans. Neil M. Cheshire and Michael J. Heath, 17.

55. More, *History of Richard III*, 101.

Richard III, a world that many scholars have charted with Machiavellian equip-ment.[56] It is, for our purposes, an anti-Erasmian realm where, as Anne Righter points out by way of Erasmus,[57] one's ability to act the part and look "like a king" (3.3.68) paves the way to political success.[58] In this theatrical setting, oaths take their place as rhetorical utterances, intended to persuade. They are subject to rhetorical classification as types of testimony, such as *orcos*, "affirming that one speaks the truth"; *euche*, "a vow to keep a promise"; and *eustathia*, "a pledge of constancy."[59] To leap ahead for a moment, Bardolph in his brief role as the peacemaker lays the most stress on euche: "He that strikes the first stroke, I'll run him up to the hilts, as I am a soldier" (H5 2.1.64–66). Pistol replies: "An oath of mickle might" (67), signaling that oaths were dramatic currency—and that Pistol might have attended a few performances of *Richard II*.

Since Shakespeare's kings are stage actors, their oaths garnish their lines. What we witness in the opening scene of *Richard II* is a burst of rhetorical showmanship, intended to be taken as such. His well-staged display of trust in Gaunt serves Richard's political end of consolidating his power. That being accomplished, the King summons two other men into his royal presence. On receiving their compliments, Richard remarks: "We thank you both. Yet one but flatters us" (R2 1.1.25). Their deep-sworn, mutual recriminations are, as the King goes on to point out, of "high treason" (27). We detect hypocrisy on a grand scale, but we don't know where to assign guilt. The defendant in the case is Thomas Mowbray, Duke of Norfolk. The accuser is Henry Bolingbroke, Duke of Hereford, heir to his father's dukedom of Lancaster, and first cousin to the King. In question is Mowbray's role in the death of Thomas of Wood-stock, Duke of Gloucester, the late uncle both of Richard and of Bolingbroke.

Lurking in the background is the suggestion that the King and Mowbray were plotting together against Gloucester, but we never really know. John Dover Wilson notes that, in *Richard II*, the circumstances of Gloucester's death remain obscure, the facts barely surfacing in the play: "Yet strangely enough Shakespeare makes no attempt to place the audience in possession of these facts."[60] We may prefer, with Dover Wilson, to attribute this gap to compres-sion or distortion "in the process of revision," or to an inconsistent blending

---

56. See, for example, Spiekerman, *Shakespeare's Political Realism*.

57. Anne Righter, *Shakespeare and the Idea of a Play*, 113 (see Chapter 1).

58. Righter, *Shakespeare and the Idea of a Play*, 111.

59. Miriam Joseph, CSC, *Shakespeare's Use of the Arts of Language*, 103–105.

60. John Dover Wilson, introduction to *King Richard II*, by William Shakespeare, ed. John Dover Wilson, lxvii.

"of two or more varying accounts" among the sources materials.[61] Or, to follow a line of thinking established by the fine Australian critic Wilbur Sanders, who refers to Shakespeare's political "agnosticism," we may suspect that Shakespeare intended to imply something more disturbing about the historical record.[62] "For thy records and what we see doth lie," he wrote of "Time" in Sonnet 123 (11). If Time's "records" rely on the truth-telling capacities of human beings, that is, on oaths, vows, and other forms of human testimony, it can be little surprise if truth does not prevail.

It is my suggestion that Shakespeare came to regard the historical record as grounds for a skeptical response, a *"Que sçay je?"*[63] that, in turn, implies our weak knowledge of reality, common ignorance of the facts, and ready capacity for rationalizing our preferences and desires. More had commented, in his *History of King Richard III*, on how "men out of hatred report above the truth."[64] In the opening scene of *Richard II*, Bolingbroke and Mowbray are both keenly aware of this problem. Both respond to it by invoking God as their witness. Bolingbroke begins his suit to the King: "First—heaven be the record to my speech!— / In the devotion of a subject's love, / Tend'ring the precious safety of my prince, / And free from other misbegotten hate, / Come I appellant to this princely presence" (1.1.30–34). Shakespeare knows what Bolingbroke knows: "misbegotten hate" corrupts the "record." Mowbray, for his part, stoutly rejects Bolingbroke's version of events. First, he swears by the cruciform hilts of his "knighthood" (78–79). Then he speaks directly to the point: "Oh, let my sovereign turn away his face / And bid his ears a little while be deaf, / Till I have told this slander of his blood / How God and good men hate so foul a liar!" (1.1.111–14). Thus "hate" answers "hate."

In terms of the sources for *Richard II*, if Shakespeare drew on two French manuscripts, the anonymous *Chronicque de la Traïson et Mort de Richart Deux Roy Dengleterre* and the *Histoire du Roy d'Angleterre Richard*, by Jean Créton, he would have encountered a strong anti-Lancastrian flavor that is alien to his main source, Holinshed's *Chronicles*. Naseeb Shaheen, ranging over all known and contested sources for the play, makes the following case: "the

---

61. Wilson, introduction, lxviii.

62. Wilbur Sanders, *The Dramatist and the Received Idea: Studies in the Plays of Marlowe and Shakespeare*, esp. 158–93. Sanders defines "agnosticism": "not a retreat from moral responsibility, but a refusal to accept moral-oversimplifications" (190); and again: "a breaking down of all simple one-way attitudes" (193). Sanders suggests that the "barren controversies" of Tudor political debate may have sensitized Shakespeare to contradiction in his source material (153).

63. Michel de Montaigne, *The Complete Works*, trans. Donald M. Frame, 477 and 477n38.

64. More, *History of Richard III*, 35.

emphasis on Richard's betrayal as being parallel to Christ's occurs only in the *Traïson*, in Créton, and in Shakespeare, and Shakespeare's inspiration for that parallel evidently came from them."[65] Leaving the matter open, we remark a further discrepancy between historical sources in their conflicting portrayals of Gloucester. Gloucester is the moral hero of *Thomas of Woodstock*, a play Shakespeare had absorbed when he wrote *Richard II*. Its favorable portrait of Gloucester jars against the unfavorable portrait by George Ferrers in the *Mirror for Magistrates* (1559), a book Shakespeare is "generally assumed to have known . . . well, and from an early date."[66] Another accepted source, Samuel Daniel's *First Fowre Bookes of the Civile Wars* (1595), has Mowbray (who is absent from *Thomas of Woodstock*) arranging Gloucester's death by strangling; Bolingbroke denigrating the King to Mowbray; and Mowbray snitching on Bolingbroke to the King.[67] As a general matter that extends to the career of Richard II, Holinshed was aware of what he called "variance in writers."[68] Geoffrey Bullough presents a scholarly account of this intricate discord among the sources.[69] In my view, the discord generated a sensible fog, which Shakespeare allowed to linger in his play, to seep ironically into the vaunting assurances of rival oaths and to resist the audience's visceral push for judgment and satisfaction.

To manage the crisis erupting before him, and to maintain his pretense to fairness, Richard makes "a vow" (119) of impartiality toward his kinsman Bolingbroke—a vow he will break. He and Gaunt fail to pacify the two rivals. Mowbray, having sworn by his "sword" and by "God," respectfully refuses his liege lord's request that he return Bolingbroke's gage: "dear my liege, mine

---

65. Shaheen, *Biblical References*, 361. The point is contested. While Shaheen positively identifies both the *Chronicque* and Créton's *Histoire* as secondary sources, attributing the former to "a member of Queen Isabella's entourage" (Shaheen, *Biblical References*, 361), Bullough is warier (*Narrative and Dramatic Sources*, 3:369–72). Citing the authority of Holinshed, Maurice Hunt advances another factor in the comparison between Richard and Christ: "Shakespeare almost certainly knew that King Richard II . . . was thirty-three years old when he died." By means of numerological analysis, Hunt argues that Richard's prison soliloquy (5.5.1–66) "complicates, even undercuts, Richard's association with Christ." I prefer "complicates," since, contrary to the (possible) suggestion of *undercuts entirely*, we lack grounds to abrogate Richard's Christological and martyrological associations, and we have ambiguous grounds to retain them. Maurice Hunt, "Christian Numerology in Shakespeare's *The Tragedy of King Richard the Second*," *Christianity and Literature* 60 (Winter 2011): 231, 236.

66. Stuart Gillespie, *Shakespeare's Books: A Dictionary of Shakespeare's Sources*, 339. See also Robert S. Miola, *Shakespeare's Reading*, 168.

67. Bullough, *Narrative and Dramatic Sources*, 3:373.

68. Raphael Holinshed, quoted in *Thomas of Woodstock or King Richard the Second, Part One*, by Anonymous, ed. Peter Corbin and Douglas Sedge, 206.

69. See especially the headnote in Bullough, *Narrative and Dramatic Sources*, 3:353–54.

honor let me try" (184). Similarly determined, and disinclined to honor his
father, Bolingbroke, having previously invoked "heaven," proceeds to name
"God" as his witness that he will not relent: "Oh, God defend my honor from
such deep sin!" (187). The rivals are equally fervent in their self-defense, and
"God" gets quite a workout. Ultimately, Richard defers to Mowbray and Bolingbroke by resorting to medieval means: trial by combat, scheduled for the
Feast of Saint Lambert. The King appears to recognize the claims of chivalric
honor and "the independence of the aristocracy from royal interference."[70]
But it is not strange that dishonor wins the day, since trial by combat appeals
to the jurisdiction of divine powers that have been greatly provoked.

The tension at court translates physically to the combat scene, which
Shakespeare imbues with a seemingly sacred aura, as if the tilting field were
a Holy of Holies: "On pain of death, no person be so bold / Or daring-
hardy as to touch the lists" (1.3.42–43). Glittering with heralds and trumpets,
the scene appears to be building toward a resolution that will dispel the
murk. Will justice prevail? Will God make his will known? Richard arranges
a grand, echoing display of oaths that travel from his own command
(1.3.10), to formulaic interrogatories by the Marshal (11–15), to the formulaic, sworn deposition of Mowbray (16–25), back to the King (30), on to
the Marshal for another round of interrogatories (31–34), and concluding
with the formulaic, sworn deposition of Bolingbroke (35–41). It is curious
to consider that, as we hear later, the young Jack Falstaff was Mowbray's
"page" (2H4 3.24–26). The future Lord of Misrule, who, like Mowbray,
swears "by these hilts" (1H4 2.4.204), must have found all this traditional
folderol highly instructive.

Its anticlimax is a marvel. Without warning, the pageantry fizzles as Richard intervenes. In an astonishing turn of events, the King cancels the match,
profligately destroying his prior investment in ceremonial language, and possibly—it is the theory maintained by Mowbray's unfortunate son—guaranteeing his royal destruction (2H4 4.1.123–29). The next scene, when Richard
wishes aloud for Gaunt's death, will clarify the King's motives. But when he
abruptly interrupts the trial by combat, he manifests the tyrant in his nature.
Turning their potential goodness as Christian knights against the combatants,
Richard exploits their chivalrous fealty to God and King by making it the
means to secure their exile, subjecting them in their woe to yet a further
round of oaths:

70. Knowles, "*I Henry IV*," 423.

Return again, and take an oath with thee.
Lay on our royal sword your banished hands.
[*They place their hands on Richard's sword.*]
Swear by the duty that you owe to God—
Our part therein we banish with yourselves—
To keep the oath that we administer.

(R2 1.3.178–82)

In his alternation of "Return" and "banish," the King plays the *fort/da* game like a spoilt child. Then, like a cruel stage-director, he bids the men to swear on his cruciform "royal sword" and "by the duty" they "owe to God." He assumes the royal "we," invoking the King's Two Bodies and the doctrine of divine right.[71] As regards Shakespeare's sense of this doctrine, we agree with Sanders: "Shakespeare, by placing the advocacy of the old divine kingship in the hands of the unstable Richard and the older generation of statesmen, reveals his awareness that it can no longer stand unqualified."[72] With a pathetic air of personal sacrifice, the King releases Bolingbroke and Mowbray from "the duty" they owe him as their sovereign (his "part therein"). Only he says, "Our part therein," continuing to wield his sacred kingship while indulging his godlessness. Bolingbroke and Mowbray swear obediently, even as each man vehemently maintains his cause. It was, I suggest, not only nonconforming Puritans who would have gotten the message that the Sermon on the Mount had fallen on deaf ears in England.

To the extent that *Richard II* has a satirical aspect, parading the ghastly ease with which those of noble rank violate their oaths, *The Education of a Christian Prince* supplies the standard or normative frame for the satire, the moral high ground that is conspicuously lacking: "The good faith of princes in fulfilling their agreements must be such that a simple promise from them will be more sacred than any oath sworn by other men."[73] As historian Margo Todd has observed, Erasmus was in his soul a republican who detested the hereditary nobility, viewing it as at best a necessary evil. For Erasmus, kings

---

71. For *Richard II* and the doctrine of the King's Two Bodies, see Ernst H. Kantorowicz, *The King's Two Bodies*, 24–41. For a political and historical critique of Kantorowicz, see David Norbrook, "The Emperor's New Body? *Richard II*, Ernst Kantorowicz, and the Politics of Shakespeare Criticism," *Textual Practice* 10 (Summer 1996): 329–57. In Norbrook's view, "the ideal imperial body . . . has acquired a mystical status out of proportion to its historical significance" (343). For other views, see Spiekerman, *Shakespeare's Political Realism*, 72.

72. Sanders, *Dramatist and the Received Idea*, 149.

73. Erasmus, *Education of a Christian Prince*, 94.

and their ilk were aristocratic pirates and brigands, wholly inimical to the philosophy of Christ. This critique surfaces sharply in the *Adages*. In *The Education of a Christian Prince*, it defines the contrasting ethos against which the Christian prince must strive.[74] While we cannot identify Erasmus's position with Shakespeare's, it is an important subtext. In my analysis, Shakespeare is more interested in the human reality of politics as opposed to exhorting princes and magistrates to lives of virtue. I think of him as more conservative than Erasmus, more inured to the Great Chain of Being. I do not think of the author of *Julius Caesar* as a republican. And yet he was well aware of Erasmus's acuity on these matters. His historical consciousness included his consciousness of Erasmus—an educated mode of reflection that habitually lent itself to the distancing effects of irony and satire.

A living relic of an earlier time, Gaunt in his upright behavior raises questions in our minds about whether virtue can survive in Shakespeare's Ricardian world. Arguing with Gloucester's widow, he maintains a policy of loyalty to the King that is higher, more principled, than the bereaved Duchess's call for revenge (1.2.35–36). Gaunt does not doubt Richard's involvement in Gloucester's death, but he suspends judgment as to Richard's guilt, leaving it to "heaven" to decide if and to what degree the deed was done "wrongfully" (39–40). Politically, he adheres to the doctrine of the divine right of kings: "Non-resistance and passive obedience are enjoined by God."[75] Consistent with this theory and its biblical grounding, Gaunt defers to Richard as "God's substitute," / His deputy anointed in His sight" (37–38). The sacramental word *anointed* carries weight—it occurs five times in *Richard II*. It savors of the *Homilies* and the Bible. In "An Exhortacion to Obedience," the word echoes ten times in five minutes' worth of reading.[76] The inevitable reference point, repeated in "An Homilie against Rebellion," is 1 Samuel (24:4 ff., 26:9–10), which tells of David's decision not to slay Saul, the Lord's anointed King, when Saul was unknowingly at David's mercy.[77] With a powerful show of

---

74. See Margo Todd, *Christian Humanism and the Puritan Social Order*, 183–87. Todd observes Erasmus's intellectual kinship, in this respect, to Thomas More and Thomas Starkey. We may add that More's *Utopia* is savagely satirical of Europe's hypocritical reliance on oaths as the basis of treaties, and that it builds toward a fierce riff on Augustine's comparison of states to great thieving mills (*City of God* 4.4). See More, *Utopia*, 70 and 89, as well as Robert Adams's editorial note, 89n3.

75. Figgis, *Divine Right*, 6. I have removed the original italics.

76. Bond, *Certain Sermons*, 165–66.

77. More generally, the providential narrative of Israel's nationhood inspired "the perennial tendency of the British to identify themselves with the Israelites," which Shakespeare found in his study of Holinshed and Hall. Steven Marx, *Shakespeare and the Bible*, 41.

biblical wisdom, Gaunt anchors the play in traditional principles of passive obedience that his King has recklessly exploited.

The grand old man dies not a warrior but a prophet. In response to the disastrous impact of Richard's misrule, Gaunt's role shifts from the active life to the spiritual life, from loyal liegeman to English Jeremiah. In the second act, following his son's exile, the dying Gaunt adopts the voice of a "prophet new inspired" (2.1.31). When the King arrives with his notorious retinue, Gaunt's speech grows authoritative and bold: "Yet he that made me knows I see thee ill" (2.1.93). Richard unwittingly dignifies Gaunt by calling him a "fool" (2.1.115), and the dying man answers by addressing the question of Richard's guilt. I note that King Edward III was Gaunt's father and Richard's grandfather: "My brother Gloucester, plain well-meaning soul— / Whom fair befall in heaven 'mongst happy souls!— / May be a precedent and witness good / That thou respect'st not spilling Edward's blood" (2.1.128–31). While Gaunt continues to respect the distance between heavenly and worldly knowledge, the word *witness*, with support from the surrounding vocabulary, makes pointed reference to God's jurisdiction over Richard. Gaunt's spiritual authority is further suggested through an elevation in style, both in the lines I have quoted and in the speech within which they are couched, as the blank verse swells with rhymes and near-rhymes.

In effect, the dramatist confirms a larger frame of reference, which the Elizabethans would have felt in their bones. He develops a stereoscopic framework of perception, glancing, as it were, "from heaven to earth, from earth to heaven" (MND 5.1.13), which I shall hereafter refer to (for lack of a better term) as *Christian ulteriority*. In a way analogous to how the stained glass windows at York Minster, or at St. Mary's church in the town of Fairford, in Gloucestershire (forty miles from Stratford), presented biblical scenes to his Elizabethan contemporaries,[78] the light of sacred history haunts Shakespeare's stage and its presentation of historical events. This is the primary sense of *ulteriority*: it refers to the intersection of sacred history and British history. It is active through prophecy, though such activity is always rhetorical, never evangelically pure. It is similarly evoked through the threat of Judgment. Accessed through touches of allegory, it operates, for example, when Bolingbroke compares Gloucester's "blood" to Abel's, naming the younger son who offered the firstling of his flock: hence "sacrificing Abel's" "blood" (R2

---

78. For many examples, see Oscar G. Farmer, *Fairford Church and Its Stained Glass Windows*, and Sarah Brown, *Stained Glass at York Minster*.

1.1.104);[79] or when, confronted with Richard's corpse, he compares the murderer, Exton, to Abel's fratricidal brother, Cain: "With Cain go wander in the shades of night" (5.6.43).[80] In a secondary sense, it may peep allusively into view whenever characters swear by God, or address divine law, or deliberate over matters of conscience, or say something that all or part of the audience hears spiritually.

This ulteriority, the interplay of complementary perspectives, is inherent to the Christian faith. What changes over time is the language-game and, relatedly, the psychological investment in the reality of this world vis-à-vis the next. The "medieval stage . . . was a glass held up towards the Absolute, reflecting the 'age and body of the time' only incidentally."[81] While Shakespeare's Christian ulteriority owes much to the medieval stage, the Shakespearean stage is less didactic and more mediated in its representations. The action bears a humanist stamp because sacred history illuminates but does not eclipse the world that Atlas carries on his shoulders. For instance, in *Richard II*, Gaunt prophetically refers to England as "[t]his other Eden" (2.1.42), and the choric Gardener of Act 3, Scene 4 confirms that Eden is not irredeemably lost. And yet England is not Eden. The existence of the sacred, with its providential and typological signs, continues to be revealed through history, but these mediated signs can be difficult or dangerous to grasp. To a strict Calvinist living in the world, only the elect, "directed wholly towards knowledge of and obedience to God," "have eyes to trace the workings of divine providence."[82] To Shakespeare's Christian humanist sensibility, the challenge is to navigate, as much as possible, the elusive whole of experience.

With Gaunt's death, the role of persevering in one's oath to the King falls chiefly to York, "the last of noble Edward's sons" (2.1.171). Acting as Lord Governor of England while the "anointed King" (2.3.96) is off slaughtering the Irish, York characterizes his divided loyalties—between Richard and Bolingbroke—in terms of his "oath" versus his "conscience":

> Both are my kinsmen:
> Th'one my sovereign, whom both my oath
> And duty bids defend; t'other again

---

79. As Adrian Streete observes, the use of the present participle is striking. See Adrian Streete, *Protestantism and Drama in Early Modern England*, 180.

80. "It is ironic that a course of action which [Bolingbroke] had initiated as the avenger of Abel . . . finds him at its conclusion the patron of Cain." Sanders, *Dramatist and the Received Idea*, 172.

81. Righter, *Shakespeare and the Idea*, 16.

82. Wilhelm Niesel, *The Theology of Calvin*, trans. Harold Knight, 68, 72.

> Is my kinsman, whom the King hath wronged,
> Whom conscience and my kindred bids to right.
>
> (2.2.110–115)

Tension between conscience and oath-taking was, as we have seen, intrinsic to the Elizabethan settlement. York maintains his Christian oath until it is, as it were, as exhausted as he is: "Things past redress are now with me past care" (2.3.171). Despite his eventually yielding to circumstances, his fortitude as regent highlights the difference between being true and being false to one's word. For a significant time, York stands for principle. He takes Richard impressively to task for looting Gaunt's estate. He half-commands, half-advises Bolingbroke and his supporters: "To find out right with wrong—it may not be" (2.3.144). He was not the only Englishman since Thomas à Becket to come to this conclusion. Refusing to swear the Oath of Supremacy, Thomas More told Lord Chancellor Thomas Audley: "I am not bound, my lord, to conform my conscience to the council of one realm against the general council of Christendom."[83] York and his conscience, which we find impossible to dismiss as a Machiavellian stage prop, are likewise caught between shifting contexts. Like More, though less bravely, York will eventually defy his "temporal Prince."[84] In Sonnet 115 ("Those lines that I have writ before do lie"), the poet reflects on "reckoning Time, whose millioned accidents / Creep in twixt vows and change decrees of kings. . . . Divert strong minds to th'course of alt'ring things" (5–8). These verses speak very well to York's situation. Shakespeare takes up the theme of "alteration" in the more famous Sonnet 116 ("Let me not to the marriage of true minds"): "Love is not love / Which alters when it alteration finds" (2–3). Not being "Time's fool," Love isn't fooled by the alterations of Time: "Love alters not with his brief hours and weeks, / But bears it out even to the edge of doom" (11–12). Richard declines and Bolingbroke rises. Right and wrong seem to reverse polarities. York's dilemma leaves no evident opening for systematic reasoning, or for the light of natural law,[85] or for a saving passage from the Bible. The legal contexts change, forcing conscience onto shifting ground. But above the flux of time and history, the unchanging higher reality signaled by "the edge

---

83. Thomas More, quoted in C. S. Lewis, *Studies in Words*, 203.

84. The phrase is More's. See Cummings, *Mortal Thoughts*, 71.

85. For natural law in the Thomistic tradition, see Quentin Skinner, *The Foundations of Modern Political Thought*, 2:148–53; for its emergent role in the Protestant tradition, see 2:320–21, as well as Robert E. Stillman, *Philip Sidney and the Poetics of Renaissance Cosmopolitanism*, 21–28.

of doom" cannot be altered. There will be a "reckoning." Our consciences may have reasoned wrongly.[86]

A most calculating political animal, Northumberland resembles one of Shakespeare's later creations, Antonio, the usurping Duke of Milan. Regarding conscience, Antonio proclaims, "I feel not / This deity in my bosom" (TMP 2.1.279–80). Like Antonio, the conscienceless Northumberland is set defiantly in his ways. He exemplifies the meanness of instrumental thinking. The excessive flattery with which he greets Bolingbroke (R2 2.3) indicates that his will is committed to vice. Richard in the opening scene has, in fact, alerted us to the devious practice of flattery. Later on, he and Gaunt exchange sharp words on the subject, in a lively piece of *stichomythia* (2.1.87–90) that prepares us for Northumberland's flattering usage of Bolingbroke. Northumberland's rhetoric shows him to be acutely sensitive to the politics of the situation, but we must always remember that it is the Elizabethans who are judging his words and actions: it is not Mussolini in the quiet of his study contemplating *The Prince*.

Northumberland's role as kingmaker will trouble the future Henry IV well beyond their upcoming political clash. Events move quickly: it is a question of relative, not absolute, mastery over them. When York decries Bolingbroke's "rebellion" (2.3.147), Northumberland unflinchingly replies:

> The noble Duke hath sworn his coming is
> But for his own, and for the right of that
> We all have strongly sworn to give him aid;
> And let him never see joy that breaks that oath!
>
> (2.3.148–151)

We may say with Charles Harold Herford that "Bolingbroke has in fact given no pledge and taken no oath," and that, at the same time, "Northumberland seeks merely to get possession of Richard, without committing his chief."[87] It is a solid suggestion: Northumberland might well be thinking on his feet in this way. To be scrupulous, though, we lack first-hand information about the reality or unreality of Bolingbroke's pledge or oath. Who really knows? Hotspur, parleying with Blunt near Shrewsbury, tells the story differently: "when he heard him swear and vow to God / He came but to be Duke of Lancaster.

---

86. A possible reference point: "What Aquinas cannot allow is that it is, not human sinfulness, but the nature of things or the divine will which generates tragedy." Alasdair MacIntyre, *Whose Justice? Which Rationality?*, 187.

87. Nineteenth-century critic Charles Harold Herford, quoted in Spiekerman, *Shakespeare's Political Realism*, 66–67.

. . . My father, in kind heart and pity moved, / Swore him assistance" (1H4 4.3.62–67). What we can say for certain is that "Northumberland's claim takes on a life of its own."[88] It is striking how fiercely the conspirators maintain this useful idea of Bolingbroke's "coming. . . . But for his own," a pursuit of justice (the "right") that circumvents their own oaths of fealty. Northumberland repeats the story before Flint Castle, as does Bolingbroke in the base court, when, with Richard submitting to his cousin's will, the game is basically up. Nor is that all. In *2 Henry IV*, Richard's successor, now ill and under emotional strain, while pleading his version of events to the sympathetic Warwick, garbles the timeline of Richard's famous prophecy: "Northumberland, thou ladder by the which / My cousin Bolingbroke ascends my throne" (2H4 3.1.70–71). The King follows this imperfect recital of Richard's prophetic words to Northumberland (see R2 5.1.55) with an oath (an instance of *orcos*, or affirming that one speaks the truth) that he desperately wants to believe: "Though then, God knows, I had no such intent" (2H4 3.1.72). What does he mean by "then"? It was in fact after his deposition that Richard uttered his prophetic words to Northumberland. Bolingbroke was already planning his "coronation" (R2 4.1.321). We infer that Henry IV is a man who cannot get his facts straight. In rhetorical terms, his *narratio* is false. Warwick, in his speech beginning "There is a history in all men's lives" (2H4 3.1.80), articulates a skepticism towards prophecy that is meant to boost the King's morale. But the ultimate Judge, as the King well knows, will have the relevant texts by heart.

Shakespeare challenges us to unravel this mighty skein of narrative threads. Hotspur, in his parley with Blunt, accuses Henry IV of having stepped "a little higher than his vow" to Northumberland (1H4 4.3.77), while exonerating Northumberland of guilt for having innocently trusted Bolingbroke in the first place. And yet Hotspur, at least in the latter respect, knows better, having rebuked his father and his uncle for their "unjust" (1.3.173) part in supplanting Richard and championing Bolingbroke. Worcester, pleading his case before Henry IV, airs the rebel army's grievances, repeating the point that Hotspur has just made to Blunt: "You swore to us, / And you did swear that oath at Doncaster / That you did nothing purpose 'gainst the state, / Nor claim no further than your new-fall'n right, / The seat of Gaunt, dukedom of Lancaster. / To this we swore our aid" (1H4 5.1.41–46). In his long speech, which is forensic in type, focusing on past actions and past wrongs, Worcester harps on this crucial oath, repeating the gravamen of his charge against the King: "violation

---

88. Spiekerman, *Shakespeare's Political Realism*, 67.

of all faith and troth / Sworn to us in your younger enterprise" (1H4 5.1.70–71). The King denies it. His lofty retort about adorning "the garment of rebellion" with "some fine color that may please the eye" (74–75) catches echoes of the homily "Against Disobedience and Wilfull Rebellion,"[89] a response to the Catholic uprising of 1569–70 and as fine a display of the Tudor Myth as one could ask of an English cleric.[90] Past hypocrisies and present hypocrisies dance a devilish jig. Worcester is likely correct when he denigrates the King's proffered friendship, telling his confederate Vernon: "It is not possible, it cannot be, / The King should keep his word in loving us" (1H4 5.2.4–5). There is (again) something hellish in this exile from love and truth.

The fall of Richard II was of course not a new tale to the English. Shakespeare's play was a variation on a well-known story. Theologically, from the perspective of Luther or Calvin, Shakespeare was staging a past action that was strictly predestined to occur. He wrote his plot in imitation of God's plot. To quote one of the Lord's more eloquent press secretaries, "Have you not heard that I determined it long ago?" (Isaiah 37:26). This uncanny analogy can hardly be avoided: as a man or woman is destined to enact God's providence, so an actor is destined to follow a script.

What, then, did Shakespeare's retelling of events really signify? Shakespeare did not dismiss the typical Renaissance conceit, evident in More's *History of King Richard III* and variously developed by Spenser, Jonson, and Raleigh, of history as an explicator of providence and a witness to moral truth. But only in a limited sense can I ascribe to the *Henriad* a view such as the following: "By displaying the moral pattern of cause and effect throughout time, history displays the way God's natural law works, vindicating its operation in the world. Thus history directs our conduct by providing us with examples to emulate and avoid."[91] Natural law is not absent from the *Henriad*, but it operates as one truth among others. It should not be confused with providence. Deferring to providence, Shakespeare does not insist on a clear "moral pattern of cause and effect." He is skeptical about his, or anyone's, power to do so. The pattern that starts at some undefinable point with the rebellion against Richard and that ends with Henry V's victory at Agincourt is too blurred by ambiguity to be interpreted as a straightforward demonstration of natural law. It is true that Shakespeare does not reward evil characters—he "directs our

---

89. See Shaheen, *Biblical References*, 423.
90. See Bond, introduction, 44.
91. Craig Bernthal, *The Trial of Man: Christianity and Judgment in the World of Shakespeare*, 3–4.

conduct" in that Johnsonian respect. But too strong an insistence on evidencing "God's natural law" runs the risk of reducing God to natural law: it is a problem that goes back to the schoolmen and evokes theological battles between the Dominicans and the Franciscans.[92]

Natural law implies (among other things) a strong view of practical reason as being able to distinguish good from evil. Some such reasoning capacity will seem proper to human beings, unless one is willing (as Shakespeare certainly was not) to abandon the concept of evil in favor of cultural relativism. On the other hand, Luther's position holds an element of psychological truth that Shakespeare undoubtedly recognized:

> At present people are beginning to praise natural law and natural reason as the source from which all written law has come and issued. This is true, of course, and the praise is well placed. But the trouble is, everyone likes to think that the natural law is encased in his head. . . . [Therefore] it is also a fact that among those who presume to have natural reason or natural law, and boast of it, there are very many great and efficient natural fools. The noble gem called natural law and reason is a rare thing among the children of men.[93]

It is a delightful passage, ironical and urbane, and I would suggest that Shakespeare also entertains a limited idea of the powers of practical reason and the lessons of natural law. The *Henriad* does not so much provide us with laboratory examples (to emulate and avoid) as with challenges to our self-knowledge, leaving us with moral perplexities, dilemmas, and much food for thought.

I am sympathetic to the picture presented by Robert G. Hunter, who breaks down the general problem of historical interpretation as follows:

> Luther and Calvin believe that our wills are not free. They also believe that the majority of us will spend our eternities in hell. . . . The divine justice which punishes a man who has no freedom of choice must be called mysterious if it is not to be called monstrous. . . . The mysteries which Shakespeare confronts in these plays remain mysteries when the plays are over and are, if anything, more profoundly disquieting than they were before his imaginative considerations of them."[94]

---

92. See Richard E. Rubenstein, *Aristotle's Children: How Christians, Muslims, and Jews Rediscovered Ancient Wisdom and Illuminated the Dark Ages*, 247–51.

93. Luther, quoted in R. S. White, *Natural Law in English Renaissance Literature*, 37. Cf. Brabantio's appeal to "all rules of nature" (OTH 1.3.103).

94. Robert G. Hunter, *Shakespeare and the Mystery of God's Judgments*, 1, 2. Though Hunter was not addressing the *Henriad*, his argument strikes me as relevant.

We can list a few of these mysteries, as we see them in the *Henriad*. Is human freedom active in the world? Or only the illusion of human freedom? What kind of light is natural law? What is our role in the face of God's mysterious power? Is history a spectacle of damnation, "chronicled in hell," to quote Sir Pierce of Exton (R2 5.5.116)? What is the meaning of history?

In all these respects, the career of Bolingbroke raises more questions than it answers. To discern good from evil is no easy matter where he is concerned. Addressing Richard in the base court, Bolingbroke rises from his knee to profess, "My gracious lord, I come but for my own" (3.3.196). This, as we have seen, is the party line. But does Bolingbroke himself know what he means by "my own"? A remark of More's is relevant here: "opportunity and likelihood of success put a man in courage of that he never intended."[95] Does Bolingbroke, in this respect, betray a lack of self-knowledge as to his intention? Is he the victim of flattery? Possibly it is calculating for the future King to appear to show fealty to the fallen King, whose image adorns English coins, including the "coin" of Gaunt's plundered estate (2.1.161). York will later compare Bolingbroke to "a well-graced actor" (5.2.24), a phrase ripe with the suggestion of duplicity. Being sensitive to "value" (2.3.19) and to the state of his "treasury" (2.3.60), Bolingbroke capitalizes on the practice of oath-making as a ready verbal means of exchange among his newfound allies. We soon learn, to his apparent credit, that he "has sworn to weed and pluck away . . . the caterpillars of the commonwealth . . . Bushy, Bagot, and their complices" (165–67). He goes on to order the executions of the King's councilors, Bushy and Green, *in the King's name.* Juxtaposed against Bolingbroke's successful manipulation of oaths, however, the prospect of divine wrath prods the Elizabethan conscience, which (perhaps surprising to some) had never heard of speech act theory.[96] In a Christian universe, because transcendent truth exists prior to the speech act, what is to be tried and tested is a character's ability to speak and to act freely in accordance with transcendent truth—a transcendence to which speech act theory does not subscribe. By denying or resisting transcendent truth, a character indicates a lack of freedom on his or her part, be it on account of pride or lust, or some other sin. In such instances, God's will is not done. If Gaunt was right, that "the tongues of dying men" (2.1.5) command

---

95. More, *History of Richard III*, 36.

96. "God is more important in the casuistical literature than in J. L. Austin's *How to Do Things with Words* (1962). But Shakespeare's use of binding language still has points of contact with Austin and with arguments between John Searle, Jacques Derrida, and Judith Butler on speech acts." Kerrigan, *Shakespeare's Binding Language*, 35.

attention, then Green's dying words cannot be dismissed out of hand: "My comfort is that heaven will take our souls / And plague injustice with the pains of hell" (3.1.33–34). This statement suggests that Bolingbroke is not acting on the side of truth and virtue. Its pathos is persuasive. Rightly or wrongly, it is prophetical. It sounds the mystery of God's will for England, a mystery that confronts the medieval past as well as the Tudor present.

But if this will is a mystery, why does it matter it all? Why not see it in a Machiavellian light as an illusion? After all, Machiavelli's counsel to the prince appears to be admissible: "because men are wretched creatures who would not keep their word to you, you need not keep your word to them."[97] My reply is that Shakespeare has much more interest in politics as drama than in politics as the end-all and be-all of human affairs. He is reserved but clear about the limits of political power. For instance, with superb economy, he uses the briefest of scenes to contrast the reach of providence against the reach of mortal sovereignty. We watch as Salisbury fails to convince the Welsh captain to keep his army together for "another day" (2.4.5). The scene lasts twenty-four lines—a numerical pun. The Welsh army defers to rumors and omens, and Richard's tardiness costs him his throne. The King arrives from Ireland, delivers his grand speech, "Not all the water in the rough rude sea, / Can wash the balm off an anointed king" (3.2.54–55), only to be bluntly informed by Salisbury: "One day too late" (3.2.67). Bolingbroke's impression notwithstanding—"Four lagging winters and four wanton springs / End in a word; such is the breath of kings" (1.3.214–15)—Richard's breath is no match for "contrarious winds" (1H4 5.1.52).

The mind of providence is like a black swan, trivializing our best calculations. Little is explained about this higher power, except that we must submit to it. It was a lesson that Shakespeare took from the Sermon on the Mount, including the Lord's Prayer, where the advent of God's kingdom is dependent on God's will being done, not ours. With rare exception, manifestations of providence in the *Henriad* are more puzzling than revelatory. Like Richard in his dungeon, setting "the word itself / Against the word" (5.5.13–14), we are stymied by contradictory signs. To the Gardener in York's garden (3.4), and to the Gardener's Man, who echoes Gaunt's "demi-paradise" speech, Richard is paying the inevitable price for his malfeasance. The garden allegory has considerable authority, but it is not the final word. To the Bishop of Carlisle, whose truth is valorized by his risking a martyr's death, Bolingbroke is a "foul

---

97. Niccolò Machiavelli, *The Prince*, trans. George Bull, 55.

traitor" (4.1.136). What we hear in this dramatic clash of perspectives is the sound of our own ignorance.

If Marx was right that "history repeats itself, the first time as tragedy, the second time as farce," we may find the play's opening quarrel to be reenacted as farce when, before Parliament, Bagot accuses Aumerle of Gloucester's murder. As a gloss on the disputatious opening, Act 4, Scene 1 overlays the entire action in grotesquery. Like Sanders, I find Shakespeare's art to be deliberate in this respect: "That this is a thematic development is made plain by its obvious parallel with the first scene—the tabling of accusations, the wordy warfare of challenge, and the visual parallelism provided by the down-flung gages."[98] Not to mention the snarling fastidiousness about rank—the scene is a hypocritical pageant of dishonorable honor-mongering. After Bagot makes his opportunistic accusation against Aumerle, we watch as Fitzwater, Percy (i.e., Hotspur), and another lord gang up against York's outnumbered son. They are competing for the patronage of Bolingbroke, who (like the Richard of 1.1) is dispensing justice of a kind. Shakespeare deliberately continues to withhold the circumstances of Gloucester's murder. To be clear: the presence of this scene, with its crude accusations, militates against "the case that if the audience assumes Richard's culpability (as shown in *Woodstock*), then 'his confused actions throughout Acts I and II' can be viewed as deriving from a guilt, or guilts, out of which there is no clear path."[99] Richard, in Shakespeare's telling, is connected to the evil of Gloucester's death, about which we possess no dispositive facts. We violate Shakespeare's skeptical technique by importing such facts into *Richard II* from *Thomas of Woodstock*, where each particular is known. Seemingly desirous to learn the truth, Bolingbroke proposes recalling Mowbray from exile, only to be informed by his enemy, the Bishop of Carlisle, that Mowbray has died a saintly death worthy of Chaucer's Knight: "Many a time hath banished Norfolk fought / For Jesu Christ in glorious Christian field" (4.1.93–94). If this was news to the Elizabethans, it was because "Shakespeare seems to have invented this colorful bit of Mowbray's history."[100] It certainly does not clarify the past.

With neither the pernicious sniping at Aumerle nor Mowbray's heroic death reflecting well on Bolingbroke, York enters the stage. He announces

---

98. Sanders, *Dramatist and the Received Idea*, 168.

99. Gillespie, *Shakespeare's Books*, 102; Gillespie is quoting A. P. Rossiter. Likewise, Spiekerman: "The historical King Richard was presumed to have been responsible for Gloucester's death and Shakespeare's audience would have taken this for granted." *Shakespeare's Political Realism*, 60.

100. William Shakespeare, *Richard II*, ed. Anthony B. Dawson and Paul Yachnin, 239n.

Richard's willingness to abdicate the throne and then proclaims, "long live Henry, fourth of that name!" (113). Bolingbroke's acceptance prompts Carlisle's towering rebuke:

> BOLINGBROKE   In God's name I'll ascend the regal throne.
> CARLISLE   Marry, God forbid!

It is the unfathomable crux of the matter: God's will versus man's. The bishop bravely condemns the proceedings, correctly prophesies civil war (cue the Wars of the Roses), and in very Christian, biblical, and typological terms condemns the rising gang's actions.[101] The gang now includes York, who, one might argue, relieves his guilt by projecting it onto his son, Aumerle. Though York voices the doctrine of passive obedience when he counsels his Duchess, "But heaven hath a hand in these events / To whose high will we bound our calm contents" (5.2.37–38), and though he refuses to be the "bawd" of his son's "vice" (5.3.67) when Aumerle proves loyal to Richard, York fails before moral demands that are beyond his powers of comprehension. Richard condemns Northumberland directly for "the deposing of a king / And cracking the strong warrant of an oath, / Marked with a blot, damned in the book of heaven" (4.1.236–37). Though he is never confronted to his face, York does not escape Richard's typological condemnation: "Though some of you, with Pilate, wash your hands, / Showing an outward pity, yet you Pilates / Have here delivered me to my sour cross / And water cannot wash away your sin" (4.1.240–43). York's latent resemblance to Pilate turns out to be significant. Both are shrewd governors of the realm who adjudicate the question of kingship. Both wish to "remain as neuter" (2.3.159). Neither can.

The determinations of providence continue to curtail the lessons of practical political philosophy. The Abbot's conspiracy to murder Henry IV and reclaim the crown for Richard II is not the work of miscreants. The men who die for their cause have kept their vows, sworn upon the "Sacrament" (4.1.329). York discovers their plot because he is shrewdly suspicious of a sealed document on the person of his son. Such contingencies, like the "contrarious winds" that caused Richard's delay in Ireland, govern the fate of kings.

---

101. Groves, in her *Texts and Traditions*, quotes Emrys Jones to support her case that if "Shakespeare was influenced by the French tradition [Créton, et al.] which portrayed Richard as an innocent, Christlike victim, he has radically changed the import of the allusions" (124). It is true, as she says, that Richard's "Christological imagery is part of his unashamed self-exaltation" (125), but her failure to acknowledge Carlisle's accusatory reprise of this Christological imagery (4.1.126–28) weakens her argument.

Let us return to the spiritual enigma that is Bolingbroke, now Henry IV. The gradual fulfillment of Carlisle's prophecy of "this house against this house" (4.1.146; see Mark 3:25) links the last scene of *Richard II* to the first scene of *1 Henry IV*, and so too does Henry IV's culpability for the death of his predecessor. Shakespeare creatively links Henry's expression of guilt to his planning a crusade to Jerusalem,[102] where the "field of Golgatha" (R2 4.1.145), prophesied typologically by Carlisle, is held by "pagans" (1H4 1.1.24). We may suspect that the new King's show of regret is intended for public consumption. Henry's soul remains hidden, even as his speech rises from the personal "I'll make a visit to the Holy Land" (R2 5.6.49) to the royal "So shaken as we are, so wan with care / Find we a time for frighted peace to pant" (1H4 1.1.1–2). Henry dominates the stage in his role as the King dealing prudently with political realities. To that extent he may be called a "political hero." But what is his true condition? If the King is merely "a well-graced actor," then his political skill may be the means to his damnation. But isn't that the great and piercing mystery at the heart of his story—that he could gain the world and lose his soul (Matthew 16:26)? Probably not in a post-Christian reading, where theological sensitivity would only distract us from the Machiavellian or Marxist or Foucauldian order of the day. In our reading, though, it is the emergence of modern politics within a Christian form of life that speaks to Elizabethan psychological reality. And with Bolingbroke, or the Tudors for that matter, who could really tell the sheep from the goats? If history was revealed through "figures in all things" (H5 4.7.33), who could be trusted to interpret these figures correctly?

1 Henry IV

If we think of *Richard II* as a domino structure of standing oaths, set up from the opening lines, the dominoes now have all fallen. None of the surviving principals is a man of his word. In *1 Henry IV*, we enter a new world where oaths are concerned. The contrast could hardly be greater. No resounding oath of fealty, no intense swearing enlivens the opening scene, which, at 107 lines long, is not tiny.

But when the scene shifts to Hal and Falstaff, the heavens start to rattle. Soon we hear a type of oath that makes our ears buzz: "'Sblood," Falstaff

---

102. Beatrice Groves, "England's Jerusalem in Shakespeare's *Henriad*," in *The Bible on the Shakespearean Stage: Cultures of Interpretation in Reformation England*, ed. Thomas Fulton and Kristen Poole, 101.

comments, "I am as melancholy as a gib cat or a lugged bear" (1.2.72–73). Hal asks if they shall steal tomorrow, and Falstaff swears he's the man for the job: "Zounds, where thou wilt lad" (98).[103] These new and colorful expressions sprouted to life in the late sixteenth century and belong to a class of swear-words known to scholarship as "minced oaths."[104] They appear to have been a lively form of anti-Puritanism.[105] *Thomas of Woodstock* is lavish of them from start to finish, and the murderous ruffians of *Arden of Faversham*, Black Will and Shakebag, are especially fond of *zounds*. Falstaff's "'Sblood" ("by God's/His blood") is one of eight occurrences of the word in *1 Henry IV*, an unusual frequency for a Shakespeare play. Likewise, *zounds* occurs ten times in *1 Henry IV*, a word count that is similarly anomalous. The fact that Shakespeare held his fire until *1 Henry IV* adds to the evidence for the *Henriad*'s unified design. Moreover, since the actors in *Richard II* never speak in prose (or compare themselves to tomcats), the eruption of minced oaths in *1 Henry IV* is all the more striking. Verbal remnants of the Middle Ages, the family of minced oaths derived in many cases from the contraction of medieval formula naming Christ's physical attributes.[106] Other Shakespearean instances include Justice Shallow's "By God's liggens" (2H4 5.3.65; probably derived from "God's lid-kins"); Hamlet's "God's bodikin" (2.2.529), from "bodykins," that is, "By God's little body," a "diminutive formation on 'body' used in oaths referring originally to the consecrated wafer used in the Mass";[107] and "'Sfoot," sworn by the lowly Thersites in *Troilus and Cressida* (2.3.5). It is noteworthy to us Freudians that most "early modern swearing was . . . not about sex but about God."[108]

Our scrutiny of Shakespearean oaths invites a moment for laying a wreath to the memory of George Santayana, whose serenely self-assured commentary stands as a monument to the secularizing of Shakespeare: "When Iago says '*sblood*' a commentator might add explanations which should involve the whole

---

103. Kastan in his editorial notes characterizes '*Sblood* as a "mild oath" and *Zounds* as "a strong, though common oath." William Shakespeare, *King Henry IV, Part 1*, ed. David Scott Kastan 154n and 156n. Regarding the former, Cummings writes: "The evidence is strong that saying 'sblood' was as socially unacceptable as saying 'God's blood,' and was capable of giving as much offence." *Mortal Thoughts*, 152. I suppose demographics would come into play.

104. For a historical snapshot of minced oaths, see Geoffrey Hughes, *Swearing: A Social History of Foul Language, Oaths and Profanity in English*, 104–105; cited in Cummings, *Mortal Thoughts*, 151. Hughes's account is helpful but not definitive.

105. See Hughes, *Swearing*, 18.

106. Cummings, *Mortal Thoughts*, 149 and 152.

107. C. T. Onions, *A Shakespeare Glossary: Enlarged and Revised throughout by Robert D. Eagleson*, 25. Onions has "orig." for "originally."

108. Cummings, *Mortal Thoughts*, 149.

philosophy of Christian devotion; but this Christian sentiment is not in Iago's mind, nor in Shakespeare's, any more than the virtues of Heracles and his twelve labors are in the mind of every slave and pander that cries *"hercule"* in the pages of Plautus and Terence. Oaths are the fossils of piety."[109] Comforting as his words must have been to the faithful at Harvard, Santayana was blinded by his own brilliance. It turns out that, in the 1590s, at least, Falstaff's minced oaths had plenty of zing to them. Though I would not call them expressions of "Christian devotion," they were by no means "fossils." Shakespeare, I have said, exploits the moral and artistic possibilities of Christianity by adhering to Christianity. He appeals to a Christian sensibility that is sophisticated and religious, not, as some would prefer to have it, mindless and incapable of appreciating modern art. In the *Henriad*, the mincing of oaths is a form of truth-telling. It is *giving the devil his due*. It is a direct comment on the infernal glut of aristocratic swearing and oath-breaking in *Richard II*.

Given the work of Poole and others identifying the anti-Puritanism in Falstaff's verbal conduct, we cannot doubt that his mincing of oaths irritated the godly. But the satirical thrust of such oaths can be read as sympathetic to anyone forcibly subjected to the Oath of Allegiance, beginning with the 1534 Act of Succession, or, more precisely, beginning when Parliament devised the oath to uphold the 1534 Act. As we know, his refusal to fall in line cost More his life. A famous case, to be sure, but the intrusive reach of the Oath of Allegiance went well beyond it. As Tom McAlindon has noted, "The Catholic Rebellion of 1569 and the papal bull of 1570 did much to keep the oath at the center of religious and political consciousness."[110] Putting aside historical details for the moment, we recognize that Falstaff is obviously blasphemous. We recognize that his minced oaths add zest to the anti-Puritan humor. But the same oaths can be taken as a commentary on a situation that had minced everybody. That is, insofar as his blasphemy follows upon the ubiquitous oath-breaking of *Richard II*, he blasphemes against broader conditions of spiritual hypocrisy. His mincing of Christ's body impugns the worldly powers that had corrupted the spiritual church that Paul called the "Body of Christ" (1 Corinthians 12:27), a theological concept that took on political importance in the Middle Ages before it shaped Elizabethan law and politics through "the simile of the state as a human body, a 'Corporation,' whereof the king is the head and the subjects are members."[111]

---

109. George Santayana, *Interpretations of Poetry and Religion*, 148.
110. McAlindon, *Shakespeare's Tudor History*, 42.
111. Kantorowicz, *King's Two Bodies*, 15.

I turn now to some chronological details. John Shakespeare, the poet's father, is thought to have been born in 1531 (his mother, Mary, was some six years younger). As a child, John might have heard his father or other local patriarchs discussing the 1534 oath, which sent More to the block and advanced the break from Rome. The Protestant Edward VI, who bequeathed Stratford its public school, reigned from 1547 to 1553; the Catholic Queen Mary I, from 1553 to 1558; the Protestant Queen Elizabeth I from 1558 to 1603, all childless years, with widespread anxiety over her succession in the 1590s, when Shakespeare wrote the *Henriad*. Over the course of John Shakespeare's life, the Oath of Allegiance, sworn by English office-holders, entailed significant religious shifts in 1534, 1547, 1553, and 1558. Pope Pius V's late-arriving bull of 1570 (just after the rebellion failed) excommunicated the Queen, still in her thirties, and, in Pius's mind, at least, absolved her subjects from their allegiance to her. It outraged Protestants and put severe pressure on English Catholics. The Saint Bartholomew's Day Massacre (to be memorialized for the stage by Marlowe) occurred in Paris in 1572, with Catholic mobs descending on Protestants and butchering them by the thousands. Then there was the other Catholic Mary, Queen of Scots, beheaded by order of Elizabeth in 1587. In terms of religious conflict, who knew what the future would bring? More mincing of one's conscience, one's honor, one's self-respect? Who could be honest with themselves or with their neighbors under such circumstances? Was England populated by a tribe of unprincipled trimmers?[112]

Whether we are absorbed by the pre-Reformation setting of the *Henriad*, or attuned to its contemporary resonances in the 1590s, the reality of a Christian God overseeing the actors on the historical stage theologically binds the past to the present. It is evident that Shakespeare "seeks to establish a dialogue between an ideologically conflicted past and a religiously and politically troubled present." I maintain that his political sensibility was shaped by the Christian humanist means by which he inquired into the battle for secular power: one of those means of inquiry was, as we have seen, to reframe the question by deploying intervals of Christian ulteriority throughout the *Henriad*.

The mimetic pull of this ulterior reality serves to express Shakespeare's consciousness of the Reformation as an event that admitted no political triumphalism at all, on either side of its temporal horizon. His Christian mimesis is not an ornament for political myth-making. It can have quite the opposite effect. Shakespeare in this regard is indirect: he plies suggestions, allusions,

---

112. Cf. King Henry VI's commentary on oaths (3H6 3.1).

jests, and the like to layer and enrich his mimetic framework. Henry IV professes to be a "soldier" of Christ (1H4 1.1.20), expatiates on Christ's life and crucifixion, and advertises "Our holy purpose to Jerusalem" (101). In the next scene, Falstaff minces his oaths, frets over his soul, renounces "vanity" (1.2.81), invokes "God" three times (17, 81, 91), "the Lord" three times (39, 62, 95), and the world of "Christendom" (97). Prompted by Falstaff,[113] Hal quotes the Book of Proverbs: "wisdom cries out in the street and no man regards it" (87–88). All this before Poins enters and jokes about Falstaff selling his soul on "Good Friday" (113). The world of Hal and Falstaff is full of such quips. The constant God talk, in all its shades of solemnity and humor, alerts us to the relevance of biblical wisdom and biblical typology—the Geneva Bible refers to the "spiritual" meaning in this latter respect (Revelation 11:8). Falstaff is preoccupied by "the Parable of the Prodigal Son from Luke 15, and the Parable of Dives and Lazarus in Luke 16." He and "Hal are both, in different ways, prodigals."[114] Christianity's liturgical and biblical participation in secular history is, in fact, one of its distinctions. As Shaheen observes, Shakespeare broke from his sources by introducing a wealth of biblical references to dramatize the rise of Henry IV and his son.[115] "The play's language," Hamlin observes, "is pervasively biblical and religious."[116] I want to suggest that there is a Christian point to it: Caesar's politics fall into an apolitical perspective against the measure of sacred history and its ulterior depths—an allusive presence that is in effect choric. The figure of Julius Caesar, which appears three times in the *Henriad*, is itself absorbed into these cosmic depths, becoming an indeterminable type or shadow of Satan or Christ, depending on how you look at him.

John Cox puts the case with a slightly different inflection: "Evocations of sacred history do more than ironize the action . . . they provide limits to instrumental thinking about power by pointing to moral thinking about politics that had infused medieval religious drama since the early fifteenth century."[117] I take this to be a species of understatement. With no irony intended, I would describe Shakespeare, in his response to the "instrumental thinking" of political calculation, as a sophisticated medieval Christian. In this respect, he is close to Erasmus. He was more intellectually curious than Erasmus was, however, about

113. Hamlin, *Bible in Shakespeare*, 238.
114. Hamlin, *Bible in Shakespeare*, 244. See also Poole, *Radical Religion*, 35.
115. Shaheen, *Biblical References*, 407–408.
116. Hamlin, *Bible and Shakespeare*, 237.
117. John Cox, *Seeming Knowledge: Shakespeare and Skeptical Faith*, 100.

propaganda and *realpolitik*. He studied the political world as a mixed phenomenon of virtue and vice, and he exploited its inherent theatricality.

And yet despite what one can reasonably call Shakespeare's political
vision, his Christian humanist approach to history—sophisticated, medieval,
skeptical—puts him at odds with Machiavelli's political realism. The crux of
the matter is pretty simple: "Whereas most humanist historians allow for the
presence of God and providence in their analyses of the world, Machiavelli
the pragmatist categorically divorces history from theology."[118] Shakespeare
does not divorce history from theology; and yet, for some scholars, Machiavelli
holds the very key to Shakespeare's thought. We noticed this particular modernizing tendency earlier in this chapter. We may now advance our position
as follows: because instrumental thinking relies on a substratum of fact and
on reliable inferences of cause and effect, Shakespeare, having denied the dispositive authority of his sources, induces us to doubt the instrumentalist's
premises. Again, I am not denying Shakespeare's interest in politics. Bolingbroke with his impeccable timing and his showmanship is undoubtedly a
superior politician. Richard is a political simpleton. But we have seen that
Shakespeare left crucial facts unresolved in *Richard II*. Through strategic lac-
unae, including the opacity to our view of the human soul, he limits our power
to draw the kind of inferences that politicize history in a partisan direction,
or that undergird the larger ambitions of political science, be it Machiavelli's
assertion of "our free will"[119] or Plato's city-soul analogy. In a non-Platonic
and anti-Machiavellian manner, he directs our awareness to the mysterious
reality of Judgment.

To notice Shakespeare's religious sensibility is to notice his capacity for
indirection: it was by targeting the zealous Puritans—the usual suspects—that
Shakespeare could secure the means to pursue his real design, to go after
bigger game, to call *everybody's* bluff, to interrogate, for example, the Tudor
Myth of history that Spenser was celebrating in *The Faerie Queene*. Falstaff is
eminently fitted for this purpose. Licensed, as it were, by the Sermon on the
Mount, Falstaff's wit prevails as a comment on the warring oaths of all oath-
breakers—and hence on the anarchic violence that precedes and underlies the
political order. In a society of frauds, Falstaff takes others down, challenging,
for instance, Worcester—"Rebellion lay in his way, and he found it" (1H4 5.1.

---

118. Ivo Kamps, "The Writing of History in Shakespeare's England," in *A Companion to Shakespeare's Works: The Histories,* ed. Richard Dutton and Jean E. Howard, 14.
119. Machiavelli, *The Prince,* 78.

28)—who not only views his betrayal of Richard in a self-justifying light, but uses it to emphasize Henry's obligation to him: "For you my staff of office I did break / In Richard's time." (34–35). It is Falstaff's task to pay these phony knights back in kind. He is the Miller responding to their Knight's Tale, and, in Chaucer's language, he will "quite" them.

The gist of Falstaff's moral work can be grasped in the biblical terms of Erasmus's *Paraphrases*: "the Pharisees, the Scribes, and the lawyers, while they reckon shame to acknowledge their own iniquity, they have rather willed to make God a liar, than to embrace the truth."[120] Falstaff's lies, being "gross as a mountain, open, palpable" (1H4 2.4.224), do not make God a liar. Falstaff happily leaves that to a society of hypocrites, including the author—Pharisee, scribe, and lawyer rolled into one—of the statement, "when Christ so earnestly forbad swearing, it may not so be understood as though he did forbid all manner of oaths." By being a fabulous sinner with peerless capacities for excusing his own sins, Falstaff exposes not only his own hypocrisy, but the ceremonious and legalistic hypocrisy of the uncannily familiar Catholic England that Hal wants to redeem—a strangely recognizable version of the oath-bound, oath-breaking, and oath-mincing world of the Elizabethans.

Henry IV's membership in that fallen order, the "Player Kings of the flawed rule,"[121] is a blazing invitation to Falstaff's anarchic energies. Insofar as Falstaff represents the "devil" (1H4 2.4.442) and "that old white-bearded Satan" (2.4.458), he has entered the kingdom through the breach in the cosmic structure created by Henry IV's role in Richard's murder. We recognize that Falstaff is not the only one to "swear truth out of England" (2.4.303). In their first scene together, when Hal wavers about becoming a robber, Falstaff vows sacrilegiously: "By the Lord, I'll be a traitor then, when thou art king" (1.2.142–43). This unholy triad of "Lord," "traitor," and "king" has the insinuating force of prodding us to reassess our political theology. In *Richard II*, the matter of sorting king from traitor was never finally settled. Now that Henry IV wears the crown, his flawed rule is open both to legal and to military challenge. It is a sensitive situation, which Falstaff exploits to justify his lawless behavior. Enmeshed in his own elaborate lies even as he cannot resist embellishing them, Falstaff asks with a nod to Pilate, "Is not the truth the truth?" (1H4 2.4.227–28). His outrageous truth-flouting invites comparison with any

---

120. Erasmus, *The First Tome or Volume of the Paraphrase of Erasmus vpon the Newe Testament*, EEBO, image 318 of 658. I have modernized the spelling.

121. Righter, *Shakespeare and the Idea*, 109.

number of shameless liars, including, as we have suggested, Worcester, who betrays Hotspur by falsely accusing Henry IV of "now forswearing that he is forsworn" (5.2.38). But Falstaff's most dangerously pervasive suggestion is that, given the widespread illegitimacy that prevails in the kingdom, there is no such thing as a "traitor" and no such thing as a "king." These words are mere words, not metaphysical symbols housed in a systematic worldview. Nominalism, a school of thought that started with the English Franciscan William of Ockham (c. 1287–1347) and spread through the *via moderna* and Reformation theology,[122] is typical of Falstaff's verbal repertoire. Of course, it is an opportunistic nominalism, but it is thematically essential. After Hal and Poins expose his ignominious behavior at Gad's Hill, Falstaff declares: "I shall think the better of myself and thee during my life—I for a valiant lion, and thou for a true prince" (2.4–270–72).[123] Based as it is on an open lie, this backhanded compliment is not flattering to Hal's political ambitions. When, soliloquizing on the field of battle, Falstaff ends his "catechism," he again plays the nominalist: "Honor is a mere scutcheon" (5.1.139–40). It is a seriously observant remark from Mowbray's former page. It finds considerable support in the *Henriad*.

Shakespeare arranges the famous tavern scene (*1H4* 2.4) to stage an inquiry into Christian society through an orgy of oaths. The action begins with Hal's report that he is "sworn brother to a leash of drawers, and can call them by their Christian names" (2.4.5–7). Hal appears to have agitated a drawer named Francis with the "prospect . . . of an offer of a place in the prince's household."[124] He is in the process of tempting Francis to break his apprentice's oath—to become like the "revolted tapsters" (4.2.28) among Falstaff's cannon fodder. Because of Poins's hollering, Francis's reply to Hal is cut off: "Oh, Lord, sir, I'll be sworn upon all the books in England, I could find in my heart—" (2.4.49–50). Francis teeters on the verge of swearing to break his oath: "all the books" refers to Bibles,[125] though it is doubtful the good lad could have read one. He has sworn a loyalty oath to his master, the Vintner, an oath that runs parallel, on the level of the master's household, to the greater oaths of the English aristocracy.[126] His potentially breaking his

122. See Heiko A. Oberman, *Luther: Man between God and the Devil*, trans. Eileen Walliser-Schwarzbart, 117–20.

123. Cf. *The Faerie Queene*, 1.iii.5–6.

124. William Shakespeare, *The First Part of the History of Henry IV*, ed. John Dover Wilson, 146n.

125. See Shaheen, *Biblical References*, 414.

126. See Bernthal, *Trial of Man*, 14–15.

oath recalls the nobles' breaking their oaths to the King. All England is in danger of turning into a lie.

The mood of the scene, with Falstaff in the dock, followed by Falstaff's and Hal's playacting interviews, is one of edgy release from official language and its hierarchical script. As we have observed, the breaking of oaths became savagely ubiquitous in *Richard II*. The tavern denizens show that they are well versed in this development—and make it their own. By my count, without regard for variations of upper and lower case, "faith" or "in faith" occurs seven times; Mistress Quickly says "O Jesu" four times; "by'r Lady" occurs three times; "by the Lord," "marry," "'Sblood," and "Zounds" occur twice apiece; "forsooth," "by the mass," "by these hilts," "amen," "for God's sake," and "the Father" each occur once. Then you have Falstaff under vinous cross-examination testifying to his own truth, and giving the figure of *orcos* (affirming that one speaks the truth) quite a workout. Either he is in some particular respect true and good, he avouches, or he is "a shotten herring" (127–28); will shave his manly beard (136–37); will see Poins "damned" (144); is "a rogue" (150); is again "a rogue" (162); his enemies "are villains" (169–70); is a "Jew else, an Hebrew Jew" (177); is "a bunch of radish" (184); is "no two-legged creature" (186); is "a villain" (204). There is precedent for this kind of shape-shifting in the medieval Vice.[127] In this context, though, Falstaff's lies can also be understood in terms of the floating verbal currency introduced with such form and ceremony in *Richard II*. Falstaff traffics in verbal items of exchange that face an uncertain market, and if a lie will not serve his purpose, he will turn it into a joke that will. The idea is similar to what we find in Hotspur's wordplay on "cracked crowns" that "pass . . . current" (2.3.93–94), and (Hotspur again) on soldiers "of this season's stamp" that go "current through the world" (4.1.4–5). Hotspur has his strong arm to back his currency, Falstaff has his wit.

It's a lawless inning. The fat knight, we recall, has just been robbed of his robbery of a large trove of coins. He adjusts to his loss with one invention, one lie, at a time, in effect paying the proverbial piper with each newly minted "counterfeit" and never a "true piece of gold" (2.4. 486–487). Where were those true pieces of gold going before the Gad's Hill escapade? Gadshill informs us: "There's money of the King's coming down the hill; 'tis going to the King's Exchequer" (2.2.53–54). It would appear, then, that the Chaucerian "pilgrims going to Canterbury" (1.2.123–24) were robbed of Caesar's taxes,

127. Phebe Jensen, *Religion and Revelry in Shakespeare's Festive World*, 161.

and then the robbers were robbed by the young "Caesar" himself (H5 5.0.28). Among the fusions of past and present: the Lollard and hot Puritan aversion to religious oaths; the costly Irish wars of Richard II and Elizabeth I; the spiking "price of oats" (2.1.12–13); and Hotspur's complaint of Henry IV's having "tasked" (i.e., taxed) the "whole state" (4.3.94), as Richard had done. Given that the 1590s were characterized by "dearth and inflation," and that the English took to comparing Elizabeth to Richard II as a "monarch who had taxed them ruthlessly,"[128] Falstaff as a robber of taxes becomes a comment on the state as a robber by means of publicans or tax collectors. As regards the flawed King's "exchequer," Falstaff plainly has his eye on it (2.2.35 and 3.3.184). The money is up for grabs, because justice is on holiday. In the end, the historical connotations of Falstaffian misrule cannot be nailed down. If Falstaff as stage Puritan could conjure memories of Oldcastle, he could also conjure memories of Catholic folk heroes Robin Hood and Friar Tuck,[129] as when he invokes "Maid Marian" later in the play (3.3.115; see also 2H4 5.3.104).

By precipitating a universal breakdown in trust, the flawed King has licensed the moral scourge, Falstaff, to range outside the lines of the stage Puritan, touching nerves and consciences across the spectrum of religious belief. His anarchic oaths establish a witty counterpoint to the violent oath-breaking of those in power. He renders unto Caesar with a vengeance. And that is one reason why Caesar's coins are everywhere. Falstaff would mint them out of Bardolph's "nose" and "cheeks" (3.3.79–80). Marching off to war, he'll "answer the coinage" (4.2.8). One recalls the charge leveled against Marlowe, by Richard Baines in his famous "Atheism" letter of 1593, that Marlowe had claimed "he had as good Right to Coine as the Queen of England."[130] Falstaff is free to do and say what he likes, and, in a sense, *how free* is the question. In this respect, Harold Bloom follows A. C. Bradley: both view Falstaff's transcendent freedom as a hallmark of Shakespeare's genius. For Bradley: "The bliss of freedom gained in humor is the essence of Falstaff."[131] For Bloom: "Falstaff, who is free, instructs us in freedom—not a freedom *in* society, but *from* society."[132] For critic Harry Morris, by contrast, "Falstaff is the major figure

128. Kastan, introduction, 64. James Shapiro, *A Year in the Life of William Shakespeare 1599*, 121.

129. For Robin Hood and Friar Tuck in the crosscurrents of the Reformation, see Jensen, *Religion and Revelry*, 118–28 and 161, respectively.

130. Richard Baines, quoted in Marlowe, *Doctor Faustus*, ed. Kastan, 128.

131. A. C. Bradley, "The Rejection of Falstaff," in *Henry the Fourth Parts I and II*, ed. David Bevington, 89.

132. Harold Bloom, *Shakespeare and the Invention of the Human*, 276, his italics.

through whom the four last things are most closely pursued."[133] The last four things are not free. They are Death, Judgment, Heaven, and Hell; and if Morris's view of Falstaff's spiritual gravity impinges upon the radical freedom celebrated by Bradley and Bloom,[134] one is nonetheless struck by Falstaff's weighty connections to Christianity. These include, as Bernard Spivak tactfully observes, his inexorable basis in the morality plays: "It is hard for us, if not impossible, to regard Falstaff as a villain in any sense, Shakespeare having marvelously exploited his affinity with the comic aspects of the Vice. But Falstaff's high comedy is still sufficiently close to its origins in the double nature of his allegorical forbear to prevent him from being a comic figure merely. In him the direct accent of the Vice's wit is *not quite free* from the faint echo of the Vice's evil."[135] This subtext will intensify in *2 Henry IV*.

The middle plays of the *Henriad* are designed so that Hal's initially secret drive to reknit the body politic comes into conflict with Falstaff's anarchic energies. To critics who think Hal is "a most princely hypocrite" (2H4 2.2.51), I will seem, at times, to be advancing a rather naïve view of the subject.[136] But we shall see. When he plays his royal father in the tavern, Hal momentarily interrupts the saturnalia of a riotous scene that is in effect a swear-fest. "The complaints I hear of thee are grievous" (1H4 2.4.437), he tells Falstaff, now that their acting roles are reversed. Falstaff assumes the Prince's part: "'Sblood, my lord, they are false" (438). Hal seizes on the minced oath: "Swearest thou, ungracious boy?" (2.4.430). As the King's understudy, Hal projects an ostentatious grace of freedom from what Article 39 calls "vain and rash swearing," while instantly condemning it in others. With a poignant flourish of the old Cicero (*Tolle hanc spem, tolle hoc praesidium*), Falstaff pleads not to be banished. Hal answers with a promise that, in its simplicity, would have pleased the strictest Puritan: "I do, I will" (2.4.476). The pronounced lack of swearing combines with an instance of Caesarian asyndeton. Impersonating Henry IV, whose performance he means to improve upon, the future Christian Caesar foreshadows the end of saturnalia by indicating that his word will keep

---

133. Harry Morris, *Last Things in Shakespeare*, 270.

134. Bloom follows A. C. Bradley's separating of Falstaff from his Christian conscience; Bradley proposes that Falstaff's interest in religion comes down to his "amusing himself with remorse at odd times when he has nothing else to do." Bradley, quoted in Bloom, *Shakespeare and the Invention*, 297.

135. Bernard Spivak, *Shakespeare and the Allegory of Evil: The History of a Metaphor in Relation to His Major Villains*, 204, my emphasis.

136. For an engaging response to the anti-Hal school of thought, see McAlindon, *Shakespeare's Tudor History*, 122–40.

its metaphysical and monetary value: a Caesarian point underscored as the scene closes with Peto's reading aloud Falstaff's debt to Mistress Quickly in shillings, *denarii,* and *obuli.*

Hal's "I will" recalls his signature line, from the soliloquy that concludes his first encounter with the audience, "Redeeming time when men think least I will" (1.2.211). Likewise, it anticipates his promise to his disappointed father, "I will redeem all this on Percy's head" (3.2.132). *Redeem,* which means to "buy back," is an important word in the *Henriad*'s theological and numismatic vocabulary. Shakespeare's usage echoes contemporary English Bibles, which feature the resonant phrase ("redeeming time") in Paul's letters.[137] In the case of Hal, the audacity of "I will redeem" suggests a need for accord between his will and God's. In his soliloquy and in his roleplaying, Hal presumes to signal his destiny, which is to atone for past sins and to ransom the English from their fallen state: to repair verbal and monetary losses by replacing bad oaths with true, by recovering the value of currency, and by making good on old debts. The soliloquy that Arthur Quiller-Couch called the "most damnable piece of workmanship to be found in any of [Shakespeare's] plays"[138] may be damnable (Shakespeare was open to things being damnable), but it also suggests a point that is easily overlooked: a Christian culture could recognize as a fundamental and necessary appeal to spiritual authority what, to the ideological mind, looks like a Machiavellian talent for crafty cunning. To adopt the broader argument of Cummings, Hal's using the word *redeem* in soliloquy directs us toward his relation with God, insofar as Shakespearean soliloquies in general suggest "an implied presence beyond the self."[139]

While Hal aims at becoming the true king, Falstaff's interrogations and exposures lend focus to the burgeoning of counterfeit realities, including the impersonating of Henry IV by his nobles on the field at Shrewsbury.[140] Any argument for traditional moral thinking on Shakespeare's part must survive this pervasive threat of nominalism, which is the threat of nominal value without substance. In the tavern scene, the law's approach prompts Falstaff to lay on the flattery, saying to Hal: "Never call a true piece of gold a counterfeit. Thou are essentially made without seeming so" (2.4.486–88). We are not sure whether "true piece of gold" refers to Falstaff or to Hal: it seems to float

---

137. See Shaheen, *Biblical References,* 412–13.

138. Arthur Quiller-Couch, quoted in J. I. M. Stewart, *Character and Motive in Shakespeare: Some Recent Appraisals Examined,* 125.

139. Cummings, *Mortal Thoughts,* 182.

140. For an overview of this topic, see Kastan, introduction, 62–69.

between them. As for the second sentence, it is cheap flattery, yes, but is it wholly lacking in dramatic irony? Hal shoves it back in Falstaff's face, mimicking his syntax: "And thou a natural coward without instinct" (489).[141] What I want to suggest, though, is that Falstaff says more than he knows, because Hal will eventually display his kingly mettle or essence, that is, his quality of being "essentially made" or stature as the true king, by upholding both his kingly word ("I do, I will") and his "vow" to his kingly father (3.2.159). Kastan, in his superb edition of the play, refutes this type of reading: "'Never call a true piece of gold a counterfeit' proves inapplicable as a political metaphor; in the political world of the play 'no true piece of gold' can be found and counterfeits therefore pass as current."[142] My counterargument runs as follows. At Shrewsbury field, when Hal encounters the counterfeit-killing sword of "the Douglas," the dram of truth in Falstaff's phrase ("Thou are essentially made without seeming so") kicks in. The Prince's heroic action in rescuing his overmatched father at least realizes the *possibility* of his redeeming his word. Hal's rousing vaunt, as he faces Douglas, suggests that at least one true piece of English gold will be passing current: "It is the Prince of Wales that threatens thee, / Who never promiseth but he means to pay" (5.4.42–43). Is this a counterfeit? Hal does not think so: "It is the Prince of Wales." It is as if he were ripping off a mask. He likewise passes from seeming to being—by dint of his own will, if not of God's—when he declares to Hotspur: "I am the Prince of Wales" (5.4.63). In this way, the currency in question starts to feel more like true currency. It also improves in value through the dramatic contrast between Hal and his foes, Douglas and Hotspur of the "cracked crowns," as well as between Hal and Falstaff, who anarchically challenges the exclusive royal prerogative for minting coins. "Thou hast redeemed thy lost opinion," the grateful King tells his son, "And showed thou mak'st some tender of my life" (48–49). The phrase *legal tender*, meaning "lawful currency," is not recorded until the eighteenth century. But *tender* in the sense of "lawful tender," an "offer of money, or the like, in the discharge of a debt or liability; *esp.* an offer which thus fulfills the terms of the law and of the liability" (OED 1b), enters the Shakespearean canon at least two other times (MND 3.2.8 and SON 83.4; see also HAM 1.3.107). No doubt the King's primary sense is "tender consideration, regard, care, solicitude."[143] But given the proximity of

---

141. Shakespeare, *King Henry IV, Part 1*, ed. Kastan, 235n. I am indebted here to Kastan's luminous notes.

142. Kastan, introduction, 64.

143. Onions, *Shakespeare Glossary*, 281.

"pay" and "redeemed," Shakespeare generates an aura of secondary meanings: redeeming the value of the King's monetary and verbal currency against counterfeits; guaranteeing the exchange value of a Lancastrian oath; binding together with true oaths "the nominal value of the currency" and "the substantial value of the metal."[144]

But Shakespeare, we reply in Kastan's stead (if we may), allows Hal only the violent, political performance of truth, not its reality. I reply in turn that (a) Shakespeare does not divorce the political world from (real) theological considerations and (b) Shakespeare's rhetoric is not a medium for the absolute validation of truth. It is joined at the hip to performance. It may or may not persuade us to believe something to be the case.

To attend to the relation between politics and theology is to follow Shakespeare observing the fallenness of humanity with such penetration that the very existence of truth starts to seem like an ironical feature of life on earth.[145] Such must be the existence of heaven to the damned. For Shakespeare, the high challenge of discerning true from false requires an exacting Christian perspective on history and drama. What Erasmus calls the "pomp of state" sweeps the boards: "If all that makes a king is a chain, a scepter, robes of royal purple, and a train of attendants, what after all is to prevent the actors in a drama who come on the stage decked with all the pomp of state from being regarded as real kings?"[146] An actor plays a king who gives instructions on how to act like a king (1H4 3.2.46–87). Another actor counterfeits a counterfeit king. But the self-referential quality of these plays—their abundance of metadramatic effects, their virtuosic punning on their own performance—does not abandon Shakespeare's Christian interrogations to the formal play of the signifier. (Nor should we discount the risk of excessive metadrama, namely, the audience's growing weary of "a self-evident sham."[147]) When we hear from Henry IV's own mouth that England is among "the kingdoms that acknowledge Christ" (3.2.111), Shakespeare wants his audience to consider this theatrical kingdom and this rhetorical acknowledgement. Is it all just show? Let us revisit an earlier quotation from Erasmus: "the Pharisees, the Scribes, and the lawyers, while they reckon shame to acknowledge their own

144. The quoted phrases are from Kastan, introduction, 65.
145. "[T]here is so much difficulty in finding the truth that it would be more ludicrous to say that deceit could not exist than to say that truth could not exist." Augustine, *Soliloquies*. *Augustine's Inner Dialogue*, trans. Kim Paffenroth, 60.
146. Erasmus, *Education of a Christian Prince*, 17.
147. Flann O'Brien, *At Swim-Two-Birds*, 21.

iniquity, they have rather willed to make God a liar, than to embrace the truth." Erasmus is commenting on hypocrisy. A hypocrite, etymologically, is an actor. To put a hypocrite on stage is potentially to expose the hypocrite in all of us. Hal recognizes Falstaff as a hypocrite, "that reverend Vice" (1H4 2.4.448). But Falstaff's roguish charm is that, in this pharisaical kingdom, he is more or less an open hypocrite, acknowledging not so much the kingdom of Christ as his own iniquity: "Thou knowest in the state of innocency Adam fell; and what should poor Jack Falstaff do in the days of villainy? Thou see'st I have more flesh than another man, and therefore more frailty having more flesh" (3.3.165–69). The "days of villainy" is an exposure not only of Falstaff but of England and English history under the effects of the Fall. What survives of truth—whatever survives of Eden—must survive this disconnection from God. It is all that Shakespeare and Hal (I will return to this connection) have to build on.

Falstaff's finest display of hypocrisy occurs, unsurprisingly, when every eye in the house is glued to him. Though this epitome of self-serving play-acting does not make a God a liar, it casts more than a little suspicion on humanity. Shakespeare manages to unite satirical rowdiness and saturnalian release in the resurrection scene that marks the zenith of Falstaff's power. The effect is potent enough to overcome, at least for the moment, the ugly spectacle of carnage. Bullough notes in dating the play, "Falstaff's attitude to his soldiers . . . would be topical in 1596/1597."[148] To fight the Spanish and the Irish, Elizabeth had conscripted unknown numbers of men and lads, among whose ranks many were abused by their officers and lost to history.[149] Horrific as all this was and is, we are mesmerized by Falstaff's versatility as a vessel of satire. Those "peppered" "ragamuffins" (5.3.35–36) sound like a gargantuan meal. The brutal topicality suggests that Falstaff could swallow just about anything. This type of rough satire blends with saturnalian comedy in what appears to be the resurrection—not of Christ—but of the Lord of Misrule. After tricking Douglas by lying doggo, Falstaff astonishes us by means of the immortal stage directions, *Falstaff riseth up.* Satire and saturnalia cooperate because this resurrection of the counterfeit dead combines a volcanic explosion of comic energies with a staggering satire on Christian war— the sacrilegious rite that Hotspur loved too much and that Erasmus detested. Erasmus understood war among Christians as a violent means of rendering

---

148. Bullough, *Narrative and Dramatic Sources*, 4.155.
149. Alongside Bullough, see, more recently, Shapiro, *A Year in the Life*, 52–53.

unto Caesar the things that are Caesar's: "Having sworn the oath of Christ, will you turn aside to the behavior of Julius. . . ?"[150] For Erasmus, such "behavior" was grounds for damnation. No champion of the just war tradition, Erasmus was a total peacenik. By contrast, Mowbray's valiant death is consistent with the teachings of Aquinas and John of Gaunt. If we look for "Christian service and true chivalry" (R2 2.1.54) at Shrewsbury, however, we find ourselves engulfed by a moral fog. Henry IV is not fulfilling his "holy purpose to Jerusalem" (1H4 1.1.101). The good of his cause has yet to be determined. On the day of battle, it is as likely that hypocrisy will triumph over hypocrisy, as that good will triumph over evil.

Shakespeare loads Falstaff's weightiest monologue with minced oaths and swearwords, as well as with memorable language from the fifteenth chapter of Paul's First Letter to the Corinthians, the essential Christian teaching on the resurrection of the dead—"one of the principal points" of the Gospel, as the gloss in the Geneva Bible for 1 Corinthians 15 tells us. Making allowance for grammatical inflection, I have adopted italics for keywords in the speech that overlap with 1 Corinthians 15:

> *Falstaff riseth up.*
> Emboweled? If thou embowel me today, I'll
> give you leave to powder me and eat me too *tomor-*
> *row.* 'Sblood, 'twas time to counterfeit, or that hot ter-
> magant Scot had paid me, scot and lot too. Counterfeit?
> I lie, I am no counterfeit. To *die* is to be a counterfeit,
> for he is but the counterfeit of a *man* who hath not the
> *life* of a *man*; but to counterfeit *dying*, when a *man*
> thereby *liveth*, is to be no counterfeit but the *true* and
> perfect *image* of *life* indeed. The better part of valor is
> discretion, in the which better part I have *saved* my
> *life*. Zounds, I am afraid of this gunpowder Percy,
> though he be *dead.* How if he should counterfeit too
> and *rise?* By my *faith*, I am afraid he would prove the
> better counterfeit. Therefore I'll make him sure; yea,
> and I'll swear I killed him. Why may not he *rise* as well
> as I? Nothing confutes me but eyes, and nobody sees
> me. Therefore, sirrah [*stabbing him*], with a new
> wound in your thigh, come you along with me.
>
> (5.4.111–28)

---

150. Erasmus, *Education of a Christian Prince*, 18.

The mad echoes of the letter to the Corinthians; the uncanny oaths, "'Sblood" and "Zounds"; the gentler "yea, and I'll swear," evocative of Matthew 5:37 and its fraught reception; the unmerciful desecration of Hotspur's corpse (Christians are responsible for corporal acts of mercy and these include burying the dead): all suggest the sharp Christian sensitivities behind Shakespeare's pen. Falstaff's comic talent for self-exposure is never more wonderful than in his remark to the playgoers whose eyes are fixed on him, "Nothing confutes me but eyes, and nobody sees me." Lack of witnesses is a universal enticement to vice and hypocrisy; it is opposed by the fear of Judgment. Here one confronts the universalizing force of Christianity in its representation of fallen man as a self-divided and hypocritical being, a creature longing for God and "life" in Paul's sense, yet a creature idolizing "life" in Falstaff's sense: a creature sworn to reject the devil and all his works, and therefore a creature who should not be fighting, swearing, and breaking the law of Moses and the law of Christ as if man were the devil incarnate.

As we know, Hal had previously called Falstaff "a devil," "that reverend Vice," "that gray Iniquity," "worthy but in nothing," and "that old white-bearded Satan" (*1H4* 2.4.442, 448, 453–54, 458). In this case, actions speak louder than words. Falstaff belies his own name by rising instead of falling, and the threat of nominalism (which is implicit in every lying oath) usurps the stage with a kind of comic tyranny. If there is no escaping Falstaff, it's because we are staring at ourselves. Politics becomes a sideshow. The playwright brings the counterfeiting theme to its climax by counterfeiting God himself, as Falstaff in his mock-resurrection assumes the devil's role as the ape of God.[151]

There was precedent for this diabolic topsy-turvy on the English stage. Shakespeare may have heard about *Antichrist*, play 22 of the belated Chester cycle, which made its appearance on the threshold of the English Renaissance. Scholars date *Antichrist* from the sixteenth century, with performance running into the 1570s.[152] Peter Happé comments that the play is "built on the device

---

151. C. S. Lewis claimed to have traced the medieval aphorism *diabolus simius dei* ("the devil is the ape of God") back to Tertullian, but no exact source in Tertullian has ever been confirmed. See Mark Edwards, "C. S. Lewis and the Early Christian Church," in *C. S. Lewis and the Early Church: Essays in Honor of Walter Hooper*, ed. Judith Wolfe and B. N. Wolfe, 24n2. H. W. Janson concluded, after careful study, "It seems likely . . . that the *diabolus simia Dei* was not coined until the High Middle Ages, or even later." H. W. Janson, *Apes and Ape Lore in the Middle Ages and the Renaissance*, 25–26n39. I would also note an instance from Calvin's sermons: "the Devil is always *an Ape of God and a counterfeiter of his works.*" John Calvin, *Sermons of Master Iohn Caluin, vpon the Booke of Job*, trans. Arthur Golding, EEBO, image 348 containing page 624, my emphasis. I have modernized the spelling.

152. David Mills, "The Chester Cycle," in *Medieval English Theatre*, ed. Richard Beadle and Alan J. Fletcher, 125.

of making Antichrist ape many of the actions and attributes of the true Mes-
siah, including death on behalf of his followers and a resurrection."[153] The
character of Antichrist feigns his own death. Being duly buried, he seems to
rise from the dead by his own power. No one identifies him as the ape of
God, but his repertoire of "false miracles"[154] surely fits the bill.

This context is important because, as I have suggested, we cannot share
the Elizabethan feeling for Falstaff without recognizing his roots in medieval
theater. We cannot understand the rejection that awaits him unless we see how
an Elizabethan audience was predisposed to accept it.

2 Henry IV

Whether it was the case that Shakespeare planned 2 Henry IV independ-
ently from the start, or whether he wrote it to capitalize on Falstaff's gate
receipts, we can infer that, either way, this great sequel offered the playwright
a chance to reflect on 1 Henry IV, to reassess his characters and themes, and,
in that respect, at least, to comment on what he had written. In moving from
Richard II to 1 Henry IV, Shakespeare moved outwardly from the vortex of
warring oaths and contradictory source materials to the creation of Falstaff
as a comedic and satirical vehicle for exposing the universal vice and hypocrisy
of that land of counterfeits: Christian England. Having won our hearts with
Falstaff's wit, he now faced the hard task of dwelling on Falstaff's darker
side—the side we have already witnessed in the fat knight's indefensible treatment of his "ragamuffins." This task, of representing Falstaff's fall, was inseparable from the job of dramatizing Hal's rise.

The entire undertaking continues to reflect Shakespeare's skepticism
toward the historical record. One thinks in the first instance of Rumor, "an
allegorical figure whose appearance draws on Fame, a mythic creature whose
multiple tongues and eyes are indicative of the unreliability of historical repor-
tage." "Rumor," as James Bulman explains, "is akin to the allegorical figures
of Morality plays and Tudor interludes." Among the likely sources for the
figure's appearance in Shakespeare is a pageant designed by Thomas More,
dating from around 1492 and "printed in 1557."[155] Rumor's Induction leads
directly to Northumberland's receiving irreconcilable reports about his son—
a dizzying start to the action and a further comment on the problems of

153. Peter Happé, *Cyclic Form and the English Mystery Plays: A Comparative Study of the English Biblical Cycles and Their Continental and Iconographic Counterparts*, 245.
154. John Cox, *The Devil and the Sacred in English Drama, 1350–1642*, 152.
155. Shakespeare, *King Henry IV, Part 2*, ed. Bulman, 152n and 161n.

sources and methods in history. Falstaff continues to take self-interested aim at sanctimonious fictions. One detects the glee with which Shakespeare, by way of Falstaff, seizes on the Tudor Myth—a royal counterfeit in its own right—in order to defile it: "'When Arthur first in court'— / Empty the jordan" (2H4 2.4.33–34). This seeming accident of speech mingles the archetype of Tudor kingship and the contents of a chamber pot. One also senses metadramatic commentary by Shakespeare on his position as playwright and trickster, for instance, in Shallow's description of young Jack Falstaff's breaking "Scoggin's head at the court gate" (3.2.30), a likely reference to King Edward IV's jester, John Scoggin, who lent his name to a book called *Scoggin's Jests,* licensed in 1565–66. Shallow's complex anachronism (Edward IV was crowned the first time in 1461) may have been Shakespeare's way of flaunting his fool's license, wielding the authority of tradition to back up the risky practice.

The grand arc of oaths and oath-breaking sustains us here as well. Let us examine one moment in particular that epitomizes Shakespeare's take on England's royal houses. At Gaultree Forest, Prince John's breaking of his oath to the rebel leaders—the Archbishop of York, Lord Hastings, and Lord Mowbray (who is the late Duke of Norfolk's son)—enlivens the play with a sensational *coup de théâtre.* Leading the King's forces, Prince John roundly chastises the Archbishop: "You have ta'en up, / Under the counterfeited zeal of God, / The subjects of His substitute, my father" (4.2.26–28). This appeal to the theology of the King as God's "substitute" harkens back to Gaunt's defense of passive obedience: "God's is the quarrel; for God's substitute, / His deputy anointed in His sight, / Hath caused [Gloucester's] death" (R2 1.2.37–39). Richard II likewise spoke of "Our substitutes at home" (1.4.48). In *2 Henry IV,* the chain of logic supports similarly absolutist claims: if the King is God's substitute, and if Prince John has been "substituted" for the King (1.3.84), then Prince John is arguably in a position not only to pull rank on the Archbishop, but also, rather impressively, to imply divine "justification for the English law of succession."[156] The Davidic kingdom gleams in the Lancastrian background, an ulterior reality transcending time, as it had similarly done during Richard's reign as the "anointed" King.[157]

156. I take the phrase from Figgis, *Divine Right*, 5.
157. For an impressive range of works and contexts that fostered the possibility of this Davidic presence, see David Evett, "Types of King David in Shakespeare's Lancastrian Tetralogy," *Shakespeare Studies* 14 (1981): 139–61. See also Noah Millman's perceptive "Whence Comes Legitimacy?" *The American Conservative* (March 16, 2017), https://www.theamericanconservative.com/articles/whence-comes-legitimacy/.

And yet, given our memories of *Richard II*, and given the rebel leaders' belief in their legitimate grievances (a belief that the younger Mowbray's presence encourages), the question of counterfeits cannot easily be dismissed. It rears its curious head when Prince John accuses the rebels of "the counterfeited zeal of God." When Westmorland, who may have masterminded the dirty business, asks Prince John how he likes the articles of the rebels' petition, Prince John swears robustly:

> I like them all, and do allow them well,
> And swear here, by the honor of my blood,
> My father's purposes have been mistook. . . .
> My lord, these griefs shall be with speed redressed,
> Upon my soul, they shall.
>
> (4.2.54–60)

The Archbishop buys it: "I take your princely word for these redresses" (66). But it must be Shakespeare's moral purpose that, if we have been attentive, we are not so easily hoodwinked. We have heard stentorian lungfuls of swearing. We have measured what a "princely word" is worth. We have been catechized in the truth of such "honor." Prince's John's clever ambiguities recall Portia, in *The Merchant of Venice*, which was written about the same time, resorting in the courtroom scene to what Cicero in *De Officiis* calls "chicanery and an excessively clever but malicious interpretation of the law" (see Chapter 2). In either play, it is much the same revelation of a legal system at odds with its Christian pretensions. Prince John beats Portia at her own game, exulting like Marlowe's Barabas over his "Christian" victims: "I promised you redress of these same grievances / Whereof you did complain, which, by mine honor, / I will perform with a most Christian care" (113–15). Then the moment of instrumental reason arrives—in the form of nefarious deceit:

> But for you rebels, look to taste the due
> Meet for rebellion as such acts as yours. . . .
> God, and not we, hath safely fought today. (116–17, 121)

Having double-crossed his enemies, Prince John can rule confidently against "rebels" and "rebellion." In his mouth, and despite his late heroics at Shrewsbury, these words are not so much the tokens of justice as they are the weapons of state propaganda. That is one reason why the early fifteenth-century stage action can prefigure the short-lived Northern Uprising of 1569–70 and its appropriation by the Tudor regime. An instant propagandist, Prince John shamelessly drags God into it, as the victors make God a liar. Bulman notes Shakespeare's divergence from the chronicles: "In both Stow and Holinshed, Westmorland himself negotiates with the rebels at Gaultree, Prince John being only 16 at the time. By having Prince John—here clearly older than the historical prince—negotiate the peace, Shakespeare suggests a fellowship of deceit and attaches to the royal household a duplicity not attributed to it in the sources."[158] By savaging royal integrity as an odious lie, Shakespeare and his company were delivering a shrewd rebuke to the smug propaganda enshrined in the Book of Homilies, in particular, "Against Swearying and Perjurie" and "Against Rebellion," the latter a direct response to the events of 1569–70.

I am suggesting that Shakespeare uses the pivotal moment of Prince John's godless maneuvering to compare the past to the present, casting neither in a savory light. It comes as a relief when Falstaff takes Sir John Coleville prisoner, insults Prince John with the counterfeit theme ("if you do not all show like gilt twopences to me" [4.3.49–50]), and demands his "right" (54). We should remember the moral impetus behind this satire. For Shakespeare, the Sermon on the Mount ought to have pushed any person regardless of wealth or status toward greater self-knowledge with respect to the whole of reality. Shakespeare is not a preacher, but nonetheless he engages the Elizabethan conscience. His satirical thrusts, in *2 Henry IV* as in *1 Henry IV*, continue to constitute a moral interrogation of the English people on Christian grounds.

The playwright had at his disposal various dramatic means of exploiting the universal reality of Judgment, occasions of death being chief among them. In *2 Henry IV*, the approach of two great deaths starts to activate mimetic potentialities that serve, as we suggested earlier, a recognizably medieval design. To quote Dover Wilson on the judgmental scheme in question: "the forces of iniquity were allowed full play upon the stage, including a good deal of horse-play, provided they were brought to nought, or safely locked up in Hell, at the end."[159] Early in *2 Henry IV*, the flawed King knows he is dying; the Lord of Misrule is sicker than he knows. It is the "gout"-ridden Falstaff (1.2.243) who, having dipped into Galen, confidently diagnoses the King's condition: "apoplexy . . . a kind of lethargy . . . a kind of sleeping in the blood, a whoreson tingling . . . a kind of deafness" (1.2.110–16). The King is piteously wracked with insomnia when we finally meet up with him in Act 3, Scene 1. In his second appearance, in Act 4, Hal takes him for dead. On

158. Shakespeare, *Henry IV, Part 2*, ed. Bulman, 239n.
159. John Dover Wilson, *The Fortunes of Falstaff*, 17–18.

Falstaff's side, a "doctor" is inspecting Falstaff's urine (a possible source for this situation is *Scoggin's Jests*): a "good healthy water, but, for the party that owed it, he might have more diseases than he knew of" (1.2.1–5). The Lord Chief Justice (1.2.24) and Poins (2.2.98) pick up the theme, the Lord Chief Justice adapting "physician" to a legal and moral sense, Poins applying it to Falstaff's spiritual condition. Doll Tearsheet (who is notably sensitive to language) administers Christian charity: "when wilt thou leaving fighting o'days and foining o'nights, and begin to patch up thine old body for heaven?" (2.4.230–32). The King is fated to die offstage in the chamber in Westminster Abbey where he "first did swoon" (4.5.32), which, accentuating the prophetic problem of "figures in all things," is "called Jerusalem" (2H4 4.5.233).[160] Falstaff, for whom the "grave doth gape . . . thrice wider than for other men" (5.5.53–54), is fated to die offstage, reciting the Twenty-Third Psalm[161] and crying "God, God, God" (H5 2.3.18–19). Both men have fitfully expressed a longing for repentance. Neither has redeemed the time. Their powers collapse as the season of "playing holidays" (1H4 1.2.198) wanes. Awareness of the approach of Judgment redounds back upon the audience.

The second part of *Henry IV* relies for its titular integrity largely on the emotional power of one scene, in which Hal steals off with the "golden rigol" (4.5.36), the idol—we note the implicit rhyme—of his seemingly dead father. Act 4, Scene 5 is built on soul-baring and on oaths that call God to witness. With the crown and a sickbed as props, Shakespeare thwarts the potential for hollow melodrama through the dignity with which he endows the primary affections. The scene is noble in sentiment, presenting the royal father and son as honorable and self-sacrificing. But this dignity rests on oaths that, while they resist a cynical interpretation due to the circumstances of the King's illness, nonetheless leave a great deal unresolved. Caught red-handed with the crown, Hal swears to his father, "God witness with me, when I here came in, / And found no course of breath within your Majesty, / How cold it struck my heart!" (148–50). While we are inclined to believe Hal at this moment, we also want to say: not "coldly" enough to stop him from trying on a new hat. His father's final advice begins with a confession: "God knows, my son, / By what bypaths and indirect crook'd ways / I met this crown" (182–84). This is truer than "Though then, God knows, I had no such intent" (3.1.72), but one

---

160. Groves accepts "the irony perceived by Henry IV" (at 4.5.237), but advances a Protestant context that adds "a kind of affirmation." Groves, "England's Jerusalem," 87, 99. It seems to me that Groves runs the serious risk of sending Henry IV to heaven.

161. Per editors Bevington, Craik (cited below), and Dover Wilson.

can imagine Richard II's response—not to mention that of the Deity being invoked. The King ends the father-son colloquy between guilt and hope, "How I came by the crown, O God forgive / And grant it may with thee in true peace live!" (4.5.217–218). That the decision lies with God in both respects is no trifling concern.

The genuinely moving emotions of this scene emerge in stark contrast against a strikingly different vein of artistic action, one more characteristic of the play's earthy tang. Part 2 of *Henry IV* finds much of its footing in the underplot, that is, in Falstaff's maneuverings. As we noted, Rumor steps out of the past to start the play. What we soon discover is that, in a departure from *Richard II* and *1 Henry IV*, allegorical names proliferate: Fang, Snare, Sneak, Smooth, Doll Tearsheet, Tisick, Shallow, Silence, Dumbe, Pistol, Moldy, Nightwork, to name a few. Falstaff's name also fits in this category, and it is Falstaff who calls Justice Shallow a "Vice's dagger" (3.2.318). Marshalling this force of allegorical suggestion, Shakespeare lessons us in the native dramatic tradition, glancing with sidelong foreboding at the dangerous disorder attending Falstaff's levity. This disorder achieves its highest threat-level when Falstaff hears the "good news" that Hal is King: "Let us take any man's horses; the laws of England are at my commandment. Blessed are they that have been my friends, and woe to the Lord Chief Justice!" (5.3.138–41). Falstaff's aping of the Beatitudes and commandeering the Commandments would have impressed the Elizabethans, especially given the context of Pistol's grand announcement: "And tidings do I bring, and lucky joys" (2H4 5.3.96), which apes the angel in the Gospel of Luke (2:10): "I bring you tidings of great joy."[162] It is Pistol who changes the moral balance between *1 Henry IV* and *2 Henry IV* where Falstaff is concerned. Falstaff's ancient or standard-bearer, he is a raw piece of evil, half-mad and not easy to ignore. His false proclamation—on the Shrovetide verge of Lent—is unsettling. In case you were nodding, Shakespeare drives it home: "And shall good news be baffled?" (106). The connotations were undoubtedly negative. In a gush of ebullience, his great and penetrating wit overcome by sheer greed, Falstaff rushes off to London in order to realize the late King's worst nightmare (4.5.116–36).

G. K. Hunter, casting doubt on the seminal work of Dover Wilson on Falstaff and the morality tradition, warns that "we only sidestep" the problem

---

162. Cf. Faustus, "Come, Mephistopheles, / And bring glad tidings from great Lucifer." Marlowe, *Doctor Faustus*, ed. Kastan, 2.1.26–27.

of Falstaff's rejection "if we suppose that the non-human components in the [Hal-Falstaff] relationship cancel out the human ones."[163] I agree with Hunter that, in some respects, Dover Wilson overstated his case. If he is overly schematic, though, his sense of the medieval background is indispensable. Moreover, there is nothing "non-human" about Pistol or his relation to Falstaff: one cannot dismiss Pistol's inversion of the Gospel message as mechanical or schematic. Aping God, it echoes his master's technique.

Following Dover Wilson and J. I. M. Stewart (in polemical contradistinction to the Bradley-Bloom axis), I agree that Falstaff is set up to fall by a process that is carefully prepared for him. Stewart puts it this way: the "Falstaff-Hal story subsumes diverse traditional significances for the most part already embodied in the drama, and the rejection scene is unexceptionable to an audience aware of and properly balancing these."[164] I agree that Shakespeare has made his audience "aware" of "diverse traditional significances" derived from the medieval drama. The difficulty lies in "properly balancing these" significances in order to accept Falstaff's rejection. It is part of Shakespeare's design that the "diverse traditional significances" have a foot in the medieval past. They hold true, but their truth requires an attunement to more recent experience. Falstaff is not a static abstraction. We don't become attached to static abstractions. To the contrary, we find that, the better we understand the rejection scene, the more we are moved by it. It resembles a "tragic collision" in a broadly Hegelian sense: "within a collision of this kind both sides of the contradiction, if taken by themselves, are *justified*; yet, from a further point of view, they tend to carry into effect the true and positive content of their end and specific characterization merely as the *violation* of the other equally legitimate power."[165] What Hegel means, if I understand him, is that, in a tragic clash between two equally just protagonists (think of Antigone and Kreon), each side is right in its way, but all either side gets out of being right is hurting the other side. Though Hegel is not our final authority on tragedy, it is evident that this collision of powers excites our moral interest and our passions. In terms of Athens and Jerusalem: Falstaff, the "Elizabethan Socrates,"[166] is not right and just, but his critique of society is. Hal, a Davidic

---

163. G. K. Hunter, "Shakespeare's Politics and the Rejection of Falstaff," in *Henry the Fourth Parts I and II*, ed. David Bevington, 259.

164. Stewart, *Character and Motive*, 134.

165. Georg Wilhelm Friedrich Hegel, *The Philosophy of Fine Art*, 4:297–98, his italics.

166. Bloom, *Shakespeare and the Invention*, 275, 298. For Falstaff's Socratic precedents in Erasmus and Rabelais, see Grace Tiffany, "Shakespeare's Dionysian Prince: Drama, Politics, and the 'Athenian' History Play," *Renaissance Quarterly* 52 (Summer 1999): 366–83.

figure (more on that below),[167] is not right and just, but his goal is. Accordingly, as the corrective regime of Henry V begins, the Falstaffian perspective stays with us. The drama's action concludes with the disgraceful Prince John chatting things over with the honorable Lord Chief Justice. The legitimacy problem lingers. In the "obscure interplay" between "the psychological integrity of the drama" and the "overriding myth which the characters must obey,"[168] the playwright does not encourage us to worship state power, or to confuse it with God's omnipotence. He does not complete the mythical pattern by asserting the final legitimacy of the new reign. He does not—to return to the moment of Falstaff's hearing the "good news"—suggest that the Lord Chief Justice and the Beatitudes have any correlation at all.

This spiritual wilderness is relieved by intervals of Christian ulteriority, which direct us to look for Judgment beyond the political business of events on the ground. Hal had joked curiously with Poins: "Well, thus we play the fools with the time, and the spirits of the wise sit in the clouds and mock us" (2H4 2.2.134–36). Shaheen and others point out that this catches a Pauline echo from any of various English Bibles, "Walk circumspectly, not as fools, but as wise, redeeming the time" (Ephesians 5:15–16). As often happens, Shakespeare adopts the language of wisdom and folly, so characteristic of Paul and Erasmus, to delight his audience with the kind of conscience-searching considerations that they loved. Bulman detects a further biblical reference. Still on 2.2.134–36, he directs us to the fourth line of the Second Psalm: "*But he that dwelleth in the heaven shall laugh: the Lord shall have them in derision.*"[169] Contemplating the future Henry V as a type of King David soon to be anointed, Shakespeare may have had, moreover, not only the fourth line of this psalm but its general context in mind. The Geneva Bible's gloss on the Second Psalm is pertinent to the spiritual action: "The prophet David rejoiceth that notwithstanding his enemies' rage, yet God will continue his kingdom forever & advance it even to the end of the world, And therefore exhorteth Kings and rulers, that they would humbly submit themselves under God's yoke, because it is in vain to resist God. Herein is figured Christ's kingdom." It would follow, then, that Shakespeare was already associating Hal with this prophetic movement toward the end of history. Henry IV's weird answer

---

167. For grounds for linking Henry V to "David the true mirror of a Christian king" (158), see Evett, "Types," especially 154–58.

168. Stewart, *Character and Motive*, 135.

169. Shakespeare, *Henry IV, Part 2*, ed. Bulman, 241n, italics in original. I have modernized the spelling.

to Warwick's hopeful prognostications about the wayward Prince gains significance in this context:

> 'Tis seldom when the bee doth leave her comb
> In the dead carrion. (2H4 4.4.79–80)

Whether or not the King fully understands what he is saying, his words allude to "the story in Judges 14:5–14 of Samson's killing a young lion in whose mouth he subsequently found bees and a honeycomb." For the Church Fathers, as Robert Knapp explains, the passage told "of the kings of the world who roared before Christ but afterwards proclaimed and defended the sweet words of the evangelists."[170] Further, as Groves observes, "Shakespeare's audience members were used to thinking of themselves as living out the call to inhabit the new [*sic*] Jerusalem."[171] And yet, does the conclusion follow that, after Henry IV failed to reach the city of Jerusalem, his son and heir, Henry V, would lead the English toward its spiritual or typological fulfillment in the New Jerusalem? To answer in the affirmative would seem to point us in the non-Shakespearean direction of state propaganda and officially sanctioned history. Fortunately, the playwright has strewn obstacles in the path of this fulfillment by means of Falstaff's rejection and Hal's Caesarian arrogation of authority. He would go on to construct other obstacles as well, both to compensate for the loss of dialectical energies resulting from Falstaff's departure, and to satisfy his own stubborn moral nature.

Henry V

In bringing the *Henriad* to a triumphant close, Shakespeare ran the risk of stifling his audience's participatory *conscience*—a word that gets worked soundly in *Henry V*.[172] When it is bandied, for example, from the King to the Archbishop and back to the King, in Act 1, Scene 2, it serves to indicate the moral pressure on one speaker and to provoke a torrent of casuistry from the other. What does it say about his conscience that the King would lean publicly on the Archbishop's conscience, when the Archbishop is plainly compromised by financial considerations? The remaining uses of *conscience* go

---

170. Robert S. Knapp, *Shakespeare: The Theater and the Book*, 25 and 25n33.

171. Groves, "England's Jerusalem," 101.

172. For more on conscience in *Henry V*, see William W. E. Slights, "The Reformed Conscience," in *Stages of Engagement: Drama and Religion in Post-Reformation England*, ed. James D. Murdock and Kathryn R. McPherson, 21–39, esp. 33–39.

seven times to Fluellen, for whom it is a verbal tic expressive of a humorous type, and four more times to the King, for whom it continues to be an index of moral pressure, as before the gates of Harfleur, "conscience wide as hell" (3.3.13). This pressure, to which Fluellen contributes insistently if indirectly, is critical because it encourages us to study the King's character. Too much triumphalism for Henry V would have alienated Falstaff's audience. Just as important, as I will argue, it would have alienated Shakespeare from his task. It would have offended his own conscience.

Shakespeare saw Christ's kingdom on the horizon as Henry V approached his destiny, but to lay too transparent a stress on the biblical pattern of "the end of the world" would have violated his skeptical technique and put *Henry V* back in the Middle Ages along with its subject-matter. Think of it this way: the more that typological meanings direct our attention, the less moral work we have to do on our own. From an artistic point of view, this is the risk that Shakespeare took in *Henry V*, the most nationalistic play in the tetralogy. It replaces Rumor with the Chorus. It replaces the moral scourging of Falstaff with the Chorus's incitements to imagination in the service of epic patriotism. The King's avowal of his Welsh blood has pro-Tudor significance, as does the Chorus's bow to "our gracious Empress" (5.0.30). We may well ask why Shakespeare would exalt Henry V, a God-mouthing, war-dealing monarch whose first action in the play savors suspiciously of his father's advice to "busy giddy minds / With foreign quarrels" (2H4 4.5.212–13). How, by the light of an Erasmian understanding, could a Christian king assume "the port of Mars" (Prol. 6)? What a strange leap, this sudden appeal to absolute truth: "Yet sit and see / Minding true things by what their mockeries be" (H5 4.0.52–53). It is only a partial defense to claim that Shakespeare was limited by his material. He was guilty of not betraying the national memory of England's greatest Christian warrior-king, as enshrined in the chronicles and on the stage. He failed to impugn Henry V by developing a Falstaffian counter-current to the play's main action. It can be maintained that Bardolph, Nym, and Pistol caricature the King's raiding of France, and that the hanging of Bardolph is a personal betrayal. There is something to this, of course. But Shakespeare did not give us much incentive to attach ourselves to these remnants of Falstaff.

The goal of England's new ruler, to which he must sacrifice Falstaff, is to reknit the body politic and, in doing so, to restore the integrity of oaths. He needs to match his word to his deed, and both to the will of God. King Harry—what's left of Hal—undertakes to pay "the debt he never promisèd" to achieve his "reformation" (1H4 1.2.203, 207). The familiar historical meaning of this term—*the Protestant Reformation*—was engrained in the English psyche before the 1590s. Shakespeare had risked a serious play of words in the first tetralogy, in which the murderous Jack Cade "vows reformation" (2H6 4.2.63). In *Henry V*, the dramatist returns again to this type of punning figure, known as *syllepsis* (the pun is self-contained), when the Archbishop of Canterbury praises the new King to the Bishop of Ely: "Never came reformation in a flood / With such a heady currance, scouring faults" (H5 1.1.34–35). For purposes of establishing "a dialogue between an ideologically conflicted past and a religiously and politically troubled present," *reformation* was your man. By the very nature of its synchronic echoing, which suggests the perennial need of reformation under all regimes, Shakespeare insists on our searching behind the official façade of events to discover the eschatological drama of passionate souls. Doing so, he risks exposing his protagonist to criticism that his status as a Christian hero cannot survive. But the moral purpose of this artistic tightrope-walking does not lie, as Norman Rabkin would suggest, in testing our ability to tease out "rival gestalts."[173] Likewise, the ambiguity of *reformation* should not simply be stocked and shelved as an example of William Empson's "seventh type of ambiguity," "when the two meanings of the word, the two values of ambiguity, are the two opposite meanings defined by the context, so that the total effect is to show a fundamental division in the writer's mind."[174] I respect both Rabkin and Empson, the one a fine critic, the other a minor genius. But let us say the two fundamental meanings of *reformation* are God's and the devil's. If so, what is most fundamental is not a division *in the writer's mind*. What is most fundamental and ambiguous, in the Latin sense of the word of *driving both ways*, is the Christian worldview that precedes and informs the author's mind. This ambiguity is therefore a means of inviting others to the search for moral truth, as we confront the limits of our knowledge, under the eschatological pressure of a reality dominated by heaven and hell, which, we are reminded, appear symbolically in the structure and ornamentation of the stage itself.

The divine reality behind the political action is carefully reinforced by the biblical perspective that informs *Henry V*. As regards Henry V's role in fulfilling the redemptive arc of English history, the action of the play alludes with particular interest to the Book of Revelation. Like a great medieval

173. Rabkin, *Shakespeare and the Problem*, 62.
174. William Empson, quoted in Rabkin, *Shakespeare and the Problem*, 60. Rabkin does not discuss *reformation*. He cites Empson's seventh type as a general explicator of the play.

window, radiant with eternity, the vision of John of Patmos dominates the play's ulterior framework. And yet the interrogations of Shakespeare's Christian conscience persist, shaping the play so that the audience's identification with the victorious Henry is subject to moral scrutiny.

Shakespeare in my view alludes to Revelation in an artistic act of faith, an act of faith by a Christian writer, a deferral of his own skepticism to the "true things" of providence. We witness an authorial submission to English history that parallels what the epic protagonist does or tries to do throughout the play, persistently invoking God's "will," "hand," "peace," "arm," etc. The difficulty of trying to discern God's will in order to conform to it puts us in mind of *Hamlet*. In the case of *Henry V*, we likewise sense a parallel between the hero's situation and the author's artistic choices. We may formulate the parallel as follows: given his entanglement in temporal history and his inheritance of sin, how could Henry V hope to find blessing and vindication in the will of God? And, given his Christian skepticism and historical consciousness, what providential truth could Shakespeare hope to share in an inevitably erroneous account of English royalty?

Henry's prayer to the warrior God of Revelation (invoked by the French at 3.5.15), "O God of battles, steel my soldiers' hearts" (4.1.287–303), is the crux of the relation between poet and protagonist, each of whom "comes after all" (302). On a generous reading, it is an admission of moral defeat and of total dependence on God: in paradoxical Christian terms, that humbling recognition may be its strength. But it is also a piece of rhetoric, an impossible attempt to persuade the divine Judge "to pardon blood" (4.1.298). It is revealing that Shakespeare subjected himself to such an ordeal as a writer, exposing, as it were, the naked limits of his (and of all) rhetoric: none of Shakespeare's known sources focuses exclusively on Henry in the agonies of prayer.[175] If we can read it as an admission of spiritual defeat, I am suggesting that we can also read the prayer as an admission of artistic failure, of having means that are insufficient to the end: "Oh, for a muse of fire" (1.0.1). Focusing on Henry, we can read it as an act of self-interested rationalization, a self-conspiring that has provoked critical skepticism from Greenblatt's "magical propitiation and bad conscience" to Cox's "successful effort at self-evasion" to Spiekerman's "barely worthy of a child."[176] Spiekerman, by the way, does

175. Evett, "Types," 151–52.

176. Stephen Greenblatt, *Shakespearean Negotiations: The Circulation of Social Energy in Renaissance England*, 62; Cox, *Seeming Knowledge*, 154; Spiekerman, *Shakespeare's Political Realism*, 143.

acknowledge the prayer as an apparent challenge to his Machiavellian version of Henry. He maintains his argument that "Henry V is untroubled by the pangs of conscience" by focusing on results: "In fact, Henry's fit of conscience changes nothing . . . . Henry may stray from Machiavelli's script, but he is not less effective because of it."[177] For Spiekerman's Shakespeare, then, God has nothing to do with the victory at Agincourt. But why then write the prayer, not as a Machiavellian act of political theater, but as a soliloquy?

I am suggesting that Henry's difficulty is very close to Shakespeare's. Because neither the playwright nor his protagonist can "wash every mote out his conscience" (4.1.179), both express a powerful sense of inadequacy. As a soliloquy, the prayer bookends the "Redeeming time" soliloquy—only now that the bill has come due, only Christ can pay it. Only the supreme Judge can pardon or overlook for "today" what the King calls "the fault / My father made in compassing the crown" (4.1.290–92). What, then, of our "bending author," "[m]angling" his work with "rough and all-unable pen." (Epil. 1–4)? However artificial, the humility topos is essential to the spirit of the work. "The diffidence of the Chorus," writes Dover Wilson, "is the expression of a genuine attitude of mind."[178] The humility in evidence is not the effect of an aesthetic conscience, a Nietzschean drive to artistic perfection. It is not independent of the Christian worldview that the author of the *Henriad* represents with tireless intensity. Having chronicled Bolingbroke's "fault" in detail, having established its synecdochic bearing for all England, Shakespeare knew that he was in no position to absolve anyone of sin. More, he is himself unusually present in this play, as the Chorus makes clear from start to finish. The task of understanding providence and reading the signs of sacred history challenged him. It tested his conscience with the temptations of false prophecy, idolatry, and heretical opinion. At the same time, it connected him to his protagonist and to his audience. True, Shakespeare and the audience know that the King will triumph at Agincourt. But what does that victory mean as the culmination of the *Henriad*? How does it inform the *Henriad* as whole? In this respect, Shakespeare, like Henry, must encounter in his soul not only the "God of battles" but the God of history as well.

The Book of Revelation informs the colloquy between Bates, Williams, and the King that precedes and inspires the prayer. Williams tells the

---

177. Spiekerman, *Shakespeare's Political Realism*, 117, 142.
178. John Dover Wilson, introduction to *King Henry V*, by William Shakespeare, ed. John Dover Wilson, xiv.

unannounced, self-proclaimed "friend" (4.1.93) that the King, if his "cause be not good" (134), will have a "heavy reckoning to make" (135) "at the Latter Day" (137). Let us acknowledge that Christianity expresses its belief in the resurrection of the dead in many ways. But the playwright goes on to supply an important detail, long overlooked, that links the action of the play spiritually to John of Patmos's vision. As the sun rises on the field of battle, the King waxes prophetic:[179]

> And Crispin Crispian shall ne'er go by,
> From this day to the ending of the world,
> But we in it shall be rememberèd—
> We few, we happy few, we band of brothers.
> For he today that sheds his blood with me
> Shall be my brother. . . .
>
> (4.3.57–62)

Early in the horrible reign of Diocletian, the martyred saints and reputed brothers Crispinus and Crispianus were not crucified or thrown to the lions. They were *beheaded.* In a thoroughgoing biblical culture such as Shakespeare's, the still-current manner of their executions would have been associated with the eerie way that death by beheading enters John of Patmos's prophecy about the Millennium:

> And I *saw* the souls of them, that were beheaded for the witness of Jesus, and for the word of God, & which did not worship the beast, neither his image, neither had taken his mark upon their foreheads, or on their hands: and they lived, & reigned with Christ a thousand year.
> But the rest of the dead men shall not live again, until the thousand years be finished: this is the first resurrection.
>
> (Revelation 20: 4–5, italics in original)

My focus on Revelation takes additional support from "Crispin Crispian" both because the King invokes "the ending of the world," as Williams had done two scenes earlier, and because Henry now does so with the liturgical calendar in view, including a martyrological and fraternal reference to the shedding of blood: "he *today* that sheds his blood with me / Shall be my brother" (my emphasis). The King's place in this spiritual realm, *when he*

---

179. For "the feast of Crispine and Crispinian" in Holinshed, see Raphael Holinshed, *Holinshed's Chronicle: As Used in Shakespeare's Plays,* ed. Allardyce and Josephine Nicoll, 83.

occupies it, is necessarily prophetic and Christological. To be sure, he does not always rise to these heights. Like King David, he is more than a little flawed. And yet, hard fact for us critics, we are not necessarily in a position to judge him, even when he is at his least appealing. A gap between our powers of judgment and God's power of Judgment is built into the Christian experience of the play. What we can say is that, in his defining moment of victory, at least, the King is typologically like the "God of battles" (4.1.287), who, in Revelation, is the rider on the white horse, leading his heavenly armies to their final victory over evil: he "was called, Faithful & true, & he judgeth and fighteth righteously . . . and his name is called, THE WORD OF GOD (Revelation 19:11–13).[180]

None of this is a matter of reductive Christian allegorization. It is a matter of Shakespeare's authorial resolve that, though Henry's time was brief, it had glimpsed England's highest destiny. I find this act of expressive, literary faith to be quasi-Spenserian and proto-Miltonic, more Protestant than Catholic in character, though, piquantly, it comes in celebration of a pre-Reformation monarch. The Book of Revelation gave the playwright an image of Christ as a righteous warrior-king,[181] leading his armies to final victory, and dwelling as God with his people (beheaded martyrs first) in the New Jerusalem. Henry's marriage to Katharine of Valois, amidst chatter of "cities turned into a maid" and "maiden walls that war hath never entered" (5.2.322–23), may allude on a spiritual level to the New Jerusalem, "come down from God out of heaven, prepared as a bride trimmed for her husband" (Revelation 21:2). As a further, related consideration, we note that Falstaff's dying talk of the "Whore of Babylon"—with a "rheumatic" pun on the Roman church (2.3.37–38)[182]— completes his concern with the four last things by landing him in the Book of Revelation (17:5). As Morris points out, Mistress Quickly's malapropism about "Arthur's bosom" (2.3.10) leads us to remember Falstaff's "recurrent evocations of the parable of Dives and Lazarus," a uniquely Lucan parable that was "frequently met in the general iconography of apocalyptic art."[183] The memory the Boy shares is thus curious: "Do you not remember, 'a saw

---

180. Shaheen connects this biblical figure, by way of Isaiah 63:13, to Hal's promise to his father: "When I will wear a garment all of blood / And stain my favors with a bloody mask" (1H4 3.2.135–36). Shaheen, *Biblical References*, 418.

181. Groves argues that Shakespeare drew on the martial tradition of the Harrowing of Hell. See Groves, *Texts and Traditions*, 135–53. I note that Prince Arthur's exploits in Book 1, Canto viii of *The Faerie Queene* are keyed both to the Harrowing of Hell and to Revelation.

182. Per Bevington.

183. Morris, *Last Things*, 281, 284.

a flea stick upon Bardolph's nose, and 'a said it was a black soul burning in hell" (39–41). So Falstaff's career is not divorced from the turn to Revelation in *Henry V*.

With this larger Christian reality restored to view, I return to the sustaining architecture of oaths. For Pistol, operating at the lowest level of verbal currency, almost no one is to be trusted: "oaths are straws" (2.3.50). Captain Gower remarks of soldiers like Pistol: "they trick up [their false history of events] with new-tuned oaths" (3.6.76). In Pistol's case, the nominal value of his verbal currency is all the value there is: we recognize the Falstaffian pedigree. The ill-fated Nym (whose name means "to steal") operates at the same base level. As Nym's reluctant apprentice, the ill-fated Boy reports: "his few words are matched with as few good deeds" (3.2.38–39). Some Falstaffian wit seems to have rubbed off on this young person—Hal's gift to Falstaff. He remarks in French to Pistol's captive, the pathetic Monsieur Le Fer, who is not made of iron, "*Encore qu'il est contre son jurement de pardoner aucun prisonnier, néanmoins, pour les écus que vous l'avez promis, il est content à vous donner la liberté, le franchisement.*" With a smirking pun on *franchisement*, Shakespeare ridicules the defeated French, who so much lack the ability to redeem words with deeds that one of their men surrenders to the English *miles gloriosus*, who sells out his alleged oath (*son jurement*) for two hundred French crowns, which evidently are not worth very much. Shakespeare's attention to bad oaths continues in the final humiliation of Pistol at Fluellen's hands, with the leek, the beating, and a degrading "groat" for payment (5.1.57). Gower appropriately calls Pistol a "counterfeit cowardly knave" and asks him, "Will you . . . dare not avouch in your deeds any of your words?" (5.1.68, 71–72). To expose Pistol in this brutal fashion is the necessary means, when all the world's a stage, for distinguishing false actors from true actors. As we know, Pistol is much affected by the stage. He apes the rodomontade of bombastic aspirants to regal power like Marlowe's Tamburlaine.[184] And yet, his swaggering theatrical affectations deceived Monsieur Le Fer, and briefly deceived Fluellen. By removing the counterfeits from circulation, Shakespeare bolsters the currency of those who are true to their word. And while Rabkin is right to draw our attention to the grim "postwar world the play so powerfully conjures up,"[185] the moral emphasis does not fall on social consciousness in the sense of Woolf's Mrs. Ramsay. It is Christianity that is left on the proverbial hook.

---

184. G. K. Hunter, *English Drama 1586–1642: The Age of Shakespeare*, 42n18.
185. Rabkin, *Shakespeare and the Problem*, 57.

The common soldier Williams represents the next level of verbal currency. Fluellen's interactions with Pistol frame the King's interactions with Williams, to the effect of highlighting Williams's true "word" (4.1.219, 4.7.174, 4.8.32). Arguably, the King is not being very honest himself, in the business of Williams and the glove, but the bluff humor of the situation wins out:

> KING   Soldier, why wear'st thou that glove in thy cap?
>
> WILLIAMS   An't please Your Majesty, a rascal that swaggered with me last night, who, if 'a live, and ever dare to challenge this glove, I have sworn to take him a box o'th'ear; or if I can see my glove in his cap, which he swore, as he was a soldier, he would wear if 'a lived, I will strike it out soundly.
>
> KING   What think you, Captain Fluellen, is it fit this soldier keep his oath?
>
> FLUELLEN   He is a craven and a villain else, an't please Your Majesty, in my conscience.
>
> KING   It may be his enemy is a gentleman of great sort, quite from the answer of his degree.
>
> FLUELLEN   Though he be as good a gentleman as the devil is, as Lucifer and Beelzebub himself, it is necessary, look your Grace, that he keep his vow and his oath.
>
> (4.7.118–37)

Williams's reference to "a rascal that swaggered" conjures up Pistol more than it does the King, though the ambiguity stands: "Your Majesty, a rascal that swaggered." We note that the actor who played Pistol must have delivered a fine performance. The first quarto title page of *2 Henry IV* (1600) reads in part: "The second Part of Henry the fourth, continuing to his death, *and coronation of Henry* the fifth. With the humours of sir John *Falstaff, and swaggering Pistol.*" The first quarto title page of *Henry V* (also 1600) refers to "The Chronicle History of Henry the Fifth, With his battle at Agincourt in *France*. Together with *Ancient Pistol.*"[186] In *2 Henry IV*, when Pistol makes his first entrance, Doll Tearsheet and Mistress Quickly respond to him by using some variation of "swagger" nine times (4.2). The homiletic simplicity of the Pistol/Williams contrast is disturbed by Fluellen's remark about the swaggerer in question: "Though he be as good a gentleman as the King is, as Lucifer and Beelzebub himself, it is necessary, look your Grace, that he keep his vow and his oath." For a heartbeat, an antithetical reading of *Henry V* opens up,

---

186. Shakespeare, *King Henry IV Part 2*, ed. Bulman, 431, and William Shakespeare, *King Henry V*, ed. T. W. Craik, 373. I have modernized the spellings and kept the original italics.

where the King, a swaggerer, stands on a continuum with the arch-rebels Lucifer and Beelzebub, who are recognized for their gentlemanly qualities, as they peep at us with God only knows what knowledge. They have not been absent from the English campaign or the day of battle. But Williams refuses to be "forsworn" (4.8.12). Unlike Pistol, he keeps his "word" (4.8.32) by striking Fluellen, another man of his word, who unknowingly wears Williams's glove. The King intervenes, and, after Williams pleads his case, rewards him by stuffing the glove with "crowns" (4.8.57), definitively bringing the nominal value of the currency in line with substantial value of the metal. The nominal value is now as good as the King's word, which is as good as Fluellen's word, which is as good as Williams's word, which is as good as the British soldiers' word, which is as good as the word of Christian martyrs. At the highest level of verbal currency, the "word of God" (Revelation 19:13) and the word of Henry V come into symbolic conjunction through the military determinations of providence and its true English vessels. So the victory at Agincourt serves a redemptive purpose, for the King's language and coinage, as well as for English history. This and thus despite Henry's spotted political heroism.

But the play ends on an elegiac note, an anticlimax in which the God of history recedes. When Charles VI, the French King, worries that French children "grow like savages . . . To swearing" (5.2.59–61), the remedy, as Henry V is quick to remark, lies in "full accord to all our just demands" (5.2.71). In the same confident fashion, Henry's preference for "downright oaths" (5.2.146) suits his brisk courtship and flatters the English reputation for blunt honesty. But still, if we are not distracted by Henry's humorous demeanor, we will find that the references to "swearing" and "oaths" supply an important context for the nuptials. When Charles VI gives Katharine to Henry, he does so in the hope of their children establishing "Christian-like accord" between England and France (5.2.352)—a millennial peace, and an Erasmian pipedream. King Henry ends the action with the celebratory promise of transformative oaths to come:

> Prepare we for our marriage, on which day,
> My lord of Burgundy, we'll take your oath,
> And all the peers', for surety of our leagues.
> Then shall I swear to Kate, and you to me;
> And may our oaths well kept and prosperous be!
>
> (5.2.369–73)

After this happy vision of "oaths well kept and prosperous," the Chorus returns one last time to the stage, to announce, in the form of a sonnet, a very different chapter in English history: when Henry V died young, his and Katharine's heir, Henry VI, failed to keep France. In other words, the wished-for "Christian-like accord" broke down. None of the oaths was "well kept." The millennium failed to materialize. Whatever our reading of the *Henriad*, the abrupt and unhappy ending unsettles it.

Historian Edward Hall, absorbing the work of Polydore Vergil, had linked the murder of Richard II to the succession of evils that finally culminated in God's scourge, Richard III, being defeated by God's paladin, Henry Tudor. Hence Tillyard's view of interlocking tetralogies. The suggestion may follow that Henry V's prayer was granted with exacting precision, that retribution for past sins did not come on the day of battle at Agincourt ("Not today, O Lord, / Oh, not today, think not upon the fault / My father made in compassing the crown!"), and that the design of providence was not fulfilled until the Wars of the Roses and Henry Tudor's decisive victory at Bosworth Field.[187] On a different view, however, Henry Tudor was vulnerable to charges of illegitimacy on both sides of his family tree. Curiously enough, Holinshed mentions a dissenting account of the Tudors' patriarchal origins in the *Polychronicon*, though he goes on in the same spirit as Hall, reporting that, after the widowed Katharine married a Welshman called Owen Tudor, she gave birth to four children, including Edmund Tudor, the father of Henry, who, as Henry VII, became the founder of the Tudor dynasty, the father of Henry VIII, and the grandfather of Elizabeth. Spenser polished this Welsh apple in *The Faerie Queene*. Shakespeare did so in his earlier tetralogy. In fact, he had depicted Henry Tudor praying to God on the eve of battle (R3 5.3.108–17). And yet, with the Epilogue of *Henry V*, he chose not to amplify heroic continuity, preferring instead to burden his audience with their loss of a redeeming time. Though no saint, Henry V had "achieved" "the world's best garden" (Epil. 7). By contrast, what could the present achieve? Where the medieval past was redeemed through the providential correspondence between the victorious Henry V and the victorious God of battles, the Tudor period could not, to follow the Chorus's elegiac suggestion, lay claim to the same typological arc. The dawn of the Tudors meant the coming of the English Reformation and the rise of Tudor political mythology, all of which played out too ambiguously in Shakespeare's mature mind to warrant celebration.

---

187. With thanks to Noah Millman. See Tillyard, *Shakespeare's History Plays*, 330–31.

CHAPTER 4

Free Will in *Hamlet*?

FIRST SAILOR   God bless you, sir.
HORATIO   Let him bless thee too.
FIRST SAILOR   'A shall, sir, an't please him.
(HAM 4.6.7–9)

In the previous chapter, I argued that Shakespeare in writing *Henry V* encountered the distinctly Christian situation of trying to discern God's will in order to conform to it. The argument turned on the idea of a parallel between the hero's decisions and the author's artistic choices, and, more specifically, on conscience being the means to this parallel. *Hamlet* presents much the same scenario of trying to discern God's will, and with the same type of parallel. In this case, though, the plot is driven not by the circumstances of a providential destiny, but by a conscience-harrowing ghost.

The English word *conscience* possesses shades of meaning that Shakespeare recognized. To parse these meanings, we can turn for help to that master of erudition, C. S. Lewis. In *Studies in Words*, Lewis explains that, in its simplest meaning, *conscience*, which derives from the Latin noun *conscientia*, is a psychological faculty that "bears witness" to events but does not dictate right or wrong. He cites two illustrative examples from *Richard III*: the murderer who says that "conscience makes a man a coward" and Richard's apostrophe to "coward conscience." He then addresses how *conscience* came to mean "the internal lawgiver." Having examined the sources of this "great semantic shift" in Saint Paul, he adduces a later instance of mixed usage (witness and lawgiver) in *Henry V*.[1] I would extend this hint from Lewis to suggest that the witnessing sense cooperated with the lawgiving sense for the author of *Henry V*: both the hero and the author pay close witness to their moral choices; and for both, conscience has the power to dictate right and wrong. Despite challenges and difficulties, conscience does not disrupt the functioning of the social self in its station in life. A balance is maintained. But for Hamlet, as well as for the

---

1. C. S. Lewis, *Studies in Words*, 190, 188, 191, 192, 204. The passage of mixed usage comes from the disguised King (4.1.118–19).

Shakespeare of *Hamlet*, conscience is caught in the grips of a full-blown crisis of authority. It interferes with the social self.

In or around 1599, in between writing *Henry V* and *Hamlet*, Shakespeare wrote *As You Like It* and *Julius Caesar*.[2] The one is a witty pastoral frolic, the other a troubled vision of the Rome of the Stoics. The comic heroine Rosalind has her play's sole remark about conscience. She makes this remark to Orlando, who, apparently, cannot see through her disguise as Ganymede. The love-struck young man protests that he is sincere, "I would I could make thee believe I love." Rosalind replies, "Me believe it? You may as soon make her that you love believe it, which I warrant she is apter to do than to confess she does. That is one of the points in the which women still give the lie to their consciences" (3.2.375–81). In the green world of *As You Like It*, "the lie" is on the side of the comedy. Rosalind's conscience does not dictate right or wrong. It only bears witness to the truth. It is her disguised womanly self that gives her witnessing conscience the lie. Rosalind (as we know) is charmingly theatrical.

In *Julius Caesar*, the lie is on the side of the tragedy. Brutus's soliloquy in Act 2 is a study in self-evasion. It has the Augustinian potential, *qua* soliloquy, to be "a form of colloquium with God."[3] But Shakespeare's Brutus, a pagan speaking before an audience of Christians, is unaware of their God. This is why we can point to the rhetorical tradition of Augustine: the audience is so keenly aware of the Christian God that, during the course of Brutus's casuistical speech, it supplies the Christian conscience lacking in the speaker. We cannot understand the play at all if we disregard its most basic rhetorical situation: the dramatic irony of the audience's understanding the characters' real moral position better than they do.

Alone in his orchard, Brutus has Caesar on his mind:

> And since the quarrel
> Will bear no color for the thing he is,
> Fashion it thus: that what he is, augmented,
> Would run to these and these extremities;
> And therefore think him as the serpent's egg
> Which, hatched, would, as his kind, grow mischievous;
> And kill him in his shell.
>
> (2.1.28–34)

---

2. See Bart Van Es, *Shakespeare in Company*, 312–14.

3. Brian Cummings, *Mortal Thoughts: Religion, Secularity & Identity in Shakespeare and Early Modern England*, 182.

The "quarrel" is of course the case against Caesar. Brutus suspects that Caesar's murder will be a tough sell to the commoners because the conspirators lack a legitimate reason for carrying it out. To get what he really wants, Brutus has recourse neither to conscience nor to reason but to his will: "Fashion it thus." He projects what Christians would recognize as his own sins of pride and envy onto a "serpent's egg" of his imagination, the serpent being emblematic in the Elizabethan mind of Satan in the garden of Eden. That is why we are in Brutus's orchard. With no one bearing witness except Brutus himself, the audience, and their God, Brutus's stoical mind defers at this fateful moment to the ethos of heroic competition between aristocratic, honor-driven males.[4] Brutus is not delayed by an internal lawgiver. He is driven by what Augustine in *The City of God* would call his *libido dominandi*, his "lust of rule."[5] His critical lapse in judgment occurs despite the emphasis in stoical teaching on cultivating the truth. Lacking a Christian conscience, Brutus is unable to know himself at his moment of crisis.

Then again, he has no Christian conscience to make him a coward. It was Shakespeare's decision to link Hamlet to Wittenberg that fostered such unheroic conditions for the stage. As an innovation on the known sources, this theological masterstroke guaranteed Martin Luther a significant role in the future world of *Hamlet* scholarship. It took a long time to happen, however, and when it did Johnson was in the grave and Coleridge in his final decade. Not until 1826 did S. W. Singer write the pioneering note on the Diet of Worms that is now standard editorial fare. The ball did not really get rolling until J. Dover Wilson set it in motion in *What Happens in Hamlet* (1951).[6] It is worth underscoring: the Shakespeare of Johnson and Garrick, of Coleridge and Hazlitt, of Eliot and Woolf, was never subjected to theological scrutiny befitting the Elizabethan age.

Now that Shakespeare's interest in Luther has been established, we can suggest that the famous Reformer haunts the opening scene of *Julius Caesar*, where we locate the second and last occurrence of *conscience* between *Henry V*

---

4. The stoical ethos of *Julius Caesar* is well summarized in *De Officiis*, in the paragraph beginning, *In primisque hominis est propria veri inquisitio atque investigatio*. Marcus Tullius Cicero, *On Duties [De Officiis]*, trans. Walter Miller, 14 (I.iv.13).

5. Augustine, *The City of God*, trans. Marcus Dods, 3.

6. See Raymond B. Waddington, "Lutheran *Hamlet*," *English Language Notes* 27 (1989): 27, 39n3, 39n4. For other Lutheran analyses of the play, see R. Chris Hassel, Jr., "Hamlet's 'Too, Too Solid Flesh,'" *Sixteenth Century Journal* 25 (Autumn 1994): 609–22, and Edward T. Oakes, SJ, "*Hamlet* and the Reformation: The Prince of Denmark as 'Young Man Luther,'" *Logos* 13:1 (2010): 53–78.

and *Hamlet*. A number of tradesmen are idling about Rome in violation of the sumptuary laws. The tribune Marullus asks one of them: "But what trade art thou? Answer me directly." The worker replies: "A trade, sir, that I hope I may use with a safe conscience, which is indeed, sir, a mender of bad soles" (1.1.12–14). Luther, who "was fond of citing his lowly origins,"[7] was known for ministering to the spiritual needs of working people. Cobblers, in particular, seem to have peopled his imagination. The following passage from the Large Catechism, penned by Luther in German, appeared in Latin translations of 1529 and 1544, as well as in the 1584 Latin edition of *The Book of Concord*: "Let us therefore learn the first commandment well and realize that God will tolerate no presumption and no trust in any other object; he makes no greater demand of us than a hearty trust in him for all blessings. Then we shall be on the right path and walk straight ahead, using all of God's gifts exactly as a cobbler uses his needle, awl, and thread (for work, eventually to lay them aside). . . . Let each person be in his station in life according to God's order, allowing none of these good things to be his lord or idol."[8] Luther's preaching on vocation underscores the same humble practices: "For if we could be content with those things which we have, and quietly use the gifts of God, and so rejoice with our wife, our children, and families giving thanks to God for the same, and with a good conscience doing our duty in our vocation, who could be so happy as we?"[9]

Clearly, Shakespeare's cobbler wants to satisfy a Christian "conscience." He is lacking in Brutus's ambition. And if the blatant pun on "soles/souls" sails right over the heads of Marullus and his fellow tribune, Flavius, the joke is on them: the Elizabethans knew better.

---

7. The passage continues: "Both his father and his mother, he liked to say, had peasant backgrounds. This is misleading." Michael Massing, *Fatal Discord: Erasmus, Luther, and the Fight for the Western Mind*, 20.

8. Martin Luther, quoted in *The Book of Concord: The Confessions of the Evangelical Lutheran Church*, ed. Theodore G. Tappert, 371.

9. Martin Luther, *A Commentarie vpon the Fiftene Psalmes, Called Psalmi Graduum, that is, Psalmes of Degrees: Faithfully Copied Out of the Lectures of D. Martin Luther; Very Frutefull and Comfortable for All Christian Afflicted Consciences To Reade; Translated Out of Latine into Englishe by Henry Bull*, EEBO, 141–42. (I have modernized the text). Luther also wrote: "When a prince sees his neighbor oppressed, he should think: That concerns me. I must protect and shield my neighbor . . . . The same is true for shoemaker, tailor, scribe, or reader. If he is a Christian tailor, he will see: I make these clothes because God has bidden me to do so, so that I can earn a living, so that I can help and serve my neighbor. When a Christian does not serve the other, God is not present; that is not Christian living." Martin Luther, "A Sermon on Christian Righteousness, or the Forgiveness of Sins, Preached at Marburg in Hesse, 1529, Martin Luther, Wittenberg, 1530," quoted in Greg Peters, *The Monkhood of All Believers*, 164. The memorable anecdote, in *The Book of Concord* (275), about the shoemaker of Alexandria, was written by Philip Melanchthon.

The name of Erasmus is not one we readily associate with *Hamlet*. Granted, the rhetorical fingerprint of *De Copia* is more or less ubiquitous in Shakespeare. As Marion Trousdale demonstrates in her admirable *Shakespeare and the Rhetoricians*, *Hamlet* is no exception. Nor, for that matter, is *Julius Caesar*.[10] On the level of theology, though, it is the great debate between Erasmus and Luther (1524–25) that creates an unexpected opening for Erasmus—one long overlooked, if only because the main texts, Erasmus's *On the Freedom of the Will* and Luther's *On the Bondage of the Will*, were not translated into English for centuries.

That Shakespeare had some knowledge of the great debate cannot be doubted. The participants and their disagreement were too significant to be ignored. Ben Jonson, for instance, took sides in his commonplace book, *Discoveries*,[11] championing Erasmus over Luther. The debate marked the permanent divisions between humanism and the Reformation—which is why Quentin Skinner referred to it as a "definitive breach."[12] The debate's impact on Shakespeare's mind was to foster an atmosphere of ideas that was by its nature traceable to many analogous sources, and reducible to none. To reconstruct this atmosphere entails risks: it is not a matter of nailing things down. But if we begin with Hamlet's and Horatio's being students at the University of Wittenberg, where Luther had held the chair in biblical theology, we may proceed by means of Shakespeare's text to Luther's argument for predestination and the bondage of the will, and thus to the debate in which that argument achieved its most memorable expression. If we go so far, it is impossible to exclude Erasmus.

Recent studies by Brian Cummings and Ricardo Quinones have clarified the debate's historical significance. For Cummings, its real meaning, aside from "the celebrity of its participants," is that "literature and theology cannot, after all, escape each other."[13] Taking Cummings's penetrating observation as a starting point, we may say that Shakespeare elaborates upon it: "literature and theology cannot escape each other—nor can they be reconciled." In *Hamlet*, the discourses of literature and theology, of humanism and reform, jostle and jar as a consequence of their occupying the same text. Hamlet himself

---

10. See, for example, Jeffrey J. Yu, "Shakespeare's *Julius Caesar*, Erasmus's *De Copia*, and Sentential Ambiguity," *Comparative Drama* 41 (Spring 2007): 79–106.

11. *The Cambridge Edition of the Works of Ben Jonson*, ed. David Bevington, Martin Butler, and Ian Donaldson, 7:535–36.

12. Quentin Skinner, *The Foundations of Modern Political Thought*, 2:4.

13. Brian Cummings, *The Literary Culture of the Reformation: Grammar and Grace*, 148.

embodies this instability. He wants to hold "as 'twere the mirror up to nature" (3.2.22) and a "glass" (3.4.20) to his mother's soul. He asks the players to "reform" their bad acting (3.2.38), after declaring, "The play's the thing / Wherein I'll catch the conscience of a king" (2.2.605–606). Hamlet, in other words, may be said to combine and to condense the registers and impulses of literature and theology, humanism and reform.

For Quinones, "Erasmus represented the advanced stage of European consciousness in his time, while Luther was suspicious of consciousness, its traps, its lures, its self-flatteries and self-promotions."[14] Shakespeare absorbs and recasts what Quinones calls the agonistic "dualism" of the great debate, internalizing both sides of the argument. If he achieves the greatest authorial consciousness that we know, he compounds it with suspicion of that consciousness, of "its traps, its lures, its self-flatteries and self-promotions." In this respect, the author of *Hamlet* bears comparison to the Luther who wrote, "If I lived and worked to eternity, my conscience would never be assured and certain how much it ought to do to satisfy God. For whatever work might be accomplished, there would always remain an anxious doubt whether it pleased God or whether he required something more, as the experience of all self-justifiers proves."[15] This speaks to "conscience" making "cowards of us all" (3.1.84) with peculiar force. It speaks to the difficulty of knowing precisely what one knows and precisely where one stands in relation to God. Relevant here is the etymological link between "the noun *conscientia* and the adjective *conscius*."[16] Like the English word *conscious*, both Latin words concern knowing, and both, through the variable force of the prefix, can insinuate the complexities of knowing what one knows. Luther was tortured by such psychological complexities. Erasmus, by contrast, was not obsessed with determining the mental grounds of moral knowledge. Erasmus gravitated toward health, not morbidity, and took for granted the operations of a healthy conscience. As regards conscience, Erasmus in the *Enchiridion* sounds positively medieval. For Luther, the younger man rising in fame, the free play of Erasmus's protean consciousness was lacking in essential depth. Yet Erasmus understood Luther perfectly well.

---

14. Ricardo Quinones, *Dualisms: The Agons of the Modern World*, 58. If there are lingering doubts about the general importance of the debate between Luther and Erasmus, they likely stem from the introduction by E. Gordon Rupp to *Luther and Erasmus: Free Will and Salvation* (the standard English edition of the main texts in the debate). Quinones restores the debate to its central place in the history of European culture and corrects Rupp (Quinones, 23–97, 405n8).

15. Martin Luther, *On the Bondage of the Will*, in *Luther and Erasmus: Free Will and Salvation*, ed. E. Gordon Rupp and Philip S. Watson, 329.

16. Lewis, *Studies in Words*, 181.

Like Thomas More, Luther points conscience in a new direction as the ground under Christendom fissures. To follow Cummings on Luther: "Conscience becomes associated with faith, with identity, rather than with ethics and behavioral psychology."[17] When he declared at the Diet of Worms (Hamlet's famous allusion occurs at 4.3.20–21), "My conscience is captive to the Word of God," Luther was rejecting the faculty psychology and moral reasoning of the scholastics. Further, he wanted to liberate conscience "from papal decree and canon law,"[18] and to impose "on it the responsibility to render service to the world."[19] He upheld this view of conscience in the great debate.[20] But "ultimately," as Heiko Oberman explains, "the moral pressure of the Devil . . . led him to do battle against that fatal human disease, the oppressive 'superego' of conscience."[21] Luther's apprehensions about conscience are less well known than his heroics at the Diet of Worms, which advanced western civilization toward a secular ideal of conscience that would have shocked his medieval soul. One thinks of Robert Bolt's *A Man for All Seasons*, where Luther's adversary More is anachronistically celebrated for his individual code of conscience.[22] More's conscience was traditional and scholastic, but not without its own glimmerings of a later, more self-oriented modernity. In a general sense, we can trace Hamlet's battles of conscience to the cultural crisis that Luther and More precipitated, a crisis of faith and tradition. But given Hamlet's past at Wittenberg, we will defer in this chapter to the pressure exerted by Luther. This exhausting pressure of conscience, even as it thwarts Hamlet's humanistic desire for action and the active life, becomes a spur to his creator's consciousness, or larger recognition, of the almost impossibly tense relations between literature and theology. And though we cannot call that consciousness Erasmian, we will understand it better if we grasp its Erasmian qualities.

I want to argue that the great debate is a conceptual source text for *Hamlet*, a kind of ideational template, and that its resonances in the play extend from the thematic tension between free will and predestination, to the divisions of

17. Cummings, *Mortal Thoughts*, 80.

18. Martin Luther, quoted in Heiko O. Oberman, *Luther: Man between God and the Devil*, trans. Eileen Walliser-Schwarzbart, 203.

19. Oberman, *Luther*, 204.

20. Luther, *On the Bondage*, 127, 128, 309.

21. Oberman, *Luther*, 291; quoted in Dominic Erdozain, *The Soul of Doubt: The Religious Roots of Unbelief from Luther to Marx*, 23.

22. Cummings, *Mortal Thoughts*, 67–68. For the senses of *conscience* in More, and its relation to conscience in Luther, see 67–91.

conscience, to the competing worlds of humanism and reform, out of which complexity and dissonance Shakespeare salvages what moral coherence he can. In his consciousness of this fractured dialectic, of this difficult reality of scarcely complementary forces at work in the mind and in society, Shakespeare may have been provoked by Luther's theological use of the theater as metaphor. The man who wrote, "All the world's a stage" (AYL 2.7.138), knew about the anti-theatrical arguments of Stephen Gosson and Philip Stubbes, who had the insect power to harass and annoy, motivated, as they were, by "the Protestant abhorrence of ceremony and spectacle."[23] Luther had the power of mind to penetrate more deeply. He rebukes Erasmus: "Man has free choice—if, of course, God would hand over his own to him! . . . But that is not the way for theologians to talk, but for stage players."[24] Luther found the very phrase "free choice" to be "too imposing, too wide and full," a "misuse of language," better suited to actors and acting than to theology. He associated it with the deluded notion that "man is lord of heaven and earth." [25] In a different context, he referred to "all of profane history" as a "puppet play of God's," while using the "expression 'God's play' for what takes place in justification."[26] Luther in his theological brilliance put an anti-humanistic spin on the ancient metaphor of the *theatrum mundi*. The world, in his view, was indefensible in terms of either free will or humanism, and Shakespeare certainly leaves open an anti-humanistic reading of his play.[27]

But the playwright engages both sides of the debate by employing methods characteristic of Erasmian skepticism: recourse to ambiguity and suspension of judgment. To quote Erasmus in his failed efforts at de-escalation:

---

23. Russ McDonald, *The Bedford Companion to Shakespeare: An Introduction with Documents*, 319.

24. Luther, *On the Bondage*, 143.

25. Luther, *On the Bondage*, 142–43.

26. Ernst Robert Curtius, *European Literature and the Latin Middle Ages*, trans. Willard R. Trask, 140. Curtius is quoting Luther in Erich Seeburg, *Grundzüge der Theologie Luthers* (1940). I note that when Luther "entered the monastery [at Erfurt], he left almost all his books behind, but insisted on taking along copies of Plautus and Virgil, authors he would quote all his life." Oberman, *Luther*, 123. Evidently, he "stressed [Plautus's] pedagogical uses as a mirror of morality." Stuart Gillespie, *Shakespeare's Books: A Dictionary of Shakespeare's Sources*, 413.

27. For example, John Carroll asks of *Hamlet*, "Where is the cleansing metaphysical exhilaration at the end, the exhausted audience rising out of the ashes with the inspired feeling that, in spite of all, life is fresh and good? . . . That out of the tragic wreck the annihilated individual transcends the bounds of his or her own self and is united with the grander scheme of things?" John Carroll, *The Wreck of Western Culture: Humanism Revisited*, 44–45. More recently, Rhodri Lewis writes of Shakespeare, "*Hamlet* indicates that he came to find humanist moral philosophy deficient in the face of human experience as he observed it." Rhodri Lewis, *Hamlet and the Vision of Darkness*, 26. For sources of the philosophical debate between humanism and anti-humanism in *Hamlet*, see Ronald Knowles, "*Hamlet* and Counter-Humanism," *Renaissance Quarterly* 52 (Winter 1999): 1048–52.

"so far am I from delighting in 'assertions' that I would readily take refuge in the opinions of Skeptics, wherever this is allowed by the inviolable authority of the Holy Scriptures and by the decrees of the Church."[28] Luther's central point, repeated almost *ad nauseam*, was that the argument over free will was essential (*pace* Erasmus), that the debate itself was meaningful precisely because the question of free will was paramount—and so the assertive Luther achieved his definitive breach. Shakespeare, I have said, absorbs and recasts the agonistic "dualism" of the great debate, internalizing both sides. He takes very seriously Luther's denial of free will and his anti-humanistic doctrine of the two kingdoms: Satan's and God's. Luther's being in the right is a possibility that haunts this much-haunted play. Suspending judgment, the author of *Hamlet* does not resolve the great debate or the topics that follow closely in its wake. He applies Erasmian techniques of ambiguity and silence to frame questions that, within his understanding, must remain open: whether we have free will, what is the meaning of tragedy and tragic suffering, and how far Christianity can countenance the violence inherent in humanism, which, as regards *Hamlet*, we may approach in an Erasmian spirit as "the wider plain of the Muses,"[29] including the plain of Ilion.

This framing of questions leaves us to attend to moral and interpretive dilemmas that are the signs of Shakespeare's severest limitations as a moralist—limitations that strike us as an expression of spiritual crisis on Shakespeare's part, though we do not have the biographical facts to get a clear picture of that crisis, or to connect Shakespeare's daily experience to the writing of the play.[30] But we may suggest that Shakespeare's life as a playwright—his labor writing lines for men and women in the passionate grip of life—gave intimate focus to the doubts and questions about the will and salvation that he grapples with in *Hamlet*. A theologian discusses any number of mysteries in order to carve out a system or to assert a truth; a tragedian, having to express these mysteries in the flesh, may prefer to suspend judgment. Even so, Shakespeare could neither suspend, nor outthink, the thought of Final Judgment. Hamlet's delay, including his notorious decision against murdering Claudius in Act 3, Scene 3, reflects his obsessive anxiety about the afterlife. Lewis's vision of the case may be narrow, but it is not blind: "Hamlet's use of *conscience* at the end of the famous soliloquy . . . means

28. Erasmus, *On the Freedom of the Will*, in *Luther and Erasmus: Free Will and Salvation*, ed. E. Gordon Rupp and Philip S. Watson, 37.
29. Erasmus, *Freedom of the Will*, 36.
30. With a nod to T. S. Eliot's 1919 essay "Hamlet and His Problems."

nothing more or less than 'fear of hell.'"[31] I would like to compromise on this point, though I suspect Lewis would not. The "conscience" that makes "cowards of us all" does indeed suggest a fear of hell. But in my view, it carries Reformation associations that go beyond that one great driving concern. It is pertinent that the word *consciousness* emerges contemporaneously with *Hamlet*. It does so on the basis of what Lewis (referring to the variable force do the prefix) calls the "together sense," which, importantly, links it to *conscience*.[32] It was through the early modern pressure placed on *conscience*, as evident in the great debate and the annals of the Reformation, that Shakespeare developed his *consciousness* of the historical, theological, and literary problems at hand.

Some brief qualifications are in order. First, in keeping with previous sections of this book, we should acknowledge that Shakespeare's use of methods characteristic of Erasmian skepticism took place amidst broader currents of "skeptical faith" in sixteenth-century England: not only Erasmus and More but also skeptical writings newly translated from antiquity all played a role in shaping skeptical Christian sensibilities.[33] Second, and closely related to the first item, Montaigne factors in.[34] Certain strands of thought connect my reading of the play to the "Apology for Raymond Sebond," in particular, to Montaigne's emphasis on "the inanity, the vanity and nothingness, of man."[35] Even so, John Cox's point that Shakespeare, unlike Montaigne, employs biblical references that convey "the moral imperative that is inherent in the Christian sense of destiny"[36] applies to *Hamlet* and pulls in the direction of the great debate with its hundreds and hundreds of biblical references. Third, given our concern with the raw power of Luther's doctrine of justification in his debate with Erasmus, I will have no more to say regarding Luther's pastoral writings. I will be focusing on the Luther of the great debate. To borrow from

31. Lewis, *Studies in Words*, 207. He does acknowledge some other possible shades of meaning.

32. Lewis, *Studies in Words*, 210–11. The OED's first attestation of *consciousness* is from Sir Edwin Sandys's *A Relation of the State of Religion in Europe*: "Laying the ground of all his pollicie, in feare and ielousie issuing from a certaine consciousnesse of his owne worthlesness." Sandys completed his work in "Paris, in the April of 1599." Theodore K. Rabb, "The Editions of Sir Edwyn Sandys's *A Relation of the State of Religion in Europe*," *Huntington Library Quarterly* 26 (August 1963): 323.

33. As noted in Chapter 1, the phrase "skeptical faith" derives from John D. Cox, *Seeming Knowledge: Shakespeare and Skeptical Faith*, xii.

34. For *Hamlet* and Montaigne, see Rolf Soellner, *Shakespeare's Patterns of Self-Knowledge*, 187–88, and James Shapiro, *A Year in the Life of William Shakespeare 1599*, 297. See also note 171 in my Introduction.

35. Michel de Montaigne, *The Complete Works*, trans. Donald M. Frame, 397.

36. Cox, *Seeming Knowledge*, 231.

Skinner's account of Luther's position, we are not addressing free will in the ordinary, practical sense of men and women being free "to eat, drink, beget, rule."[37] The Luther of the debate happily conceded free will on this everyday level. It was to him a sop he could throw to Erasmus—with more than a dash of scorn. We are also passing over the question of purgatory, which scarcely enters the debate, with Luther himself dismissing it among "irrelevancies" and "trifles"; in any case, it has probably attracted sufficient attention in recent decades. Fourth and last, I am suggesting that it was due in part to the great debate that Erasmian ideas, particularly on free will, were circulating in the English religious bloodstream when Shakespeare took up *Hamlet*. Observing that "in most accounts of English opposition to Calvinism, anti-predestinar-ianism simply appears in the 1590s," Gregory Dodds offers a notable correc-tion to our sense of the late-Elizabethan period: "anti-predestinarian thought was present . . . in the writings and thought of Erasmus. . . . Erasmus's legacy was . . . firmly established in English religious culture." In Dodds's account, Erasmian ideas influenced the controversy over free will that boiled over at Cambridge University in 1595, leading to the formulation of the Lambeth Articles (see Chapter 1). Erasmus's influence would only grow with the rise of the Arminian movement.[38] If Calvin's deterministic worldview inspired a continuing, countervailing interest in Erasmus among English divines, we may infer that Luther's position in the debate cast a long shadow.

Hamlet's soliloquy in Act 3, Scene 1 is not about the freedom of the will or its bondage, but it does consider the kindred topic of the will and eternal salvation. Luther addresses this topic in his denunciation of Erasmus's "mod-erate Skeptical Theology": "it is not irreverent, inquisitive, or superfluous, but essentially salutary and necessary for a Christian, to find out whether the will does anything or nothing in matters pertaining to eternal salvation . . . For what we are doing is to inquire what free choice can do, what it has done to it (*'Quid patiatur'*), and what is its relation to the grace of God."[39] *Quid patiatur*, Luther's Latin phrase, can be translated "what it may suffer," a point I make to strengthen the connection to Hamlet's range of concerns, without suggest-ing a direct and palpable textual link. Hamlet starts his speech in a humanistic vein, pondering how action and suffering relate to being, not to salvation. But his dilemma leads him in the direction of the Christian afterlife, and, as the

37. Skinner, *Foundations*, 2:6. Luther, *On the Bondage*, 286.

38. Gregory D. Dodds, *Exploiting Erasmus: The Erasmian Legacy and Religious Change in Early Modern England*, 112, 112–15, 193–200.

39. Luther, *On the Bondage*, 116.

soliloquy develops, he thinks on how "dread of something after death . . . puzzles the will" (3.1.79–81). Let us revisit the opening lines:

> To be, or not to be, that is the question:
> Whether 'tis nobler in the mind to suffer
> The slings and arrows of outrageous fortune,
> Or to take arms against a sea of troubles
> And by opposing end them.
>
> (3.1.57–61)

For Rhodri Lewis in his book *Hamlet and the Vision of Darkness*, these words "are confused, and are not under Hamlet's control . . . [T]hey comprise another study in superficial humanism . . . held together not by logic or by art, but by a kind of negative whimsy."[40] Let me say that I appreciate the boldness of Lewis's account, by which it seems that Erasmus's warning against "a multitude of inane thoughts and words thrown together without discrimination"[41] was prophetic of this very passage—so burnished by fame that we have lost our ability to read it. But still, we are left to wonder why Luther's Christianity makes no appearance in *Hamlet and the Vision of Darkness*. For if we recognize Luther's impact when we read these famous lines, we may find that both art and logic militate against Lewis's verdict, even as we discover that art and logic are doing some strange things.

What I want to suggest is that Shakespeare, as the soliloquy begins, is fiddling with his placement of rhetorical *contraria*. We have just heard Erasmus's warning against "a multitude of inane thoughts and words thrown together without discrimination." How did one avoid such ramshackle writing? It was by arranging rubrics or headings "according to the principle of affinity and opposition,"[42] as Erasmus explains in book two of *De Copia*. Imagine you have your commonplace book open before you. You understand that the process of invention is necessary to your speechwriting ambitions: you cannot write your speeches until you become good at it. So, says Erasmus, here's how to get a handle on things. The idea is to group a selection of *sententiae* (i.e., commonplaces), *exempla*, and other promising materials under an appropriate heading, and to follow that section either by its *contrarium* or opposite, or at least

---

40. Lewis, *Hamlet and the Vision*, 267.
41. Erasmus, *On Copia of Words and Ideas*, trans. Donald B. King and H. David Rix, 11.
42. Erasmus, *On Copia*, 87; quoted in Marion Trousdale, *Shakespeare and the Rhetoricians*, 58.

by a closely related section. The *sententiae* and *exempla* that fit under the heading *Life* ("to be") might in this way be juxtaposed against the *sententiae* and *exempla* that fit under the opposite heading *Death* ("not to be"), or under the closely related heading *Illness* ("sicklied o'er with the pale cast of thought" [3.1.86]). In a commonplace book like Hamlet's "tables" (1.5.108), each heading would garner its particular trove of stock rhetorical items, such as "a fable, an apologue, an *exemplum*, a strange occurrence, a sententia, a witty or otherwise unusual expression, an adage, a metaphor or a parable."[43]

In Hamlet's soliloquy, Shakespeare subjects Erasmus's "principle of affinity and opposition" to a serious kind of deliberate confusion. He does this by short-circuiting his parallel syntax. He reneges on the parallelism that would impose order on his headings ("To be, or not to be"), along with their respective materials. Although the appearance of orderly syntactical logic presents itself, propped up by the word "or" at lines 57 and 60, the speech proceeds ambiguously, because parallel development is absent where one would expect it. For instance, Hamlet offers a prior example of parallel development when he addresses the Ghost, "Be thou a spirit of health or goblin damned, / Bring with thee airs from heaven or blasts from hell" (1.4.40–41). Likewise, almost immediately prior to the soliloquy, we hear an aside from Claudius: "The harlot's cheek, beautied with plast'ring art, / Is not more ugly to the thing that helps it / Than is my deed to my most painted word" (3.1.52–54). Assuming parallel syntax, at least for starters, and cued by the series of infinitives, we would expect Hamlet's dilemma to run as follows: (a) To be, or (b) not to be, that is the question: whether 'tis nobler (a) to take arms or (b) to suffer. But that is not what happens. By the same token, if the syntax is, in fact, strictly parallel, we must interpret Hamlet as saying that "to be" entails passive suffering and being subject to "outrageous fortune," while "not to be" entails action and taking "arms against a sea of troubles."[44]

---

43. Erasmus, *On Copia*, 89. I am indebted to Trousdale, *Shakespeare and the Rhetoricians*, 57–58.

44. Trousdale sees both "to suffer" and "to take arms" in terms of action, observing a finely wrought "positive-negative alteration" throughout the speech. Trousdale, *Shakespeare and the Rhetoricians*, 58–59. Somewhat like Trousdale, Kastan characterizes both "to suffer" and "to take arms against" as "'to be' options." David Scott Kastan, *A Will to Believe: Shakespeare and Religion*, 137. Neither critic is dead wrong; but they miss the ambiguity that comes from Shakespeare's deliberate blurring of life and death, action and passive suffering. I disagree as well with G. K. Hunter, who argues: "In 'to be or not to be' Hamlet begins by taking up the [s]toical potentialities of his own situation." Hunter is led, as he acknowledges, to "suppose that [Hamlet] is here talking about actions against enemies, not about suicide." G. K. Hunter, "The Heroism of Hamlet," in *Hamlet: A Reading and Playing Guide*, ed. John Russell Brown and Bernard Harris, 100. I find that the text does not support this supposition: for Hamlet, suicide is a mode of action.

Later in the soliloquy, Hamlet proceeds by juxtaposing classical associations between suicide and action, on the one hand, and, on the other, Christian associations between "patient merit" (3.1.75) and a life of passive suffering in which suicide is ruled out. He goes on to develop these thematic counterpoints, as I have suggested, by way of a Lutheran "conscience" (3.1.84) that frustrates his "nobler," humanistic impulses entirely, vetoing both the will to commit suicide (the "native hue of resolution" at 3.1.85) and "enterprises of great pitch and moment" that, with the unnerving "regard" of conscience, "turn awry" "their currents" and "lose the name of action" (3.1.87–89). With respect to suicide—that stoical Roman triumph—and to larger "enterprises" such as those associated with young Fortinbras, theological considerations do not so much correct as undo the humanistic impulse to act.

It is not that Hamlet is approaching a spiritual breakthrough, a Tower Experience (*ein Turmerlebnis*) à la Luther, for that would set the drama against itself, vanquishing humanistic action from the play. Rather, in what can be termed an Erasmian move on Shakespeare's part, Hamlet speaks as one of the "fools of nature . . . With thoughts beyond the reaches of our souls" (1.4.54–56). In effect, his soliloquy expresses his puzzlement before the intellectual and spiritual crisis "of the time" (2.2.524), which I interpret as the rupture between humanism and reform, between worlds that cannot be made to harmonize as one whole. By the light of Aristotle's *Metaphysics* (XII.6–7), which Luther abhorred,[45] *being* ought to pull in the direction of *activity* and *actuality*. We assume that Shakespeare, had it suited his purposes, could have propounded this metaphysical cliché with unerring clarity. But instead of arranging the opening lines of Hamlet's soliloquy "according to the principle of affinity and opposition," he skews our categories of thought.

The Mousetrap plunges us further into the question of free will. Its very title suggests the overruling dictates of fate, equating man and mouse, *vir* and vermin, in a manner not flattering to human intelligence or human agency. Readers of *The Spanish Tragedy* will recognize its relevance, particularly its astounding play within the play. Discussing Kyd's work, Lukas Erne sees a conflict between Calvinism, which "stresses divine predestination," and "Neoplatonic thinkers such as Pico della Mirandola and Ficino," who "stress

---

45. "The whole Aristotle is to theology as darkness to light." Luther's *Disputation against Scholastic Theology*, quoted in Duncan B. Forrester, "Martin Luther and John Calvin," in *History of Political Philosophy*, 3rd ed., ed. Leo Strauss and Joseph Cropsey, 321. Also: "Should Aristotle not have been a man of flesh and blood, I would not hesitate to assert that he was the Devil himself." Luther, quoted in Oberman, *Luther*, 121.

human free will." While Erne does not broach the possible impact of Luther or Erasmus on Kyd, he makes a point that applies equally well to *The Spanish Tragedy* and to *Hamlet*: "Whether Man is seen as God's puppet or as the author of his own role and script, histrionic metaphors work to describe either view."[46] Hamlet evokes the famous example of Kyd's Hieronymo and his *Soliman and Perseda* by inserting "a speech of some dozen or sixteen lines" (2.2.541) into *The Mousetrap*. Like Shakespeare himself, Hamlet imposes his will on a world of players; according to Shakespeare's script, he imposes it on Gertrude and Claudius, whose reactions he strives to "interpret," much as he would "interpret" Ophelia's "love" if he "could see the puppets dallying" (3.2.244–45). But the case for human agency remains undecided. As in Hieronymo's case, there is "no way of deciding," because "predeterminism and self-determinism, frame and play within are both contradictory and complementary, articulating an irreconcilable tension."[47] As Erne suggests, the tension is inherent and structural: we are all actors trying to write our own scripts. Hamlet in trying to pull the strings cannot decisively escape the specter of predeterminism, which lurks, for instance, within the curiously incest-driven role of "Lucianus, nephew to the King" (3.2.242). It is a tension that Shakespeare realized to the quick.

Fixing our attention on vows of love, Shakespeare makes them a test case for the will: "If she should break it now!" Hamlet exclaims, supplying an uncanny cue for the Player King's comment: "'Tis deeply sworn" (3.2.222–23). Cooperation with God's purpose regarding the union of woman and man (see Matthew 19:6) was a crucial idea for Shakespeare: the status and efficacy of the sacraments was, on some level, a question and a concern; more generally, this cooperation was a means of examining the ideal of love and the nature of the will in light of human sexuality and human frailty. In *Hamlet*, where Christian marriage is at stake, it would be grossly ahistorical to approach true-love vows as speech acts in our contemporary sense. I refer the reader to my previous chapter: "in a Christian universe, because transcendent truth exists prior to the speech act, what is to be tried and tested is a character's ability to speak and to act freely in accordance with transcendent truth—a transcendence to which speech act theory does not subscribe. By denying or resisting transcendent truth, a character indicates a lack of freedom on his or her part, be it on account of pride or lust, or some other sin. In such instances,

---

46. Lukas Erne, *Beyond* The Spanish Tragedy: *A Study of the Works of Thomas Kyd*, 103.
47. Erne, *Beyond* The Spanish Tragedy, 106–107.

God's will is not done." *The Mousetrap*, as a kind of *Hamlet* in miniature, calls the morality of the larger play into question by a layered interrogation of human agency and its contested Christian grounds. The artistic problem for Shakespeare is thus a self-reflexive moral conundrum: what claim could the dramatist make for his art, what could "the purpose of playing" (3.2.20) be, if the stage were essentially a puppet show—a reduction of man consistent with a world where "marriage vows" are "false as dicers' oaths" (3.4.45–46), and "reason panders will" (3.4.89)?

On the question of free will hangs the answer to what kind of "a piece of work is a man"—is he a divine masterpiece or a bit of overheated "dust" (2.2.304–309)? The great debate was the moment when the clarity of the question and the consequences of the answer achieved their seminal expression. My suggestion here is that the conflict between the freedom of the will and its bondage prompted doubts and anxieties that inform Hamlet's manic-depressive utterance about the nature of "man." In my reading, these doubts and anxieties connect Hamlet to Shakespeare, permeating the work in a structural pattern that the author painstakingly laid out through number symbolism, though no critic I know of has ever noticed it. It is a question for another time why the numerological aspect of Shakespeare's writing remains under-appreciated.[48] The essential point is that number symbolism in *Hamlet* offers a metadramatic commentary on what kind of "a piece of work is a man." This number symbolism is rooted in the significance of Hamlet's age at the defining moment of his death. It overlays the play as a whole, with special emphasis in *The Mousetrap*.

Horatio's account of the duel between Old Fortinbras and Old Hamlet extends to the ambitious maneuvers of young Fortinbras while it silently touches the birth date of young Hamlet (1.1.83–111). This hint sinks like a depth bomb from view until it rattles us with the gravedigger's remark at 5.1.147–48: "It was the very day that Hamlet was born." It is the same grave-digger who mentions that Hamlet is now "thirty years" old (5.1.162). So we

---

48. "Numerology as a thematic concern is certainly well-nigh omnipresent in the literature of the Renaissance, its 'evidence' extending from the firm declaration of St. Augustine . . . to the count-less efforts mounted thereafter to comprehend, explicate, and apply the mysteries variously pen-etrated." C. A. Patrides, *Premises and Motifs in Renaissance Thought and Literature*, 67. Patrides cites the Augustine of *On Christian Teaching* (*De Doctrina Christiana*), II.xvi. Maurice Hunt supplies examples of Shakespearean numerology in Sonnet 6, *Richard II*, *The Winter's Tale*, *1 Henry IV*, and *Julius Caesar*. See Maurice Hunt, "Christian Numerology in Shakespeare's *The Tragedy of King Richard the Second*," *Christianity and Literature* 60 (Winter 2011): 227–45. A key biblical text for numerology is Wisdom 11:17 (11:20 in NRSV).

detect a linking device, an act of calculated and deliberate artistry, in the repetition of *thirty* (and the use of *thirties*) in the opening words of the Player King:[49]

> Full thirty times hath Phoebus' cart gone round
> Neptune's salt wash and Tellus orbèd ground,
> And thirty dozen moons with borrowed sheen
> About the world have times twelve thirties been,
> Since love our hearts and Hymen did our hands
> Unite communal in most sacred bands. (3.2.153–58)

The Player King evokes the 360-degree figure of a circle. He does so repeatedly. To begin, we imagine the Ptolemaic orbits of the sun ("Phoebus' cart") and moon as circular. Then we have the ambiguous evidence of the Player King's opening couplet: "Full thirty times hath Phoebus' cart gone round / Neptune's salt wash and Tellus orbèd ground." I take it that the Player King is referring to thirty zodiacal cycles, not to thirty days;[50] this interpretation would draw support from a case of parallel phrasing in *Measure for Measure*: "penalties / Which have . . . hung by the wall / So long that nineteen zodiacs have *gone round*" (1.2.163–65, my emphasis). Since a "full" zodiac comprises twelve constellations or signs, we can multiply twelve "thirty times" to equal 360. The most striking instance of the Player King's evoking the 360-degree figure of a circle is his chiastic tautology, "And thirty dozen moons with borrowed sheen / About the world have times twelve thirties been." The cyclical nature of the action is driven home by the form, with rhyme and meter supporting the idea of regular movement returning upon itself. Further, the phrase "with borrowed sheen" reinforces the temporal correspondence between the ambiguous solar couplet and the unambiguous lunar couplet that attends it. Being thirty years of age (the equivalent in solar terms of "Full thirty" zodiacal cycles of "Phoebus' cart"), or thirty-dozen moons old, Hamlet bears this association throughout the play.

I have yet to clarify the *why* behind this number symbolism. Let us note that, for reasons of spatial symmetry, it is satisfying that the play and its hero "come full circle" (LR 5.3.177) in the thirty years between Old Hamlet's victory and the accession of young Fortinbras to the Danish

---

49. For a review of the relevant scholarship and some learned speculation, see Steve Sohmer, *Shakespeare's Mystery Play: The Opening of the Globe Theatre 1599*, 234–36.

50. "Strictly, the first *thirty times* would indicate 30 days, while *thirty dozen moons* indicates 30 years." William Shakespeare, *Hamlet*, ed. Ann Thompson and Neil Taylor, 308n. Possibly this underrates the significance of "*Full* thirty times."

throne.[51] But the main idea, which harkens back to Hamlet's manic-depressive speech about the created nature of man (2.2.304–309), is the mystery of what it means for the tragic hero to have come full circle. In this respect, the circle-figure is so perfectly ambiguous that it operates as the sign of the either/or perspectival indeterminacy unfolding before the protagonist and us.

To Shakespeare's audience, the circle-figure was rich with symbolic possibilities. John Donne employed the figure in his "Valediction: Of Weeping": "On a round ball / A workeman that hath copies by, can . . . quickly make that, which was nothing, *All*."[52] Cesare Ripa, an influence on Ben Jonson, wrote that the circle of the Zodiac "*è simbolo della ragione, & è debita, & conueneuole misura dell'attioni perfette.*"[53] To George Puttenham, the circle bore "a similitude with God and eternitie."[54] If we may again summon the Florentine Neoplatonist Marsilio Ficino, we find divine love connected to each individual in a circle that "influences the human soul" and develops in it "an inclination toward love itself." This "response, which is caused by divine love, manifests itself in the love of God and an activity of the soul."[55] In connecting divine love to "an activity of the soul," Ficino assumes a more traditional metaphysic. Jörg Lauster has recently compared Ficino and Erasmus on the basis of several quotations that reflect their shared Neoplatonic sensibility. But while Erasmus, in one of his more renowned adages, does refer to the circle in terms of "eternity,"[56] he does not, so far as I know, identify the circle-figure with divine love or the soul. In any case, the association between the circle and "love" occurs in the Player King's speech through the thirty-year anniversary of a "sacred" marriage. Granted, this union is destined to be undone by death and deceit, though, in fact, we see the Player Queen breaking her vows only in the dumb show, because Claudius interrupts the actual performance.

In its wealth of potential meanings, the circle could also (as Donne shows us) signify "nothing." Within Act 3, Scene 2, "nothing" refers to the nothingness

---

51. On "the spatial character of Renaissance thought," see Alastair Fowler, *Triumphal Forms: Structural Patterns in Elizabethan Poetry*, 17.

52. John Donne, *Selected Poetry*, ed. John Hayward, 46.

53. Cesare Ripa, *Iconologia*, quoted in D. J. Gordon, "The Imagery of Ben Jonson's 'The Masque of Blacknesse' and 'The Masque of Beautie,'" in *England and the Mediterranean Tradition: Studies in Art, History, and Literature*, 116–17. The Italian can be rendered as "is a symbol of reason, and what is due, and fitting measure of a perfect action."

54. George Puttenham, *The Arte of English Poesie*, 111.

55. Jörg Lauster, "Marsilio Ficino as a Christian Thinker: Theological Aspects of His Platonism," in *Marsilio Ficino: His Theology, His Philosophy, His Legacy*, ed. Michael J. B. Allen and Valery Rees, 62.

56. Erasmus, *The Adages of Erasmus*, ed. William Barker, 140.

of "dumb shows and noise" (12) as well as to the female genitalia as the pro-duction site of matter and flesh (119; see also 114). Indeed, "nothing" per-meates all five acts, evoking the question of what is at stake in human speech, perception, action, and suffering. In terms of perspectival indeterminacy, Hamlet, at the time of his death, will either participate in the all of God's loving will, or he will have achieved nothing, a vast amount of it, calling to mind Luther's fundamental antithesis "between the 'alls' and 'nones' of which Paul speaks,"[57] between the all of God's grace and the nothing of our free will. Luther does not employ the circle-figure, but "nothing" is the constant refrain of his argument, his hedgehog's defense against the Erasmian fox: "For if it is not we, but only God, who works salvation in us, then before he works we can do nothing of saving significance, whether we wish it or not."[58] The examples could be greatly multiplied.

A Lutheran reading of Sonnet 59 ("If there be nothing new . . .") illumi-nates our present context. The poet asks if writers improve over centuries: "Whether we are mended, or whe'er better they / Or whether revolution be the same" (11–12). In this comparison between the Ancients and the Moderns, the verb *to mend* conveys the spiritual suggestion of "to free (a person, character, habits, etc.) from sin or fault; to improve morally; to reform" (OED 4). This meaning is not infrequent in Shakespeare, though neither Vendler nor Burrow mentions it with respect to Sonnet 59. It is not a pun. It is closely aligned with the primary meaning that Burrow gives, "improved, set to right."[59] Its recla-mation is a matter of theological sensitivity, not of wrenching a word from its meaning. One thinks of the "mender of bad soles" and his line to Flavius, "I can mend you"—to which the uncomprehending tribune replies, "What mean'st thou by that? Mend me, thou saucy fellow?" (JC 1.1.14, 17–18). If we hear in the sonnet's opening line an echo of Ecclesiastes,[60] the spiritual weight of "mended" finds a biblical footing. If we lose the possibility of Christian mending, we also lose the thought of predestination in "whether revolution be the same," which Bevington glosses as whether "the revolving of the ages brings only repetition." The possibility of there being "nothing new" between the "antique book" (7) and Shakespeare's sonnet coheres with the anti-human-istic potentialities of *Hamlet*. Without grace, there is nothing and "nothing

---

57. Luther, *On the Bondage*, 316.

58. Luther, *On the Bondage*, 319.

59. William Shakespeare, *The Complete Sonnets and Poems*, ed. Colin Burrow, 498n.

60. Margreta de Grazia, "Revolution in Shake-speares Sonnets," in *A Companion to Shakespeare's Sonnets*, ed. Michael Schoenfeldt, 61.

new." Further, a Lutheran reading of the sonnet would highlight the capacity for deceiving oneself that emerges in the closing couplet, "Oh, sure I am the wits of former days / To subjects worse have given admiring praise," a certainty that, on close examination, infects the "admiring praise" with which the poet has been addressing his own subject, the "Fair Youth." Along similar lines, a Lutheran reading of the play would have Hamlet locked in the endless historical repetition of vanity and sin—a world not far from Eliot's *Waste Land*.

What can the gravediggers tell us about the powers and limits of free will? The lines of the First Clown swarm with rhetorical vices, figures of speech that reveal his ignorant misapplication of a word, or, more explosively, Shakespeare's sleight of hand with theologically charged language:

> FIRST CLOWN   Is she to be buried in Christian burial, when she willfully seeks her own salvation?
> SECOND CLOWN   I tell thee she is; therefore make her grave straight. The crowner hath sat on her, and finds it Christian burial.
> FIRST CLOWN   How can that be, unless she drowned herself in her own defense?
> SECOND CLOWN   Why, 'tis found so.
> FIRST CLOWN   It must be *se offendendo*, it cannot be else. For here lies the point: if I drown myself wittingly, it argues an act, and an act hath three branches—it is to act, to do, to perform. Argal, she drowned herself wittingly.
> SECOND CLOWN   Nay, but hear you goodman delver—
> FIRST CLOWN   Give me leave. Here lies the water; good. Here stands the man; good. If the man go to this water and drown himself, it is, will he, nill he, he goes, mark you that. But if the water come to him and drown him, he drowns not himself. Argal, he that is not guilty of his own death shortens not his own life.
> SECOND CLOWN   But is this law?
> FIRST CLOWN   Ay, marry, is't—crowner's quest law.
> SECOND CLOWN   Will you ha' the truth on't? If this had not been a gentlewoman, she should have been buried out o' Christian burial.
>
> (5.1.1–24)

Being theologically sensitive, the audience was well prepared to get the opening joke, to recognize "salvation" as a rustic blunder for "damnation."[61]

---

61. The opening line of *Hamlet* 5.1 recalls the opening lines of 3.3 in *Much Ado About Nothing*:
DOGBERRY Are you good men and true?
VERGES Yea, or else it were pity but they should suffer salvation, body and soul.

Convinced that Ophelia has committed suicide, the First Clown identifies the natural, earthly level of meaning, the everyday level of what people might will to do, with the supernatural level, where he determines that Ophelia has willed her own damnation—her suicide suggesting, to a Lutheran or a Calvinist, that she was damned from the start. He confounds, so to speak, Luther's "two kingdoms" and their rival dispensations regarding the will: "just as in his own kingdom [man] is directed by his own counsel, without regard to the precepts of another, so in the Kingdom of God he is directed by the precepts of another without regard to his own choice."[62] It is the First Clown's way of probing what Luther called "the vital spot."[63] This vital spot, the place where the will touches the limits of its own sovereignty, troubled gentles and commoners alike, courtiers and groundlings, lords and liverymen, ladies and nurses, bawds and drabs, lawyers and law students, masters and apprentices, since anyone with a brain could grasp the doctrine of double predestination (which originates in Luther) and apply it to his or her own life: "the eternal will of God not only elects some to salvation, but effects as well the reprobation of others who are thereby doomed to everlasting destruction."[64]

As the Second Clown indicates, the ruling on Ophelia's suicide was placed legally in the hands of the "crowner," or coroner, who is said to have "sat on her," that is, to have sat in judgment on her, but with a hint of obscenity that Webster remembered in *The White Devil*.[65] Given the nature of the case, the crowner can hardly avoid trespassing on God's jurisdiction. This same civil servant, whose title invokes the authority of the Crown, represents the divine office of the King, as if Shakespeare were enjoying a subversive antithesis in *crown* and *clown*.[66] It is the crowner's ruling (on Ophelia's behalf) that the clowns question and ridicule. Their grumbling probably carried the audience's sympathy—with the exception of those who had paid the higher admission fees.

62. Luther, *On the Bondage*, 183.

63. Luther, *On the Bondage*, 333.

64. Paul R. Sellin, "The Hidden God," in *The Darker Vision of the Renaissance: Beyond the Fields of Reason*, ed. Robert S. Kinsman, 159. Regarding Calvin's debt to Luther on this point, and their minor differences, see 165–69.

65. "Methinks none should sit upon thy sister but old whoremasters" (3.1.13–14). John Webster, *The White Devil*, ed. Benedict S. Robinson.

66. From Elizabeth's "Golden Speech," November 30, 1601: "To be a king and wear a crown is a thing more glorious to them that see it than it is pleasant to them that bear it. For myself, I never was so much enticed with the glorious name of a king or royal authority of a queen as delighted that God hath made me His instrument to maintain his truth and glory, and to defend his kingdom from dishonor, damage, tyranny, and oppression . . . . [To] God only and wholly, all is to be given and ascribed." Elizabeth I, quoted in *Sources and Debates in English History 1485–1714*, ed. Newton Key and Robert Bucholz, 102.

As Michael MacDonald and Terence Murphy note with respect to coroners' rulings on doubtful deaths and to this scene in particular, "aristocrats and gentlefolk were treated more leniently than their social inferiors, and everyone knew it."[67] In any case, the coroner's ruling has been called into doubt. And as the subsequent clash of opinion between Laertes and the "churlish priest" (5.1.240) would suggest, no one can really know how God judges Ophelia.

A widely accepted source for the First Clown's remarks on suicide is a famous Elizabethan legal battle about the drowning of Sir James Hales, a 1560 lawsuit that hinged on the relation of will and act. As Harold Jenkins observes in the "Longer Notes" to his edition of *Hamlet*:

> Shakespeare's knowledge of the arguments about suicide in the case of Hales v. Pettit, however come by, seems beyond question. . . . The grave-digger's division of an act into three branches (which turn out to be identical) is a recognizable caricature of the argument of the defending counsel that the act of self-destruction "consists of three parts: The first is the Imagination, which is a reflection or meditation of the mind, whether or not it is convenient for him to destroy himself, and what way it can be done. The second is the Resolution, which is a determination of the mind to destroy itself, and to do it in this or that particular way. The third is the Perfection, which is the execution of what the mind has to do. And this Perfection consists of two parts, *viz.* the beginning and the end. The beginning is the doing of the act which causes the death, and the end is death, which is only a sequel to the act."[68]

When Shakespeare heard about the case, possibly as "a conversational joke in the Inns of Court and the City taverns,"[69] he was evidently struck by the ingeniously half-witted argument of the defending counsel, Serjeant Walsh, on behalf of Dame Hales's right to her property. The playwright must have been especially impressed by the curious logic of Walsh's attempt—a failure in the mind of the judges who ruled against him—to separate the "two parts" of the third part of the act, "the Perfection" (a Latinism based on *perficio*, to perform or bring to completion), so that Hales would not be held responsible for the result of his suicide, his death being "only a sequel to the act." (If

---

67. Michael MacDonald and Terence R. Murphy, *Sleepless Souls: Suicide in Early Modern England*, 126.

68. From editor Harold Jenkins's "Longer Notes" in William Shakespeare, *Hamlet*, ed. Harold Jenkins, 547.

69. O. Hood Phillips, *Shakespeare and the Lawyers*, 78. On Walsh's losing the case, see 77–78.

Hales were held not responsible for his own death, the Crown could not claim his widow's property.) What changes, in Shakespeare's handling of the material, is that Shakespeare takes a case about suicide and property and applies it to a case about suicide and salvation. It is a change that alerts us to the angle of Shakespeare's interest in the case—to what precisely caught his eye.

We might ask, then, did Shakespeare's interest in the great debate prepare his receptivity to Hales v. Pettit? Certain affinities and analogies hold between the two. Tripartite arguments were common, but we may observe that Walsh's tripartite argument (however inept) is similar in topic to Erasmus's tripartite analysis of human action: *quidam orthodoxi patres, tres gradus faciunt operis humani: primus est cogitare, secundus uelle, tertius perficere. Atq; in primo quidem ac tertio nullum locum tribuunt libero arbitrio quicquam operandi . . . Caeterum in medio, hoc est, in consensu, simul agit gratia et humana voluntas: sic tamen, ut principalis causa sit gratia, minus principalis, nostra voluntas.*[70] In my translation: "certain orthodox Fathers distinguish three stages of human action: the first is to think, the second is to will, the third is to perform. In the first and third, they attribute no action to free will . . . . Yet in the middle stage, that is, with one accord, grace and human will act together, but in such a way that grace is the principal cause and our will is the secondary cause."[71] We have no way of placing this text in the hands of Walsh or Shakespeare. If the power of suggestion counts, though, it is just possible to hear Erasmus's use of *perficio* in the third part of Walsh's tripartite argument. Erasmus addresses the whole problem of the will with respect to action, while Walsh is most concerned with the act achieved by the will—an act that Walsh divides in two (compare Erasmus's hair-splitting middle stage), thereby curbing the will's power and limiting its reach.

It may be that what Shakespeare heard in Walsh's quiddities was an unwitting parody of scholastic reasoning and its psychological apparatus. Bad logic attracts humor and must have sustained the legal in-joke all along. In the analogies that hold between the legal reasoning of Walsh, the tripartite argument of Erasmus, and the gravediggers' conversation, we may sense that Shakespeare was, once again, clowning with scholastic modes of argument. It is a salient irony of the great debate that Erasmus, in order to defend the freedom of the will, was driven to an uncharacteristic reliance on scholastic analysis, on a type of dialectic that he had mocked in the past and that Luther contemptuously dismissed as "*carnalis.*"[72] I do not want to suggest that Shakespeare

70. Erasmus, *De Libero Arbitrio*, n.p.
71. Cf. Erasmus, *On the Freedom*, 80.
72. Luther, *On the Bondage*, 262.

was sounding the death-knell of scholasticism; one need only consider the impact of Aquinas on Hooker to refrain from such an inference. But I must conclude that the playwright was attracted to a pointed example of legal reasoning defeating itself—revealing, as Luther would insist on theological grounds, "the words of the law are spoken . . . not to affirm the power of the will, but to enlighten blind reason and make it see that its light is no light."[73] It was, in a manner similarly related to intellectual overreach, typical of Luther to stress an element of radical discontinuity between our intentions and what follows: "for everyone things have turned out differently from what he thought they would."[74] And we may hear Luther in the Player King's rejoinder to his Queen: "Our wills and fates do so contrary run / That our devices still are overthrown; / Our thoughts are ours, their ends none of our own" (3.2.209–211); as well as in Hamlet's monumental nod to human blundering: "'tis the sport to have the engineer / Hoist with his own petard" (3.4.213–214). Granted, these non sequiturs are only broadly analogous with the legal reasoning of Serjeant Walsh, but we are trying to understand Shakespeare's angle of interest in the case.

The author's difficulty persists in his effort to harmonize the two worlds of humanism and reform: if God completely overrules human agency in this play about souls, the dramatist is left with a theater of, for, and by puppets. The telling phrase "will he, nill he" (5.1.17) speaks not only to the suicide's case, but also to the dramatist's—whose "name is Will" (SON 136.14). It is extremely hard to locate agency. When the First Clown takes it on himself to clarify things, he assumes a transparent connection between will and damnation, but, in his boldly ruling on Ophelia's death, he unwittingly delivers a grave satire on presumptuous ignorance. In other words, the issues at hand have become a snare for those who presume to pronounce on them. At the same time, even as theology faces the kind of mystery that Luther called an "insoluble problem,"[75] the playwright cannot escape his dilemma: souls in *Hamlet* desperately need to be saved, and yet "the purpose of playing" cannot be to save them. The drama, as Hamlet suggests, should serve a moral purpose. But it would be idolatry to consider it a substitute for religion.

We return, then, to *The Mousetrap*'s question of how the action of the play comes full circle. Does Hamlet end as a self-deceiving puppet of fate, or as

73. Luther, *On the Bondage*, 190.
74. Luther, *On the Bondage*, 121.
75. Luther, *On the Bondage*, 331.

an instrument of grace, or possibly as a conquering soul cooperating with the will of God? The core issue of the great debate resounds in the final scene, starting when Hamlet comments on his aborted voyage to England, "There's a divinity that shapes our ends / Rough-hew them how we will" (5.2.10–11). It is taken for granted that "a divinity" means "a divine power," but one wonders if Shakespeare intended a pun on "theology," that would-be substitute for God. He is certainly attending closely to theological language. In the wording of this memorable affirmation lies an ambiguity involving the modal auxiliary *will* ("Rough-hew them how we *will* rough-hew them") and the use of *will* as a regular verb akin to *wish* or *intend*. The first alternative throws a predestinarian light on our future; the second leaves us more to do on our own and therefore puts things in a more cooperative light, as if our "rough-hewing" contributed to God's definitive and final shaping of our destinies. The ambiguity lies within the emphasis. Shakespeare extends this ambiguous terrain when Hamlet comments to Horatio: "Ere I could make a prologue to my brains, / They had begun the play" (5.2.30–31), a histrionic metaphor that hovers between agency and non-agency.

Hamlet takes confidence from his belief that the sea-voyage was providential and that, on some half-conscious level, he is now cooperating with providence. The circumstances behind his return to England are strange, improbable to our ears, though, to the Elizabethans, piracy was an ordinary evil. One curiously providential detail stands out in his letter to Horatio: Hamlet tells how he "boarded" the pirates' vessel and "On the instant they got clear of our ship, so I alone became their prisoner" (4.6.18–20). A further curiosity: it is unexpected, though not implausible, that Hamlet had brought his father's signet ring with him when he set sail from Denmark (5.2.49). Without it, he could not have sealed the "new commission" (5.2.32) that sent Rosencrantz and Guildenstern to their doom. The pirates, who appear to have been Shakespeare's innovation, were staple characters in romance as well as real persons in ancient and modern history.[76] Shakespeare makes suggestive use of them, deviating from the Hamlet story told by the Frenchman François de Belleforest in his popular *Histoires Tragiques*, which relied on Saxo Grammaticus's *Historiae Danicae*. In Belleforest, Hamlet spends a wild time in England before returning to Denmark to find the Danes celebrating his obsequies.

---

76. For pirates in Elizabethan life and literature, as well as critical debate about the incident, see Karl P. Wentersdorf, "Hamlet's Encounter with the Pirates," *Shakespeare Quarterly* 34 (Winter, 1983): 434–40, to which I am indebted here. Wentersdorf was coauthor with Heinrich Mutschmann of *Shakespeare and Catholicism* (1952), which is discussed in my Introduction.

What prompted Shakespeare to transform this traditional episode? Rather famously, Rabelais, in *The Fourth Book of Pantagruel* (1552), used a sea-voyage to epitomize human cooperation with grace. To what extent, if any, Shakespeare knew Rabelais's text is uncertain.[77] But we find precedent for Rabelais's symbolic use of the sea-voyage in Erasmus's side of the great debate, specifically rebutted by Luther,[78] and in representative works of the Italian Renaissance.[79] What this particular set of comparisons suggests is that Shakespeare refused to make a Christian humanist triumph of the business. Hamlet does not steer a ship through a dangerous storm. In fact, he feels like a prisoner: "Methought I lay / Worse than the mutines in the bilboes" (5.2.5–6). This is Hamlet's low point in terms of freedom, and Shakespeare's most powerful image of the bondage of the will. And yet, improvising providentially, or improvidently provident, Hamlet finds himself entering into a mysterious action beyond the designs of man or woman. If our "indiscretion sometimes serves us well / When our deep plots do pall" (5.2.8–9), we are reminded of Claudius's "discretion" (1.2.5), and of Claudius's deep plots. It is Hamlet's folly, his being the Christian fool, that puts him, we may infer, in a better position than the King.

This sympathetic reading of Hamlet is open to challenge. In discovering Claudius's commission, substituting his own, and sentencing Rosencrantz and Guildenstern to death, Hamlet claims "heaven ordinant" (5.2.48). Roy Battenhouse, seizing on Hamlet's cruelty toward his old friends, may stand here for those who think Hamlet closes his eyes "against the truth,"[80] that, in other words, he prefers damnation. Then again, it may be that even Roy Battenhouse is unwittingly playing the First Clown by asserting more than he knows. The God of *Hamlet* is not very nice by our standards, but it was no stain on his authority for him to approve Hamlet's tricking his faithless companions, who, in the game of wills, it must be said, had already sold theirs to Claudius.[81] At the same time, yet still leaving us on ambiguous grounds, Hamlet's confidence that his actions are

---

77. For Shakespeare and Rabelais, see Chapter 3.

78. Erasmus, *On the Freedom*, 79; Luther, *On the Bondage*, 288.

79. Ernst Cassirer, *The Individual and the Cosmos in Renaissance Philosophy*, trans. Mario Domandi, 77.

80. Roy Battenhouse, "Comment and Bibliography," in *Shakespeare's Christian Dimension: An Anthology of Commentary*, ed. Roy Battenhouse, 382. For a more recent exponent of this position, see Oakes, "*Hamlet* and the Reformation." For a strong critique of Hamlet's character from an Aristotelian standpoint, see Scott F. Crider, *With What Persuasion: An Essay on Shakespeare and the Ethics of Rhetoric*, 9–33.

81. "As the instrument of heaven, Hamlet may be a benevolent agent exempt from the consequences of his act or he may be a tainted weapon, used by providence but nonetheless damned for his offenses." Waddington, "Lutheran *Hamlet*," 35–36.

pleasing to God, and the fact that his coward-making conscience lodges no complaint, may evoke Luther's belief that a conscience informed by grace knows it and can act with "the utmost possible certainty."[82] But still, we may conclude that Hamlet's certainty is a parody of Luther's teaching.[83]

Before his culminating duel with Laertes—a duel of strange chances that either mock or affirm his trust in providence—Hamlet answers Horatio's concern for him by alluding to Christ's preaching to his disciples (Matthew 10:29): "There is special providence in the fall of a sparrow." He elaborates on what is evidently the thought of his own death: "If it be now, 'tis not to come; if it be not to come, it will be now; if it be not now, yet it will come. The readiness is all. Since no man of aught he leaves knows, what is't to leave betimes? Let be" (217–22).[84] Russell Hillier, advancing the critical tradition of Hamlet's likely salvation, argues that the Prince's "affecting 'Let be' is a creative, not a defeatist utterance, a fiat akin to the divine fiat of Genesis 1, where creator and creature are reconciled to one another and cooperate in the unfurling of a providential plan."[85] It must be admitted, though, that Hamlet, while affirming the providential plan, professes little actual knowledge of it. "Let be" is said, in effect, in response to our being "fools of nature." Hillier bridges the gap—between Hamlet's purportedly Calvinist knowledge of providence[86] and his act of cooperating with grace—by means of enthusiastic textual interpretation. To be fair, the critic scores a credible point: "Let be" is not defeatist. Possibly it expresses a moment of cooperation between Hamlet's will and his creator's. Possibly it expresses not Hamlet's creativity so much as his wise passiveness—an Erasmian Stoicism—before questions and operations that he cannot begin to decipher.

No easy conclusions follow. Humanism and theology do not, as in Rabelais, squarely support each other. Rather, they tend to expose each other's blind spots. Like the pagan Pyrrhus, the Christian Hamlet avenges his father.[87] But at what cost? The cycle of humanistic violence returns:

---

82. Luther, *On the Bondage*, 309.

83. For the theological problems complicating the issue of certainty that attended the formulation of the Lambeth Articles, see Cummings, *Literary Culture*, 287–96.

84. For textual cruxes in this passage, see Naseeb Shaheen, *Biblical References in Shakespeare's Plays*, 562.

85. Russell M. Hillier, "Hamlet the Rough-Hewer: Moral Agency and the Consolations of Reformation Thought," in *Shakespeare and Renaissance Ethics*, ed. Patrick Gray and John D. Cox, 181.

86. Hillier compares Hamlet to the privileged Calvinist believer who can "trace a providential pattern" (Hillier, "Hamlet the Rough-Hewer," 181).

87. For a review of the long debate over the morality of revenge in *Hamlet*, see Eleanor Prosser, *Hamlet and Revenge*. Kastan, in his *Will to Believe*, infers a Christian basis for revenge "on him that

> So as a painted tyrant Pyrrhus stood,
> And, like a neutral to his will and matter,
> Did nothing.
> But as we often see against some storm
> A silence in the heavens, the rack stand still,
> The bold winds speechless, and the orb below
> As hush as death, anon the dreadful thunder
> Doth rend the region, so, after Pyrrhus' pause,
> A rousèd vengeance sets him new a-work . . . .
> Out, out, thou strumpet Fortune! All you gods
> In general synod take away her power!
> Break all the spokes and fellies from her wheel,
> And bowl the round nave down the hill of heaven
> As low as to the fiends! (2.2.480–97)

For a brief moment, Pyrrhus stands as a "neutral to his will and matter." The short line ("Did nothing."), with its arresting full stop (cf. "Pyrrhus's pause"), links his motionless silence to the blankness on the page: whether, in the end, he is the master of his fate, or whether "the heavens" determine every detail, we do not know. It may shed a little light, though, to notice that the Trojan War played a thematic role in the great debate, and that references to it on Luther's side are especially frequent. Erasmus compared the primal battle between Achilles and Hector to the theological divide within Christendom.[88] Luther's response was to refer to the Church Fathers and other venerable authorities of the Roman Church as "this Troy of ours," which, at last, "through so many wars," has been "taken." Luther in fact acknowledged that he, for a long time, viewed the traditional authorities favored by Erasmus as "invincible."[89] In Luther's revised view, the view he holds in the debate, "this Troy" at last has fallen. We are meant to appreciate Luther's ironic identification

---

doeth evil" from Romans 13:4 (133). I. J. Semper evidences *The Golden Legend* for a "purgatorial ghost acting as an agent of divine justice" that "may have influenced Shakespeare." I. J. Semper, *Hamlet without Tears*, 18. Semper also refers to Aquinas on revenge. In the *Summa Theologica* (II-II, q. 64, art. 3), Aquinas approves of Moses' commanding bloody vengeance in the name of God against those who worshiped the golden calf (Gen. 32:27–30). For Aquinas, this act of revenge is lawful as being properly delegated by God's agent on earth (i.e., Moses) to private individuals. See Semper, *Hamlet without Tears*, 20. Semper's defense of a Catholic position is not and cannot be conclusive, but Greenblatt's dismissal of it cannot be conclusive either: "there is no evidence that Hamlet's circumstances in any way match those that might justify the assassination of Claudius." Stephen Greenblatt, *Hamlet in Purgatory*, 308n44.

88. Erasmus, *On the Freedom*, 95–96.
89. Luther, *On the Bondage*, 145.

of himself with the barbaric Greeks. The game, he says, is up. Christian humanism, for both Erasmus and Luther, could provide a shared rhetorical means of signifying theological conflict, even as Luther proceeded to drive a powerful wedge between humanism and theology.

I hope that to speak of Shakespeare's revisiting this Christian humanist battlefield is, at this juncture, not a stretch. The First Player's speech culminates in an appeal for divine intervention that, however briefly, fuses a Homeric world with a Christian one, which emerges with the "fiends" of a Christian hell. Most strikingly, the reference to a "general synod" evokes Christianity and its long history of theological deliberations, including the recent synod that generated the Lambeth Articles.[90] If the speech foretells Hamlet's act of "vengeance" against Claudius, yet it leaves us to contemplate—like everlasting ecclesiastics in an eternal synod—the relationship between the circle-shaped "wheel" of Fortune and the totality of God's providence, including the mystery of the will.

The play's action concludes rapidly and darkly. We experience a flicker of heavenly hope when the mortally wounded Laertes says, "Exchange forgiveness with me, noble Hamlet" (5.2.331). Hamlet complies, but Laertes is apparently already dead. The Prince's last utterance underscores the limits of human knowledge: "The rest is silence" (5.2.360).[91] It may be that Erasmus would accept this uncertain dénouement: "nor should we through irreverent inquisitiveness rush into those things which are hidden, not to say superfluous: . . . whether our will accomplishes anything in things pertaining to eternal salvation; whether it simply suffers the action of grace; whether what we do, be it for good or ill, we do by necessity or rather suffer to be done to us. . . . There are some things which God has willed that we should contemplate, as we venerate himself, in mystic silence."[92] According to Dodds, this view of "things" was upheld by Robert Cecil, in response "to the Cambridge dispute which led to the Lambeth Articles" of 1595. Seeing "precisely the position laid out by Erasmus and adopted by Elizabeth," Dodds quotes court observer Humphrey Tyndall's paraphrase of Cecil's response that "the matters were too high mysteries for his understanding."[93] But before we award pride of place to Erasmus, we must remember that Hamlet's "silence" is not necessarily a "mystic silence" before the "high mysteries" of God. It is possible that the "fell sergeant,

---

90. See Chapter 1.
91. That lovely 360 is the product of Bevington's editorial conflation of Q2 and F.
92. Erasmus, *On the Freedom*, 39.
93. Dodds, *Exploiting Erasmus*, 114–15.

Death" (5.2.338) was destined to find Hamlet enmeshed in unholy murder, leaving yet more to do for the gravediggers and the priests. Horatio fills the breach with his lyrical "flights of angels" (5.2.362), but then Fortinbras enters on cue, coming full circle in his own right, directing us to "his rights of memory in this kingdom" (391). "Remember me," indeed (1.5.92). The world reverts to form, and England, to judge by its ambassadors, is hardly the wiser. Nonetheless, we may observe that the playwright has attempted to illuminate the meaning of the most serious human actions, an effort that can be compared to chiaroscuro in painting, as humanism and theology cohere in a shadowy synthesis. In this sense, the indeterminacy of Hamlet's fate is the sign of Shakespeare's effort to master his own moral and dramatic limitations and come to grips with what he could and could not say. Through this labor of conscience and consciousness, Shakespeare maintained the play's action by pursuing the fate of the soul "beyond the reaches" of humanism or theology, where the interpretation of words and actions breaks down and God alone can judge.

CHAPTER 5

On Not Understanding
King Lear's Hidden God

Have ye no regard, all ye that pass by this way? Behold, & see, if there be
any sorrow like unto my sorrow, which is done unto me, wherewith the Lord
hath afflicted *me* in the day of his fierce wrath.

(Lamentations 1:12, italics in original)

In the Preface to this book I described my general approach: "Addressing
how Shakespeare fuses Christian ideas and meanings with non-Christian ideas
and meanings, I present Shakespeare's Christian humanism as an effort at
imaginative synthesis that varies from play to play." Some would argue that
King Lear, the subject of this final chapter, marks not so much a synthesis as
a collapse into nihilism. Pagan and Christian elements combine like certain
unstable forms of oxygen and nitrogen, in catastrophic loss and mutual devastation. The hope for a providential fusion of these elements is, it turns out,
an ironic prelude to the entirely disillusioning fifth act. If the previous chapters
kept us in the humanistic game, if the dizzying interaction of Athens and
Jerusalem supplied a means for appreciating an always difficult ad hoc synthesis, the Shakespeare of *Lear* appears to bring the Christian game of wisdom
and folly to an abrupt halt. David Kastan's reading is indicative of how things
stand: "As Lear desperately imagines that the dead Cordelia breathes, he
admits that 'If it be so / It is a chance which does redeem all sorrows / That
ever I have felt.'. . . But the feather does not stir and Cordelia does not live.
Sorrows here are not redeemed, nor are they redemptive."[1]

---

1. David Scott Kastan, "Shakespeare and the Idea of Tragedy," in *A Companion to Shakespeare's
Work: The Tragedies*, ed. Richard Dutton and Jean E. Howard, 12. For anti-redemptive views similar
to those of Kastan, see Harold Bloom, *Shakespeare and the Invention of the Human*, 505–06; Stephen
Greenblatt, *Shakespearean Negotiations: The Circulation of Social Energy in Renaissance England*, 125; and
James Shapiro, *The Year of Lear: Shakespeare in 1606*, 301–04. As anti-redemptionists, these four major
critics are preceded in their position in some respects by A. C. Bradley, *Shakespearean Tragedy* (1904),
240–42, but especially by William R. Elton, King Lear *and the Gods* (1966). Elton in his influential
book contends against Christian readings of *King Lear* as a "traditional drama of redemption" (71),
finding that "the obstacles to an orthodox theological reading of *King Lear*, in which the protagonist

Forty-odd years ago, in a different era, René Fortin presented a good argument that such unambiguous rulings—and they are legion—do the play an injustice: "Any critic intending to offer an unequivocal reading of its ending should recall that he is witnessing a play that has throughout insisted upon the problematics of seeing and that this theme dominates the final lines of Lear."[2] Fortin's 1979 essay "Hermeneutical Circularity and Christian Interpretations of *King Lear*" develops his contention about "the problematics of seeing" by recognizing how textual questions are framed and by observing the effect of presuppositions.[3] I think these hermeneutic concerns are healthy and sane—often they are theologically sensitive—but I am less sanguine than Fortin was about achieving a tolerant pluralism among critics of *King Lear*. As if in perverse reaction against the play's self-evident concern with spiritual blindness, critics have made *King Lear* Exhibit A for Shakespeare's post-Christian avant-gardism. "The timing of these two deaths," writes Marxist critic Jonathan Dollimore on the fates of Cordelia and Lear, "must surely be seen as cruelly, precisely, subversive . . . . The play concludes with two events which sabotage the prospect of both closure and recuperation." Dollimore commends Nicholas Brooke, who, "in one of the best close analyses of the play that we have, concludes by declaring: 'all moral structures, whether of natural order or Christian redemption, are invalidated by the naked fact of experience.'"[4] Park Honan, for whom the play is "pre-Christian and post-Christian at once," is similarly unequivocal about what he is seeing: "There is no spiritual development in this whole ordeal . . . . Lear, finally, is divested of most of his illusions."[5] In case there are any lingering illusions (formerly known as interpretive problems), James Shapiro writes to dispel them: "though the others onstage know, as do we, that Lear is engaged in wishful thinking and that the strangled Cordelia cannot possibly be alive, the folio

---

moves from sin and suffering to redemption, are more formidable than has generally been realized" (263). On the other hand (and more recently), Marjorie Garber in *Shakespeare After All* responds to the question of "whether there is any redemption in *King Lear*" (682) by counting "the direction of nihilism" (694) as no more than one interpretive option. She and René Fortin (cited below) are not far afield in this respect. Along similar lines, see also Steven Marx, *Shakespeare and the Bible*, 77–78.

2. René E. Fortin, "Hermeneutical Circularity and Christian Interpretations of *King Lear*," *Shakespeare Studies* 12 (1979): 117. Lear's final lines in our text are 5.3.316–17.

3. For a related discussion, see Christopher Ricks, *T. S. Eliot and Prejudice*, esp. 94–102.

4. Jonathan Dollimore, *Radical Tragedy: Religion, Ideology and Power in the Drama of Shakespeare and His Contemporaries*, 203, and, quoting Nicholas Brooke, 202.

5. Park Honan, *Shakespeare: A Life*, 338, 340.

version nonetheless offers playgoers the consolation of a Lear who has suffered enough and is allowed to be deluded."[6]

The professional context, as I write today, is that a Christian reading of the play faces impressive obstacles. As we saw in the Introduction, starting with the hostile reader's report that launched the pepper theory, the weapons of skeptical thought are not aimed at the post-Christian prejudices that normalize a post-Christian Shakespeare, or at whatever sensitivities determine that it's better for all concerned to promote a Shakespeare about whose faith we cannot see, hear, or speak. It remains relevant that "the period from 1904 [when Bradley's *Shakespearean Tragedy* appeared] until the early 1960s was dominated by redemptionist, Christian readings of *King Lear*."[7] Bradley, though he was divided about the play's ending, set a precedent for redemptionist critics who seized on Lear's "unbearable *joy*."[8] We are hardly conscious, though, that our own period is dominated by a continuing reaction against such redemptive readings. Yet that is most certainly the case. Breaking from this unequal contest of redemptive and anti-redemptive readings, I will argue that the Shakespeare of *Lear* is more interested in tragic suffering than in the joy of redemption, which joy, I submit, has become a critical convenience that distracts our attention from the crux of the matter. While Christianity's presence doesn't preclude redemptive possibilities, its larger effect is more disturbing. In *King Lear*, tragic suffering, not redemption, is expressive of Shakespeare's Christian faith. An unfathomable providence compels a "sensibilitie of feare infused from aboue."[9] God's anger indicts the once and future Britain.

To begin rethinking the play, I want to look at Shakespeare's use of the royal plural in the first scene. The action starts with Gloucester and Kent. From the dramatist's point of view, the two of them are (among other things) supplying the backstory and preparing us for the King's entrance with his daughters, sons-in-law, and train of followers. I want to suggest that the royal plurals of Kent and Lear foreshadow a crisis of allegiance that will gradually extend from the stage to the audience. In this respect, we may note that the play begins with the question of where affection is directed:

---

6. Shapiro, *Year of Lear*, 303. Shapiro's point is countered by Desdemona's and the Duchess of Malfi's briefly returning to life after suffocation (or strangulation).

7. Susan Bruce, ed., *William Shakespeare: King Lear*, 4.

8. Bradley, *Shakespearean Tragedy*, 241, his italics.

9. This quotation comes, by way of the OED (*sensibility*, 4a), from the Douay Bible's "Annotations" (1609). It refers to the hardening of Pharaoh's heart in Exodus 7: "He did not mollifie it, with sensibilitie of feare infused from aboue."

KENT   I thought the King had more affected the Duke of Albany than
   Cornwall.
GLOUCESTER   It did always seems so to us; but now in the division of
   the kingdom it appears not which of the dukes he values most.

                                                              (1.1.1–5)

The King makes his glittering entrance after thirty-three lines. He orders
Gloucester to go look after France and Burgundy, and comments forthwith:
"Meantime we shall express our darker purpose" (1.1.36). I am observing, in
the first place, that Lear and Gloucester both open with the royal plural.[10]
Gloucester's "us" marks the one time that the Earl voices the royal plural in
the entire play. After his fall, he uses the first-person plural very differently;
to take a notable example: "As flies to wanton boys are we to th'gods; / They
kill us for their sport" (4.1.36–37). The honest Kent wants to understand what
is happening: "I thought the King had more affected the Duke of Albany
than Cornwall." He goes on to show interest in Edmund: "Is not this your
son, my lord?" (8). Gloucester replies by taking Kent into his confidence with
lascivious chat about Edmund's origins. Kent is polite without warming to
Gloucester's manner. Coleridge has aptly remarked: "Need it be said how
heavy an aggravation the stain of bastardy must have been, were it only that
the younger brother was liable to hear his own dishonor and his mother's
infamy related by his father with an excusing shrug of the shoulders, and in a
tone betwixt waggery and shame."[11] In a Christian land, adultery was a mortal
sin. Somewhat coyly, Shakespeare appears to palliate Gloucester's indiscretions
with a pun on "conceive" (1.1.12). We seem as yet a world away from Poor
Tom's ravings about "the act of darkness" (3.4.86), or from Goneril's punning
use of "conceive" (4.2.24) in her adulterous flirtation with Edmund. But given
what we are about to find out, most especially the evil effects of Gloucester's
"good sport" (1.1.23), Gloucester's "us" does considerable work. If we hear
it as extending to Edmund, we would infer that Gloucester and his bastard
son had been discussing "the division of the kingdom," in which case
Edmund's unfilial reference to "half his revenue" (1.2.54) finds an unexpected,
royal inspiration: being quick of "study" (1.1.31), Edmund develops his own

---

10. As René Weis points out, the royal plural was "used by other important personages" and
may in Gloucester's case carry the secondary meaning of "'myself and other members of my family,'
as Edmund is present." William Shakespeare, *King Lear: A Parallel Text Edition*, ed. René Weis, 80n.
Cf. *Macbeth* 2.1.24.
11. Samuel Taylor Coleridge, *Shakespearean Criticism*, ed. Thomas Middleton Raysor, 1:52.

ideas about "the division of the kingdom." If we hear Gloucester's "us" as more purely self-regarding, it links two powerful egos ripe for a fall—a fall that is dramatized through their pronoun usage.

As the King of Britain, Lear stands in a curiously sensitive relation to King James I, who is widely credited with coining the phrase "Great Britain." Lear's history, as every schoolboy knew, was part of the great providential march that culminated in the Tudors and the Stuarts. Lear's use of the royal plural would have encouraged Shakespeare's audience to project the aura of native kingship onto his character. John Baxter makes a pertinent point: the "royal 'we' is made possible because the king as a figurehead represents the whole community."[12] Without insisting that Lear in his initial appearance commanded the audience's allegiance, we may suggest that he invited it. Like James, he was a British monarch and a royal patriarch. The play's connection to the historical idea of "Great Britain," so dear to James's heart (though, as we shall see, not to everyone's), aligns Lear with James, as do numerous topical resonances. To follow James Shapiro, King James VI of Scotland, in his 1599 treatise *Basilikon Doron* (Gk. "royal gift"), had warned his eldest son, Prince Henry, against "dividing your kingdoms." The book gained many attentive readers when the Scots King became James I of England in 1603. Its "warning about 'dividing your kingdoms' is closely echoed in the opening lines of *King Lear* in Gloucester's remark about the 'division of the kingdoms.'" Moreover, the comment by Kent that begins the play, "I thought the King had more affected the Duke of Albany than Cornwall," was calculated to tease: "Jacobean playgoers knew that King James's elder son, Henry, was the current Duke of Albany, and his younger one, Charles, the Duke of Cornwall."[13] To describe Lear, in his first appearance, as a distorted image of James is right: the opening scene presents something of a contemporary mirror, and Lear has not yet harmed the royal elevation that he and James enjoy.

Lear's "we shall express our darker purpose" has a grandiose ring that decays according to our knowledge of the plot. The King inhabits his royal pronouns, subject and possessive, with a self-gratifying sense of his own depths. He basks in the luxury of his ritualistic splendor. Bevington glosses the phrase "darker purpose" as "undeclared intention," which is right. Its ambiguities threaten to overtake its primary meaning only if, like the actors themselves, we know what lies ahead. If we do, or if we are preternaturally

---

12. John Baxter, *Shakespeare's Poetic Styles: Verse into Drama*, 133.
13. Shapiro, *Year of Lear*, 33, 40. Bevington, following F, has "division of the kingdom."

sensitive to "darker" possibilities, we wonder if Lear's "darker purpose" is darker than he knows. From the opening, the disruptive lurking presence of dramatic irony signals the advent of a larger perspective that will engulf the play. We sense this disturbing irony and its unknown depths when Cordelia delivers her abrupt line, "Nothing, my lord." The successive *nothings* (1.1.87, etc.) that usher Lear into the abyss supply a harsh antidote to the royal "we" and a catalyst to whatever self-knowledge he achieves: "I am a very foolish, fond old man" (4.7.61). Gloucester, in his fashion, soon gets unto the act (1.2.36, etc.). From start to finish, *nothing* is a stumbling block. Its moral danger lies in the temptation to assimilate it to what we think we know. To claim or declaim that "Nothing will come of nothing" (1.1.90) is, given the moment's intense pressure, to presume or overstep, as any theologically sensitive person would have known the doctrine of creation *ex nihilo*.[14] The word's multitudinous variance within the play, militates, like the grinding force of experience, against our ability to frame a coherent perspective. Such a perspective remains hidden from us.

While Lear initially invites the allegiance of loyal subjects, France's resounding use of the royal plural—Burgundy never uses it—comes after the King has disinherited Cordelia, divided his kingdom in two, and exiled Kent. Lear's "We" addresses Burgundy at line 193, but the context has abruptly changed.[15] Working his way through this royal desolation, France rises to the heights:

> Thy dowerless daughter, King, thrown to my chance,
> Is queen of us, of ours, and our fair France.
> Not all the dukes of wat'rish Burgundy
> Can buy this unprized precious maid of me.
>
> (260–63)

At this juncture, France's royal pronouns have no claim on our allegiance—not if we mingled with the peers at Whitehall on its St. Stephen's Day performance, December 26, 1606, likely its debut,[16] and not if we saw *King Lear* at the Globe playhouse sometime later. The brevity of his appearance works

---

14. Cf. Antonio in *The Duchess of Malfi*: "Do not weep. / Heaven fashioned us of nothing and we strive / To bring ourselves to nothing." John Webster, *The Duchess of Malfi*, ed. Leah S. Marcus (3.5.79–81).

15. For more on Lear's pronouns, see Angus McIntosh and Colin Williamson, "*King Lear*, Act I, Scene I. A Stylistic Note," *The Review of English Studies* 14 (February 1963): 54–58.

16. Liturgical reasons for a St. Stephen's Day debut are laid out by Joseph Wittreich, *"Image of that Horror": History, Prophecy, and Apocalypse in* King Lear, 116–19. The question is not settled, however. See Bevington, A-17–18.

with his isolated position to keep France at a distance. He brings no topical associations to help orient the situation in his favor. He does not evoke the contemporary French King, Henry IV. He is no one's figurehead—a lack of relation that is peculiar and important, given that France acts as a true Christian king ought to act, embracing spiritual, not worldly, worth. Lear and Burgundy, in their shameful rejection of Cordelia, serve as foils to set off France's Christian magnanimity. His rich rhetoric of the royal plural is morally arresting: he is chivalrous and faithful where Burgundy is cautious and practical. He shows righteous indignation, not self-love.

In his ideal nature, France bears the markers of romance and allegory. Most important, he initiates the sharp contrast between Christian and pagan worlds that distinguishes *King Lear* from its main source, the monolithically Christian *True Chronicle History of King Leir*, where the Christian God plays a conspicuous role in human affairs. I will come back to this pregnant matter of *Lear* versus *Leir*. For the moment, though, let us observe that France's rhetoric, coming after Lear's swearing by Hecate and Apollo, is distinctly biblical:

> Fairest Cordelia, that art most rich being poor,
> Most choice, forsaken, and most loved, despised,
> Thee and thy virtues here I seize upon,
> Be it lawful I take up what's cast away.
>
> (254–57)

Naseeb Shaheen connects line 254 to two passages from Saint Paul, both from Second Corinthians, "Our Lord Iesus Christ, that he being riche, for your sakes became poore" (8:9), and "As poore, and yet make many riche" (6:10). The combined effect of these two references, as Shaheen lists them, is negligible. In the nature of his work, he cannot help but succumb to a leveling effect: the vast patchwork of biblical allusions overwhelms the thread of any particular allusion. Yet the same scholar makes the extremely valuable observation that, although *The True Chronicle History of King Leir* "contains some thirty clear biblical references," Shakespeare "borrowed none" of them. In fact, "none" of his sources "influenced Shakespeare's biblical references."[17] What we hear from France, then, is the first sharp injection of Christian language into this ostensibly pagan play.[18] I would argue that these biblical

---

17. Naseeb Shaheen, *Biblical References in Shakespeare's Plays*, 604–05.

18. Shaheen (*Biblical References*, 607) catches an allusion to Ephesians in Cordelia's "Obey you, love you, and most honor you" (1.1.98). But the effect is not sharp or prolonged.

allusions are *urgent*. They are the key to recognizing the Shakespeare of *Lear* as a Christian writer who criticizes and challenges Christians, but who does so on Christian grounds. They show him imaginatively synthesizing pagan Britain and Christian Britain. They show him fusing Christian ideas and meanings with non-Christian ideas and meanings. They mark the first strong instance of a carefully crafted technique that reflects Shakespeare's originality and purpose in one of his greatest works.

That the biblical reach of France's lines goes beyond Second Corinthians is a point that neither Shaheen nor the play's many editors have addressed. Peter Milward is surely right about the biblical atmosphere that permeates France's address to Cordelia. For instance, Milward connects France's words to Matthew 27:46 (which echoes Psalm 22:1), where the dying Christ asks, "My God, my God, why hast thou forsaken me?"[19] Moreover, if Cordelia has been "forsaken" in a Christ-evoking sense, if, that is, her forsakenness connects her to Christ on the cross, then France's reclaiming what has been "cast away" begs consideration. In my years discussing these lines at a Jesuit college, Catholic students have often heard France's words with an ear to one of Jesus's sayings: "The stone which the builders rejected has become the cornerstone" (Matthew 21:42).[20] It is stonecutters who produce cornerstones, and *King Lear* is (significantly or not) the only Shakespeare play with the word "stonecutter" in it (2.2.59). Regan and Cornwall occupy a "hard house— / More harder than the stones whereof 'tis raised" (3.2.63–64). Preaching of stones and builders, Jesus continues to recite Psalm 118, his source text for this pericope: "The stone which the builders refused, the same is made the head of the corner. This was the Lord's doing, and it is marvelous in our eyes" (Matthew 21:42). But then he breaks from Psalm 18 quite unexpectedly: "Therefore say I unto you, the kingdom of God shall be taken from you" (Matthew 21:42–43; see also Mark 12:10–11). It is a startling appropriation of the Psalmist's verses. It resembles the supersessionist language that has incited centuries of anti-Semitism, but there is the matter of intention. As a Jew, Christ was invoking the major prophets: Isaiah, Jeremiah, and Ezekiel (though Daniel is also a major prophet, he was not based in Jerusalem, as the others were). Like his prophetic forebears, he was warning the inhabitants of Jerusalem of imminent disaster. In the Acts of the Apostles (4:11), Peter,

---

19. Peter Milward, SJ, *Biblical Influences in Shakespeare's Great Tragedies*, 163–64.

20. My students hear it in the language of the New Jerusalem Bible, which I have quoted for the nonce.

imprisoned in Jerusalem, preaches the same text to leaders of the Jewish community. He identifies Jesus as "the stone" that the builders rejected. The same Peter (or his proxy) revisits it yet again at 1 Peter 2:7. Since Christ's warning echoes throughout the New Testament, I would suggest that Shakespeare's audience heard traces of it when France takes up "what's cast away," especially given the sudden density of biblical inversion. Amongst the divisions and rivals, the effect would be to stir the audience's shifting sympathies and allegiances. France's royal pronouns may connect subliminally, after all.

This experience of shifting sympathies will carry the audience a considerable distance—to the very end, in fact. To take another in a series of illuminating instances: one hears the royal plural in Cordelia's lines: "No blown ambition doth our arms incite, / But love, dear love, and our aged father's right. / Soon may I hear and see him!" (4.4.27–29). Shakespeare invites us to sympathize when the Queen of France upholds "our aged father's right." This invitation stands despite the nearby presence of "British powers" (4.4.21). Following this emotional cue, we observe that, as Cordelia rallies us to her father, her language grows Christological. Shaheeb casts a cold eye on "O dear father, / It is thy business I go about" (4.4.23–24): "Cordelia's words are a clear reference to Luke 2:49 ['I must go about my father's business'], making these lines in *Lear* a favorite passage for those who would place a religious interpretation on Shakespeare's plays."[21] Be that as it may, let us remember that, as Shaheen informs us, Shakespeare's religious allusions are his own. Shaheen directs us to another strongly Christological passage later in Act 4, lines spoken by the Gentleman to Lear's receding back: "Thou hast one daughter / Who redeems nature from the general curse / Which twain have brought her to" (4.6.205–07). Informed by this desert blossoming of Christology, the audience continues to waver in allegiance between the British and the loving Cordelia with her French invaders. When that charming piece of evil, Edmund, says, "The battle done and they within our power" (5.1.70), his words—embedded in a wickedly self-loving soliloquy—are not likely to win over the audience's hearts and minds. And yet, he's referring to the home team. The actor's way of delivering the line will reflect his take on Edmund's character as a whole. Is he gloating? Is he suddenly all business? Do we hear the royal plural lurking in his heart? Is Edmund *our* figurehead? Regan is all in for the royal plural, which she would share with Edmund: "That's as we list to grace him"

21. Shaheen, *Biblical References*, 616.

(5.3.63). We are the British—it's our language, after all—but the French host has managed to stake a claim to our spiritual allegiance. It has no claim on our national allegiance, and the fact that it materializes only in the form of vague figures rushing across the stage gives it a dreamlike ambience. No one ever speaks a word of French, and we never hear a French accent after the opening scene. The French King—strange fellow—returns to his country in the middle of the invasion. France's army is led, at least in the 1608 quarto (Q1), by someone called "Monsieur La Far" (4.3.8). The obscure name of this shadowy personage evokes the "far country" in the parable of the Prodigal Son, in the language both of the Bishops' Bible and the Geneva Bible (Luke 15:13). If we look for the parable of the Prodigal Son, Shaheen would readily point it out to us, when Cordelia is heard pitying her father (using the familiar *thou*): "and wast thou fain, poor father, / To hovel thee with swine and rogues forlorn / In short and musty straw?" (4.7.39–41). Here "fain" means not "glad" or "pleased," or even "content under the circumstances," but "forced" or "constrained."[22] Cordelia is responding to her father's powerlessness. Her message is more in the nature of allegory than of realism. She must play the forgiving father to Lear's prodigal son, and we must decide whether we are on the side of God's forgiving love or, like the older brother in the parable, we are on our own side.

The pointedly Christian language that France introduces into the play serves Shakespeare's purpose of testing his audience—an audience whose tastes and expectations he had practically created—with the moral play of contraries. France champions "love" (1.1.242, 255, 259) with a Christian intelligence that connects him to Cordelia (1.1.252 and 4.4.28) and distinguishes their love from "love" in the uncharitable usages of Lear, Goneril, Regan, and Edmund. If we recall Shakespeare's prior use of the figure *syllepsis* (in *Henry V*, for example), in which the pun is self-contained, we notice its potential for moral ambiguity in this rhetoric of contraries. "To 'love' a person," writes Erasmus in his famous essay from the *Adages*, "The Sileni of Alcibiades," "in common parlance, is either to corrupt by over-indulgence or to lay schemes against both chastity and reputation, hostile actions which it is hard to surpass."[23] From an Erasmian point of view, the Christian meaning of love stands in "topsy-turvy" relation to the worldly meaning of love (a meaning akin to

---

22. C. T. Onions, *A Shakespeare Glossary: Enlarged and Revised throughout by Robert D. Eagleson*, 96. Bevington has "constrained."
23. Erasmus, *The Adages of Erasmus*, ed. William Barker, 253.

"nothing") that occupies the vicious minds of Edmund and Lear's older daughters. The Latin adjective Erasmus often uses to get this argument across is *praeposterus*, as in, *Atque hinc praeposterum de rebus multitudinis judicium*.[24] As I mentioned in Chapter 1, the word evidently entered the English language through a 1533 translation of Erasmus's *Enchiridion*. It is (generally speaking) part of the Erasmian legacy in Shakespeare, occurring in his works, both adjectivally and adverbially, some dozen times. As an Erasmian feature of Shakespeare's Christian worldview, it informs the interplay of wisdom and folly throughout *King Lear*, which, in turn, shapes the perspectival clash between good and evil. Goneril's characteristic contempt for fools is expressive of her evil character. To be a fool in her parlance is, one recognizes, to be better than she is. Her husband, she says, is a "fool," a "moral fool," a "vain fool" (4.2.28, 59, 62). The scorn she pours on him, "Milk-livered man / That bears a cheek for blows" (4.1.51–52), evokes its Christian inversion: "Resist not evil: but whosoever shall smite thee on thy right cheek, turn to him the other also" (Matthew 5:39). Shakespeare's advance in *Lear*, as a Christian work of art, is toward a new kind of holy preposterousness, a sacred folly that the world and its sin-laden "business" (a frequent word, usually weighed down by the *sin* it contains) cannot accommodate, can only imprison, injure, or kill: "And my poor fool is hanged!" (5.3.311).

So "forsaken" and "cast away" is wise folly in this world that Erasmian wit, failing in its educational mission, morphs into Shakespearean madness. Enid Welsford comments on this harsh new intensity: "That Shakespeare's ethics were the ethics of the New Testament, that in this play his mightiest poetry is dedicated to the reiteration of the wilder paradoxes of the Gospels and of St. Paul, that seems to me quite certain." Further, she grasps the unpleasant corollary of this obsessive dedication to Christian paradox: "the metaphysical comfort of the Scriptures is . . . omitted, though not therefore necessarily denied."[25] We may add: to omit "the metaphysical comfort of the Scriptures" is severely to test the audience's allegiance to the message of the Gospels, not with worldly pleasures and earthly delights, as in Spenser's Bower of Bliss, but in the face of the hell that reigns on earth when that message is *abandoned*. So long as what Erasmus terms the "common parlance" speaks through us, we are implicated in its results.

---

24. "Hence the mob's topsy-turvy judgment about things." A Latin text of the *Sileni Alcibiadis* is available online: http://ihrim.huma-num.fr/nmh/Erasmus/Proverbia/Adagium_2201.html. Accessed January 17, 2020.

25. Enid Welsford, *The Fool: His Social and Literary History*, 271.

King Lear is thus instructive in its cruelty, at least to a point. It is a play not only where ambitious evil murders love, but where love suffers its greatest defeat in an action that stupefies the intellect. The unreasoning nature of Cordelia's death seems to exploit, for purposes of horrendous satire, the scholastic doctrine that only "good or being can act or be causes."[26] Indeed, Lear had long "believed in a universe controlled by divine authority"; he is steadily stripped of that belief until its final extinction comes with Cordelia's death.[27] Occurring after mindless delay, and despite Edmund's belated change of heart, Cordelia's murder punishes the logical mind. That is why, if we ask of our wise fools, why was *their* love destroyed, we are generally referred to nihilism, hard realism, Beckett, and so on. One is accustomed to reading *King Lear* as a play that arraigns God: a Book of Job "without God's voice from the whirlwind."[28] "The real point of Cordelia's death," proclaims the author of that brief but pithy essay, "The Theology of *King Lear*," "is precisely that it is pointless."[29] It follows that to tear down the façade of meaningfulness we must puncture the lines that prop up this façade. In the last scene, in particular, one thinks of Edgar's prematurely declaring, "The gods are just" (5.3.173), and of Albany's vain invocation, "The gods defend her!" (261). But what if, taking Lear's cry against "men of stones" (5.3.262) to our own "hard hearts" (3.6.77),[30] what if we are led to ask (standing at the Globe or seated behind the King) not simply, why did God let this happen? But, since our allegiances are flickering and our consciences uneasy, are we to blame? Are we responsible for the ruins before us?

This last question leads beyond our routine hypocrisies and prudent evasions to a more degrading possibility. It comes as an afterthought, an unexpected effect of the catastrophe, a silent, creeping recognition scene: are we Britons implicated in the death of love? Shakespeare's two uses of "redeem"—both connected to Cordelia[31]—would then redound back on our apparently predestined failure, implicating us in our broken hopes, augmenting

---

26. Etienne Gilson, *The Christian Philosophy of St. Thomas Aquinas,* trans. L. K. Shook, CSB, 158.

27. Norman Maclean, "Episode, Scene, Speech, and Word: The Madness of Lear," in *Critics and Criticism,* ed. R. S. Crane, 87.

28. Hannibal Hamlin, *The Bible in Shakespeare,* 330.

29. Paul Cheetham, "The Theology of *King Lear*," in *King Lear: William Shakespeare,* ed. Linda Cookson and Bryan Loughrey, 62.

30. For "hard hearts," see David Beauregard, *Catholic Theology in Shakespeare's Plays,* 159–60. The hardening of Pharaoh's heart (Exodus 9:12) is a prooftext in the great debate between Erasmus and Luther.

31. See 4.6.206 and 5.3.271.

our despair. In the Lamentations of Jeremiah, the weeping prophet hopes "there may be hope" (3:29). But he ends without it: "thou hast utterly rejected us: thou art exceedingly angry against us" (5:22). The anti-redemptionist habit, as we have seen, is to blame God's absence for the lack of divine intervention. Beckett again: "The bastard! He doesn't exist!" But what if the Shakespeare of *King Lear* repels our interest in *theodicy* (a word we can't blame on the Reformation); what if he antagonizes our pathetic self-interest in whether God's ways are just? One thinks of that Job-like moment in *Cymbeline* when Jupiter speaks: "How dare you ghosts / Accuse the Thunderer . . . ?" (5.4.94–95). Lear swears twice by "Jupiter" (1.1.181, 2.4.20), but the Thunderer does not intercede for "old men" (2.4.191). Do we "dare" blame him for disappointing *us*? What, then, if Shakespeare's emphasis is on England's national failings—on human fallenness, sinfulness, ignorance, and unloving nothingness?

Such a cultural counterattack would resemble the species of sermon known as a Jeremiad—the generic title for sermons that aim at national restoration on the prophetic model of ancient Israel. A major Elizabethan example would be William Perkins's 1592 sermon, *A Faithful and Plaine Exposition upon the Two First Verses of the Second Chapter of Zephaniah.*[32] To approach *Lear* as a Jeremiad is to ask, have we alienated God's allegiance; have we lost his covenantal blessing?[33] "The ultimate sanction," writes Michael McGiffert with reference to the prophet Hosea, "was the doom of Lo-Ammi—*not my people.*"[34] We may consider, in this general context, that the biblical prooftext for the incomprehensibility of God does not come from the Book of Job, as one might expect, but from the thirty-second chapter of Jeremiah.[35] The idea of a hidden God, the *Deus absconditus* of Aquinas and Luther (for Luther, a *Deus absconditior*), derives from Isaiah 45:15.

Before entering further into this prophetic background, I want to return to what Fortin called the "problematics of seeing" by way of one last examination of personal pronouns. These are from the play's closing lines. They are

---

32. For Perkins's sermon and its context among contemporary English Jeremiads, with detailed attention to theological problems both of works and grace, and of church and state, see Mary Morrissey, "The Paul's Cross Jeremiad and Other Sermons of Exhortation," in *Paul's Cross and the Culture of Persuasion in England, 1520–1640*, ed. Torrance Kirby and P. G. Stanwood, 421–438. For more on the English Jeremiad, see Michael McGiffert, "God's Controversy with Jacobean England," *American Historical Review* 88 (December 1983): 1151–1174.

33. For covenant theology and the English Jeremiad, see Morrisey, "Paul's Cross," esp. 429.

34. McGiffert, "God's Controversy," 1153, his italics.

35. Karl Rahner, SJ, "Thomas Aquinas on the Incomprehensibility of God," *The Journal of Religion* 58, Supplement (1978): S108.

assigned to Albany in the quarto and to Edgar in the folio. I take this opportunity to say that, excepting some minor considerations, I do not have space to lead our discussion through *King Lear*'s labyrinth of textual variants, their possible sources, and their possible meanings:

> EDGAR [ALBANY in Q1]
> The weight of this sad time we must obey;
> Speak what we feel, not what we ought to say.
> The oldest hath borne most; we that are young
> Shall never see so much nor live so long.
>
> (5.3.329–32)

As we can see, Shakespeare deploys the first-person plural at both ends of his play. And as it happens, whether we follow the quarto or the folio, the final speaker is in a position to wield the royal plural. I don't think it is the primary sense, and yet the intensive repetition of "we" revives the question of allegiances at this final moment of cataclysm and soul-baring. The battle for military supremacy has been won, but the aftershocks of spiritual defeat cannot be shaken off.

Alongside four invitations of "we," the closing lines administer a strong dose of the "problematics of seeing": "we that are young / Shall never see so much nor live so long." As regards the significance of seeing "so much," an ironic reading is hard to escape. Did *we* see anything? Did we *understand* anything? For Shakespeare and his audience, the blindness of those who see only with their eyes was proverbial. Hence the seducer in *A Lover's Complaint*: "My parts had power to charm a sacred nun, / Who disciplined, ay, dieted in grace, / Believed her eyes when they t'assail begun, / All vows and consecrations giving place" (260–63). Hence Aragon's reference in *The Merchant of Venice* to "the fool multitude, / That choose by show, / Not learning more than the fond eye doth teach, / Which pries not to th'interior" (2.9.26–28). What counts more than any single reference, though, is the audience's sensitivity to an archetypal western concept that, having been received through the widespread testimony both of natural and of supernatural witnesses, ramified beyond measure in the realm of Elizabethan and Jacobean rhetoric.

A serious study of spiritual or metaphorical blindness would go back through apophatic theology and the Augustinian tradition to the Bible, and, on the Greco-Roman side, to the myths of Oedipus and Tiresias, Plato's Cave (one thinks of Poor Tom as Lear's "good Athenian" at 3.4.179, in the torch-lit hovel), and Homer's legendary blindness; from the ancient to the modern world, it would prove inseparable from the history of skepticism, including Christian skepticism. But since we are not writing a book on the subject, let us go back to the most important source of all: the Bible. The man born blind is an everyman figure for Christians. After Jesus heals him on the sabbath, there is much alarm in Jerusalem. With his eyes opened, he is driven out of town. Jesus finds him and offers the following explanation: "I am come unto judgment into this world, that they which see not, might see: and that they which see, might be made blind" (John 9:39). The story of "Doubting Thomas" is likewise about seeing: "Jesus said unto him, Thomas, because thou hast seen me, thou believest: blessed are they that have not seen, and have believed" (John 20:29). The Geneva gloss on "they that have not seen" is Augustinian and robustly Protestant, "Which depend upon the simplicity of God's word, and ground not themselves upon man's sense and reason."[36] Most important, in his teachings about seeing and not seeing, the Christian God-man says things that ought to remind historically inclined persons that *King Lear* was written for an audience raised on these teachings: "Therefore speak I to them in parables, because they seeing, do not see: and hearing, they hear not, neither understand. So in them is fulfilled the prophecy of Isaiah, which *prophecy* saith, 'By hearing ye shall hear, and shall not understand, and seeing ye shall see, and shall not perceive'" (Matthew 13:13–14; see also Mark 4:12, Luke 8:10, John 12:39–41, Acts 28:26–27). With biblical gravity, then, Shakespeare was confronting his audience with the problem of what it was seeing.

Shakespeare's creative revision of his main source, *The True Chronicle History of King Leir* (c. 1590), connects to several of our concerns so far: the play's topicality; its biblical and prophetic background; the problematics of seeing. Earlier, for instance, we commented on Shakespeare's innovative treatment of France, whose biblical inversions convey a spiritual authority that, we now note, is entirely lacking in France's counterpart in *King Leir*, the virtuous but bland King of Gallia. Scholars agree that Shakespeare took a good deal of raw material from the chronicle play, transforming his borrowings into something different in kind, a great tragedy as opposed to a sentimental, tragicomic hodgepodge. It is William Elton who raises the crucial issue, in his landmark 1966 book, King Lear *and the Gods*, of whether Shakespeare, in rejecting the simplicities of *King Leir*, was distancing himself from Christianity. In Elton's

---

36. For Shakespeare's attention to the Geneva Bible's gloss or margin, see Barbara Mowat, "Shakespeare Reads the Geneva Bible," in *Shakespeare, the Bible, and the Form of the Book: Contested Scriptures*, ed. Travis DeCook and Alan Galey, 25–39.

comparison, the author of *King Lear* is said to "banish the numerous direct Christian references" of the older play. According to Elton, Shakespeare realized the need for "de-Christianizing changes" in order to discredit "a belief in providence, especially a personal providence."[37]

It seems not to have occurred to Elton that Shakespeare might discredit certain appropriations of providence because he was in fact a tough-minded Christian. Bear in mind the dating: the near success of the 1605 Gunpowder Plot demanded and received a strong official response. The government's "providentialist narrative" prominently included a January 1606 addition to the Prayer Book.[38] I suggest that Shakespeare's changes were made not to de-Christianize the old play but to meet the times with prophetic urgency, articulated through a startling rearrangement of biblical material.

Shakespeare's revision of his source play has been studied in great detail; it will be helpful for our purposes to review only its main outlines.[39] Building on the work of Dorothy Nameri,[40] Peter Pauls has observed how Shakespeare adapted the older play's concern with "disguises" to "his overall theme of appearance and reality." Similarly, Pauls draws attention to how Shakespeare uses letters and messages to "distort the truth and reveal it."[41] The theme of appearance and reality, as Pauls describes it, pertains to our concern with seeing and not seeing; in fact, Pauls detects "much more emphasis on Lear's blindness in Shakespeare's version." Pauls also remarks that *King Lear* features "little of the poetic justice which is such a large part of the source play." Quite right. Shakespeare throws the human craving for poetic justice back in our faces. Albany's brave words, which crumble under the weight of events, would have suited the source play's happy ending better than they suit the ending of *King Lear*: "All friends shall taste / The wages of their virtue, and all foes / The cup of their deservings" (5.3.308–310). Evil is more potent in *King Lear*: "Goneril and Regan are much like their counterparts in the source, although Shakespeare has made them even

37. Elton, King Lear *and the Gods*, 63, 71. For a more recent version of this thesis, see David Loewenstein, "Agnostic Shakespeare?: The Godless World of *King Lear*," in *Shakespeare and Early Modern Religion*, ed. David Loewenstein and Michael Witmore, 155–71.

38. Shapiro, *Year of Lear*, 102.

39. For verbal parallels, see Peter Pauls, "*The True Chronicle History of King Leir* and Shakespeare's *King Lear*: A Reconsideration," *Upstart Crow* 5 (1984): 94–96.

40. Nameri writes, "The various disguises in *Leir* are dramatic conventions employed to enhance the romantic flavor of the story. They are devoid of the specific dramatic-thematic functions that Shakespeare assigns" to Kent and Edgar. For Nameri, these "dramatic-thematic functions" serve the gradual process of "insight." Dorothy E. Nameri, *Three Versions of the Story of King Lear*, 1:65, 67.

41. Pauls, "*True Chronicle*," 104, 96, 104.

more cruel." Cordelia "is given less than half the number of lines Cordella" (her counterpart) has. As Cordelia's role is condensed, the accent shifts from Cordella's outward beauty to Cordelia's beauty as "an inner quality which is not universally acclaimed."[42] Stephen Lynch sums up this process of character revision and thematic innovation: "the moderate character conflicts in the old play are refashioned by Shakespeare into stark dramatic oppositions: Kent's insight opposed to Lear's blindness, and the selfless and spiritual love of France in opposition to the egotism and materialism of Lear." Most important, in sharp contrast to the chronicle play, *King Lear* "continually stresses inward spiritual values."[43]

The phrase "inward spiritual values" is neither Shakespearean nor pleasingly scientific, but it coheres with the teachings of the Christ who proclaimed, "for behold the kingdom of God is within you" (Luke 17:21). *The Imitation of Christ* (1418), the devotional manual by Thomas à Kempis, much loved in Shakespeare's England, mounts Luke 17:21 above its second chapter, in which the author preaches at length on "the inward life of man."[44] Erasmus in his *Enchiridion* distinguishes between "the inner and outer man and his two parts as found in Holy Scripture."[45] Augustine, as quoted by Launcelot Andrewes, says with characteristic emphasis: "Inward charity is of far greater esteem than outward, because it cureth the principal part of man."[46] My point is that we cannot dismiss the idea of "inner spiritual values" and be true to Shakespeare's audience. It was his interest in exposing the soul, "the principal part of man," that led Shakespeare to transform the triumphant Cordella into the sacrificial Cordelia, whom Lear learns to "see better." Naturally, though, I do not find Lynch's pursuit of "redemption" to be especially valuable.[47] It is the flipside of what Elton, Kastan, and many others have to say: the loss of providence, the general horror of Lear's world. It is wiser to put our hope of redemption aside for the time being, in order to recognize that redemption may not be in the cards.

42. Pauls, *"True Chronicle,"* 99, 101, 102, 103.

43. Stephen J. Lynch, "Sin, Suffering, and Redemption in *Leir* and *Lear*," *Shakespeare Studies* 18 (1986): 164, 171.

44. Thomas à Kempis, *Of the imitation of Christ, three, both for wisedome, and godlines, most excellent bookes; made 170. yeeres since by one Thomas of Kempis, and for the worthines thereof oft since translated out of Latine into sundrie languages by diuers godlie and learned men: now newlie corrected, translated, and with most ample textes, and sentences of holie Scripture illustrated by Thomas Rogers*, EEBO, 70.

45. Erasmus, *The Essential Erasmus*, ed. and trans. John P. Dolan, 47.

46. Lancelot Andrewes, *A Pattern of Catechistical Doctrine*, quoted in Judy Kronenfeld, *King Lear and the Naked Truth: Rethinking the Language of Religion and Resistance*, 105.

47. Lynch, "Sin," 162.

The Christianity that Shakespeare wanted in his play is neither gentle nor reassuring. It is marked by a sharp quality of anachronism that is foreign to the source play. *The True Chronicle History of King Leir* betrays not a glimmer of historical self-consciousness. Shakespeare's play, by contrast, makes a forceful show of its pagan setting, and then riddles us with weird details: "godson" (2.1.91), "steeples" and "cocks" (3.2.3), the Fool's prophecy, overtly Christological language, inversions of folly and wisdom, Poor Tom's devils, "holy water" (4.3.31), "the promised end" (5.3.268). Shakespeare, we might say, delivers the play's Christian meaning to those with eyes to see. He does so by stripping Christianity of its customary dress and exiling it from power. His warning, like his method, is indirect. It is a national warning that the chronicle play doesn't endorse in the least. Its relevance is porous with ambiguity, lodged, for all intents and purposes, in the interrogative mood, and left for the playgoer to contemplate.

Due to this ambiguity about who and what is being addressed, I hesitate to classify the play as a type of Apocalypse. The Geneva margin says that Revelation is a vision of "things which were hid before." The thematically ambiguous act of seeing precludes the play from being such a vision. Due to the 1606 "Acte to Restraine Abuses of Players," Shakespeare found himself prohibited from even writing the word *God*. He seems to have flown under the official radar at least once, with Lear's monotheistic "God's spies" (5.3.17), another reference to seeing. I agree with Joseph Wittreich that *King Lear* asserts "a context for itself in the apocalyptic drama of St. John's Revelation and in prophetic tradition generally."[48] The context of the Apocalypse is real. Indeed, from a Christian perspective the Apocalypse transcends history and is always present. But its presence in the play is dependent upon prophetic warnings that are paramount. It emerges powerfully in Kent's famous exchange with Edgar in the closing scene: "Is this the promised end?" / "Or image of that horror?" (5.3.268–69). Even here, though, the language is not specific to the Book of Revelation, but refers more generally to "the end of the world, as foretold both by Old Testament prophets and by Christ himself in his eschatological discourse."[49] The play traffics in eschatology, an abiding concern of Shakespeare's, which the playwright compresses in his final scene, overwhelming our ability to attach meanings to signs, that is, our ability to see and

48. Wittreich, "*Image*," xi.
49. Milward, *Biblical Influences*, 201. Milward has "OT" for Old Testament; for Christ's "eschatological discourse" he cites Matthew 24, Mark 13, and Luke 21; he also cites 1 Peter 4:7 and Psalm 55:5.

understand. The visionary tableau of Cordelia in Lear's arms evokes, as Peter Milward has remarked,[50] Michelangelo's Pietà. At the same time, as regards the prophetic tradition, Lear's cry of "Howl, howl, howl!" (5.3.262) harkens back to Jeremiah, "Howl, ye shepherds, and cry, and wallow yourselves in the ashes" (25:34), as well as to Isaiah, "Howl you, for the day of the Lord is at hand: and it shall come as a destroyer from the Almighty" (13:6). These Old Testament passages are heard in James 5:1 and in the liturgy for Holy Saturday.[51]

Despite its apocalyptic pressures, I am suggesting that *Lear* is best approached through the prophetic tradition and its parabolic fulfillment in Christ. In composing *King Lear*, the playwright commented on the present by means of the past, in the sense that Jesus commented on the present by means of the past, and Christians subsequently interpreted the Old Testament as prefiguring the future. It has been established that Shakespeare wrote for an audience that, having many of Christ's teachings by heart, would be alert to the sounds of Matthew 13:13–14 ("they seeing, do not see"). The Geneva margin at this Matthean text directs us first to Isaiah 6:9, followed by Mark 4:12, Luke 8:10, John 12:40, Acts 18:26, and Romans 11:8. This prophetic trajectory was well known. So it becomes highly significant that *King Lear* is "set in a pagan Britain roughly contemporary with the prophet Isaiah."[52] Isaiah's calling occurs in "the year of the death of King Uzziah" (6:1). Among the versions of Lear that precede Shakespeare's, with variations in spelling and alternative plotlines, Geoffrey of Monmouth mentions Isaiah's contemporaneity with Cordeilla's foe and nephew Cunedagius,[53] while Holinshed makes Cordeilla's reign contemporary with Uzziah's.[54] The chronology gave Shakespeare historical grounds for connecting Lear's Britain to the world of the prophets. Further, we are operating under the English Jeremiad's assumption that the covenantal theology of Jeremiah 31:30–33 is in effect. The apocalyptic knowledge of the prophets was fulfilled in the person and teachings of Christ. This great intertextual vein of minatory terror informs *King Lear*'s warnings about seeing and understanding.

Shapiro is likely correct about the impression made by the ending of *Lear* on its more sensitive observers at court. They would have sensed "the image

---

50. In a rare 1969 work called *The New Testament and English Literature*. See Dennis Taylor, "Peter Milward."

51. Milward, *Biblical Influences*, 200.

52. Stephen Greenblatt, *Will in the World: How Shakespeare Became Shakespeare*, 360.

53. Geoffrey Bullough, *Narrative and Dramatic Sources in Shakespeare*, 7:316.

54. Bullough, *Narrative and Dramatic Sources*, 7:319.

and horror of the collapse of the state and the obliteration of the royal family akin to the violent fantasy of the Gunpowder plotters."[55] The same scholar makes a valuable observation about the playwright: "It would be hard to find many individuals in Jacobean England more intricately linked than he was to those whose lives were touched by the Gunpowder Plot.[56] I would agree that Shakespeare was well aware of the insane events of November 5, 1605. That it was, in fact, a Catholic plot is inextricably but opaquely bound up with Shakespeare's play, from its inception to its reception.[57] What I understand as Shakespeare's attraction to predominantly Protestant materials (e.g., the English Jeremiad), in order to construct the play's prophetic armature, does not rule out the possibility, even the likelihood, that the Catholic situation cut him to the heart. His daughter Susanna's recusancy occurred in 1606.

Met with this tremendous convergence of public and private worlds, the playwright, I am suggesting, registered what had happened in prophetic terms. In particular, his artistic obsession with the act of seeing was intended to evoke the prophetic context of Matthew 13:13–14 ("they seeing, do not see"). We will soon be integrating this context with matters of high theological import. First, let us observe how the play's leitmotif progresses to its climax in the last scene:

> LEAR
> Had I your tongues and eyes . . .
>   Lend me a looking glass . . . .
>
>   (5.3.263, 267)
> LEAR   Mine eyes are not o'th'best . . . .
>
>   (284)
> KENT
> If Fortune brag of two she loved and hated,
> One of them we behold.
>
>   (285–86)
> LEAR   This is a dull sight.
>
>   (287)
> LEAR   I'll see that straight.
>
>   (292)

---

55. Shapiro, *Year of Lear*, 302.

56. Shapiro, *Year of Lear*, 116.

57. For Edgar as persecuted Jesuit, see Peter Milward, SJ, *Shakespeare's Religious Background*, 72. For the English Catholic reception of the play, see Joseph Pearce, *The Quest for Shakespeare: The Bard of Avon and the Church of Rome*, 155, 155n9.

ALBANY   Oh, see, see!

(310)

LEAR

Do you see this? Look on her, look, her lips,

Look there, look there!

(316–17)

EDGAR   Look up, my lord.

(318)

EDGAR

we that are young

Shall never see much nor live so long.

(331–32)

Through this thematic repetition of verbs of seeing arranged with related
words (*eyes*, *looking glass*, *sight*), the play both demands and resists our efforts
at understanding. The materialist autopsy reports of Lear and Cordelia ignore
this dazzling ambiguity, which completes the great pattern of the play. In
this respect, let us trace the leitmotif's full arc with some memorable
instances:

GONERIL   Dearer than eyesight . . . .

(1.1.56)

KENT   See better, Lear . . .

(1.1.159)

GLOUCESTER   Come, if it be nothing I shall not need spectacles.

(1.2.35–36)

EDMUND   Look, sir, I bleed.

(2.1.40)

KENT   Nothing almost sees miracles

But misery.

(2.2.168–69)

FOOL   Then comes the time, who lives to see't . . .

(3.2.93)

CORNWALL   Lest it see more, prevent it. Out, vile jelly!

(3.7.86)

GLOUCESTER   I stumbled when I saw.

(4.1.19)

EDGAR   Oh, thou side-piercing sight!

(4.6.85)

GLOUCESTER   I see it feelingly.

(4.6.149)

By most accounts, Gloucester and Lear learn to "see better," if only by fits and for a short time. Whether their suffering is finally redemptive, whether or not the last act crushes all hope and renders their spiritual insights moot, these are secondary questions that, while important, do not go to the heart of the matter. The heart of the matter is the audience's participation in the act of seeing, which develops through Shakespeare's testing of allegiances and which draws, with marked originality, on the Hebrew prophets as Christ alludes to them in Matthew 13:13–14, etc. This prophetic context would have led Shakespeare's audience in the biblical direction of shared guilt and the consequences of betraying a jealous God.

It is pertinent that Isaiah's visionary powers represent a towering indictment of the spiritual blindness around him.[58] Erasmus, in the Foreword to the last edition of his Latin New Testament, updates this indictment for sixteenth-century Europe, quoting from Isaiah 56:10–11: Israel's "watchmen are blind; they are all ignorant. . . . [T]hey all look to their own way."[59] Isaiah tells how he saw God, who is unseen by others: "In the year of the death of King Uzziah, I saw also the Lord sitting upon a high throne" (6:1, see also 1:1). After the prophet describes his vision, an angel touches his mouth with "a hot coal" (6:6), purging his "sin" (6.7), so that he can deliver the message that Christ will make his own in the fullness of time. The Lord commands Isaiah, "Go, and say unto this people, Ye shall hear indeed, but ye shall not understand: ye shall plainly see, & not perceive. / Make the heart of this people fat, make their ears heavy, and shut their eyes, lest they see with their eyes, and hear with their ears, and understand with their hearts, and convert, and heal them" (6:9–10). In effect, Isaiah is called to go out and fail, in a process that the Geneva Bible's headnote for Isaiah 6 justifies sequentially, citing the chapter's verses: "1. Isaiah showeth his vocation by the Vision of the divine majesty. 9. He showeth the obstinacy of the people. 11. The destruction of the land. 13. The remnant reserved."[60] The Old Testament idea that God arranges history in the form of a morality tale is known to modern scholars as the Deuteronomic doctrine.[61] It is in evidence here. The gloss pretends to

---

58. Greg Maillet also discusses Isaiah with respect to *King Lear*, though our analyses differ considerably. See Greg Maillet, *Learning to See the Theological Vision of Shakespeare's King Lear*, esp. 3–4. For more on *King Lear* and Isaiah, see Wittreich, *"Image"*; and Hope Traver, "'King Lear' and 'Isaiah,'" *Shakespeare Association Bulletin* 9 (October 1934): 181–85.

59. Erasmus, *The Praise of Folly and Other Writings*, ed. and trans. Robert M. Adams, 137.

60. I adopt Roman type for quotations from the Geneva commentary, originally in italics.

61. See Marx, *Shakespeare and the Bible*, 61.

make moral sense of God's actions ("as they will not learn thereby to obey his will, and be saved"), but the logic behind the land's "great desolation" (6:12) is not self-evident.

This moral miasma persists as a challenge for critics of *King Lear* who read the play as an indictment of God's justice. Because prophetic justice resists appropriation, it belies their common premise: "If God is indeed good and just, and if indeed he governs all things, then everything happens for a reason."[62] To follow Hannibal Hamlin, who defines the "Christian believer" in such terms, we would expect God to be a reasonable fellow. But the God of the prophets is not necessarily going to be reasonable. A rough analogy would be the father with legitimate concerns about his child's bad behavior, but whose punishment is not proportional to the offense. The prophets are seers who warn against abandoning the poor. They decry injustice and champion the divine law. They inveigh against false gods. But that the God who sent them should know ahead of time that they will not be heeded, that he should proceed to punish his people even in light of his divine foreknowledge, preserving a saving remnant only after allowing slaughter and deprivation on a massive scale, is a mystery that reason cannot fathom. The theological inferences to be drawn were, as we shall see over the following pages, immense.

Isaiah's visionary mode is subsequently adopted by Jeremiah and Ezekiel. Jeremiah preaches to a "foolish and senseless people, who have eyes, but do not see" (Jeremiah 5:21). He goes to the potter's house where the Lord declares, "O house of Israel, cannot I do with you as this potter?" (18:6; see also Isaiah 45:9 and Romans 9:20–21). It is not a comparison intended to reassure Israel about God's ways. It is not a comparison that inspires confidence in theodicy. Luther comments acidly on those, like Erasmus, who dislike being compared to clay pots in the hands of a divine potter: "This is what Reason can neither grasp nor endure."[63] Jeremiah advises King Zedekiah of Judah, who stubbornly ignores him. Subsequently, the "King of Babel slew the sons of Zedekiah, before his eyes. . . . Then he put out the eyes of Zedekiah & the King of Babel bound him in chains" (52:10–11). Ezekiel, after repeating the words of Isaiah about having eyes in vain (Ezekiel 12:2), could apply them literally to the blinding of King Zedekiah (12:12–13), that is, if we follow the Geneva margin. God's decision to give his people "statutes that

---

62. Hamlin, *Bible in Shakespeare*, 305.
63. Martin Luther, *On the Bondage of the Will*, in *Luther and Erasmus: Free Will and Salvation*, ed. E. Gordon Rupp and Philip S. Watson, 258.

were not good" (Ezekiel 20:25) provokes a torrent of paratextual explication; but it combines with the degrading pornography of Ezekiel's twenty-third chapter, the famous allegory of the two sisters, to leave the Geneva explainers hard-pressed: the anti-liturgical "cup of destruction" (23:33) overflows beyond measure. It is this enigmatic history of prophetic vision condemning willful blindness that Jesus alludes to in all four Gospels by way of Isaiah 6:9–10. It is this disturbing prophetic knowledge, cultivated by Luther and Calvin alike,[64] that defines the stakes for seeing and not seeing in *King Lear*.

The challenge to understand Lear in the storm, at high volume, forms one of the finest provocations of Shakespeare's prophetic writing. Out on the heath, the old King would outroar the wind, rain, and thunder, which are not on his side, not, at least, as they are for King Leir. When Shakespeare's Lear addresses the heavens, it is not clear that anyone is listening but the Fool:

> Blow, winds, and crack your cheeks! Rage, blow!
> You cataracts and hurricanoes, spout
> Till you have drenched our steeples, drowned the cocks!
> (3.2.1–3)

The eschatological impact of these lines derives from the New Testament, where Christ refers to Noah's flood as a prefiguration of the Apocalypse (Matthew 24:37–39 and Luke 17:26–27). The author of the Second Letter of Peter develops this motif. That the allusion is distinctly Christian is confirmed by Lear's referring to "our steeples" and "cocks." Ever since Pope Nicholas I pronounced his universal decree in the ninth century, wood and metal roosters have perched on church domes and steeples as a symbol of Peter's denial of Christ. This denial must have been on Shakespeare's mind when he connected "cocks" to the Flood. Figuratively, Peter's denial is the antitype of denials, from antediluvian times onward. Before the Flood, the "wickedness of man was great in the earth, and all the imaginations of his thoughts *were* only evil continually" (Genesis 6:5, italics in original). God comes to "repent" his creation of man (Genesis 6:7). The Flood happens as foretold to the righteous Noah: the "rain was upon the earth forty days and forty nights" (Genesis 7:12), so that "every man" (Genesis 7:21) perished due to his evil. In Shakespeare's storm, in which Lear denounces "ingrateful man" (3.2.9), the Flood's permanent apocalyptic significance is palpable. It activates the framework of

---

64. For example, Luther, *On the Bondage*, 166; John Calvin, *The Institution of the Christian Religion*, 3.24.13.

perception that I have called Christian *ulteriority*, referring, in a primary sense, to the intersection of sacred history and British history. We are reminded that the 1608 quarto is titled a *True Chronicle History*, and that the word *chronicle* has strong biblical overtones. For Christians across confessional lines, Isaiah and Jeremiah had railed against the perversion of the temple, and Ezekiel had seen its visionary restoration. Ulteriority in Lear's speech leaps into the present moment, because Shakespeare's allusion to the Flood impugns not only the evils besetting Lear, but "our steeples" as well. Their awkward presence signals disturbing possibilities. Was the Church of England incapable of repentance? Had the Church of Rome denied Christ?

Lear ascends to high prophetic mode by condemning society and threatening retribution: "Let the great gods, / That keep this dreadful pother o'er our heads, / Find out their enemies now. Tremble, thou wretch, That has within thee undivulgèd crimes / Unwhipped of justice!" (3.2.49–51). Eye contact, anyone? The "wretch" in question is undoubtedly present before the great Richard Burbage—the actor playing Lear to Robert Armin's Fool[65]—whether standing among the groundlings in the yard or seated in the topmost tier of the galleries on a cushioned bench. It is not enough for Lear to insinuate his godlike knowledge of "undivulgèd crimes." He broods over severe punishment, and the whip-cracking, proto-Miltonic enjambment after "crimes" snaps the syntax home. A theater being a house or playhouse, "this hard house" (3.2.63) may be said to play host, if we follow Lear's eyes, to godless scofflaws who conceal their depravity, to a nation that might conceivably be damned:

> Hide thee, thou bloody hand,
> Thou perjured, and thou simular of virtue
> That art incestuous! Caitiff, to pieces shake,
> That under covert and convenient seeming
> Has practiced on man's life! Close pent-up guilts,
> Rive your concealing continents and cry
> These dreadful summoners grace! I am a man
> More sinned against than sinning.
>
> (53–60)

In a harsh metonymy, Lear commands our "guilts" to tear through the appearance of moral propriety and to plead for "grace." As Bevington notes, "*Summoners* are the officers who cited offenders to appear before ecclesiastical courts" (his

---

65. Bart Van Es, *Shakespeare in Company*, 185.

italics). But the sense is metaphorical: it strengthens an apocalyptic perspective. Lear's role as prophet emerges through his accomplishing of three goals: (1) he lays down a terrifying indictment; (2) he threatens an apocalypse on account of derelictions; and (3) he preaches conversion of the heart. In this tradition, one preaches to the people so that they can avoid disaster before it's too late or, ultimately, since it is too late, to foretell and to cultivate a saving remnant.

Lear's Jeremiad is matched, at the end of Act 3, Scene 2, by the Fool's prophecy, which is based on anonymous verses that were mistakenly attributed to Chaucer. Wittreich has noticed that these verses have a biblical ring. He writes, "the Fool's prophecy derives particularities and form" from Isaiah 24:

> The Lord maketh the earth empty . . . he turneth it upside down . . .
> And there shall be like people, like Priest, and like servant, like master, like maid, like mistress, like buyer, like seller, like lender, like borrower, like giver, like taker to usury.[66]

Isaiah 24 conveys the idea of a breakdown in social order, an indiscriminate leveling—what the Geneva margin calls a "horrible confusion." Did Shakespeare sense the Isaian subtext? We can compare the Fool's prophecy:

> When priests are more in word than matter;
> When brewers mar their malt with water;
> When nobles are their tailors' tutors,
> No heretics burned but wenches' suitors,
> Then shall the realm of Albion
> Come to great confusion.
>
> When every case in law is right,
> No squire in debt, nor no poor knight;
> When slanders do not live in tongues,
> Nor cutpurses come not to throngs;
> When usurers tell their gold i'th'field,
> And bawds and whores do churches build,
> Then comes the time, who lives to see't,
> That going shall be used with feet.
>
> (3.2.81–94)

While maintaining that Shakespeare stands behind these F-only lines, Gary Taylor observes that the "Fool's prophecy . . . reinforces Lear's denunciation"

---

66. Wittreich, *"Image,"* 70, quoting Isaiah 24:1–2. I have modernized the spelling.

of guilty hypocrites—a series of furious rebukes that "can, of course, be directed (overtly or ambiguously) to the audience itself."[67] I agree with Taylor; but whether or not we detect an Isaian subtext for the Fool's prophecy, we are still left to ponder, what exactly do we make of the Fool's gift for anticlimax? As regards the Fool's opening scenario, its topicality is plain enough. John Kerrigan remarks, the "first four lines of this second-hand rhyme tell us what is happening *now*, in the 1600s. . . . It takes no great wit to conclude from such abuses that the 'Realme of *Albion*' has come to great confusion." And what of the utopian impossibilities that follow? For Kerrigan, "the Fool's prophecy is a studiously careful exercise in the avoidance of prophecy." In other words, the ending's anticlimax, which is apparently unique to Shakespeare, undoes the vatic pretension of any attempt at predicting the future, as, for instance that egregious wizard "Merlin" (3.2.95) had done, prophesying the advent of Elizabeth I in *The Faerie Queene* (3.3.49.6). Though he overlooks the irony that "see't" takes from its context in the play, Kerrigan has a valid point that "in *King Lear* irony flows from the disappointment of reasonable hopes"; in his view, it follows that the Fool wisely refrains from commenting on the future.[68] But still, we may reply that, first, irony flows from other sources in the play than from reasonable hopes being dashed; and second, the Fool's prophetically denouncing the present amounts to something greater than "a studiously careful exercise in the avoidance of prophecy." Too much is being risked. Let us immediately discard René Weis's verdict of "intellectual despair," that "the Fool is saying that both the world as it is and the world as ideally it should be are equally confusing and meaningless."[69] The fact that Shakespeare's satirizing England under King James entailed risks is only one reason why the Fool's prophecy is not meaningless. I would emphasize that the futility of prophesying and its personal cost to the prophet are features that connect the Fool to Isaiah, Jeremiah, and Ezekiel. The Fool's utopian horizons, like those of the major prophets, are premised on the "great confusion" of national catastrophe.[70] In other words, the prophetic context counts. If Taylor is correct in his hypothesis that Shakespeare added the Fool's

67. Gary Taylor, "*King Lear*: The Date and Authorship of the Folio Version," in *The Division of the Kingdoms: Shakespeare's Two Versions of King Lear*, ed. Gary Taylor and Michael Warren, 384.

68. John Kerrigan, "Revision, Adaptation, and the Fool in *King Lear*," in *The Division of the Kingdoms: Shakespeare's Two Versions of King Lear*, ed. Gary Taylor and Michael Warren, 225, his italics; 224.

69. Shakespeare, *King Lear: A Parallel Text Edition*, ed. Weis, 204n.

70. For the Fool's satirical utopianism in relation to the Christian humanism of Erasmus and More, see Maillet, *Learning to See*, 59–62.

prophecy during revisions circa 1609–1611, then, strangely enough, we can see the Fool's lines as reflecting the failed prophetic warnings of the 1608 quarto—a failure that Shakespeare had, if you will, already prophesied. The problematics of seeing return: "Then comes the time, who lives to see't." The corrupt "authority" that Lear denounces in his madness—"change places and handy-dandy, which is the justice, which is the thief?" (4.6.153) —does not repent. "A man may see how this world goes with no eyes": "Robes and furred gowns hide all" (150–51, 165). As it was in Chaucer's time, so it was in Jeremiah's, so it is today: the blind, unsurprisingly, remain blind.

We can follow Shakespeare among the prophets by considering their devotion to the poor. An important Jacobean perspective, as Judy Kronenfeld has observed, is that "*King Lear* relates to the outpouring of homiletic literature that came at a time when there was an increase in poverty and/or concern about the poor, and an increase in governmental response to poverty."[71] Lear voices such concern in a moment of poignant self-accounting that transcends both his and his audience's sense of time and place. As the storm rages on, he lingers outside to "pray" (3.4.27), and only Kent stays with him. The King is no longer locked in himself, nor yet are his wits "gone" (3.6.87):

> Poor naked wretches, whereso'er you are,
> That bide the pelting of this pitiless storm,
> How shall your houseless heads and unfed sides,
> Your looped and windowed raggedness, defend you
> From such seasons as these? Oh, I have ta'en
> Too little care of this! Take physic, pomp;
> Expose thyself to feel what wretches feel,
> That thou mayst shake the superflux to them
> And show the heavens more just.
>
> (3.4.28–36)

Lear's seeming apostrophe, "Take physic, pomp," has power to disturb an audience of churchgoers. The rich in their habitual injustice, the prophets give warning, call down heaven's vengeance. The Lord asks through Isaiah, "Is this not the fasting that I have chosen? . . . Is it not to deal thy bread to the hungry, & that thou bring the poor that wander, unto thy house? When thou seest the naked, that thou cover him, and hide not thine self from thine own flesh?" (Isaiah 58:6–7). Among two or three thousand spectators at the

---

71. Kronenfeld, *King Lear and the Naked Truth,* 173.

Globe, or delivered at Whitehall before King James and crew, Lear's sermon (with its biblical "thou") was bound to pierce a few hard hearts. To come back to "pomp": James's court masques were "beyond extravagant, costing an unbelievable sum of three thousand pounds or more for a single perform-ance."[72] Shakespeare never wrote one. As for disparity of wealth, the con-temporary enclosure of common pastures (by no means a new development in English history) enriched greedy landlords but injured the landless, the tenant farmers, shepherds, and mill workers of "Poor pelting villages" (2.3.18). The economic conditions that led to the enclosure riots of 1607 were no doubt causing grief.[73] Poor Tom is waiting in the wings when we hear, rather piercingly, "Expose thyself to feel what wretches feel, / That thou mayst shake the superflux to them / And show the heavens more just." The disguised Edgar, who is disguised through his lack of clothes, incarnates the poor and marginalized.

But where Lear's previous speech had ended with a swerve of self-evasion ("I am a man / More sinned against than sinning"), as if he would direct the "dreadful summoners" elsewhere because he himself was comparatively less in need of "grace," in the present speech he effects a more dangerous swerve. If the wealthy through their hypothetical charity could show "the heavens more just," we must infer that Lear is indicting the heavens. The "storm" is "pitiless" and "such seasons as these" attack the most vulnerable. Recognizing the question of this cosmic scandal, we are likely to connect Lear's words to Job's interrogation of God's justice: "The earth is given into the hand of the wicked: he covereth the faces of the judges thereof: if not, where is he? Or who is he?" 9:24). Or to Jeremiah's demanding question: "O Lord, if I dispute with thee, thou art righteous: yet let me talk with thee of thy judgments: wherefore does the way of the wicked prosper?" (Jeremiah 12:1). The Geneva scholiasts redouble their efforts at such moments. For instance, the gloss to Jeremiah 12:1 reads: "This question has always been a great temptation to the godly, to see the wicked enemies of God in prosperity, as Job 21:7, Psalms 37:1, 73:1, Habakkuk 1:3."[74] If even the "godly" experience the reflex to make God bear some of the blame for worldly injustice, if even for true saints it is a "great temptation," can we admit that we are tempted too? And if so, whose side are we on? Where does our allegiance lie?

---

72. Shapiro, *Year of Lear*, 2.

73. See *Sources and Debates in English History 1485–1714*, ed. Newton Key and Robert Bucholz, 116–17.

74. Abbreviations in original.

As we accompany the old King into exile,[75] poverty and nakedness stare at us. Have we fed the poor? Have we clothed their nakedness? Have we broken the Ten Commandments with our abominations? Let me emphasize that I am not so much reading *Lear* as an allegory of the Old Testament prophets (Lear does not stand for Isaiah or Jeremiah) as I am arguing that the play partakes of their prophetic ethos, which Shakespeare's audience would have recognized, though generally we do not—which may explain the success of Stephen Greenblatt's surprising insight that the play is about the "fear of retirement and dread of dependence upon children."[76] In any case, Edgar as Poor Tom speaks with unassailable authority to those with ears to hear him: "Obey thy parents; keep thy word's justice; swear not; commit not with man's sworn spouse; set not thy sweet heart on proud array" (3.4.79–82). Jeremiah might have put it this way: "Will you steal, murder, and commit adultery and swear falsely and burn incense unto Baal, & walk after other gods whom ye know not?" (Jeremiah 7:9). Baal, I must concede, fails to make an appearance in the play, though Edmund's "Nature" bears a family resemblance (1.2.1). In his Arden edition of *King Lear*, R. A. Foakes hears Edgar's lines as "parodying several of the Ten Commandments in the Bible (Exodus 20: 3–17), to honor one's parents, not to bear false witness (in other words, maintain the righteousness or justice of your words in accordance with divine law), not to take the Lord's name in vain (or swear; see also Matthew 5:34), not to commit adultery, and to avoid covetousness."[77] The idea of Edgar's "parodying" the Ten Commandments ought not to deflect Shakespeare's high moral seriousness. It may be that, without divine grace, all humanity can do is to parrot and parody the Ten Commandments. Given the intricacies of Shakespeare's mind, we might accept Foakes's suggestion in terms of a *serious parody*. But, in any case, it would be a mistake to laugh off Poor Tom's penetrating babble. To employ an earlier point: since Shakespeare's biblical allusions in the play are his own, independent of his source material, we have reason to notice the sharp injection of such language when it occurs. In this respect, Poor Tom's preaching the Ten Commandments does the same kind of work as Lear's moral eruption in the storm and the Fool's prophecy. Violating the play's setting in place (though not in time), it stands out as a marker of Shakespeare's moral intention.

75. I note that Shaheen, in *Biblical References*, 78, connects Lear's fantastic comments about Poor Tom's "Persian" garments (3.6.79) to the Book of Daniel.

76. Greenblatt, *Will in the World*, 361.

77. William Shakespeare, *King Lear*, ed. R. A. Foakes, 277n.

Shakespeare's Christian mimesis, as discussed in the Introduction, accommodates the Christian reality of Edgar's prophetic calling. Edgar as Tom is not in disguise in the realist sense of Sam Spade and Philip Marlowe. Rather, Edgar descends *through* Tom into the lower echelons of the cosmic order. He journeys spiritually. Despite their textual source in Samuel Harsnett's *Declaration of Egregious Popish Impostures* (1603), his devils are not the hoaxes of sham exorcists. They refer to supernatural agents that link past Britain to present Britain, "where the same devils continue their destructive ways."[78] The fall of "Lucifer" in Isaiah 14:12 supports this continuity. Further, though we are in pre-Christian Britain, Tom, like the Suffering Servant of Isaiah 53, is a type of Christ. Let me rephrase that a little more gently. In this fallen world, he is *like* a type of Christ. The line we cannot cross is aestheticizing the text to the point where we lose Shakespeare's moral intention. So while I do not want to "Christianize" the play beyond what it is, we cannot, in all honesty and candor, simply ignore that Shakespeare weaves a Christian thread into the fabric of *King Lear* that is foreign to his sources and conspicuously out of place in ancient Britain. Why not write a tragicomical romance, a more sophisticated, up-to-date version of *The True Chronicle History of King Leir*? *Pericles* was just around the corner, the play where no less an eminence than E. K. Chambers detected a Catholic conversion.[79] All the salient Christian details of Edgar's soliloquy in Act 2, Scene 3—the "tree" (2), the blanketed "loins" (10), the "Bedlam"/Bethlehem connection (14), the "nails" (16), the kenosis of Lear's *godson*, for crying out loud— these contribute to our sense of Poor Tom as a prophetic type or prefiguration of the Christ whom the sinful Britons have denied. I think that is what we need to keep in mind. Shakespeare is not "someone constantly ready to appropriate religious matter wherever it enhances his artistic vision, but who invariably subordinates it to the requirements of the individual artefact."[80] Shakespeare is someone who promiscuously adapts Christian material to a Christian universe. To restate a preliminary point: he criticizes and challenges Christians, but he uses Christian means to do so.[81]

---

78. An exceptionally fine point by Shapiro. See his *Year of Lear*, 82. For Shakespeare and Harsnett, see F. W. Brownlow, *Shakespeare, Harsnett, and the Devils of Denham*, 107–31.

79. E. K. Chambers, *William Shakespeare*, 1:86.

80. Alison Shell, *Shakespeare and Religion*, 231 (also quoted in Introduction).

81. Two minor points: Poor Tom's warning against "proud array" may well allude to a number of remarks by the apostle Paul, but none of these is as elaborate as what we find on the subject in Isaiah 3:16–24. And, more curiously, Poor Tom "eats cow dung for salads" (3.4.130–31), while Ezekiel bakes his bread on "cow's dung" (4:15). Here I quote the Great Bible, still in use in some English churches at the time. See Hamlin, *Bible in Shakespeare*, 15.

It may be argued that the Jeremiad model breaks down for two reasons. First, insofar as Jeremiah and his fellow prophets are concerned with the fate of a nation whose origins and whose past were common knowledge, the analogy wavers for *King Lear*, because, if we think of "Great Britain" as a nation, we have to contend with significant dissent. The Gunpowder plotters were opposed to the political union of England and Scotland, while King James was quick to invoke the failed apocalypse on behalf of his cause.[82] This ambiguity of national definition lends itself to Shakespeare's art, because the playwright is more intent on testing self-knowledge than on rallying his audience to Christian nationalism. Shakespeare's Jeremiad is not the forging of a nation's identity: it is the suspension of a nation's identity. Like the Gunpowder Plot, King Lear's history—which Shakespeare rewrote for maximum moral shock effect—puts pressure on the conscience of every subject that confronts it. Providence makes its violent determinations in reality and on the stage, but in neither instance is the purpose of God's plan transparent. Anything but.

As regards the first argument against the Jeremiad model, I have admitted its validity while, in fact, submitting it as evidence in my case. A second possible objection, already touched on, is that *King Lear* defies the Geneva margin's logic of sin and punishment: the death of Cordelia is particularly incomprehensible. It jars with the existence of a benevolent and omnipotent deity. *King Lear* therefore frustrates the norms of Christian theodicy. I reply that the devastation of Jerusalem and its inhabitants, extending to collateral damage beyond reckoning, is likewise incomprehensible. We have seen Luther's response to Erasmus regarding the clay-pot metaphor that Jeremiah takes up from Isaiah. For Luther, God's will is "hidden": "God hidden in his majesty neither deplores nor takes away death, but works life, death, and all in all. For there he has not bound himself by his word, but has kept himself free over all things."[83] Luther's *Deus absconditus* withdraws beyond our categories of thought: "Cause and reason can be assigned for a creature's will, but not for the will of the Creator, unless you set up over him another creator."[84] The basic premise was well known in England. John Colet, the friend of Erasmus and More, was a "significant English link in asserting the 'unknown God' concept."[85] Negative theology, "as in Dionysus the Pseudo-Areopagite and as

82. Shapiro, *Year of Lear*, 94, 101.

83. Luther, *On the Bondage*, 201.

84. Luther, *On the Bondage*, 237.

85. Elton, King Lear *and the Gods*, 30n56. Other sources named in the same note: "Augustine, John Scotus Erigena, Anselm, Bonaventure, and Eckhart."

developed by the cabalists, helped spread the *Deus absconditus* idea in the Renaissance."[86] In fact, the *Deus absconditus* idea had obvious medieval roots. Aquinas is expert in negative or apophatic theology.[87] The sixty-fourth chapter of Book 3 of *The Imitation of Christ*, the final chapter of most English editions, is titled: "That high matters, and secret judgments of God should not be searched after." A representative passage: "I say reason not why this man is so rejected, or that man in such favor; why this man is so miserably afflicted, that man so highly advanced. . . . These things are beyond the reach of man; neither is any reason, or disputation meet enough to search out the counsel of the Almighty."[88] Calvin addressed the idea primarily through the Book of Job.[89] He did not agree with Luther on the question of the Eucharist; he was the more theocratic thinker; but in this respect the two major Reformers found much to agree about: "Like Luther, Calvin posits a hidden God outside of nature, history, and Christ."[90] On this second count, then, the Jeremiad model breaks down only if, like the Geneva scholiasts for Isaiah 6, we justify the God of the prophets in human terms.[91] But we may prefer to read Jeremiah as closer in its divine incomprehensibility to *Lear*.

Having come this far, I want to advance my position that a theology for which God's wrath defies human comprehension is essential to *King Lear*. Elton, while he was well aware of Luther's idea of a *Deus absconditus*—including its sources and diverse channels of influence—makes it serve his case for "the skeptical disintegration of providential belief." For Elton, "the devastating fifth act shatters, more violently than an earlier apostasy might have done, the foundations of faith itself."[92] I reply that the *Deus absconditus*, being no friend to human understanding, would be no friend to what Elton, with a firmness reminiscent of Bertrand Russell, calls "the foundations of faith itself." "Cause and reason" (Luther's terms, quoted above) are powerless to

---

86. Elton, King Lear *and the Gods*, 30n56.

87. See Gregory P. Rocca, *Speaking the Incomprehensible God: Thomas Aquinas and the Interplay of Positive and Negative Theology*.

88. Thomas à Kempis, *Of the imitation of Christ*, 268. I have modernized the spelling.

89. Hamlin argues for Calvin's *Sermons on Job* impacting Shakespeare by way of Arthur Golding's translation (Hamlin, *Bible in Shakespeare*, 312–14, 318–19). Ivor Morris had previously discerned "very close correspondences," but did not conclude that "Shakespeare was familiar with Calvin's exposition" (by way of Golding). Ivor Morris, *Shakespeare's God*, 28–30.

90. Susan E. Schreiner, "Exegesis and Double Justice in Calvin's Sermons on Job," *Church History* 58 (September 1989): 336.

91. At other times, the scholiasts take the opposite tack, underscoring the limits of "our apprehension" (gloss on Job 9:23).

92. Elton, King Lear *and the Gods*, 335, 337.

make sense of faith's "foundations." More recently, Hamlin has referred to "the notion of 'the hiddenness of God'" as "a kind of theological escape hatch," a characterization that likewise diminishes the theological clout and psychological interest of the notion under review. In a subjoined note, Hamlin admits a scruple: "This may seem a somewhat dismissive description of negative or apophatic theology, which attempts to describe God in terms of what cannot be said of him." With all due respect, it makes no difference, historically, that, to Hamlin and, I would assume, to most scholars of the period, "the idea of a hidden God does seem a rather convenient and suspiciously irrefutable solution."[93]

Critic Paul R. Sellin in his extraordinary essay of 1974, "The Hidden God," connects Luther and Calvin to the fostering of an "irrational mentality" that had a much wider impact than scholars such as Elton and Hamlin would allow.[94] In reviewing the religious mentality in question, Sellin concludes that it "in one form or another captured the mind of northern Europe during the sixteenth and seventeenth centuries." He finds evidence of this widespread theological mindset in Marlowe's *Doctor Faustus*:

> Faustus stirs the tragic emotions because he has been given a winning dimension on the human level. . . . [W]hat Marlowe seems to have assumed was an audience prepared to yield to the notion of an undecipherable Providence whose processes are hidden both to the onlooker and to the protagonist on whom they work. He also expected it to accept a heaven that refuses to conform to human standards of punishment or reward, on the one hand, and yet not to react, on the other hand, with feelings of shock and outrage so strong as to obliterate the requisite emotions or to elevate the defiance of Providence into a kind of alternate salvation for the tragic hero. . . . Accordingly the poet sought to present a spectacle of an excellent man placed in a situation where the obligatory exercise of virtue brought with it permanent destruction of life and happiness, for he was certain that to such an object his audience would respond with and take delight in the feelings evoked by regrettable loss.

If Sellin's characterization of Faustus as "an excellent man" is open to challenge, it cannot be doubted that Faustus possesses "winning" qualities—a great mind, a love of knowledge and beauty, a capacity for friendship, a desire to

93. Hamlin, *Bible in Shakespeare*, 327, 327n64.
94. Paul R. Sellin, "The Hidden God," in *The Darker Vision of the Renaissance: Beyond the Fields of Reason*, ed. Robert S. Kinsman, 147–96. For Catholic background, see 175; see also Fortin, "Hermeneutical Circularity," 119, which also supplies a relevant quotation from Hooker.

repent. And yet, his *eternal* damnation is God's will. Sellin's verdict on *Lear* follows: "Perhaps the most heartrending appeal to the irrational mentality that I have described is the death of Cordelia in *Lear*. . . . [It] is clearly designed to affect minds both sensitive to a notion of destiny operating on principles seemingly hostile to human standards of the right and just and predisposed to sorrow at spectacles of undeserved suffering at its hands."[95] As in our reading of *Lear*, heaven "refuses to conform to human standards." And what may be most crushing to our humanist pride is that our knowledge of history itself, of King Lear and King James, of Machiavellian progeny and the Gunpowder Plot, of unholy slaughter between nations and between faiths, is entirely dependent upon God's "indecipherable" will. If we try to deduce God's purpose with our powers of natural reason, we are forced to recognize our true condition as fools. Cordelia's forgiveness of her father in Act 4, Scene 7 is foolish in this respect: not rational, not reducible to cause and effect, a love we cannot merit or possess. At the end of *King Lear*, this restorative love is physically lost. I agree that its "transcendent goodness" is not negated,[96] and yet, the "gored state" (5.3.326), like Israel in the Old Testament, must face a wrathful God and his Judgment. Lear's self-knowledge is no help to him. Nor is our own. Like the prophet of Lamentations, we are destined to suffer and to weep.

As a literary historian, Sellin is theologically sensitive. Buttressed by references to Christian experience in Spenser, Jonson, and Donne, as well as to later writers Herbert, Marvell, Milton, and Vaughan, he develops his connection between Reformation theology and the emergence of high tragedy on the Shakespearean stage, from the prentice work of *Romeo and Juliet* to the heights of *Hamlet* and *Lear*:

> Perhaps Renaissance irrationality as I have described it stimulated a number of changes in attitudes toward human life, values, happiness, Providence, and the hereafter. These attitudes, in turn, were peculiarly conducive to those feelings for the plight of others which we consider tragic. As the public changed, of course, so did the assumptions on which artists built their works. A new range of emotions lay readily open for exploration, and once dramatists learned to appeal to these emotions they were led to mold the kinds of objects—that is, deeds, characters, and feelings—which one finds in the best tragedies of the age.[97]

95. Sellin, "Hidden God," 188, 172, 184, 185–86 (I have inserted a comma into the text), 188.
96. John Cox, *Seeing Knowledge: Shakespeare and Skeptical Faith*, 85.
97. Sellin, "Hidden God," 176.

Despite this powerful linkage of English literature and the history of Christianity, we may continue to insist, nonetheless, that Shakespeare wrote *King Lear* to extend and to intensify the currents of atheism in his lifetime. Such was the burden of Elton's admirable scholarship. But still, it is hard to imagine Shakespeare explaining his work in such terms to the King's Men. The tortured rationalizations that Elton supplied to accommodate his reading of *Lear* to its original audience are a case in point.[98] Kastan's argument is not overly elaborate or tortured in this way, but his conclusion is strained: "tragic suffering neither instructs nor improves; at best it numbs."[99] Are we really to assume that *Lear*'s immense range of thought and feeling, through all its soaring heights and plunging depths, among the finest pulsations of thought ever conceived in art, was intended in the end to "numb" its audience? Where the redemptionists could at least claim to satisfy a Jacobean playgoer, the anti-redemptionists play cat and mouse with him before knocking the poor fellow unconscious. Elton was quick to dismiss G. Wilson Knight, but Knight's once-famous essay "*King Lear* and the Comedy of the Grotesque" can at least do justice to Shakespeare's audience: the "very heart of the play [is] the thing that man dares scarcely face: the demonic grin of the incongruous and absurd in the most pitiful of human struggles with an iron fate."[100] Sellin's argument and Knight's, I maintain, are complementary. Knight's "iron fate" and Sellin's cosmic irrationality are alike rich in pathos and conducive to weird humor. Sellin suggests that a "new range of emotions lay readily open for exploration." Knight observes how, after a sublime build-up "to tune our minds to a noble, tragic sacrifice," a new kind of grotesque comedy intervenes: Gloucester "falls from his kneeling posture a few inches, flat, face foremost."[101] Likewise, the powder in the basement does not explode. A hidden God, indeed.

If we look for support for Sellin's thesis, we may discover it in the innovative work of Blair Hoxby. Hoxby shifts our common understanding of tragedy away from the German idealist tradition, which "places a premium on action and collision, not suffering," and toward the "poetics that emerged around 1550 with the first major commentaries on Aristotle's *Poetics*." "The most important conviction that emerges from the early modern poetics of tragedy," Hoxby writes, "is that *pathos* is the one indispensable element of tragedy." Further, the "importance of scenes of passive suffering to early

---

98. Elton, King Lear *and the Gods,* 338.
99. Kastan, "Shakespeare and the Idea," 13.
100. G. Wilson Knight, *The Wheel of Fire: Interpretations of Shakespearian Tragedy,* 198.
101. Knight, *The Wheel of Fire,* 194.

modern tragedy's effects is underlined by the challenges that they pose to critics such as Bradley who endeavor to read Shakespeare's tragedies through the lens of Hegel." As regards *King Lear*, Hoxby shows that Bradley's allegiance to Hegel puts him at odds with the play, "whose 'principal characters . . . are not those who act, but those who suffer.'" Our interest here is that, if we follow Hoxby's recovery of an eclipsed poetics, we find its emphasis on "passive suffering" and "*pathos* as the essence of tragedy"[102] to be consistent with Sellin's reconstruction of an audience that "would respond with and take delight in the feelings evoked by regrettable loss." In both cases, the emphasis shifts to what Sellin identifies as a predisposition "to sorrow at spectacles of undeserved suffering." In both cases, a narrow focus on redemptive action would miss the point.

Hoxby does not pursue the possible connection between Reformation theology and the "importance of scenes of passive suffering" in Shakespearean tragedy. But as Russ Leo has shown in considerable detail, the religious understanding of tragedy was well advanced when Shakespeare wrote *King Lear*. Of particular interest for us is Erasmus's reception of Euripides in the *Adages*; for instance, the final words of the *Hecuba*, in Erasmus's Latin: *Nam sic urget nescia flecti et / Cogit dira necessitas.*[103] These lines, spoken by the Chorus, bring a dark play to its fatalistic end: "For thus necessity, cruel and unable to be turned, drives and compels [us]."[104] The young Thomas Lodge extended these Erasmian concerns. Writing in critical reaction against Stephen Gosson's *Schoole of Abuse* (1579), Lodge, in his *Defence of Poetry* (1579, the pamphlet is variously titled), applies an allegorical sensibility: "What made Erasmus labor in Euripides's tragedies? Did he endeavor by painting them out of Greek into Latin to manifest sin unto us? Or to confirm us in goodness?"[105] Citing this passage from Lodge, Emrys Jones suggests that Erasmus's "*Hecuba* and his *Iphigenia* would have stood a strong chance of being widely read for

---

102. Blair Hoxby, *What Was Tragedy?: Theory and the Early Modern Canon*, 5, 6 (the author identifies the German idealists as "Friedrich Schiller, Friedrich Schelling, the Schlegel brothers, and Georg Wilhelm Friedrich Hegel"), 8, 10 (quoting Bradley's *Shakespearean Tragedy*), 10.

103. Russ Leo, *Tragedy as Philosophy in the Reformation World*, 20.

104. Translation by Aaron Seider.

105. Thomas Lodge, "Defence of Poetry, Music, and Stage Plays," in *Elizabethan Critical Essays*, ed. G. Gregory Smith, 1:68 (I have modernized the spelling). The longest lived of the "University Wits," Lodge is best known for his prose romance *Rosalynde*, which Shakespeare looted for *As You Like It*. It is arguable that his 1591 prose romance *The Famous True and Historicall Life of Robert Second Duke of Normandy* impacted the writing of *King Lear*; see Donna B. Hamilton, "Some Romance Sources for *King Lear*: Robert of Sicily and Robert the Devil," *Studies in Philology* 71 (April 1974): 173–91. His conversion to Rome is another interesting fact about him.

educational purposes (particularly perhaps in the middle decades of the six-teenth century, when his influence was especially strong").[106] In other words, Shakespeare may have known these plays.

Likewise following Erasmus, Melanchthon "imported poetics into theo-logical study . . . and recruited tragedy in particular to theological ends." In his 1545 work *Cohortatio ad Legendas Tragoedias et Comoedias* (*An Exhortation To Read Comedies and Tragedies*), Melanchthon writes: "For people are not moved by considering lighter or more ordinary misfortunes, but by having a terrifying sight cast before their eyes, which might pierce their souls and hold fast all day, to move them by way of compassion, so that they reflect upon the causes of human calamities, and each one might comport themselves to these rep-resentations." Sound strangely familiar? To be sure, the labors of Melanchthon were meticulously pious and didactic. Nonetheless, as a Christian humanist he achieved an influential synthesis of tragic poetics and Lutheran theology, highlighting "the degree to which man is not free and the human will, inef-fective."[107] In Chapter 4, we touched on Luther's reference to "all of profane history" as a "puppet play of God's." Evidently, Luther approved the work of his Wittenberg student and colleague.[108] One can only wonder if he and Erasmus would have admired *King Lear*, which places its mimesis of God's wrath beyond the rational powers of "cause and reason," but within the uncanny depths of Christian sensibility.

106. Emrys Jones, *The Origins of Shakespeare*, 97.

107. Leo, *Tragedy as Philosophy*, 13, 26 (Leo's translation), 28. For Melanchthon's legacy and its "impact . . . on Sidney's fashioning of a new poetics for the English tradition," see Robert E. Stillman, *Philip Sidney and the Poetics of Renaissance Cosmopolitanism*. Stillman and Leo are at odds, however, on the key matter of what Stillman calls Melanchthon's "carefully delimited optimism about human agency" (viii and xi). Leo's Melanchthon is closer to Luther.

108. Leo, *Tragedy as Philosophy*, 21–22.

CONCLUSION

Shakespeare and the Radical Middle

What we want is . . . to point out that at any moment the relation of a modern Englishman to Shakespeare may be discovered to be that of a modern Greek to Aeschylus.

—T. S. Eliot, 1918

Having approached Christian humanism with a focus on literature that is uncommon in contemporary Shakespeare studies, I have invoked the idea of the radical middle to support my study of Shakespeare as a great literary figure. When I say that Christian humanism occupies the radical middle between extremes that are not friendly to literary culture, I am trying to maintain the grounds of a living tradition. This work of custodianship was once the essence of criticism. Of course, I would not want to suggest that mainstream academic scholarship on Shakespeare is uninterested in literary tradition as a good in its own right. Nor would I suggest that the self-referential quality of such scholarship is a correlative of exorbitant tuition fees and professional insularity. Few professors would think of themselves as bound by a guild mentality too locked inside itself to connect Renaissance Christian humanism to the present time. Others, insisting on precise definitions, would prefer to confine their subject-matter within parameters that they police with consummate care, while using politics or pop culture to affirm their enlightened contemporary relevance.

In Shakespeare's time, the radical middle flourished between the Master of Revels and the godly Puritans who hated the theater. The state was not secular, but it enforced censorship to protect its interests. As for the anti-theatrical tradition, it appears to have commanded Shakespeare's attention without crushing his nerve. Both the agents of the state and the anti-theatrical Puritans were capable of anti-humanistic violence. Their intellectual heirs are prospering on and off university grounds. Insofar as they have no permanent ideals to fail to live up to, they keep an easy conscience where their hypocrisies of pride and finger pointing are concerned. Dickens, the scourge of Humbugs, found himself in a strong position to do justice to their brand of humorless, intolerant cant.

I hold that the radical middle was and remains a site of cultural originality, as expressed through mimetic works of art intended for a catholic (small "c") audience. It describes the conceptual space where Shakespeare was free to engage theological questions, and where his Christian skepticism could serve his literary purposes. This skepticism toward authoritative systems of truth was never an end in itself. The radical middle as I conceive it has always furthered the end of addressing and realizing the complexity of truth on a human scale. Its greatest scandal is the suggestion, which is not an evangelical ploy, that our highest potential for the renewal of literature is implicit in the immeasurable range, variety, and depth of Christian thought and feeling. This potential is inseparable from an intelligent spirit of humanistic tolerance and ecumenical appreciation, a consciousness born of the trial of centuries. In this respect, the Christian capacity to nurture art represents an intellectual survival mechanism: a drive for health and fresh air; an opening for good language; an escape from sterile conformity.

Fanatics and tyrants may shut down the radical middle for a time. The field may lie fallow for generations. Strange flowers have rooted in its ancient soil. But it survives in great literature.

> So long as men can breathe or eyes can see,
> So long lives this, and this gives life to thee.

Bibliography

Altman, Joel B. *The Tudor Play of Mind: Rhetorical Inquiry and the Development of Elizabethan Drama.* Berkeley: University of California Press, 1978.

Anon. *The Edge of Doom: The History and Hidden Wall Paintings of The Guild Chapel.* Stratford-upon-Avon Town Trust: Stratford-upon-Avon, n.d.

Anon. *Rhetorica ad Herennium.* Translated by Harry Caplan. Cambridge: Harvard University Press, 1954.

Anon. *Thomas of Woodstock or King Richard the Second, Part One.* Edited by Peter Corbin and Douglas Sedge. Manchester: Manchester University Press, 2002.

Aquinas, Thomas. *Summa Theologica.* Translated by the Fathers of the Dominican Province. 5 vols. Notre Dame: Ave Maria Press, 1981.

Aristotle. *The Basic Works of Aristotle.* Edited by Richard McKeon. New York: Random House, 1941.

Auden, W. H. *The English Auden: Poems, Essays and Dramatic Writings 1927–1939.* Edited by Edward Mendelson. London: Faber, 1986.

Auerbach, Erich. *Mimesis: The Representation of Reality in Western Literature.* Translated by Willard R. Trask. Princeton: Princeton University Press, 1953.

Augustine. *The City of God.* Translated by Marcus Dods. New York: Modern Library, 1993.

———. *Confessions: Books 1–8.* Edited and translated by Carolyn J.-B. Hammond. Cambridge: Harvard University Press, 2014.

———. *On Christian Teaching.* Translated by R. P. H. Green. Oxford: Oxford University Press, 2008.

———. *Soliloquies: Augustine's Inner Dialogue.* Translated by Kim Paffenroth. Hyde Park: New City Press, 2000.

Babcock, Robert Weston. "Saints' Oaths in Shakespeare's Plays." *The Shakespeare Association Bulletin* 6 (July 1931): 86–100.

Baldwin, T. W. *William Shakspere's Petty School.* Urbana: University of Illinois Press, 1943.

———. *William Shakspere's Small Latine and Lesse Greek.* 2 vols. Urbana: University of Illinois Press, 1944.

Barber, C. L. *Shakespeare's Festive Comedy: A Study of Dramatic Form and Its Relation to Social Custom.* Cleveland: Meridian Books, 1963.

Bate, Walter Jackson, ed. *Criticism: The Major Texts.* Enlarged ed. San Diego: Harcourt, 1970.

Battenhouse, Roy. "Comment and Bibliography." In *Shakespeare's Christian Dimension: An Anthology of Commentary,* edited by Roy Battenhouse, 382–86. Bloomington: Indiana University Press, 1994.

———. *Shakespearean Tragedy: Its Art and Its Christian Premises*. Bloomington: University of Indiana Press, 1969.

———. "Shakespearean Tragedy: Its Christian Premises." *Connotations: A Journal for Critical Debate* 3 (September 1993): 226–42.

Baxter, John. *Shakespeare's Poetic Styles: Verse into Drama*. London: Routledge and Kegan Paul, 1980.

Bearman, Robert. "John Shakespeare's 'Spiritual Testament': A Reappraisal." *Shakespeare Survey* 56 (2003): 184–202.

Beauchamp, Gorman. "Shylock's Conversion." *Humanitas* 24 (2011): 55–92.

Beauregard, David. *Catholic Theology in Shakespeare's Plays*. Newark: University of Delaware Press, 2008.

Bell, Robert H. *Shakespeare's Great Stage of Fools*. New York: Palgrave, 2011.

Bernthal, Craig. *The Trial of Man: Christianity and Judgment in the World of Shakespeare*. Wilmington: ISI Books, 2003.

Bethurum, Dorothy. "Shakespeare's Comment on Medieval Romance in *A Midsummer Night's Dream*." *Modern Language Notes* 60 (1945): 85–94.

Bevington, David, ed. *The Complete Works of William Shakespeare*. 6th ed. New York: Pearson, 2009.

———, ed. *Henry the Fourth, Parts I and II*. New York: Garland, 1986.

———, ed. *Medieval Drama*. Boston: Houghton Mifflin, 1975.

Bloom, Allan with Harry V. Jaffa. *Shakespeare's Politics*. Chicago: University of Chicago Press, 1981.

Bloom, Harold. Introduction to *Geoffrey Chaucer*, edited by Harold Bloom, xi-xiii. Bloom's Classic Critical Views. New York: Infobase Publishing, 2008.

———. *Shakespeare and the Invention of the Human*. New York: Riverhead Books, 1998.

———. *The Western Canon: The Books and Schools of the Ages*. New York: Harcourt, 1994.

Bloom, Harold, ed. *Geoffrey Chaucer*. Bloom's Classic Critical Views. New York: Infobase Publishing, 2008.

Bond, Ronald B., ed. *Certain Sermons or Homilies (1547) AND A Homily against Disobedience and Wilful Rebellion (1570): A Critical Edition*. Toronto: University of Toronto Press, 1987.

Bonneville, Hugh. *Shakespeare Uncovered*. DVD. Season 2, Episode 1. *A Midsummer Night's Dream*. Directed by Richard Denton. New York: Thirteen Productions, 2015.

Bouyer, Louis. *Erasmus and His Times*. Translated by Francis X. Murphy. Westminster, MD: Newman Press, 1959.

Bradley, A. C. "The Rejection of Falstaff." In *Henry the Fourth, Parts I and II*, edited by David Bevington, 77–98. New York: Garland, 1986.

———. *Shakespearean Tragedy*. New York: Fawcett Premier, 1991.

Brague, Rémi. *Eccentric Culture: A Theory of Western Civilization*. Translated by Samuel Lester. South Bend, IN: Saint Augustine's Press, 2002.

Briggs, John Channing. "Happiness, Catharsis, and Literary Cure." In *The Eudaimonic Turn: Well-Being in Literary Studies*, edited by James O. Pawelski and D. J. Moores, 115–33. Lanham, MD: Rowman and Littlefield, 2013.

Brown, Sarah. *Stained Glass at York Minster*. London: Scala, 2017.

Brownlow, F. W. *Shakespeare, Harsnett, and the Devils of Denham*. Newark: University of Delaware Press, 1993.

Bruce, Susan, ed. *William Shakespeare: King Lear*. Columbia Critical Guides. New York: Columbia University Press, 1998.

Bullough, Geoffrey. *Narrative and Dramatic Sources in Shakespeare*. 8 vols. New York: Columbia University Press, 1957–75.

Bulman, James C. Introduction to *King Henry IV, Part 2*, by William Shakespeare, edited by James C. Bulman. Arden Third Series. London: Bloomsbury, 2016.

———, ed. *King Henry IV, Part 2*, by William Shakespeare. Arden Third Series. London: Bloomsbury, 2016.

Burke, Kenneth. *A Grammar of Motives*. Berkeley: University of California Press, 1969.

Burrow, Colin, ed. *The Complete Sonnets and Poems,* by William Shakespeare. Oxford: Oxford University Press, 2008.

Calvin, John. *The Institution of Christian Religion, Written in Latine by Maister Iohn Caluine, and Translated into Englishe Accordyng to the Authors Last Edition, by T.N. Wherunto is Added a Table, to Fynde the Principall Matters Entreated of in Thys Boke, Conteyning by Order of Common Places, the Summe of the Vvhole Doctrine Taught in the Same. Seen and Allowed According to the Order Appointed in the Queenes Maiesties Iniunctions.* London, In White Crosse strete by Richarde Harrison, 1562. *ProQuest*. Web. 4 Nov. 2020. STC (2nd ed.) / 4416.

———. *Sermons of Master Iohn Caluin, vpon the booke of Job*. Translated out of French by Arthur Golding. [London: 1574]: Imprinted by [Henry Brynneman for] Lucas Harison and George Byshop. EEBO. STC (2nd ed.) / 4445.

Cantor, Paul. *Shakespeare: Hamlet*. Cambridge University Press, 2004.

Carroll, John. *The Wreck of Western Culture: Humanism Revisited*. 2nd ed. Wilmington: ISI Books, 2010.

Cassirer, Ernst. *The Individual and the Cosmos in Renaissance Philosophy*. Translated by Mario Domandi. New York: Harper and Row, 1964.

Chambers, E. K. *The Elizabethan Stage*. 4 vols. Oxford: Clarendon Press, 1951.

———. *The Medieval Stage*. 2 vols. Mineola: Dover Publications, 1996.

———. *William Shakespeare: A Study of Facts and Problems*. 2 vols. Oxford: Clarendon Press, 1930.

Chaucer, Geoffrey. *The Riverside Chaucer*. Edited by Larry D. Benson. 3rd ed. Boston: Houghton Mifflin, 1987.

Cheetham, Paul. "The Theology of *King Lear*." In *King Lear: William Shakespeare*, edited by Linda Cookson and Bryan Loughrey, 55–63. Harlow: Longman, 1988.

Cicero, Marcus Tullius. *On Duties [De Officiis]*. Translated by Walter Miller. Cambridge: Harvard University Press, 1921.

Coleridge, Samuel Taylor. *Biographia Literaria*, Vol. 7 of *The Collected Works of Samuel Taylor Coleridge*. Edited by James Engell and W. Jackson Bate. Princeton: Princeton University Press, 1983.

———. *Shakespearean Criticism*. Edited by Thomas Middleton Raysor. 2 vols. London: J. M. Dent and Sons, 1960.

Coonradt, Nicole M. "Shakespeare's Grand Deception: *The Merchant of Venice*—Anti-Semitism as 'Uncanny Causality' and the Catholic-Protestant Problem." *Religion and the Arts* 11 (2007): 74–97.

Copleston, Frederick, SJ. *A History of Philosophy*. 9 vols. New York: Doubleday, 1985.

Cox, John D. Afterword to *Stages of Engagement: Drama and Religion in Post-Reformation England*, edited by James D. Mardock and Kathryn R. McPherson, 263–75. Pittsburgh: Duquesne University Press, 2014.

———. *The Devil and the Sacred in English Drama, 1350–1642*. Cambridge: Cambridge University Press, 2000.

———. *Seeming Knowledge: Shakespeare and Skeptical Faith*. Waco: Baylor University Press, 2007.

———. "Shakespeare and Religion." *Religions* 9 (November 2018): 1–11.

———. "Was Shakespeare a Christian, and If So, What Kind of a Christian Was He?" *Christianity and Literature* 55 (September 2006): 539–66.

Craik, T. W., ed. *King Henry V*, by William Shakespeare. Arden Third Series. London: Bloomsbury, 2018.

Crider, Scott F. *With What Persuasion: An Essay on Shakespeare and the Ethics of Rhetoric*. New York: Peter Lang, 2009.

Cross, F. L. and E. A. Livingstone, eds. *The Oxford Dictionary of the Christian Church*. 3rd ed. Oxford: Oxford University Press, 1997.

Cummings, Brian. *The Literary Culture of the Reformation: Grammar and Grace*. Oxford: Oxford University Press, 2007.

———. *Mortal Thoughts: Religion, Secularity & Identity in Shakespeare and Early Modern England*. Oxford: Oxford University Press, 2013.

Cunningham, J. V. "'Essence' and the *Phoenix and Turtle*." *English Literary History* 19 (December 1952): 265–76.

Curtius, Ernst Robert. *European Literature and the Late Middle Ages*. Translated by Willard R. Trask. New York: Harper and Row, 1963.

Daniell, David. "Shakespeare and the Protestant Mind." *Shakespeare Survey* 54 (2001): 1–12.

Danson, Lawrence. *The Harmonies of the Merchant of Venice*. New Haven: Yale University Press, 1978.

Dawson, Anthony B. and Paul Yachnin. *The Culture of Playgoing in Shakespeare's England: A Collaborative Debate*. Cambridge: Cambridge University Press, 2001.

Dawson, Christopher. *The Making of Europe: An Introduction to the History of European Unity*. Cleveland: Meridian, 1956.

De Grazia, Margreta. "Revolution in Shake-speares Sonnets." In *A Companion to Shakespeare's Sonnets*, edited by Michael Schoenfeldt, 57–69. Chichester: Wiley-Blackwell, 2010.

———. "Soliloquies and Wages in the Age of Emergent Consciousness." *Textual Practice* 9 (1995): 67–92.

Dickens, Mamie. *My Father as I Recall Him*. Amsterdam: Fredonia Books, 2005.

Dodds, Gregory D. *Exploiting Erasmus: The Erasmian Legacy and Religious Change in Early Modern England*. Toronto: University of Toronto Press, 2009.

Dollimore, Jonathan. *Radical Tragedy: Religion, Ideology and Power in the Drama of Shakespeare and His Contemporaries*. Chicago: University of Chicago Press, 1986.

Domestico, Anthony. *Poetry and Theology in the Modernist Period*. Baltimore: Johns Hopkins University Press, 2017.

Donaldson, E. Talbot. *The Swan at the Well: Shakespeare Reading Chaucer*. New Haven: Yale University Press, 1985.

Donne, John. *Selected Poetry*. Edited by John Hayward. London: Penguin, 1950.

Drakakis, John. Introduction to *The Merchant of Venice*, by William Shakespeare, edited by John Drakakis. Arden Third Series. London: Methuen, 2010.

Duffy, Eamon. *The Stripping of the Altars: Traditional Religion in England c.1400–c.1580*. 2nd ed. New Haven: Yale University Press, 2005.

Dutton, Richard, Alison Findlay, and Richard Wilson, eds. *Theatre and Religion: Lancastrian Shakespeare*. Manchester: Manchester University Press, 2004.

Eden, Kathy. *Poetic and Legal Fiction in the Aristotelian Tradition*. Princeton: Princeton University Press, 1986.

Edmondson, Paul and Stanley Wells. Introduction to *All the Sonnets of Shakespeare*, by William Shakespeare, edited by Paul Edmondson and Stanley Wells. Cambridge: Cambridge University Press, 2020.

Edwards, Mark. "C. S. Lewis and the Early Christian Church." In *C. S. Lewis and the Early Church: Essays in Honor of Walter Hooper*, edited by Judith Wolfe and B. N. Wolfe, 23–39. New York: T and T Clark, 2011.

Eliot, T. S. *The Complete Prose of T. S. Eliot: The Critical Edition: Apprentice Years, 1905–1918*. Edited by Jewel Spears Brooker and Ronald Schuchard. Baltimore: Johns Hopkins University Press, 2014.

———. *The Sacred Wood: Essays on Poetry and Criticism*. London: Methuen, 1960.

———. *Selected Essays: New Edition*. New York: Harcourt, 1950.

———. *The Use of Poetry and the Use of Criticism*. Cambridge: Harvard University Press, 1964.

Elton, William R. *King Lear and the Gods*. San Marino: Huntington Library, 1968.

Empson, William. *The Structure of Complex Words*. Cambridge: Harvard University Press, 1989.

Engell, James. *The Creative Imagination: Enlightenment to Romanticism*. Cambridge: Harvard University Press, 1981.

Erasmus. *The Adages of Erasmus*. Edited by William Barker. Toronto: University of Toronto Press, 2001.

———. *De Libero Arbitrio: Diatribe, sive Collatio*. Cologne, 1524. Google Books.

———. *The Education of a Christian Prince*. Edited by Lisa Jardine. Translated by Neil M. Cheshire and Michael J. Heath. Cambridge: Cambridge University Press, 1997.

———. *The Essential Erasmus*. Edited and translated by John P. Dolan. New York: Meridian, 1983.

———. *The First Tome or Volume of the Paraphrase of Erasmus vpon the Newe Testament*. London: Flete strete at the signe of the sunne by Edwarde Whitchurche, 1548. EEBO. STC (2nd ed.) / 2854.5.

———. *The Free Will*. In *Erasmus & Luther: Discourse on Free Will*, edited and translated by Ernst F. Winter, 3–81. London: Continuum, 2010.

———. *On Copia of Words and Ideas*. Translated by Donald B. King and H. David Rix. Milwaukee: Marquette University Press, 2007.

———. *On the Freedom of the Will*. In *Luther and Erasmus: Free Will and Salvation*, edited by E. Gordon Rupp and Philip S. Watson, 35–97. Philadelphia: Westminster Press, 1969.

———. *The Praise of Folie*. 1549, 1560 (?), and 1577. Edited by Clarence H. Miller. Translated by Thomas Chaloner. Oxford: Oxford University Press, 1965.

———. *The Praise of Folly*. Edited and translated by Clarence H. Miller. 2nd ed. New Haven: Yale University Press, 1979.

———. *The Praise of Folly and Other Writings*. Edited and translated by Robert M. Adams. New York: W. W. Norton and Co., 1989.

———. *Sileni Alcibiadis*. http://ihrim.huma-num.fr/nmh/Erasmus/Proverbia/Adagium_2201.html. Accessed January 17, 2020.

———. *Stultitiae Laus*. Edited by John F. Collins. Bryn Mawr Latin Commentaries. Bryn Mawr, PA: Bryn Mawr College, n.d.

Erdozain, Dominic. *The Soul of Doubt: The Religious Roots of Unbelief from Luther to Marx*. Oxford: Oxford University Press, 2016.

Erne, Lukas. *Beyond* The Spanish Tragedy: *A Study of the Works of Thomas Kyd*. Manchester: Manchester University Press, 2001.

Evans, G. R. *Augustine on Evil*. Cambridge: Cambridge University Press, 1990.

Evett, David. "Types of King David in Shakespeare's Lancastrian Tetralogy." *Shakespeare Studies* 14 (1981): 139–61.

Farmer, Oscar G. *Fairford Church and Its Stained Glass Windows*. 6th ed. Bath: Harding and Curtis, 1956.

Ferry, Anne. *The "Inward" Language: Sonnets of Wyatt, Sidney, Shakespeare, Donne*. Chicago: University of Chicago Press, 1983.

Forrester, Duncan B. "Martin Luther and John Calvin." In *History of Political Philosophy,* 3rd ed., edited by Leo Strauss and Joseph Cropsey, 318–55. Chicago: University of Chicago Press, 1987.

Fortin, René E. "Hermeneutical Circularity and Christian Interpretations of *King Lear.*" *Shakespeare Studies* 12 (1979): 113–25.

———. "Launcelot and the Uses of Allegory in *The Merchant of Venice.*" *Studies in English Literature, 1500–1900* 14 (Spring 1974): 259–70.

Fowler, Alastair. *Triumphal Forms: Structural Patterns in Elizabethan Poetry.* Cambridge: Cambridge University Press, 1970.

Foxe, John. "'A Protestation to the Whole Church of England.'" In *Geoffrey Chaucer,* edited by Harold Bloom, 31–34. Bloom's Classic Critical Views. New York: Infobase Publishing, 2008.

Fripp, Edgar I. *Shakespeare: Man and Artist.* 2 vols. London: Oxford University Press, 1938.

Fulton, Thomas. "Political Theology from the Pulpit and the Stage: *Sir Thomas More, Richard II,* and *Henry V.*" In *The Bible on the Shakespearean Stage: Cultures of Interpretation in Reformation England,* edited by Thomas Fulton and Kristen Poole, 204–221. Cambridge: Cambridge University Press, 2018.

Gabrieli, Vittorio and Giorgio Melchiori. Introduction to *Sir Thomas More,* by Anthony Munday, et al., edited by Vittorio Gabrieli and Giorgio Melchiori. Manchester: Manchester University Press, 1990.

Gamboa, Brett. *Shakespeare's Double Plays: Dramatic Economy on the Early Modern Stage.* Cambridge: Cambridge University Press, 2018.

Garber, Marjorie. *Shakespeare After All.* New York: Anchor Books, 2004.

Giles, Kate. "Digital Creativity and the Wall Paintings of 'Shakespeare's Guildhall,' Stratford-upon-Avon." *Internet Archaeology* 44 (2017): https://intarch.ac.uk/journal/issue44/6/toc.html.

Giles, Kate and Jonathan Clark. "The Archaeology of the Guild Buildings of Shakespeare's Stratford-upon-Avon." In *The Guild and Guild Buildings of Shakespeare's Stratford: Society, Religion, School and Stage,* edited by J. R. Mulryne, 135–69. Burlington: Ashgate, 2012.

Gill, Sylvia. "Reformation: Priests and People." In *The Guild and Guild Buildings of Shakespeare's Stratford: Society, Religion, School and Stage,* edited by J. R. Mulryne, 31–57. Burlington: Ashgate, 2012.

Gillespie, Stuart. *Shakespeare's Books: A Dictionary of Shakespeare's Sources.* London: Continuum, 2004.

Gilson, Etienne. *The Christian Philosophy of St. Thomas Aquinas.* Translated by L. K. Shook, CSB. Notre Dame: University of Notre Dame Press, 1956.

Gordon, D. J. "The Imagery of Ben Jonson's 'The Masque of Blacknesse' and 'The Masque of Beautie.'" In *England and the Mediterranean Tradition: Studies in Art, History, and Literature,* 102–21. Oxford: The Warburg and Courtauld Institutes, Oxford University Press, 1945.

Gray, Jonathan Michael. *Oaths and the English Reformation.* Cambridge: Cambridge University Press, 2013.

Greenblatt, Stephen. *Hamlet in Purgatory.* Princeton: Princeton University Press, 2001.

———. *Renaissance Self-Fashioning: From More to Shakespeare.* Chicago: University of Chicago Press, 2005.

———. *Shakespearean Negotiations: The Circulation of Social Energy in Renaissance England.* Berkeley: University of California Press, 1988.

———. *Shakespeare's Freedom.* Chicago: University of Chicago Press, 2010.

———. *Will in the World: How Shakespeare Became Shakespeare.* New York: Norton, 2004.

Greenfield, Thelma N. "*A Midsummer Night's Dream* and *The Praise of Folly.*" *Comparative Literature* 20 (1968): 236–44.

Gross, John. *Shylock: A Legend and Its Legacy.* New York: Simon and Schuster, 1992.

Groves, Beatrice. "England's Jerusalem in Shakespeare's *Henriad.*" In *The Bible on the Shakespearean Stage: Cultures of Interpretation in Reformation England,* edited by Thomas Fulton and Kristen Poole, 87–102. Cambridge: Cambridge University Press, 2018.

———. *Texts and Traditions: Religion in Shakespeare 1592–1604.* Oxford: Oxford University Press, 2007.

Hadfield, Andrew. *Shakespeare and Republicanism.* Cambridge: Cambridge University Press, 2008.

———. "Shakespeare: Biography and Belief." In *The Cambridge Companion to Shakespeare and Religion,* edited by Hannibal Hamlin, 18–33. Cambridge: Cambridge University Press, 2019.

Halio, Jay. Introduction to *The Merchant of Venice,* by William Shakespeare, ed. Jay Halio. Oxford: Oxford University Press, 1993.

Halkin, Léon-E. *Erasmus: A Critical Biography.* Translated by John Tonkin. Oxford: Blackwell, 1993.

Halliwell, Stephen. "Aristotelian Mimesis Reevaluated." *Journal of the History of Philosophy* 28 (1990): 487–510.

Hamilton, Donna B. "Some Romance Sources for *King Lear*: Robert of Sicily and Robert the Devil." *Studies in Philology* 71 (April 1974): 173–91.

Hamlin, Hannibal. *The Bible in Shakespeare.* Oxford: Oxford University Press, 2013.

———. Preface to *The Cambridge Companion to Shakespeare and Religion,* edited by Hannibal Hamlin, xi-xiii. Cambridge: Cambridge University Press, 2019.

Hamlin, Hannibal, ed. *The Cambridge Companion to Shakespeare and Religion.* Cambridge: Cambridge University Press, 2019.

Happé, Peter. *Cyclic Form and the English Mystery Plays: A Comparative Study of the English Biblical Cycles and Their Continental and Iconographic Counterparts.* Amsterdam: Rodopi, 2004.

Hardison, O. B., Jr. *Christian Rite and Christian Drama in the Middle Ages: Essays in the Origin and Early History of Modern Drama*. Baltimore: Johns Hopkins University Press, 1965.

Harrison, William. *The Description of England: The Classic Contemporary Account of Tudor Social Life*. Edited by Georges Edelen. New York: Dover, 1994.

Harvey, E. Ruth. *The Inward Wits: Psychological Theory in the Middle Ages and the Renaissance*. London: The Warburg Institute of the University of London: 1975.

Hassel, Chris R., Jr. *Faith and Folly in Shakespeare's Romantic Comedies*. Athens: University of Georgia Press, 1980.

———. "Hamlet's 'Too, Too Solid Flesh.'" *Sixteenth Century Journal* 25 (Autumn 1994): 609–22.

———. *Shakespeare's Religious Language: A Dictionary*. New York: Continuum, 2005.

Hegel, Georg Wilhelm Friedrich. *The Philosophy of Fine Art*. Translated by F. P. B. Osmaston. 4 vols. London: G. Bell and Sons, 1920.

Hill, Geoffrey. *Collected Critical Writings*. Edited by Kenneth Haynes. Oxford: Oxford University Press, 2008.

Hillier, Russell M. "Hamlet the Rough-Hewer: Moral Agency and the Consolations of Reformation Thought." In *Shakespeare and Renaissance Ethics*, edited by Patrick Gray and John D. Cox, 159–85. Cambridge: Cambridge University Press, 2014.

Hobbes, Thomas. *The Elements of Law: Natural & Politic*. 2nd ed. Edited by Ferdinand Tönnies. New York: Barnes and Noble, 1969.

Holderness, Graham. *The Faith of William Shakespeare*. Oxford: Lion Books, 2016.

Holinshed, Raphael. *Holinshed's Chronicle: As Used in Shakespeare's Plays*. Edited by Allardyce and Josephine Nicoll. London: Dent: 1965.

Holland, Peter. Introduction to *A Midsummer Night's Dream*, by William Shakespeare, edited by Peter Holland. New York: Oxford University Press, 1994.

———. "William Shakespeare." *Oxford Dictionary of National Biography*. Accessed online June 20, 2019.

Honan, Park. *Shakespeare: A Life*. Oxford: Oxford University Press, 1998.

Hooker, Richard. *Of the Laws of Ecclesiastical Polity: Preface, Book I, Book VIII*. Edited by Arthur Stephen McGrade. Cambridge: Cambridge University Press, 1989.

Horace. "Art of Poetry." In *Criticism: The Major Texts*, edited by W. J. Bate, 51–58. Enlarged ed. San Diego: Harcourt, 1970.

Horsler, Val. *Holy Trinity Church Stratford-upon-Avon: A Visitor's Guide to Shakespeare's Church*. London: Holy Trinity Church and Third Millennium Publishing, 2010.

Hoxby, Blair. *What Was Tragedy?: Theory and the Early Modern Canon*. Oxford: Oxford University Press, 2015.

Hughes, Geoffrey. *Swearing: A Social History of Foul Language, Oaths and Profanity in English*. Oxford: Blackwell, 1991.

Hunt, Maurice. "Christian Numerology in Shakespeare's *The Tragedy of King Richard the Second*." *Christianity and Literature* 60 (Winter 2011): 227–45.

Hunter, G. K. *English Drama 1586–1642: The Age of Shakespeare.* New York: Oxford University Press, 1997.

———. "The Heroism of Hamlet." In *Hamlet: A Reading and Playing Guide*, edited by John Russell Brown and Bernard Harris, 90–109. New York: Schocken Books, 1966.

———. *John Lyly.* London: Routledge and Kegan Paul, 1962.

———. "Shakespeare's Politics and the Rejection of Falstaff." In *Henry the Fourth Parts I and II*, edited by David Bevington, 253–62. New York: Garland, 1986.

Hunter, James Davison and Paul Nedelisky. *Science and the Good: The Tragic Quest for the Foundations of Morality.* New Haven: Yale University Press, 2018.

Hunter, Robert G. *Shakespeare and the Mystery of God's Judgments.* Athens: University of Georgia Press, 2007.

Jackson, Ken, and Arthur F. Marotti. Introduction to *Shakespeare and Religion: Early Modern and Postmodern Perspectives*, edited by Ken Jackson and Arthur F. Marotti, 1–21. Notre Dame: University of Notre Dame Press, 2011.

Janson, H. W. *Apes and Ape Lore in the Middle Ages and the Renaissance.* London: The Warburg Institute, University of London, 1952.

Jenkins, Harold, ed. *Hamlet.* Arden Second Series. London: Methuen, 1982.

Jensen, Phebe. *Religion and Revelry in Shakespeare's Festive World.* Cambridge: Cambridge University Press, 2008.

Jones, Emrys. *The Origins of Shakespeare.* Oxford: Oxford University Press, 1977.

———. "*Othello, Lepanto*, and the Cyprus Wars." *Shakespeare Survey* 21 (1968): 47–52.

Jonson, Ben. *The Cambridge Edition of the Works of Ben Jonson.* Edited by David Bevington, Martin Butler, and Ian Donaldson. 7 vols. Cambridge: Cambridge University Press, 2012.

Joseph, Miriam, CSC. *Shakespeare's Use of the Arts of Language.* Philadelphia: Paul Dry Books, 2005.

———. *The Trivium: The Liberal Arts of Logic, Grammar, and Rhetoric.* Edited by Marguerite McGlinn. Philadelphia: Paul Dry Books, 2002.

Joyce, James. *Portrait of the Artist as a Young Man.* New York: Viking Press, 1964.

Julius, Anthony. "The Fantasy of Free Speech." *Times Literary Supplement* 6043 (January 25, 2019): 14–15.

Kaiser, Walter. *Praisers of Folly: Erasmus, Rabelais, Shakespeare.* Cambridge: Harvard University Press, 1963.

Kamps, Ivo. "The Writing of History in Shakespeare's England." In *A Companion to Shakespeare's Works: The Histories*, edited by Richard Dutton and Jean E. Howard, 4–25. Oxford: Blackwell, 2006.

Kantorowicz, Ernst H. *The King's Two Bodies: A Study in Medieval Political Theology.* Princeton: Princeton University Press, 1957.

Kastan, David Scott. Introduction to *King Henry IV, Part 1*, by William Shakespeare, edited by David Kastan. Arden Third Series. London: Thomson Learning, 2002.

———. "Shakespeare and the Idea of Tragedy." In *A Companion to Shakespeare's Work: The Tragedies*, edited by Richard Dutton and Jean E. Howard, 4–22. Oxford: Blackwell, 2003.

———. *A Will to Believe: Shakespeare and Religion*. Oxford: Oxford University Press, 2014.

Kastan, David Scott, ed. *Doctor Faustus*, by Christopher Marlowe. New York: Norton, 2005.

Keeton, George W. *Shakespeare's Legal and Political Background*. New York: Barnes and Noble, 1968.

Kelly, Joseph F. *The Problem of Evil: From the Book of Job to Modern Genetics*. Liturgical Press: Collegeville, Minnesota, 2002.

Kenny, Anthony. "Knowledge, Belief, and Faith." *Philosophy* 82 (July 2007): 381–97.

Kermode, Frank. "The Mature Comedies." In *Early Shakespeare*, edited by John Russell Brown and Bernard Harris, 211–27. London: Edward Arnold, 1967.

Kernan, Alvin B. "The *Henriad*: Shakespeare's Major History Plays." In *Modern Shakespearean Criticism: Essays on Style, Dramaturgy, and the Major Plays*, edited by Alvin B. Kernan, 245–75. New York: Harcourt, 1970.

Kernodle, G. R. "The Open Stage: Elizabethan or Existentialist?" *Shakespeare Survey* 12 (1959): 1–7.

Kerrigan, John. "Revision, Adaptation, and the Fool in *King Lear*." In *The Division of the Kingdoms: Shakespeare's Two Versions of King Lear*, edited by Gary Taylor and Michael Warren, 195–239. Oxford: Clarendon Press, 1986.

———. *Shakespeare's Binding Language*. Oxford: Oxford University Press, 2016.

Key, Newton and Robert Bucholz, eds. *Sources and Debates in English History 1485–1714*. 2nd ed. Chichester: Wiley-Blackwell, 2009.

Knapp, Jeffrey. *Shakespeare's Tribe: Church, Nation, and Theater in Renaissance England*. Chicago: University of Chicago Press, 2002.

Knapp, Robert S. *Shakespeare: The Theater and the Book*. Princeton: Princeton University Press, 1989.

Knight, G. Wilson. *The Wheel of Fire: Interpretations of Shakespearian Tragedy*. London, Routledge, 2001.

Knights, L. C. "Notes on Comedy." In *Determinations: Critical Essays*, edited by F. R. Leavis, 109–31. New York: Haskell House Publishers, 1970.

Knowles, James. "*1 Henry IV*." In *A Companion to Shakespeare's Works: The Histories*, edited by Richard Dutton and Jean E. Howard, 412–31. Oxford: Blackwell, 2006.

Knowles, Ronald. "*Hamlet* and Counter-Humanism." *Renaissance Quarterly* 52 (Winter 1999): 1046–1069.

Kolve, V. A. *The Play Called Corpus Christi*. Stanford: Stanford University Press, 1966.

Kronenfeld, Judy. *King Lear and the Naked Truth: Rethinking the Language of Religion and Resistance*. Durham: Duke University Press, 1998.

Lake, Peter. *How Shakespeare Put Politics on the Stage: Power and Succession in the History Plays*. New Haven: Yale University Press, 2016.

———. *Moderate Puritans and the Elizabethan Church*. Cambridge: Cambridge University Press, 1982.

———. "Religious Identities in Shakespeare's England." In *A Companion to Shakespeare*, edited by David Scott Kastan, 57–84. Oxford: Blackwell, 1999.

Lander, Jesse M. "*A Midsummer Night's Dream* and the Problem of Belief." *Shakespeare Survey* 65 (2012): 42–57.

Lanham, Richard A. *A Handlist of Rhetorical Terms*. 2nd ed. Berkeley: University of California Press, 1991.

Lauster, Jörg. "Marsilio Ficino as a Christian Thinker: Theological Aspects of His Platonism." In *Marsilio Ficino: His Theology, His Philosophy, His Legacy*, edited by Michael J. B. Allen and Valery Rees, 45–69. Leiden, Netherlands: Brill, 2002.

Leo, Russ. *Tragedy as Philosophy in the Reformation World*. Oxford: Oxford University Press, 2019.

Lewalski, Barbara K. "Biblical Allusion and Allegory in *The Merchant of Venice*." *Shakespeare Quarterly* 13 (1962): 327–43.

Lewis, B. Rowland. *The Shakespeare Documents: Facsimiles, Transliterations, Translations and Commentary*. 2 vols. Stanford: Stanford University Press, 1940.

Lewis, C. S. *The Discarded Image: An Introduction to Medieval and Renaissance Literature*. Cambridge: Cambridge University Press, 1967.

———. *English Literature in the Sixteenth Century Excluding Drama*. Oxford: Oxford University Press, 1973.

———. *Studies in Words*. 2nd ed. Cambridge: Cambridge University Press, 1967.

Lewis, Rhodri. *Hamlet and the Vision of Darkness*. Princeton: Princeton University Press, 2017.

Lodge, Thomas. "Defence of Poetry, Music, and Stage Plays." In *Elizabethan Critical Essays*, edited by G. Gregory Smith, 1:61–86. London: Oxford University Press, 1950.

Loewenstein, David. "Agnostic Shakespeare?: The Godless World of *King Lear*." In *Shakespeare and Early Modern Religion*, edited by David Loewenstein and Michael Witmore, 155–71. Cambridge: Cambridge University Press, 2015.

Lovejoy, Arthur, O. *The Great Chain of Being: A Study of the History of an Idea: The William James Lectures Delivered at Harvard University, 1933*. Cambridge: Harvard University Press, 1948.

Luther, Martin. *The Bondage of the Will*. In *Erasmus & Luther: Discourse on Free Will*, edited and translated by Ernst F. Winter, 85–120. London: Continuum, 2010.

———. *A Commentarie vpon the Fiftene Psalmes, Called Psalmi Graduum, that is, Psalmes of Degrees: Faithfully Copied Out of the Lectures of D. Martin Luther; Very Frutefull and Comfortable for All Christian Afflicted Consciences To Reade; Translated Out of Latine into Englishe by Henry Bull*. London: By Thomas Vautroullier dwelling in the Blacke Friers by Ludgate, 1577. EEBO. STC (2nd ed.) / 16975.5.

————. The Large Catechism. In *The Book of Concord: The Confessions of the Evangelical Lutheran Church*, edited and translated by Theodore G. Tappert, 362–461. Philadelphia, Fortress Press, 1959.

————. *On the Bondage of the Will*. In *Luther and Erasmus: Free Will and Salvation*, edited by E. Gordon Rupp and Philip S. Watson, 101–334. Philadelphia: Westminster Press, 1969.

Lynch, Stephen J. "Sin, Suffering, and Redemption in *Leir* and *Lear*." *Shakespeare Studies* 18 (1986): 161–74.

MacDonald, Michael and Terence R. Murphy. *Sleepless Souls: Suicide in Early Modern England*. Oxford: Clarendon Press, 1990.

Machiavelli, Niccolò. *The Prince*. Translated by George Bull. London: Penguin, 1995.

MacIntyre, Alasdair. *After Virtue*. 2nd ed. Notre Dame: University of Notre Dame Press, 1984.

————. *Whose Justice? Which Rationality?* Notre Dame: University of Notre Dame Press, 1988.

Maclean, Norman. "Episode, Scene, Speech, and Word: The Madness of Lear." In *Critics and Criticism*, edited by R. S. Crane, 94–114. Abridged ed. Chicago: University of Chicago Press, 1957.

Maillet, Greg. *Learning to See the Theological Vision of Shakespeare's King Lear*. Newcastle upon Tyne: Cambridge Scholars Publishing, 2016.

Marlowe, Christopher. *Doctor Faustus*. Edited by David Scott Kastan. New York: Norton, 2005.

————. *The Jew of Malta*. Edited by James R. Siemon. In Christopher Marlowe, *Four Plays*. Edited by Brian Gibbons. New Mermaids. London: Methuen, 2019.

Marx, Steven. *Shakespeare and the Bible*. Oxford: Oxford University Press, 2000.

Massing, Michael. *Fatal Discord: Erasmus, Luther, and the Fight for the Western Mind*. New York: Harper, 2018.

Maus, Katharine Eisaman. *Inwardness and the Theater in the English Renaissance*. Chicago: University of Chicago Press, 1995.

Mayer, Jean-Christophe. "Providence and Divine Right." In *The Cambridge Companion to Shakespeare and Religion*, edited by Hannibal Hamlin, 151–67. Cambridge: Cambridge University Press, 2019.

McAlindon, Tom. *Shakespeare's Tudor History: A Study of Henry IV Parts 1 and 2*. London: Routledge, 2018.

McCoy, Richard C. *Faith in Shakespeare*. Oxford: Oxford University Press, 2013.

McDonald, Russ. *The Bedford Companion to Shakespeare: An Introduction with Documents*. Boston: Bedford Books, 1996.

McGiffert, Michael. "God's Controversy with Jacobean England." *American Historical Review* 88 (December 1983): 1151–1174.

McIntosh, Angus and Colin Williamson. "*King Lear*, Act I, Scene I. A Stylistic Note." *The Review of English Studies* 14 (February 1963): 54–58.

Millman, Noah. "Whence Comes Legitimacy?" *The American Conservative* (March 16, 2017): https://www.theamericanconservative.com/articles/whence-comes-legitimacy/.

Mills, David. "The Chester Cycle." In *Medieval English Theatre*, edited by Richard Beadle and Alan J. Fletcher, 125–51. 2nd ed. Cambridge: Cambridge University Press, 2008.

Milton, John. *Complete Poems and Major Prose*. Edited by Merritt Y. Hughes. New York: Macmillan, 1957.

Milward, Peter, SJ. *Biblical Influences in Shakespeare's Great Tragedies*. Bloomington: Indiana University Press, 1987.

———. "Religion in Arden." *Shakespeare Survey* 54 (2001): 115–21.

———. *Shakespeare's Religious Background*. Chicago: Loyola University Press, 1973.

———. *Shakespearian Echoes: The Comedies*. Tokyo: The Renaissance Institute, 2010.

———. *Shakespearian Echoes: The Tragedies*. Tokyo: The Renaissance Institute, 2010.

Miola, Robert S. *Shakespeare's Reading*. Oxford: Oxford University Press, 2000.

———. "Thy Canonized Bones." Rev. of *The Quest for Shakespeare: The Bard of Avon and the Church of Rome*, by Joseph Pearce. *First Things* 185 (August/September 2008): 49–51.

Monta, Susannah Brietz. "'It is requir'd you do awake your faith': Belief in Shakespeare's Theater." In *Religion and Drama in Early Modern England: The Performance of Religion on the Renaissance Stage,* edited by Jane Hwang Degenhardt and Elizabeth Williamson, 115–37. Farnham: Ashgate, 2011.

Montaigne, Michel de. *The Complete Works*. Translated by Donald M. Frame. New York: Knopf, 2003.

More, Thomas. *History of King Richard III*. In *Richard III: The Great Debate: Sir Thomas More's History of King Richard III [and] Horace Walpole's Historic Doubts on the Life and Reign of King Richard III*, edited by Paul Murray Kendall, 31–112. New York: Norton, 1965.

———. *Utopia*. Edited and translated by Robert M. Adams. New York: Norton, 1975.

Morris, Harry. *Last Things in Shakespeare*. Tallahassee: University of Florida Press, 1985.

Morris, Ivor. *Shakespeare's God*. London: George Allen and Unwin, 1972.

Morrissey, Mary. "The Paul's Cross Jeremiad and Other Sermons of Exhortation." In *Paul's Cross and the Culture of Persuasion in England, 1520–1640*, edited by Torrance Kirby and P.G. Stanwood, 421–438. Leiden: Brill, 2014.

Mowat, Barbara. "Shakespeare Reads the Geneva Bible." In *Shakespeare, the Bible, and the Form of the Book: Contested Scriptures*, edited by Travis DeCook and Alan Galey, 25–39. New York: Routledge, 2012.

Munday, Anthony. *Sir Thomas More*. Edited by Vittorio Gabrieli and Giorgio Melchiori. Manchester: Manchester University Press, 1990.

Mutschmann, H. and K. Wentersdorf. *Shakespeare and Catholicism*. New York: Sheed and Ward, 1952.

Nameri, Dorothy. *Three Versions of the Story of King Lear.* 2 vols. Salzburg: Institut für Englische Sprache und Literatur, 1976.

Nauert, Charles G. *Humanism and the Culture of Renaissance Europe.* 2nd ed. Cambridge: Cambridge University Press, 2006.

Newman, John Henry. *The Idea of a University.* Edited by Martin J. Svaglic. Notre Dame: University of Notre Dame Press, 1982.

Niesel, Wilhelm. *The Theology of Calvin.* Translated by Harold Knight. Philadelphia: Westminster Press, 1956.

Noble, Richmond. *Shakespeare's Biblical Language.* New York: Macmillan, 1935.

Norbrook, David. "The Emperor's New Body? *Richard II*, Ernst Kantorowicz, and the Politics of Shakespeare Criticism." *Textual Practice* 10 (Summer 1996): 329–57.

Nuttall, A. D. *A New Mimesis: Shakespeare and the Representation of Reality.* Methuen: London, 1983.

Oakes, Edward T. "*Hamlet* and the Reformation: The Prince of Denmark as 'Young Man Luther.'" *Logos* 13 (2010): 53–78.

Oberman, Heiko O. *Luther: Man between God and the Devil.* Translated by Eileen Walliser-Schwarzbart. New Haven: Yale University Press, 2006.

O'Brien, Flann. *The Complete Novels: At Swim-Two-Birds, The Third Policeman, The Poor Mouth, The Hard Life, The Dalkey Archive.* New York: Everyman's Library, 2007.

Onions, C. T. *A Shakespeare Glossary: Enlarged and Revised throughout by Robert D. Eagleson.* Oxford: Clarendon Press, 1986.

Oser, Lee. *The Ethics of Modernism: Moral Ideas in Yeats, Eliot, Joyce, Woolf, and Beckett.* Cambridge: Cambridge University Press, 2007.

———. "Imagination, Judgment, and Belief in *A Midsummer Night's Dream.*" *Literary Imagination* 16 (2014): 39–55.

———. *The Return of Christian Humanism: Chesterton, Eliot, Tolkien and the Romance of History.* Columbia: University of Missouri Press, 2007.

———. "Shakespeare and the Catholic Spectrum." *Religion and the Arts* 16 (2012): 381–90.

Pater, Walter. *Works.* Library ed. 10 vols. London: Macmillan, 1912–1915.

Patrides, C. A. *Premises and Motifs in Renaissance Thought and Literature.* Princeton: Princeton University Press, 1982.

Patterson, Annabel. *Shakespeare and the Popular Voice.* Cambridge: Blackwell, 1989.

Pauls, Peter. "*The True Chronicle History of King Leir* and Shakespeare's *King Lear*: A Reconsideration." *Upstart Crow* 5 (1984): 93–107.

Pearce, Joseph. *The Quest for Shakespeare: The Bard of Avon and the Church of Rome.* San Francisco: Ignatius Press, 2008.

Peters, Greg. *The Monkhood of All Believers.* Grand Rapids: Baker Academic, 2018.

Pettigrew, Todd H. J. "The Christening of Shylock." *Literary Imagination* 21 (November 2019): 268–84.

Phillips, O. Hood. *Shakespeare and the Lawyers*. London: Methuen, 1972.

Plutarch. *Moralia*. Translated by Frank Cole Babbitt et al. 16 vols. Cambridge: Harvard University Press, 1927.

Poole, Kristen. *Radical Religion from Shakespeare to Milton: Figures of Nonconformity in Early Modern England*. Cambridge: Cambridge University Press, 2000.

Potter, Lois. *The Life of William Shakespeare: A Critical Biography*. Oxford: Wiley-Blackwell, 2012.

Potter, Robert. *The English Morality Play: Origins, History, and Influence of a Dramatic Tradition*. London: Routledge, 1975.

Potts, Timothy. *Conscience in Medieval Philosophy*. Cambridge: Cambridge University Press, 1980.

Prescott, Anne Lake. *Imagining Rabelais in Renaissance England*. New Haven: Yale University Press, 1998.

Prosser, Eleanor. *Hamlet and Revenge*. Stanford: Stanford University Press, 1967.

Puttenham, George. *The Arte of English Poesie*. Kent, OH: The Kent State University Press, 1970.

Quinones, Ricardo. *Dualisms: The Agons of the Modern World*. Toronto: University of Toronto Press, 2007.

Rabb, Theodore K. "The Editions of Sir Edwyn Sandys's *Relation of the State of Religion*." *Huntington Library Quarterly* 26 (August 1963): 323–36.

Rabkin, Norman. *Shakespeare and the Problem of Meaning*. Chicago: University of Chicago Press, 1981.

Rahner, Karl, SJ, "Thomas Aquinas on the Incomprehensibility of God." *The Journal of Religion* 58, Supplement (1978): S107–S125.

Rhodes, Neil. *Shakespeare and the Origins of English*. Oxford: Oxford University Press, 2004.

Ricks, Christopher. *T. S. Eliot and Prejudice*. Berkeley: University of California Press, 1988.

Ricks, Christopher and Quentin Skinner. "Up for Interpretation *or* What Is This Thing that Hearsay Is Not?" *Literary Imagination* 14 (2012): 125–42.

Riggs, David. "Marlowe's Quarrel with God." In *Marlowe, History and Sexuality*, edited by Paul Whitfield White, 15–37. New York: AMS Press, 1998.

Righter, Anne. *Shakespeare and the Idea of a Play*. Baltimore: Penguin, 1967.

Rocca, Gregory P. *Speaking the Incomprehensible God: Thomas Aquinas and the Interplay of Positive and Negative Theology*. Washington, DC: Catholic University of America Press, 2008.

Rowe, Katherine. "Shakespearean Tragic Emotions." In *A Companion to Shakespeare's Work: The Tragedies*, edited by Richard Dutton and Jean E. Howard, 47–72. Oxford: Blackwell, 2003.

Rowse, A. L. *The Elizabethan Renaissance: The Cultural Achievement*. New York: Charles Scribner's Sons, 1972.

———. *Shakespeare the Man.* Rev. ed. London: Macmillan, 1988.

Rubenstein, Richard E. *Aristotle's Children: How Christians, Muslims, and Jews Rediscovered Ancient Wisdom and Illuminated the Dark Ages.* New York: Harcourt, 2003.

Rummel, Erika. "Desiderius Erasmus." *Stanford Encyclopedia of Philosophy.* https://plato.stanford.edu/entries/erasmus/. Accessed January 15, 2020.

Rupp, E. Gordon and Philip S. Watson, eds. *Luther and Erasmus: Free Will and Salvation.* Philadelphia: Westminster Press, 1969.

Russell, Bertrand. *A History of Western Philosophy.* New York: Simon and Schuster, 1972.

Russin, Robin. "The Triumph of the Golden Fleece: Women, Money, Religion, and Power in Shakespeare's *The Merchant of Venice.*" *Shofar* 31 (2013): 115–30.

Ryrie, Alec. *Unbelievers: An Emotional History of Doubt.* Cambridge: Harvard University Press, 2019.

Sanders, Wilbur. *The Dramatist and the Received Idea: Studies in the Plays of Marlowe and Shakespeare.* Cambridge: Cambridge University Press, 1968.

Santayana, George. *Interpretations of Poetry and Religion.* New York: Charles Scribner's Sons, 1911.

Savage, Richard and Edgar I. Fripp, eds. *Minutes and Accounts of the Corporation of Stratford-upon-Avon: 1553–1566.* Vol. 1. Oxford: Publications of the Dugdale Society, 1921.

Schlegel, A. W. "Shakespeare." In *Criticism: The Major Texts,* edited by W. J. Bate, 415–23. Enlarged ed. San Diego: Harcourt, 1970.

Schnackenburg, Rudolf. *All Things are Possible to Believers: Reflections on the Lord's Prayer and the Sermon on the Mount.* Translated by James S. Currie. Louisville: Westminster John Knox Press, 1995.

Schoenbaum, S. *Shakespeare's Lives.* Oxford: Clarendon Press, 1970.

———. *William Shakespeare: A Documentary Life.* New York: Oxford University Press, 1975.

Schreiner, Susan E. "Exegesis and Double Justice in Calvin's Sermons on Job." *Church History* 58 (September 1989): 322–38.

Schreyer, Kurt A. *Shakespeare's Medieval Craft: Remnants of the Mysteries on the London Stage.* Ithaca: Cornell University Press, 2014.

Sellin, Paul R. "The Hidden God." In *The Darker Vision of the Renaissance: Beyond the Fields of Reason,* edited by Robert S. Kinsman, 147–96. Berkeley: University of California Press, 1974.

Semper, I. J. *Hamlet without Tears.* Dubuque, Iowa: Loras College Press, 1946.

Shaheen, Naseeb. *Biblical References in Shakespeare's Plays.* Newark: University of Delaware Press, 2011.

Shakespeare, William. *All the Sonnets of Shakespeare.* Edited by Paul Edmondson and Stanley Wells. Cambridge: Cambridge University Press, 2020.

———. *The Complete Poems and Sonnets.* Edited by Colin Burrow. Oxford: Oxford University Press, 2008.

————. *The Complete Works of William Shakespeare*. Edited by David Bevington. 6th ed. New York: Pearson, 2009.

————. *The First Part of the History of Henry IV*. Edited by John Dover Wilson. Cambridge: Cambridge University Press, 1968.

————. *Hamlet*. Edited by Harold Jenkins. Arden Second Series. London: Methuen, 1982.

————. *Hamlet*. Edited by Ann Thompson and Neil Taylor. Arden Third Series. London: Cengage Learning, 2006.

————. *King Henry IV, Part 1*. Edited by David Scott Kastan. Arden Third Series. London: Thomson Learning, 2002.

————. *King Henry IV, Part 2*. Edited by James C. Bulman. Arden Third Series. London: Bloomsbury, 2016.

————. *King Henry V*. Edited by T. W. Craik. Arden Third Series. London: Bloomsbury, 2018.

————. *King Henry V*. Edited by John Dover Wilson. Cambridge: Cambridge University Press, 1968.

————. *King Lear*. Edited by R. A. Foakes. Arden Shakespeare. London: Thomson Learning, 2006.

————. *King Lear: A Parallel Text Edition*. Edited by René Weis. 2nd ed. London: Routledge, 2015.

————. *King Richard II*. Edited by John Dover Wilson. Cambridge: Cambridge University Press, 1961.

————. *The Merchant of Venice*. Edited by John Russell Brown. Arden Shakespeare. London: Methuen, 1955.

————. *The Merchant of Venice*. Edited by John Drakakis. Arden Shakespeare: Third Series. London: Methuen, 2010.

————. *The Merchant of Venice*. Edited Jay Halio. Oxford: Oxford University Press, 1993.

————. *A Midsummer Night's Dream*. Edited by Harold F. Brooks. Arden Shakespeare. London: Methuen, 1979.

————. *A Midsummer Night's Dream*. Edited by Peter Holland. New York: Oxford University Press, 1994.

————. *Richard II*. Edited by Anthony B. Dawson and Paul Yachnin. Oxford: Oxford University Press, 2011.

Shapiro, James. *Shakespeare and the Jews*. New York: Columbia University Press, 1996.

————. *A Year in the Life of William Shakespeare 1599*. New York: HarperCollins, 2005.

————. *The Year of Lear: Shakespeare in 1606*. New York: Simon and Schuster, 2015.

Shell, Alison. *Shakespeare and Religion*. London: Methuen, 2010.

Shepherd, Geoffrey. Introduction to *An Apology for Poetry*, by Sir Philip Sidney, edited by Geoffrey Shepherd. London: Thomas Nelson and Sons, 1965.

————. "Religion and Philosophy in Chaucer." In *Writers and Their Background: Geoffrey Chaucer*, edited by Derek Brewer, 262–89. London: G. Bell and Sons, 1974.

Short, Hugh. "Shylock Is Content: A Study in Salvation." In *Shakespeare Criticism: Merchant of Venice: New Critical Essays*, edited by John W. Mahon and Ellen Macleod Mahon, 199–212. Florence, KY: Routledge, 2013.

Shuger, Debora Kuller. *Habits of Thought in the English Renaissance: Religion, Politics, and the Dominant Culture*. Toronto: University of Toronto Press, 1997.

———. "Subversive Fathers and Suffering Subjects: Shakespeare and Christianity." In *Religion, Literature, and Politics in Post-Reformation England, 1540–1688*, edited by Donna B. Hamilton and Richard Strier, 46–69. Cambridge: Cambridge University Press, 1996.

Sidney, Philip. *An Apology for Poetry*. Edited by Geoffrey Shepherd. London: Thomas Nelson and Sons, 1965.

———. *The Defense of Poesy Otherwise Known as An Apology for Poetry*. Edited by Albert S. Cook. Boston: Ginn and Company, 1890.

Skinner, Quentin. *Forensic Shakespeare*. Oxford: Oxford University Press, 2014.

———. *The Foundations of Modern Political Thought*. 2 vols. Cambridge: Cambridge University Press, 1978.

Skinner, Quentin and Christopher Ricks. "Up for Interpretation *or* What Is This Thing that Hearsay Is Not?" *Literary Imagination* 14 (2012): 125–42.

Slights, Camille. "In Defense of Jessica: The Runaway Daughter in *The Merchant of Venice*." *Shakespeare Quarterly* 31 (Autumn 1980): 357–68.

Slights, William W. E. "The Reformed Conscience." In *Stages of Engagement: Drama and Religion in Post-Reformation England*, edited by James D. Murdock and Kathryn R. McPherson, 21–39. Pittsburgh: Duquesne University Press, 2014.

Sloane, Thomas O. *On the Contrary: The Protocol of Traditional Rhetoric*. Washington, DC: Catholic University of America Press, 1997.

Smith, Matthew J. "w/Sincerity, Part I: The Drama of the Will from Augustine to Milton." *Christianity & Literature* 67 (December 2017): 8–33.

Soellner, Rolf. *Shakespeare's Patterns of Self-Knowledge*. Columbus: Ohio State University Press, 1972.

Sohmer, Steve. *Shakespeare's Mystery Play: The Opening of the Globe Theatre 1599*. Manchester: Manchester University Press, 1999.

Spenser, Theodore. *Shakespeare and the Nature of Man*. New York: Macmillan, 1961.

Spiekerman, Tim. *Shakespeare's Political Realism: The English History Plays*. Albany: State University of New York Press, 2001.

Spivak, Bernard. *Shakespeare and the Allegory of Evil: The History of a Metaphor in Relation to His Major Villains*. New York: Columbia University Press, 1958.

Stern, Tiffany. *Making Shakespeare: From Stage to Page*. New York: Routledge, 2004.

Stewart, J. I. M. *Character and Motive in Shakespeare: Some Recent Appraisals Examined*. New York: Barnes and Noble, 1959.

Stillman, Robert E. *Philip Sidney and the Poetics of Renaissance Cosmopolitanism*. Burlington: Ashgate, 2008.

Streete, Adrian. *Protestantism and Drama in Early Modern England*. Cambridge: Cambridge University Press, 2009.

Swain, Barbara. *Fools and Folly during the Middle Ages and the Renaissance*. New York: Columbia University Press, 1932.

Tappert, Theodore G., ed. and trans. *The Book of Concord: The Confessions of the Evangelical Lutheran Church*. Philadelphia, Fortress Press, 1959.

Taylor, Charles. *A Secular Age*. Cambridge: Harvard University Press, 2007.

———. *Sources of the Self: The Making of Modern Identity*. Cambridge: Harvard University Press, 1989.

Taylor, Dennis. "Bearish on the Will: John Shakespeare in the Rafters." *Shakespeare Newsletter* 54 (Spring 2004): 11,16, 24, 28.

———. "Peter Milward. S. J. (1925–): A Chronology and Checklist of His Works on Shakespeare, in English, Gathered in the Burns Rare Book Library, Boston College, Chestnut Hill, MA." Revised July 19, 2006. Online: https://www.bc.edu/content/dam/files/publications/relarts/pdf/Milward.pdf. Accessed January 24, 2020.

Taylor, Gary. "*King Lear*: The Date and Authorship of the Folio Version." In *The Division of the Kingdoms: Shakespeare's Two Versions of King Lear*, edited by Gary Taylor and Michael Warren, 351–451. Oxford: Clarendon Press, 1986.

Taylor, Gary and Rory Loughnane. "The Canon and Chronology of Shakespeare's Works." In *The New Oxford Shakespeare: Authorship Companion*, edited by Gary Taylor and Gabriel Egan, 417–602. Oxford: Oxford University Press, 2017.

Thomas à Kempis. *Of the imitation of Christ, three, both for wisedome, and godlines, most excellent bookes; made 170. yeeres since by one Thomas of Kempis, and for the worthines thereof oft since translated out of Latine into sundrie languages by diuers godlie and learned men: now newlie corrected, translated, and with most ample textes, and sentences of holie Scripture illustrated by Thomas Rogers*. London: By Henrie Denham, dwelling in Pater noster Row, at the signe of the Starre, 1580. EEBO. STC (2nd ed.) / 23973.

Thomas of Celano. *Dies Irae*. In *The Hymns of the Breviary and Missal*, edited by Matthew Britt, OSB, 202–4. Rev. ed. New York: Benziger Brothers, 1924.

Thomas, Keith. *Religion and the Decline of Magic*. New York: Charles Scribner's Sons, 1971.

Thompson, Ann. *Shakespeare's Chaucer: A Study in Literary Origins*. Liverpool: Liverpool University Press, 1978.

Thompson, Ann and Neil Taylor, eds. *Hamlet*. Arden Third Series. London: Cengage Learning, 2006.

Tiffany, Grace. "Shakespeare's Dionysian Prince: Drama, Politics, and the 'Athenian' History Play." *Renaissance Quarterly* 52 (Summer 1999): 366–83.

Tillyard, E. M. W. *Shakespeare's History Plays*. New York: Collier Books, 1962.

Todd, Margo. *Christian Humanism and the Puritan Social Order*. Cambridge: Cambridge University Press, 1987.

Traver, Hope. "'King Lear' and 'Isaiah.'" *Shakespeare Association Bulletin* 9 (October 1934): 181–85.

Trousdale, Marion. *Shakespeare and the Rhetoricians*. Chapel Hill: University of North Carolina Press, 1982.

Tyacke, Nicholas. *Anti-Calvinists: The Rise of English Arminianism c. 1590–1640*. Oxford: Oxford University Press, 1987.

Van Es, Bart. *Shakespeare in Company*. Oxford: Oxford University Press, 2013.

Vendler, Helen. *The Art of Shakespeare's Sonnets*. Cambridge: Harvard University Press, 1997.

Vickers, Brian. *Appropriating Shakespeare: Contemporary Critical Quarrels*. New Haven: Yale University Press, 1993.

———. Introduction to *English Renaissance Literary Criticism*, edited by Brian Vickers, 1–55. Oxford: Oxford University Press, 1999.

———, ed. *English Renaissance Literary Criticism*. Oxford: Oxford University Press, 1999.

Waddington, Raymond B. "Lutheran *Hamlet*." *English Language Notes* 27 (1989): 27–42.

Walsh, Brian. *Unsettled Toleration: Religious Differences on the Shakespearean Stage*. Oxford: Oxford University Press, 2016.

Walsham, Alexandra. *Providence in Early Modern England*. Oxford: Oxford University Press, 1999.

Webster, John. *The Duchess of Malfi*. Edited by Leah S. Marcus. Arden Early Modern Drama. London: Methuen, 2009.

———. *The White Devil*. Edited by Benedict S. Robinson. Arden Early Modern Drama. London: Bloomsbury, 2019.

Weimann, Robert and Douglas Bruster. *Shakespeare and the Power of Performance: Stage and Page in the Elizabethan Theatre*. Cambridge, Cambridge University Press, 2008.

Wells, Robin Headlam. *Shakespeare's Humanism*. Cambridge: Cambridge University Press, 2005.

Wells, Stanley. *Shakespeare & Co.* New York: Pantheon Books, 2006.

———. *Shakespeare: For All Time*. Oxford: Oxford University Press, 2003.

Welsford, Enid. *The Fool: His Social and Literary History*. Garden City, NY: Anchor Books, 1961.

Wentersdorf, Karl P. "Hamlet's Encounter with the Pirates." *Shakespeare Quarterly* 34 (Winter 1983): 434–40.

Wetherbee, Winthrop. *Chaucer: The Canterbury Tales*. 2nd ed. Cambridge: Cambridge University Press, 2004.

White, R. S. *Natural Law in English Renaissance Literature*. Cambridge: Cambridge University Press, 1996.

Wiles, David. *Shakespeare's Clown: Actor and Text in the Elizabethan Playhouse*. Cambridge: Cambridge University Press, 1987.

Wilson, Ian. *Shakespeare: The Evidence: Unlocking the Mysteries of the Man and His Work.* New York: St. Martin's, 1993.

Wilson, John Dover. *The Fortunes of Falstaff.* Cambridge: Cambridge University Press, 1970.

———. Introduction to *Henry V*, by William Shakespeare, edited by John Dover Wilson. Cambridge: Cambridge University Press, 1968.

———. Introduction to *Richard II*, by William Shakespeare, edited by John Dover Wilson. Cambridge: Cambridge University Press, 1961.

———, ed. *The First Part of the History of Henry IV,* by William Shakespeare. Cambridge: Cambridge University Press, 1968.

———, ed. *King Henry V,* by William Shakespeare. Cambridge: Cambridge University Press, 1968.

———, ed. *King Richard II,* by William Shakespeare. Cambridge: Cambridge University Press, 1961.

Wilson, Richard. "Introduction: A Torturing Hour—Shakespeare and the Martyrs." In *Theatre and Religion: Lancastrian Shakespeare*, edited by Richard Dutton, Alison Findlay, and Richard Wilson, 1–39. Manchester: Manchester University Press, 2003.

Wilson, Thomas. *Wilson's Arte of Rhetorique, 1560.* Edited by G. H. Mair. Oxford: Clarendon Press, 1909.

Winter, Ernst F., ed. and trans. *Erasmus & Luther: Discourse on Free Will.* London: Continuum, 2010.

Wittgenstein, Ludwig. *On Certainty.* In *Major Works: Selected Philosophical Writings,* edited by G. E. M. Anscombe and G. H. von Wright, translated by Denis Paul and G. E. M. Anscombe. New York: HarperCollins, 2009.

———. *Philosophical Investigations.* Edited by P. M. S. Hacker and Joachim Schulte. Translated by G. E. M. Anscombe, P. M. S. Hacker, and Joachim Schulte. Rev. 4th ed. Oxford: Wiley-Blackwell, 2009.

Wittreich, Joseph. *"Image of that Horror": History, Prophecy, and Apocalypse in* King Lear. San Marino: Huntington Library, 1984.

Wright, Thomas. *The Passions of the Mind in General.* Edited by William Webster Newbold. New York: Garland, 1986.

Yaffe, Martin D. *Shylock and the Jewish Question.* Baltimore: Johns Hopkins University Press, 1997.

Yu, Jeffrey J. "Shakespeare's *Julius Caesar,* Erasmus's *De Copia,* and Sentential Ambiguity." *Comparative Drama* 41 (Spring 2007): 79–106.

Zimmermann, Jens. Introduction to *Re-envisioning Christian Humanism: Education and the Restoration of Humanity,* edited by Jens Zimmermann, 1–15. Oxford: Oxford University Press, 2017.

Index

Abel, 134–35

allegory: biblical allegory, 7–8; distinguished from allusion, 86–87; figures in *2 Henry IV*, 162, 167

Altman, Joel, 61

anadiplosis, 70

anagnorisis, 52

Andrewes, Lancelot, 63–64, 227

antanaclasis, 95, 100, 101

anthimeria, 94

Antichrist (play), 161–62

apophatic theology, 225, 242–43

Aquinas, 20–21, 40, 72, 137n86, 204, 223, 243

ara, 100

Archer, William, 31

Arden of Faversham, 21n93, 146

Aristotle, 18, 19, 23, 44, 52–53, 121n31, 194

Armin, Robert, 235

Arminianism, 64, 191

The Arte of Rhetorique (Thomas Wilson), 44, 62, 87, 102–3

Article 39, 115, 116–17

As You Like It, 49, 182, 247n105

atheism, 9–11, 83, 109n84

Auden, W. H., 113–14

Auerbach, Erich, 33n132

Augustine, 25n104, 36, 133n74, 182, 183, 227

Bacon, Francis, 58

Baldwin, T. W., 7, 61

Barber, C. L., 102, 119

Baro, Peter, 63–64

Barrett, William, 63–64

Barth, Karl, 32

Battenhouse, Roy, 10n49, 22n99, 32, 206

Bearman, Robert, 37–39

Beatitudes, 45, 122, 168, 169

Beckett, Samuel, 222, 223

Bethurum, Dorothy, 66, 79

Bible: allegory in, 7–8; attitude toward civil authority, 75, 113–15, 121–23; interpretation of, 109–11; models of kingship, 133–34, 169; references in *Hamlet*, 190; references in *1 Henry IV*, 149; references in *2 Henry IV*, 169–70; references in *The Merchant of Venice*, 86, 89–90, 96, 99–100, 107–11; references in *A Midsummer Night's Dream*, 68, 75; references in *Richard II*, 134–35; references to New Testament in *King Lear*, 217–20, 225, 227; references to Old Testament prophecy in *King Lear*, 223, 228–29, 232–42; Revelation and Christian ulteriority in *Henry V*, 172–77. *See also* Paul, Saint; Sermon on the Mount

Bloom, Allan, 124

Bloom, Harold, 32–33, 66, 154–55, 211n1

Bradley, A. C., 32, 155–56, 211n1, 213, 247

Brague, Rémi, 26n109, 33n132

Bretchgirdle, John, 46, 50

Briggs, John, 73n80

Brooke, Arthur, 19, 21, 22, 23

Brooke, Nicholas, 212

Bullough, Geoffrey, 21n91, 65n63, 78n102, 98n54, 130, 159, 229n53, 229n54

Burbage, Richard, 235

Burke, Edmund, 43

Burke, Kenneth, 106n73

Cain and Abel, 134–35

Calvin, John: account of faith as knowledge, 40, 41, 112; on church and state, 117; on the "Delphic maxim," 27n110; on the Devil, 161n151; on hiddenness of God, 243–44; and interpretation of scripture, 109; on salvation and predestination, 63–64, 74n86, 139, 140, 191, 201n64; somber tone, 4; on spiritual blindness, 234

Calvinism/Calvinist theology: and allusions to predestination in Shakespeare's plays, 96–97, 194, 201; on certainty of election, 63, 82; on discernment of divine providence, 135, 207; on salvation and predestination, 63–64, 74n86, 139, 140, 191, 201n64; theological controversy in 1590s England, 60, 63–65, 191. *See also* Calvin, John; predestination

Cantor, Paul, 25–26

Carter, Thomas, 7

Castellio, Sebastian, 40

catharsis, 73, 78–79

Cecil, Robert, 209

Cecil, William, 83

Chambers, E. K., 6n21, 6n22, 33n132, 241

Chaucer, Geoffrey: considered a Wycliffite by Foxe, 8, 66; *The Knight's Tale*, 65–71, 79–83; and religious doubt, 41n170; and satire, 120

Chesterton, G. K., 91

Christ: Antonio as type of, 107–8; and biblical references in *King Lear*, 217–19, 225, 227, 229, 232, 234, 241; in Book of Revelation,

About the Author

Lee Oser was educated at Reed College and Yale University. He teaches at College of the Holy Cross, in Worcester, Massachusetts. He is a former president of the Association of Literary Scholars, Critics, and Writers (ALSCW).

Literary Criticism

T. S. Eliot and American Poetry (1998)

The Ethics of Modernism: Moral Ideas in Yeats, Eliot, Joyce, Woolf, and Beckett (2007)

The Return of Christian Humanism: Chesterton, Eliot, Tolkien, and the Romance of History (2007)

Fiction

Out of What Chaos (2007)

The Oracles Fell Silent (2014)

Oregon Confetti (2017)

Also Available from
The Catholic University of America Press

R. V. Young, *Shakespeare and the Idea of Western Civilization*. 978-0-8132-3524-0.

James Matthew Wilson, *The Vision of the Soul: Truth, Goodness, and Beauty in the Western Tradition*. 978-0-8132-2928-7.

Anthony Lo Bello, *Origins of Catholic Words: A Discursive Dictionary*. 978-0-8132-3230-0.

Caryll Houselander, *The Dry Wood*. Catholic Women Writers. 978-0-8132-3461-8.

Sheila Kaye-Smith, *The End of the House of Alard*. Catholic Women Writers. 978-0-8132-3562-2.

Thomas Woodman, *Faithful Fictions: The Catholic Novel in British Literature*, second edition. 978-0-8132-3564-6.

Michael Cavanagh, *Paradise Lost: A Primer*. 978-0-8132-3246-1.

José Maria Eça de Queirós, *The Falling Snow and Other Stories*. Translated by Robert Fedorchek. 978-0-8132-3504-2.

Harold Frederic, *The Martyrdom of Maev and Other Irish Stories*. Edited by Jack Morgan. 978-0-8132-2781-8.

Drama in English from the Middle Ages to the Early Twentieth Century: An Anthology of Plays with Old Spelling. Edited by Christopher J. Wheatley. 978-0-8132-2787-0.

A Thomas More Source Book. Edited by Gerard B. Wegemer and Stephen W. Smith. 978-0-8132-1376-7.

Adam Schwartz, *The Third Spring: G.K. Chesterton, Graham Greene, Christopher Dawson, and David Jones*. 978-0-8132-1982-0.

Revelation and Convergence: Flannery O'Connor and the Catholic Intellectual Tradition. Edited by Mark Bosco and Brent Little. 978-0-8132-2942-3.